White

W9-DGW-387

SECOND EDITION

FROM THE FRONT LINES

Student Cases in Social Work Ethics

JULIET CASSUTO ROTHMAN

University of California, Berkeley

PEARSON

Boston   New York   San Francisco
Mexico City   Montreal   Toronto   London   Madrid   Munich   Paris
Hong Kong   Singapore   Tokyo   Cape Town   Sydney

Series Editor: *Patricia Quinlin*
Series Editorial Assistant: *Annemarie Kennedy*
Marketing Manager: *Kris Ellis-Levy*
Senior Production Editor: *Annette Pagliaro*
Editorial Production: *Walsh & Associates, Inc.*
Composition Buyer: *Linda Cox*
Manufacturing Buyer: *JoAnne Sweeney*
Cover Administrator: *Kristina Mose-Libon*
Text Design and Composition: *Publishers' Design and Production Services, Inc.*

For related titles and support materials, visit our online catalog at www.ablongman.com.

Between the time Website information is gathered and then published, it is not unusual for some sites to have closed. Also, the transcription of URLs can result in unintended typographical errors. The publisher would appreciate notification where these errors occur so that they may be corrected in subsequent editions.

Library of Congress Cataloging-in-Publication Data

Rothman, Juliet Cassuto
    From the front lines : student cases in social work ethics / Juliet Cassuto Rothman.—2nd ed.
        p.   cm.
    Includes bibliographical references and index.
    ISBN 0-205-41269-6
        1. Social case work—Moral and ethical aspects.   2. Social workers—Professional ethics.
    I. Title

    HV43.R69 2004
    174'.93613—dc22

                                                                                        2003063233

Printed in the United States of America

10 9 8 7 6 5 4 3 2   08   07   06   05   04

For My Students . . .

who wanted "a casebook of our own, just for social workers."
In grateful appreciation for all your help, your support,
and your dedication to this project.
	Without you, this could not be.

CONTENTS

■ ■ ■ ■ ■

INTRODUCTION

Elements of Ethical Decision Making   1

CHAPTER THREE

NASW Ethical Standard Three: Social Workers' Ethical Responsibilities to Practice Settings   95

CHAPTER FOUR

NASW Ethical Standard Four: Social Workers' Ethical Responsibilities as Professionals   144

CHAPTER FIVE

NASW Ethical Standard Five: Social Workers' Ethical Responsibilities to the Social Work Profession   170

CHAPTER SIX

NASW Ethical Standard Six: Social Workers' Ethical Responsibilities to the Broader Society   198

CHAPTER SEVEN

Applying the NASW Ethical Standards of Practice: Your Turn!   243

CONTENTS BY PRACTICE CONTEXT

CONTRIBUTORS

Shahla R. Adam, MSW

Tom Bertone, MSW, CSC

Patricia Y. Braun, MSW

Josephine K. Bulkley, J.D., MSW

Jeanine Castilho da Silva, MSW

Amy Craig-Van Grack, MSW

Patricia deJesus, MSW

Eileen A. Dombo, MSW

Elena B. Glekas, MSW

Julie B. Goodale, MSW

Thomas W. Gray, Ph.D., MSW

Mel Hall-Crawford, MSW

Stephen Hardstack, MSW

M. Thérèse Jones, MSW

Mary A. Kardauskas, SHCJ, MSW

Marian D. Kaufman, MSW

Karen Altenberg Libman, MSW, MBA

Linda K. Lopez, MSW

Joanna P. Martin, MSW

Aimee H. Mclain, MSW

Kimberly Platt, MSW

Robin E. Rolley, J.D., MSW

Shereen Rubenstein, MSW

Sarah M. Russell, MSW

Mickey J.W. Smith, MSW, CAC

Diane Inselberg Spirer, MSW, M.S.

Gigi Stowe, MSW

Jose Carlos Vera, MSW

Daniel W. Wilson, MSW

Karen A. Wilson, MSW

PREFACE

Major ethical issues are inherent in the work of any profession. Yet, as social workers, we often confront problems that are unique and especially difficult, because the work we do has a strong impact on every aspect of the lives of those we serve. We have many obligations—to our clients, their families and communities, and the wider society.

Our responsibilities range from care and decision making for those unable to care for themselves, to the advancement of self-determination for and the empowerment of vulnerable and oppressed client groups, to working for the public interest, or the common good of society as a whole. We are the custodians of many of the resources of our society, and we determine how they may be allocated in a just and equitable manner. We administer major social-welfare programs; protect the best interests of children, the elderly, and the disabled; and support families and individuals in developing their optimal potential.

We work in social agencies, schools, the justice system, hospitals, nursing homes, residential treatment centers, clinics, employee-assistance programs, child-welfare programs, governmental and policy-making agencies, and a multitude of other settings. In each of these settings, we work to optimize the "fit" between our client populations and the world they live in. It is our very versatility, along with our multiple and often conflicting obligations, that creates some of the ethical dilemmas that we all encounter in the course of our work.

We confront our various and conflicting ethical responsibilities armed with our personal values, professional skills, and understanding of the society in which we, as well as our clients, live. For guidance, we turn to the Code of Ethics of the National Association of Social Workers, included in full in the Appendix of this text, and to ethical principles drawn from theories that support our professional values: respect for the value and dignity of every human being and a concern for the well-being of others. We confront our clients' problems in the context of an ever-changing, ever-more-complex world. We confront them with a heightened awareness of the role that our own values, beliefs, and experiences play in our understanding of their problems and needs.

Our understanding of our clients and of our own roles in working with them has evolved with the maturation of the profession. In the early days, the days of the "friendly visitor," it was often believed that the problems that people encountered were caused by some moral failure on their parts. It was the role of early social workers to lead these unfortunates toward a "better" life by influencing their values and behavior. "If you become like me," the friendly visitor might have said, "you will no longer have problems. You must learn to think like me, act like me, believe like me."

The settlement-house movement approached the problems of clients from a different perspective. Settlement-house workers lived in the communities they served and tried to provide a wide variety of services that were needed by members of the communities. They worked with immigrant groups and with those living in poverty in all of the major cities of the nation.

With time, it became obvious that the problems people faced were often not rooted within the individuals themselves; rather, they were created by the clients' environments or by circumstances not of their own creation. This led to a proactive stance within the profession, an advocacy for programs and policies to improve the condition of the poor and disadvantaged.

In the mid-twentieth century, social workers were profoundly affected by the work of Sigmund Freud and others, and the profession began to focus interest on the development and refinement of clinical skills, work with individuals, and the application of psychological theories to practice. The ethical issues of concern to earlier practitioners were temporarily subsumed under the impetus toward clinical professional development.

The years since World War II have brought a strong resurgence in the concern with ethical issues in the profession. The Holocaust; the "brainwashing" believed to have occurred in the former Soviet Union; the war in Vietnam; the ethnic conflicts in the former Yugoslavia, the former Soviet Union, and Africa; problems in the Middle East; and global terrorism have stirred both our souls and our minds, causing us to begin to focus, once again, on ethical concerns.

Research and literature in the area of ethical issues for social workers appear regularly in books and professional journals, offering us both information and data and a forum for learning. The case studies in this book add to the growing body of knowledge about ethical issues in our profession. They offer a unique perspective: that of student social workers in the field encountering ethical issues on a day-to-day basis, having to face these issues and resolve them, in a manner consistent with both their own values and those of the profession.

The title of the book may evoke images of war and thus seem inappropriate to a social-work ethics textbook. Yet, I believe that there are parallels that can be drawn between social work and soldiering that make the title a meaningful one. At times, our work may place us on the front lines of a very real struggle: a struggle for rights, justice, survival, dignity and respect, recognition, peace, and the possibility of a good life.

Like soldiers in battle, we are given training and guidelines. We are given protocols and guidance, supervision and policies. We are sent out into a very different "field" than that of the soldier. But it is a field nonetheless, and upon it, alone, we must encounter difficult situations and make decisions, knowing that the effect of these decisions may go well beyond our immediate time and space and affect the course of many lives. Like the soldier, we do not have the luxury of inaction, for inaction in itself is an action.

Confronting ethical issues may seem daunting to students and practitioners. After all, ethics is its own discipline, with its own body of knowledge and its own methodology. How can we, without years of study, feel that we are qualified and able to make ethical decisions? We are social workers, not ethicists.

Yet, in the course of our work, we can and do make ethical decisions frequently, perhaps more frequently than we realize. It is possible, I believe, for social workers to make reasoned, reflective, and careful ethical decisions without the benefit of years of study. After all, we make ethical decisions in our personal lives all the time. We have a great deal of experience doing this!

What is asked of us, as professionals, is that we carefully consider and define the issues; that we gather the information needed to make an informed decision; that we allow ourselves to be guided by the Code of Ethics to which we all subscribe; that we recognize and consider the effect of our own values and beliefs and our own life experiences upon our decision-making process; that we honor the values and beliefs of those affected by our decisions: our clients, our agencies, our communities, and society at large; that we reason and reflect upon the choices available to us; and that we act with integrity in the manner that we believe will be best for all concerned.

The Introduction of this book takes the reader on a brief but intense journey through the elements of making an ethical decision. These apply specifically to social-work ethical decision making, but there is much here that can be used to reflect on the manner in which the reader and others make ethical decisions in their lives in general. I believe that learning about ethical decision making should be of value not just for professional practice, but for the whole person as well. As mentioned earlier, we all make ethical decisions all the time. All that reading and learning can do is to make readers more conscious and aware of the elements they themselves bring into their decision making and of the process they use to make decisions.

Each of the six chapters includes cases that are focused around one of the ethical standards of the NASW Code of Ethics. The order of the Code is preserved in the arrangement of the chapters. Within each chapter, the particular ethical standard is discussed, and examples of cases involving that standard are presented to the reader.

The collection includes thirty cases, each unique in terms of the particular combination of setting, issue, worker, and client and/or policy. Cases illustrate both common kinds of dilemmas and more unusual ones; cases where the writer did an extensive and exhaustive research and literature review and cases where less material was used; cases illustrating the use of different theories and methods; cases where the writer carefully examines the impact of his or her own values on his or her decision; and cases where this is not accentuated. In some instances, I would have made the same decision as the worker, though perhaps for slightly different reasons. In others, I would have made a very different decision. In still others, I would have framed the ethical problem differently from the way the writer has chosen. Similarly, the reader may find himself or herself agreeing with some writers and disagreeing, slightly or vehemently, with others.

The rationale for this diversity is to illustrate that it is possible to make ethical decisions using a variety of approaches, and in more or less depth, as long as certain elements are always a part of the process: adequate information, reference to the Code of Ethics or to some set of principles and theories, awareness of all of the value systems that impact the decision and are impacted by it, and a process of reason and reflection.

At the end of each case, I have included five questions to help readers consider other related issues. I hope that these will engender good discussion: Ethics flourishes best in an atmosphere of open discussion, respect, and consideration for the views and opinions of others. I also hope that, in reflecting on each writer's approach and in considering the questions at the end of the chapter, the reader will feel an increased sense of confidence in his or her own ability to make ethical decisions. References and bibliographies are included with all cases to facilitate further study.

As the classical philosopher Aristotle says in the Nichomachaean Ethics, "Ethics is an inexact science." It is not necessary—in fact, it is not possible—for social workers to make the same decisions for the same reasons as do other social workers. We are each unique; we bring that uniqueness with us to our work. Therefore, we cannot seek absolute consistency among ourselves in ethical decision making. All that can be asked of each of us is that we make the most thoughtful, reflective decision that we can, with sincerity, honesty, and integrity.

ACKNOWLEDGMENTS

This project was born on a sunny winter afternoon, early in a new semester, when, once again, I heard the familiar litany, "Why do we have to use ethics cases from other discipline's books? Why can't we have our own casebook?"

"O.K.," I said, tired of this often-repeated complaint, "I'll write one. But you must prepare good cases. I'll use material from them and put a casebook together."

And so, *From the Front Lines* was born.

Over a period of years, the students in my ethics classes at National Catholic School for Social Service have worked extra hard to prepare cases they thought would be of interest to students everywhere. They helped me classroom-test the book. They read the revised and abstracted versions of their work that I prepared, to ensure that I had preserved the flavor and urgency of their ethical dilemmas. They assisted me always with their enthusiasm, loyalty, and interest. I would like to thank each and every one—those whose cases are included here, and those who, for various reasons, were unable to contribute a case to this endeavor.

It is the sincere hope of each of us that our book will help to stimulate thought and discussion in this essential area of our professional education. In the years that I have been teaching at the University of California at Berkeley's School of Social Welfare, I have continued to explore ethical dilemmas students encounter in practice. This has both provided additional knowledge and insight and confirmed the vital importance of addressing ethical issues carefully and thoughtfully in practice.

I would like to acknowledge the following reviewers who critiqued this book; their comments were very helpful and contributed toward the final version of the text: Sally G. Goren, University of Illinois–Chicago; Sharon Hall, University of Houston–Clear Lake; and Margaret R. Calista, Marist College. Reviewers for the second edition—whose time and input is also appreciated—were Valerie Chang, Indiana University; Eva Bowie Ellis, Jackson State University; and Jean M. Granger, California State University–Long Beach.

The following materials were cited in the book with permission:

Beauchamp, T. L., and J. F. Childress, From *Principles of Biomedical Ethics* by T. L. Beauchamp and J. F. Childress. Copyright © 1994 by T. L. Beauchamp and J. F. Childress. Used by permission of Oxford University Press.

Gewirth, Alan. (1978). *Reason and Morality.* Copyright © 1978. Published by the University of Chicago Press. Used by permission of The University of Chicago Press.

Loewenberg, Frank, and Ralph Dolgoff. From *Ethical Decisions for Social Work Practice*, sixth edition, by Frank Loewenberg and Ralph Dolgoff. Copyright © 2000. Reproduced by permission of Thomson Learning.

NASW. *NASW Code of Ethics.* Copyright 1996, National Association of Social Workers, Inc.

Rothman, Jack. "Client Self-Determination: Untangling the Knot," *Social Service Review*, 6(4), pp. 598–612, published by The University of Chicago Press. Used by permission of The University of Chicago Press.

ELEMENTS OF ETHICAL DECISION MAKING

Ethical problems pervade every aspect of social work. Often, they are difficult to identify, for they mask themselves deep within clinical issues, funding issues, or agency policy issues. At times, a sincere consideration and concern for the immediate problem diminishes workers' understanding of the broader professional and societal issues that must inform ethical decision making. The following examples may help to clarify the problem.

An adolescent who has been referred by a teacher to a school social worker for service because of classroom behavior and suspected drug abuse sits silently, week after week, refusing to engage with the worker. His parents are aware of the referral, agree that it is needed, and assume that their son is accepting help. However, his problematic behavior is continuing in the classroom, and the question of substance abuse is still unresolved. It is easy to label such a client as resistive or to question the worker's skills or methods. These are clinical issues. Embedded deep within, however, is an important ethical dimension. Should his parents be informed about his refusal to talk with the worker? What if the teen simply doesn't want service? Should he be coerced, against his will, to engage with the worker? Should active engagement be made a condition of continuing to attend school, or is it enough if he just sits in the worker's office an hour a week? What about his rights—to self-determination, to dignity and respect, to privacy and confidentiality?

An elderly resident of a senior citizen's housing project has become unable to care for himself. His memory is slightly impaired, and he forgets to take vital medications. He recently fell and could not reach a telephone to ask for help. His meals are nutritionally unbalanced—he tends to open cans of pork and beans daily with little variation, and fresh fruits, vegetables, and dairy products are rarely a part of his diet. He spends long hours alone in his apartment, watching television. The housing manager has referred him to the social worker for nursing home placement, which, she feels, would provide him with the medication monitoring he needs, ensure his physical safety and nutritional health, and offer opportunities for socialization and activities. The worker agrees that the resident would be much better off in a supervised setting, but he adamantly refuses to go. The worker, believing that her obligation is to the client's best interest, feels that she must intervene for his own good. A question of genuine care and concern? Yes, but also a question of self-determination and of the rights of competent individuals. Does his refusal to enter a nursing home make him de facto incompetent?

1

A young woman comes for service to a neighborhood mental health clinic. She and the worker identify the self-esteem issues she would like to work on and develop a contract with goals set within the agency's eight-session framework for treatment. An excellent relationship is developed, which enables significant work and an increase in self-confidence. During her seventh session, she reveals another important, related issue, a long-standing problem with a sibling that also has impact on her self-esteem. She asks the worker to extend treatment by enough visits to address this important area. There is little question in the mind of the worker: Of course this client needs continued visits. She just won't mention them to her supervisor. She doesn't agree with the agency's eight-session limit, anyway, and she has to think of her client's needs first. But there are many issues related to deliberately ignoring agency policy. What about her contract with her practice setting? What about her relationship with her supervisor, who is herself being placed at risk by the worker's actions? What are some of the repercussions that might occur should the funding source discover that the conditions of funding are not being met? What of the next client, who also has needs, but who can't be served for several more weeks? And, while trying to support her client, what message is she sending to her about honesty and fidelity, about obligations, about the kind of person that she is?

An agency for Hispanics with HIV, whose funding is derived from the local Hispanic community, is designed to serve this specific population only. Its mission, policies, and purpose is clearly stated, and it even provides bilingual workers to address the needs of this special population. However, the amount of funding, and thus the very existence of the agency, is dependent on the numbers of persons served annually. This number has been steadily decreasing, and the existence of the agency itself is threatened. If the agency is closed, there will be no services at all for this at-risk minority population. There are many individuals who live in the community, and in neighboring communities, who are HIV positive and in need of service but are not Hispanics. Slowly and silently, these people are being accepted for service by the agency. The rationale makes a great deal of sense to the staff: The need for services that the agency can provide is there. It is not being met by any other agency in the community. And, of course, these clients are boosting the numbers of clients that the agency is serving, thereby ensuring its continued existence and services to the Hispanic HIV population. The benefits are obvious. But what of the harms? Is the agency engaging in deception by misusing funds designated for one population for services to another? Does the end (keeping the agency in existence) justify the means (abandoning its stated mission and policies)? Are there any other courses of action possible?

A social worker is part of a multidisciplinary team in a major medical center that must decide who will be the recipient of a liver that is available for transplant. Each member of the team provides information in his or her area of expertise to the general team meeting, and a decision is made jointly by all members. The pathologist addresses issues of tissue match; the physician, general health; the nurse, potential compliance with medical regimen; the pastor, spiritual needs. The social worker's area of expertise is the potential recipient's personal and social functioning. She takes a complete psychosocial history, from which she must extract salient pieces of information that impact on the team's decision. Yet the client reveals certain kinds of information in confidence, expecting her to maintain confidentiality. Should a history of alcohol abuse be included? Should a history of wife battering, which has not been formally charged in a court of law? A criminal record? A potential for mental instability? A history of multiple teen pregnancies and TNAF dependence? A mild mental disability? Where is the line between "necessary information" and the potential recipient's right to privacy? What psychosocial factors should be considered in determining who receives scarce organs? Should any be considered at all?

Each of these examples illustrates instances when social workers must make decisions based not only on clinical judgment and expertise, but also on ethical principles and values. Immediately, major problems surface: *Which* principles? *What* values? Drawn from *whose* understanding of human nature and philosophical position?

In order to assist workers in considering the ethical dimensions of the work that they do, it is necessary to consider problems within a basic framework that provides a consistent structure as well as specific guidelines for decision making. This introduction addresses the various elements that make up the framework of ethical decision making. Chapters 1 through 6 provide cases that present ethical problems for discussion and consideration.

There are several components to ethical decision making that must be considered in arriving at an ethical position that is clear and theoretically sound, that can be communicated to others and logically supported, and that lies within the ethics and value base of the social work profession. First, the ethical problem must be defined. Second, information relevant to the problem must be obtained. Third, an appropriate theoretical base must be determined, then professional values explored, client values understood, and the impact of personal values recognized. Finally, options must be weighed and a sound decision reached. Each of these steps will be explicated below.

It is important to recognize that, wherever possible, clients should be involved in the ethical decision-making process. Client involvement supports client self-determination, validates client values and personal ethics, promotes client self-awareness, teaches and models a careful and reflective process, and greatly increases the potential for success.

All clients can be involved in ethical decision making that pertains to them at some level, from small children to confused elderly clients, from monolingual non-English speakers to people who are unable to communicate verbally, from angry teens to compliant newcomers, from homeless people in the streets to the prison population.

Thus, it is recognized that, during the following discussion of the decision-making process, client involvement is essential when the ethical problem involves a client. Because some of the ethical dilemmas with which social workers are confronted do not involve clients directly, and because the Code of Ethics contains many provisions that are not necessarily related to direct client services, there are ethical issues that pertain to the worker alone. However, when the dilemma involves client care and services, it is also assumed that the client will be directly involved in the process.

DEFINING THE ETHICAL PROBLEM

Because social work ethical issues are usually embedded in complex personal or social issues, one of the most difficult tasks in ethics decision making is focusing on the problem that must be addressed. In order to do that, ethics cases generally begin with a brief description of the setting, followed by a presentation of the case. There is often a substantial amount of information that has been gathered about the client, practice setting, policy, community, or other subject matter being considered. The worker's first task is to sort through all the material, until the "bare bones" of the ethical issue can be viewed clearly.

This often goes against social workers' training and professional habits of thoroughness and responsibility and, at first, can be a painful exercise. Coming from a broad person-in-environment framework, where the interplay of elements forms the subject matter of the service, this shift is difficult, but necessary. If the worker is addressing the confidentiality issue regarding information revealed by a minor child, for example, the occupations of the parents, the relationship among family members, the kind of school the child is attending, as well as her grades and school performance, her interests, and her afterschool activities are not part of the *ethical* "presenting problem." That problem is more likely to involve the rights of minor children, the rights of parents, the worker's professional obligations, the policies of the agency providing the service, and the worker's service contract with parents and child.

Clearly, there may be more than one ethical issue involved in a case. Each must be separated out and addressed individually. Attempting to address more than one issue at a time blurs the lines of process, confusing the issues and creating unclear and at times unreasonable conclusions. While it is important to *recognize* that there may be more than one issue, it is best to determine the central issue and to begin with that. In that process, the other issues may resolve themselves. If they continue as problems after the central issue has been resolved, they can be addressed separately.

Once an issue has been clearly identified, it may be phrased as an *ethical dilemma* for purposes of consideration and potential resolution. An ethical dilemma presents a choice that must be made between two mutually exclusive courses of action. These may be two goods, or benefits, or the avoidance of two harms. The choices that the worker, client, agency, or policymaker have to consider (the two sides of the dilemma) must be evenly balanced and of equal worth. If one side of the dilemma is more valuable, right, good, or desirable than the other side, then there is no dilemma, for the choice would obviously lean toward the more desirable side.

Dilemma formulations are always tied to overall goals and objectives, which must be identified first. Examples might be enhanced self-esteem, optimal opportunities for growth and development, maximization of mental and physical health, well-being of the client, and so on. Goals tend to be fairly general: That's why dilemmas arise in determining the "best" way to meet them. For clarity, dilemmas take the form of _____ v. _____, and include *Self-determination* v. *Worker's Perception of Best Interest of Client, Confidentiality* v. *Duty to Warn,* and *Agency Policy* v. *Primacy of Client.*

At times, it may appear that there are more than two sides to a dilemma. It will not be possible to work with the problem under those conditions, and further deliberation will enable the worker to restate the problem so that it is presented in an accessible form.

The example given of the worker whose role is to provide psychosocial assessments and who is unsure about what information should ethically be included can serve to illustrate some of the complexities of dilemma formulation. Certain kinds of information have been revealed to the worker in confidence. Should that confidence be violated? Under what circumstances? For example, should negative information that results from *actions* of the potential organ recipient be treated differently than negative information for which the client is not responsible? Mental retardation is not the "fault" of the client. Alcoholism, depending on which theory the worker espouses, may or may not be the client's responsibility, while wife battering generally tends to be. Should a certain standard of behavior be considered in determining eligibility for donor organs? Is it the worker's obligation to share all available information or to respect the client's right to privacy? Is the worker's primary responsibility to the potential recipient (her client for purposes of assessment and evaluation), her interdisciplinary team, the hospital, or society in the sense of social justice? The overarching issue to be considered is allocation of resources, which in this case are livers.

Possible dilemma formulations might include:

Primacy of Client Interests v. *Obligation to Social Justice*
Distribution by Merit v. *Distribution by Equal Share*
Privacy and Confidentiality v. *Obligation to Colleagues*
Primacy of Client Interests v. *Obligation to Practice Setting*
Distribution by Contribution to Society v. *Distribution by Equal Share*

It is easy to see where potential problems lie. Primacy of client interests appears in two formulations, with different balanced positions on the opposite side. The worker might be tempted to formulate the dilemma as *Primacy of Client Interests* v. *Obligation to Practice Setting* or *Obligation to Social Justice*. After all, both of these alternatives fit comfortably opposite Primacy of Client Interests!

When considering which principles of distributive justice to use, similar problems could occur. Equal Share can form one side of the dilemma. However, one can state the dilemma as *Equal Share* v. *Merit* or *Contribution to Society* or *Need* or *Individual Effort*. Such a complex dilemma statement is impossible to address, for each of the four positions on the right side of the dilemma needs to be considered both separately from the others and against each of the others. The dilemma *can* be formulated in a resolvable way, however, by stating *Allocation by Equal Share* v. *Allocation using Specific Criteria*.

Once the problem has been stated as a dilemma, it is possible to undertake the next element in the decision-making process—the gathering of relevant information.

GATHERING INFORMATION

It is not possible to make a good ethical decision without some research, discussion, and exploration. The particulars of the case will inform the kind of information that will be needed.

To illustrate this point, let us return to the second case presented as an example of underlying ethical issues, that of the elderly gentleman who refuses to enter a nursing home. The central ethical dilemma may be stated as in the first example offered above: *Self-determination* v. *Worker's Perception of Best Interest of Client.*

Information gathering related to this particular problem might include research about clients who remain at home in precarious conditions, exploration of resources or services available in the home for elderly clients, statistics on injuries to elderly clients who live alone and on nursing home admissions, laws about personal freedoms, research on adjustment of patients to nursing home settings, studies about life satisfaction at home and in an institutional setting, information about the client's medical conditions and any limitations that these might cause, an exploration of the client's family and support network, an examination of policies and relevant laws for residents of senior citizens' housing, and so on.

In addition to the information gathered specific to the client's situation, it is also helpful to explore the broader principles, rights, obligations, and needs that define the dilemma. Thus, in this instance, learning about self-determination—what it means, the conditions under which it may be limited, and the values and laws that support it—will help the worker to gain a deeper level of understanding. The same process should be undertaken in exploring a client's best interest. This might include professional obligations, an understanding of the pros and cons of paternalism, and the importance of addressing "point-of-view" issues in conceptualizing best interest, among others.

In the fourth example, that of the agency serving the HIV-positive Hispanic population, there are various dilemma statements possible, for there are a number of dilemmas present. One might be *Agency Mission* v. *Community Need.*

The specific issues and the dilemma statement, again, determine what information will be useful for resolving the dilemma. It might be helpful to

1. Explore the agency's mission statement.
2. Gain a historical perspective on the agency.
3. Understand the intent of the funding sources and the auspices that direct how the funds are used.
4. Discover the extent of HIV in the Hispanic population within the community.
5. Determine if other resources exist within the community for addressing the problems of HIV clients.
6. Understand completely the unique resources provided by this particular agency.
7. Learn the extent of individuals with HIV who are non-Hispanic and in need of services in the community.
8. Determine the extent to which Hispanics utilize agencies.
9. Define the reasons that services are requested at this particular agency (presenting problem).
10. Understand the cultural differences between Hispanics and non-Hispanics that impact on their utilization of the agency's services.

In terms of broader concepts and principles, it might be helpful to learn about resource allocation issues, advocacy and policy change processes, the obligation of employees to agency mission and purpose, and the relationship between agency and community.

These examples illustrate how the problem definition, the dilemma statement, the setting, and the client or client population will determine the kind of information the worker will need.

Information that can be helpful is often accessible within the agency itself: Colleagues, supervisors, program directors, and agency administrators often have experience and insight to offer regarding the resolution of ethical dilemmas. Agencies similar in purpose, population, or philosophical orientation can also provide a basis of comparison and another kind of experience. Government agencies that serve the population or address the problem can provide insight as well. The Office on Aging, for example, may have useful information to assist the worker addressing the dilemma of the elderly gentleman who is refusing nursing home placement.

With "facts" in hand, a theoretical framework, the NASW Code of Ethics, and personal, client, societal, and other values that impact on decision making can be considered. Each of these is a separate element in the process. They may be explored sequentially or simultaneously, not necessarily in the order found in the following sections.

THEORETICAL CONCEPTS

Examining Ethical Theories

Ethics is a branch of philosophy, generally drawing from broader philosophical theories in order to formulate concepts. These theories address the nature of humankind, the meaning of life, the nature of the universe, and other wide, overarching concerns. While theories differ in the way in which the answers to these broad questions are determined and how they relate to each other within the theory, all philosophical theories tend to consider the value and worth of human beings, the dignity of life, the central role of "happiness," however that is defined, and the relationship between members of a society.

Ethical theories, a more narrow focus, generally are grounded in these broader concepts. When exploring an ethical theory, it is necessary to consider three important questions:

1. The authoritative question: Where does the theory turn for validation of its basic premises? Some possibilities include the Bible, the government and its laws, a knowledgeable person, a philosophical construct, and so on.
2. The distributive question: Whose interests does the theory address? Again, there are several possible answers to this question as well, such as every person's, every living thing's, every citizen's, every member of the community's, and so on.
3. The substantive question: What goals or actions are desirable ends within this theory? We often think of "happiness," individually defined, as the overarching end toward which all other ends tend to move. In considering these other ends, it is necessary to attempt to define the conditions for "happiness." These may include concepts such as personal freedom, health and safety, and human relatedness.

Theories that may be helpful in considering the kinds of problems social workers address fall into two general categories: those that place the "good" and "right" in the motive, or starting premise, called *deontological* theories, and those that place the "good" and "right" in the ends achieved, called *teleological* or *consequentialist* theories.

Some well-known deontological theories include those based on religious texts and direction; those based on natural laws (such as Immanuel Kant's); those based on common sense, intuition, and duties (such as W. D. Ross's); and those based on the social contract (such as John Rawls's). Teleological theories are often based on some form of utilitarianism and consider "the greatest (resultant) good for the greatest number" or costs and benefits as their foundational principle. Other important theories include value-based ethics, modern variations of Aristotelian ethics, and the ethics of care, as presented by the work of Carole Gilligan et al.

The Role of Free Will and Choice

It is also important to recognize that there is a precondition vital to all ethical decision making: free will, or the ability to make choices. If individuals are unable to chose between meaningful alternatives, ethical decisions are not possible.

There are several factors that are necessary to the exercise of choice, or free will. These include the ability to understand, reason, and reflect clearly and logically about the problem. Ethics is a discipline based on *thinking,* and this ability is vital to the project.

Additionally, there must be "real" choices available. In the first example presented, that of the adolescent who refuses to engage with the worker, "making" him talk may not be a choice (unless the worker is willing to use force or very strong coercion). The choice of sharing or not sharing information with the client's parents may be a "real" choice, or it may be constrained by school policy, which mandates a specific position. Of course, the worker has the *choice* of whether to follow the school policy, but that becomes a different dilemma entirely.

Having choices is a necessary but not sufficient condition of ethical decisions. One must be able to put the choice into effect, to operationalize it. In the case of the agency that serves HIV-positive Hispanics, the staff may "choose" to serve the broader community. They may appeal to the funding source to broaden the mission and amend the policies. However, the agency's strong identity with the Hispanic community may deter non-Hispanics from coming for service. Simply "choosing" to serve everyone in the community may not be sufficient. It may be necessary to change the image of the agency, to engage in public presentations, and to approach community leaders in order to broaden the client base. The ability to put choices and goals into action is a vital part of ethical considerations.

FROM THEORIES TO PRINCIPLES

Ethical theories provide a conceptual structure for examining problems. As has been noted, these are grounded in a philosophical consideration of broader issues relating to the nature of humankind, the meaning of life, and so on. However, they often remain too broad to provide clear direction for decision making. It is necessary to draw principles from these that can be operationalized to give the worker guidance.

Principles ensure consistency and justice in the application of theory to specific ethical problems in practice. They decrease the worker's dependence on personal values and biases by providing objective criteria that may be applied in many different circumstances.

Principles may vary, depending on the theory from which they are drawn. This variation may cause differences in the final decision that is reached. How principles are stated and, more important, how they are prioritized strongly affect the final position that emerges.

Social workers' needs in terms of ethical decision making require a set of principles that lend themselves well to the kinds of ethical problems encountered in practice. Three of these will be presented briefly here in order to provide a guide to some of the most frequently used frameworks for social workers. They are by no means exclusive—there are many other sets of principles that can guide ethical decisions also. It is suggested that workers consult more detailed descriptions of these guidelines prior to applying them in practice contexts.

Alan Gewirth's Principles Hierarchy

Frederic Reamer (1990) uses a framework for ethical decision making drawn from the philosophy of Alan Gewirth. Gewirth bases his hierarchy of principles on the fundamental right of all humans to freedom and well-being (pp. 59–65). He develops three *core goods* that enable or enhance these rights. Core goods include *basic goods,* which are necessary to well-being, such as food, shelter, life, health, and, interestingly, mental equilibrium; *nonsubtractive goods,* the loss of which would seriously compromise fundamental rights, such as honesty and fidelity in individual relationships, reasonable labor, and comfortable living conditions; and *additive goods,* which increase or enhance well-being, such as education, self-esteem, and material wealth.

In *Reason and Morality* (1978), Gewirth recognizes that conflicts occur when decisions must be made that affect another person or persons. His guidelines provide a hierarchy that may be used to resolve these:

> ***Principle 1***   Rules against basic harms to the necessary preconditions of action (the core goods, food, health, shelter, etc.) take precedence over rules against harms such as lying, revealing confidential information (nonsubtractive goods), or threats to additive goods such as education, recreation, and wealth.
>
> ***Principle 2***   An individual's right to basic well-being (core goods) takes precedence over another individual's right to freedom.
>
> ***Principle 3***   An individual's right to freedom takes precedence over his or her *own* right to basic well-being.
>
> ***Principle 4***   The obligation to obey laws, rules, and regulations to which one has voluntarily and freely consented ordinarily overrides one's right to engage voluntarily in a manner that conflicts with these laws, rules, and regulations.
>
> ***Principle 5***   Individuals' rights to well-being may override laws, rules, regulations, and arrangements of voluntary associations in cases of conflict.
>
> ***Principle 6***   The obligation to prevent basic harms such as starvation and to promote basic public goods such as housing, education, and public assistance overrides the right to retain one's own property.

Loewenberg and Dolgoff's Ethical Principles Screen

Loewenberg and Dolgoff (2000) develop a decision-making model that can be used in addressing professional issues, including ethical ones, similar to the present guidelines. The process includes identifying the problem and who is involved; determining the values, goals, and objectives relevant to the issue held by all who are involved; developing and assessing alternative courses of action; selecting the most appropriate; and implementing it (p. 63).

The essential ethical components of Loewenberg and Dolgoff's system provides clear directions for addressing the values and ethical principles that will impact decision making.

Guidance is to be sought from the NASW Code of Ethics. If there are relevant sections of the Code that can provide direction, these must be used. If there are no relevant sections, or if different sections of the Code give conflicting directions, social workers should apply the Ethical Principles Screen, which prioritizes seven principles to guide decisions (p. 69). These are:

> *Principle 1: Principle of the Protection of Life.*   Biological life must always take precedence over any other principles, because it is in the context of life that ethical decisions are made.
>
> *Principle 2: Principle of Equality and Inequality.*   Similar circumstances and situations should be treated the same. However, if there are relevant significant differences, these should be taken into consideration and unequal treatment may be accorded where it would lead to greater equality.
>
> *Principle 3: Principle of Autonomy and Freedom.*   Clients' autonomy and self-determination should always be considered, unless their autonomous actions and choices would threaten the life of self or other. The right to freedom, however, is less compelling than the prevention of harm or death.
>
> *Principle 4: Principle of Least Harm.*   Social workers should avoid causing harm and prevent harm from occurring to clients or others. Where harm is unavoidable, social workers should choose the course of least harm, or most easily reversible harm.
>
> *Principle 5: Principle of Quality of Life.*   Enhancing quality of life for clients and others in society should be a goal of social work interventions.
>
> *Principle 6: Principle of Privacy and Confidentiality.*   The right to privacy of clients and others should be enhanced wherever possible and in accordance with laws. However, it may be necessary to break confidentiality when serious harm or death to clients or others may result from maintaining such confidentiality.
>
> *Principle 7: Principle of Truthfulness and Full Disclosure.*   Social workers should be honest and provide full and truthful information to clients and others in order to support a relationship grounded in trust and honesty. (Loewenberg and Dolgoff, 2000, pp. 70–71)

Use of these principles should provide clear guidelines for decision making in social work and come from a uniquely social work-based perspective. However, it must be recognized that each of these terms (*life, equality, freedom, harm, quality of life, privacy,* etc.) may be defined differently by every worker, every client, every supervisor, and every agency and that these differences in definition seriously impact the decision-making process.

A Bioethics Perspective: The Medical Model

Beauchamp and Childress also provided a useful system for social-work ethical decision making in *Principles of Biomedical Ethics* (1994). It is especially useful for social workers in healthcare host settings, because the commonality of language between disciplines that it provides is an invaluable tool of communication.

This perspective seems easy to use because of its seeming simplicity, which involves the application of four principles with which most professionals of any discipline are familiar. However, conscientious use requires an understanding not only of the principles, but also of the rules that may be drawn from them, rules that can ultimately guide action.

Beauchamp and Childress's process is developed in four hierarchical tiers. (Beauchamp & Childress, 1994, p. 15). The highest and most abstract relates to *ethical theories*. The next level down, *principles,* is somewhat less abstract. More concrete and specific than principles is the level of *rules,* while the most concrete level, that of *particular actions and judgments,* can provide the direct guidance that is needed for a specific ethical dilemma and case situation.

Ethical theories have been briefly described earlier. The next level, principles, is presented in the order used by Beauchamp and Childress, but these principles are not necessarily prioritized.

> *Principle 1: The Principle of Respect for Autonomy.*   Autonomy is often referred to by social workers as *self-determination.* Respect for autonomy justifies informed consent and informed refusal (Beauchamp & Childress, 1994, pp. 125–128).
>
> *Principle 2: The Principle of Nonmaleficence.*   This principle has an old and distinguished history, and it simply states that one ought to do no harm (Beauchamp & Childress, 1994, p. 189).
>
> *Principle 3: The Principle of Beneficence.*   This principle states that doing no harm is not sufficient—there is an additional obligation to actively pursue the welfare of others (Beauchamp & Childress, 1994, p. 260).
>
> *Principle 4: The Principle of Justice.*   Justice is often understood in terms of fairness and is most commonly related to distributive issues of allocation. The principles often used to arrive at determinations of justice are equal share, need, effort, contribution to society, merit, and free-market exchange (Beauchamp & Childress, 1994, pp. 327–330).

From these four principles the authors draw rules, which include (1) the rule of veracity (truth), (2) the rule of privacy, (3) the rule of confidentiality, and (4) the rule of fidelity (Beauchamp & Childress, 1994, p. 395).

The application of these rules to the specific ethical dilemma that is being addressed enables the professional to reach the fourth level, that of particular actions and judgments.

Thus Beauchamp and Childress's bioethics model enables progression from a selected broad theory base to the resolution of a particular ethical dilemma in a specific situation.

Different Systems Engender Different Results

The framework selected for application to a specific case is vital: Differing results may be obtained with different frameworks. When an individual worker selects the framework, the choice often reflects the worker's personal value system. Practice settings sometimes specify the framework: This fosters consistency and fairness—all dilemmas follow the same path toward resolution (an element of formal justice, which is used by the court system, called *procedural* justice). Frameworks for deliberation may also be specified by policies, funding sources, and laws.

To illustrate the possible resolutions that can be drawn using the three systems (Gewirth's, Loewenberg and Dolgoff's, and Beauchamp and Childress's) described above, it is helpful to return to one of the cases discussed at the beginning of this introduction, the elderly gentleman who refuses nursing home placement (see p. 1).

Using Gewirth's framework, one could say that basic goods can be met in either setting—home or nursing facility. Probably, health is better provided for in the nursing home; mental equilibrium in his apartment. Nonsubtractive goods and additive goods may vary somewhat with the setting but can probably be met in either setting as well. This leaves us with Gewirth's ordered principles. Reviewing these, the applicable principle appears to be number 3. This states that an individual's right to freedom takes precedence over his right to his own well-being. In other words, the resident has the right to self-determine and to place his well-being at risk if he chooses to do so. Following Gewirth's principles, then, the worker would leave the resident in his senior citizen's apartment, perhaps building in safeguards if he will accept them.

Using the Loewenberg and Dolgoff hierarchy leads to a different resolution. Assuming that the Code of Ethics does not give clear direction in this instance, one would move on to apply the Ethical Principles Screen. There, the worker finds that the Principle of the Protection of Life, the first in the hierarchy, takes precedence over the Principle of Autonomy and Freedom, which is number 3, and the Principle of the Quality of Life, which is number 5. Thus, a worker might feel obligated to ensure the protection and care of the resident's life by placing him in a nursing home against his wishes.

Application of the medical model seems to place Principle number 1, Respect for Autonomy, in the dominant position. This is supported by Principle number 6, Privacy, which asks that the worker respect the right to privacy for this resident. Privacy of person, and self-determination, would seem to support continued residence in the senior citizens' housing project.

Of course, ethical decisions are not based exclusively on any of the three frameworks. There are other important elements that need to be considered as well. One of these is the NASW Code of Ethics, which is foundational to ethical decision making for any social work professional.

USING THE CODE OF ETHICS OF THE NATIONAL ASSOCIATION OF SOCIAL WORKERS

One of the distinguishing marks of a profession is the presence of an ethical code that sets forth and defines the responsibilities of members of the profession. The first social work Code of Ethics was adopted by the Delegate Conference of the American Association of Social Workers in 1947. After the formation of the National Association of Social Workers, a Code of Ethics was drafted and adopted in 1960. Since then, there have been numerous revisions. The most recent and extensive was adopted by the Delegate Assembly in August 1996 and is binding upon all social workers, including students in schools of social work as of January 1997. The Code of Ethics in its entirety is included in the Appendix of this book, on page 258.

Overview

The Code is divided into four sections. The Preamble summarizes the mission and core values of the profession, which are:

service
social justice
dignity and worth of the person
importance of human relationships
integrity
competence

The mission of the profession as a whole is "to enhance human well-being and help meet the basic human needs of all people, with particular attention to the needs and empowerment of people who are vulnerable, oppressed, and living in poverty" (NASW Code of Ethics, 1996).

The second section of the Code gives an overview of the purpose and functions and presents a guide for addressing ethical issues. This purpose is defined as the determination of values, principles, and standards that can provide guidance to social workers in practice. The Code is meant to be used by "individuals, agencies, organizations, and bodies (such as licensing and regulatory boards, professional liability insurance providers, courts of law, agency boards of directors, government agencies, and other professional groups) that choose to adopt it as a frame of reference" (Nasw Code of Ethics, 1996).

The third section, titled "Ethical Principles," presents the six broad principles that can be drawn from the six core values of the profession. These are:

1. "Social workers' primary goal is to help people in need and to address social problems." This principle is drawn from the value of **service.**
2. "Social workers challenge social injustice." This is drawn from the value of **social justice.**
3. "Social workers respect the inherent dignity and worth of the person." The related core value is **dignity and worth of person.**
4. "Social workers recognize the central importance of human relationships." This is drawn from the core value of the **importance of human relationships.**
5. "Social workers behave in a trustworthy manner." This principle is drawn from the value of **integrity.**
6. "Social workers practice within their areas of competence and develop and enhance their professional expertise." This is drawn from the value of **competence.** (NASW Code of Ethics, 1996)

Thus, in Section 3, each defined core value from Section 1 relates to a specific principle that can guide professional practice.

The fourth section of the Code provides specific standards, or action guides, in six areas of professional functioning. These are also used as a basis for adjudication, both public and self-regulatory, by defining accepted standards of behavior. The case material in this text is organized around the framework of these six standards. The six sections are listed as social workers':

1. Ethical Responsibilities to Clients
2. Ethical Responsibilities to Colleagues
3. Ethical Responsibilities to Practice Settings
4. Ethical Responsibilities as Professionals
5. Ethical Responsibilities to the Social Work Profession
6. Ethical Responsibilities to the Broader Society

Legal Codes and Ethical Codes

There is a delicate balance and relationship between legal codes and ethical codes in a society. In democratic societies, some or ideally all members define and ground the ethical principles that will guide behavior and relationships between individual members, groups, communities, and the government of the society. Important and complex ethical standards and expectations are often codified into laws. There is generally a lapse of time between an ethical principle or guideline's development and acceptance by a society at large and its formal passage into a code of law. This time lapse can create a tension between legal codes (which are static and consistent), ethical concepts and standards (which are always changing and evolving to incorporate changes in society), and experiences and occurrences of a more immediate nature. In general, societal ethics change and adapt to new conditions more readily than laws.

Social work professionals may find themselves caught in this tension in practice. For example, laws governing service delivery systems may not account for cultural variations among client groups. The one-size-fits-all program that provides continuity and consistency may not take into account the very special and unique situation of a particular client. Rehabilitation services that require basic changes in client behaviors to meet the requirements of society-at-large may stifle self-determination. Defined decision-making processes may require one person, rather than a family group, to take ultimate responsibility and sign a "consent" to a treatment or procedures. Agency accountability procedures may require that workers allocate resources and time in a way that does not meet individual client needs.

Effecting change in laws—"catching them up" to ethical practice—is a complex and time-consuming task. Social workers specializing in policy and management address these kinds of problems and work with legislators to change laws to enhance ethical professional practice.

Laws, Malpractice, and the NASW Code of Ethics

Laws demand and expect adherence; so do professional ethical codes. Nonadherence to laws carries legal penalties and is addressed through the justice system. Nonadherence to ethical codes may also carry legal penalties but often is monitored and addressed through the ethical boards of state professional associations or other ethical bodies as well. Social workers cannot be sent to jail for nonadherence to the NASW Code of Ethics, unless a provision of the Code is also a formal part of the legal Code. However, once a professional code has been defined and put into place, adherence to the code becomes a standard requirement of membership in the profession. Social workers can be sued for malpractice in civil court or through a professional association for violation of the NASW Code of Ethics, can be sanctioned, and can be required to make reparations. Sanctions for violations can include public sanctioning, suspension of right to practice, monetary penalties, mandated education, and termination of employment.

Laws and Personal Ethical Standards

It is essential that all professionals know and understand the personal ethical and moral code that guides them. Students can explore personal values and beliefs, prioritize them, and develop a personal ethical hierarchy. This hierarchy will guide not only personal comportment, but also the way in which ethical decisions are made in social work practice.

Adherence to current legal codes is generally a part of an individual's personal ethical system as well. People generally stop at red lights, don't read other people's mail, respect their neighbor's property, pay taxes, cross at crosswalks, serve on juries, accept the directions of law enforcement officers, call 911 in emergencies, and don't cheat on exams. They also follow the social ethical codes that guide relationship with others in society, such as treating people courteously, with respect and consideration, having goodwill, and not lying to them.

Ethical but Illegal Practice

Most of the time, individual personal ethical standards and the laws of society correspond and there is a comfortable fit between them. However, there may be times when an individual's personal system and the law differ. In that case, he or she must make difficult ethical decisions: Should "adherence to the law" be one's highest personal ethical value as well? For many of us, it is, and we would never consider breaking the law. For others, there may be a higher imperative that law, such as a responsibility to follow religious principles, a sense of primary responsibility to the good of the client, a responsibility to protect one's individual safety and integrity or that of others. These kinds of ethical professional dilemmas can be among the most difficult to address.

Using the Code to Inform Legal/Ethical Decisions

The NASW Code of Ethics can assist social workers encountering these issues, because it clearly defines professional behavior and expectations in many areas. In others, however, the Code appears purposefully ambiguous, and the play of professional standards, laws, and personal ethical standards can be a fascinating, though often challenging, part of the professional social worker's decision-making process.

CLIENT VALUES, SOCIETAL VALUES, AND
PERSONAL VALUES

The resolution to an ethical dilemma, like the treatment goals and interventions that are defined by worker and client, must be compatible with the client's values, worldview, cultural outlook, and religious beliefs. It is the responsibility of the worker to reach for an understanding of client values, so that these may be integrated into the decision-making process. They will play an important role in the ability of the worker to be of service to the client. This approach is supported by the core values of dignity and worth of the person and of both service and competence.

Returning to one of the case examples presented in the beginning of this discussion—that of the agency serving HIV-positive Hispanics and considering expanding its service to include non-Hispanics—it appears obvious that an understanding of the culture and values of this population as well as those of the population that might be added, be considered. Hispanics value both the nuclear and extended family, and decisions are often made by the family as a whole, rather than by the individual. Often, religion plays an important part in family life, as do cultural traditions that may be tied to the country of origin. The ambiance of the agency, the specific services provided, and the unit of attention support the cultural beliefs, values, and identity of the Hispanic client. How will these be impacted by the inclusion of another population, whose values, culture, and family structure may be quite different? And how can, or should, services be adapted to meet the cultural and value needs of the new population? Is the Hispanic society so insular that the impact of "outsiders" would affect the utilization of services? All of these factors, too, need to be a part of the ethical consideration.

Additionally, the worker functions within the broader society and has clear responsibilities to this society as defined in the sixth area of Ethical Standards. In general, the worker must uphold societal values, though at times he or she may advocate for changes. To uphold them, he or she must have a clear understanding of what they are. Defining "society" becomes a complex and difficult task in itself. Yet workers must find some way to address and integrate the values of the broader society as well. These might include, but should not be limited to, equality, freedom, justice, achievement and success, and self-actualization, among many others. At times, these values may conflict with those of the client and create an ethical dilemma of their own. At other times, the impact of societal values on the client, and the client's self-image, becomes an important element in the consideration of dilemmas.

The values that often impact most strongly on the resolution of any ethical dilemma are those of the worker. These generally include the values of the profession, but also the values that come out of the worker's unique life experiences, training, and belief system. Personal values affect the way in which a dilemma is phrased, the theories and principles utilized in arriving at a resolution, and the ranking of guidelines in the Code of Ethics. This impact is unavoidable. It is a given of the human condition that each person views the world from a unique point of view. However, awareness of one's own values, beliefs, and biases can help workers to diminish their role in resolving the ethical problem.

The ethical dimension of society, the client system, and the worker become a vital part of the decision-making process. The ethical position of supervisors, colleagues, and agency directors can impact strongly as well. For example, in the case of the client who asks for extended sessions in order to address a long-standing and important issue, that of her relationship with her sibling, she is relating her request to her values of self-esteem, independence, optimal functioning, and human relationships. The worker, who desires to extend services, might value human relationships, service, and the dignity and worth of the individual, as well as independence in decision making, successful work, and fidelity. If she has truth high on her personal values hierarchy, however, she will probably discuss the client's request, and her proposed action, with her supervisor. As soon as she does this, the supervisor's values impact on the problem. The supervisor may decide to allow the service to be extended, placing client service above her own obligation to her practice setting, freedom and independence above loyalty to her employer. Or, she may decide that service cannot be rendered, because her understanding of service means providing help to all who are in need, thus requiring the worker's time for other clients. She may also have justice and fairness high on her list of ethical values and believe that these would not be served if she permitted the worker to continue with the client above and beyond the extent of services available to all clients.

Workers *must* understand that sharing an ethical dilemma with a colleague or a supervisor causes his or her values to become a factor in the equation, which must be considered as well.

DEFINING OPTIONS AND ARRIVING AT A RESOLUTION

When all of the elements needed to make a sound ethical decision are gathered, the worker must consider options for action. Like the three preconditions for choices presented in the earlier discussion of free will, options must be well reasoned and considered, they must reflect real possible courses of action, and it must be possible for the worker to implement them or to set them in motion.

Options for action may be derived from either side of the dilemma equation or may collapse the dilemma by either finding a way of combining the two sides or finding a solution that is appropriate but does not support either.

In the example presented earlier of the client who asks for service beyond the eight-interview limit, the dilemma can be formulated as *Primacy of Client Interests* v. *Obligation to Agency Policy*.

Several options can be suggested for either side. In support of primacy of client interests, the worker can decide to see the client for additional service as requested, without telling anyone at her agency; she can tell her supervisor that she plans to offer this additional service and bear the consequences of her decision; she can tell her supervisor, and ask that an exception be made for compelling reasons; or she can advocate for a change in agency policy.

In support of Obligation to Agency Policy, she can refuse service to the client and terminate as required; she can consult with the supervisor and follow recommendations; she can refer the client to an agency offering similar services without the eight-session limit; or she can terminate with the client and suggest that the client reapply for service, which would again give her eight interviews, possibly with another worker. She can also consider other options entirely: She can refer the client to the agency's group program, which is not confined to the eight-session limitations; she can avoid confrontation with the client over this issue by not returning telephone calls and being unavailable to her, and so on. Obviously, however, each of these options is not equally desirable.

With all of the options defined, social workers should think about the feasibility of each. If an option cannot be put into action because there is an insurmountable barrier limiting it as a true option, that option will need to be discarded. If an option will not lead to the expected goal, it also may be discarded. The other options may be considered using a cost-benefit analysis.

A simple cost-benefit analysis framework can be used to assist social workers in thinking about the possible options for action. Using a separate system for each possible resolution, the worker can list all of the potential benefits and harms or costs of a particular course of action in two separate columns. A system can then be developed to weigh each cost and benefit. Social workers will find that some costs are so high that they eliminate the option completely. Other costs impact unfairly and unevenly on others and so affect the desirability of a particular option.

As options are carefully discarded, the worker will determine the best course of action and implement it. If unforeseen problems and obstacles arise that render that option unworkable, the social worker may fall back on another option or begin the option-formulation process over again, adding and subtracting options based on previous experiences.

CASE PRESENTATIONS

In Chapters 1 through 6, cases will be presented that illustrate a wide variety of issues and specific problems. The Code of Ethics' six Ethical Standards sections will be used to categorize the issues addressed. It is recognized that many dilemmas are not neatly contained within one section of the Code, but, rather, may span two or more sections. In these cases, assignment to sections has been somewhat arbitrary and has been based on the attempt to provide balance and diversity within each section.

While the Code is utilized as a framework for the ordering of the case presentations, it is recognized that many readers prefer to focus on cases that are specifically related to their field of practice or interest. To facilitate access to cases in this manner, an additional listing is provided following the Contents page that organizes the cases in this manner (Contents by Practice Context).

Cases included in this collection are actual ethical dilemmas students encountered in the course of their field experience. The format of the presentations has been adapted to provide consistency throughout, and deliberation, discussion, and information have been limited in order to make the material more useful and accessible to the reader. The actual dilemma resolution was, in each case, a more involved and detailed process than is presented here.

Each case includes the writer's formulation of the dilemma and the data that provides the knowledge base for an informed decision. There is a clear delineation between these more objective sections of the ethical decision-making process and the subjective reasoning process and ethical reflection that are unique to each writer. It is important to remember that the resolution presented is that of the writer and not necessarily of the reader or of the editor. Each worker brings his or her own unique reasoning process, experiences, values, and biases to the dilemma, and the resolution is reached within that framework. As noted earlier, it is not possible to discount or eliminate the subjectivity inherent in ethical dilemma resolutions.

While every attempt has been made to present the case, the dilemma formulation, and the relevant data free of the writer's personal bias, it is recognized that this is not a fully attainable goal, but only an ideal. Each writer, in choosing the way in which the dilemma is phrased and in deciding what to research and which theories to use, has already made certain ethical decisions. It is hoped that the impact of these on the general presentation will be minimal and that they will not interfere with the reader's ability to assess the ethical dimensions in his or her own terms.

Organization of Chapters

Chapters 1 through 6 follow the framework that is used in the six Ethical Standards sections of the NASW Code of Ethics. Each will begin with a review of the relevant section of the code. Following this, cases will be presented that relate, in whole or in part, to that section. Where more than one section of the Code is used in addressing the dilemma, the case has been placed in a relevant section. References to all the sections of the Code used in addressing the dilemma are included in each case. A bibliography placed at the end of each chapter includes both references to citations in the text and suggestions for further reading on the subject. Chapter 7 is designed to enable the reader to apply the decision-making process to twelve case situations in which ethical issues are embedded.

Organization of Case Material

The cases included are all real dilemmas MSW students encountered in the field. Because they are real, there is variation in the way the dilemmas are presented and the research and literature utilized in the theoretical framework that structures the decision-making process and in the very depth in which issues are explored. These are meant to portray a variety of approaches to ethical dilemmas. The reader may find that he or she does not necessarily agree with the way the dilemma is defined, the choices of research material, the theoretical framework that informs the process, and the author's resolution. The reader's different view of the dilemma is in itself a useful learning experience: There are many possible ways to consider most dilemmas.

Each student's first and perhaps most difficult task was that of defining the dilemma, of identifying the ethical issues, and of separating them from the clinical ones. The research presented is meant to provide some information to assist the reader (and the writer) in working with the dilemma. It is recognized that the selection of research materials and the way in which they are used also contain ethical components.

The reader should also be aware that, when given the freedom to choose an ethical framework, people confronted with a dilemma will not always make the same choices. Choices in the theoretical frameworks used to address the problems reflect the variety of approaches that are available to assist social workers. The specific choice of a theoretical framework is in itself an ethical issue, as is the manner in which the dilemma is phrased.

These subjective elements—how the dilemma is viewed and phrased, how research is selected to explore the problem, and which theoretical framework is used—often relate to the worldview and value system of the writer rather than to any "objective" standard.

Because of the wide variety in content, values, and reasoning processes reflected in the cases included here, the editor has attempted to present them in a consistent format to aid the reader. Each case begins with a brief presentation of the practice context and the case. The dilemma is focused into the _____ v. _____ format discussed in this introduction. The second section presents some of the data from research, literature, agency policy manuals, and discussions with colleagues that will be used to develop options and support positions. In the third section, the writers share some of their own reasoning processes and values and the choices they defined as possible courses of action, followed by the resolution that they utilized in addressing the problem.

The cases have been adapted in order to fit comfortably into a textbook format. Every attempt has been made to preserve the necessary information and the thoughts that led to the worker's decision.

Following each case presentation, five questions are offered suggesting additional areas for thought and discussion, related to issues addressed in the case. These will give the reader the opportunity to consider ethical aspects not necessarily included in the case presentation and, from a more personal perspective, to explore his or her value system and beliefs and to "practice" ethical reasoning and decision making. The reader can develop his or her own resolution to the case presented. It is often helpful to discuss ethical dilemmas with colleagues: The five questions may offer a useful starting point for such discussions.

As noted above, the bibliography for each case has been placed at the back of the chapter containing the case. These bibliographies are useful in providing sources of further information and research for the interested reader, as well as in documenting the sources that the writers used in gathering data for this project.

REFERENCES

Beauchamp, T. L., & Childress, J. F. (1994). *Principles of biomedical ethics* (4th ed.). New York: Oxford University Press.

Gewirth, A. (1978). *Reason and morality.* Chicago: University of Chicago Press.

Loewenberg, F. M., & Dolgoff, R. (2000). *Ethical decisions for social work practice* (6th ed.). Itasca, IL: F. E. Peacock.

National Association of Social Workers. (1996). *NASW code of ethics.* Washington, DC: Author.

Reamer, F. (1990). *Ethical dilemmas in social service.* New York: Columbia University Press.

■ ■ ■ ■ ■

CHAPTER ONE

NASW ETHICAL STANDARD ONE

Social Workers' Ethical Responsibilities to Clients

INTRODUCTION

Provisions of Code

The first section of the Code of Ethics relating to Ethical Standards presents the social worker's ethical responsibilities to clients. It defines and clarifies various professional responsibilities for the welfare and well-being of each client.

The first subsection (1.01) addresses Commitment to Clients, stating that, in general, clients' interests are primary; however, there may be circumstances where the legal obligations of workers or the obligation to the larger society may supersede client loyalty. Workers are made aware that clients should be advised about these limitations.

This is immediately followed by the subsection addressing client self-determination (1.02), and then informed consent (1.03). Client self-determination is upheld by informed consent, and the Code specifies that services should be provided only when clients have given such consent. Problems that may be encountered relate to informed consent, such as language difficulties, lack of decisional capacity, involuntary clients, services rendered through electronic mediums, and audio- or videotaping. The obligation of workers who act on behalf of clients who are not competent to consent is addressed in subsection 1.14.

Clients often assume that workers are competent to render services. Subsection 1.04 addresses the responsibility of social workers to represent themselves as competent only within their education, training, license, certification, and so on. Competent professionals also are knowledgeable about human behavior, cultural diversity, and oppression, as addressed in subsection 1.05.

Subsection 1.06 addresses the difficult area of conflict of interest, proscribing dual relationships with clients or former clients and exploitation of these clients for personal interest and obligating workers to inform clients in cases where there may be any potential conflicts of interest.

The right to privacy and confidentiality has always been a very basic and vital part of rendering professional service. Both the obligation to observe these and the circumstances under which workers may disclose information are presented in subsection 1.07. Also included in this section is the worker's obligation to inform clients of the limits of privacy and confidentiality. Clients have the right of access to their records, but workers must protect the confidentiality of other individuals identified within them (1.08).

Subsection 1.09 addresses sexual matters within professional relationships, limiting sexual relationships with clients, former clients, persons who have close relationships with clients, and the provision of services to former sexual partners due to the potential for harm to the client that exists in such relationships. Physical contact is limited (1.10) where there exists the possibility of harm to the client and, where used appropriately, must be both culturally sensitive and within clear boundaries. Sexual harassment is proscribed (1.11), as is the use of derogatory language (1.12).

Professional guidelines regarding payment for services are addressed in subsection 1.13, the importance of continuity of services in 1.15, and termination of services in 1.16.

The Cases

The majority of the approximately 120 students whose cases were considered for this collection were aware of strong ethical dilemmas in their obligation to clients. However, as noted earlier, it is often difficult to separate ethical issues from clinical ones. As in the first example in the Introduction to this book (p. 1), if a client is not relating to a worker or is not sharing information about himself or herself, this may easily be perceived as a clinical issue. Does the worker not have adequate skills to work with this client? Is this client being "resistive"? Is it an issue of "control"? It may be necessary to take a step back from the immediate situation to consider a different perspective: Does the client have a "right" to refuse to participate in therapy? The worker, concerned for the client's "best interests," may believe that these can best be served by therapy. The client may disagree and insist on the right to self-determination. This moves, then, from a clinical issue to an ethical one.

The opposite problem can also occur. A worker in a child welfare agency is unsure of whether his primary responsibility is to the young individual with whom he is working or to the family system. Whose needs, whose interests, should be considered as primary? This may look like an ethical dilemma, but it may in fact not be one. Deciding who the client is is often an issue of agency policy, source of referral, clinical need, client preference, or worker preference. Once this determination has been made, the ethical dilemma collapses as the worker's primary responsibility is clarified.

The cases presented in this section demonstrate some of the major ethical issues for social workers relating to clients. Cases where a worker's obligation to clients is in conflict with other obligations, such as to the welfare of society, to the employing agency, to colleagues, and to the social work profession, are presented in succeeding chapters.

In the first case presented, a 2-year-old child is placed in a long-term foster home/adoptive home. A mentally disabled adult male foster sibling states that he has sexually abused her. Although no evidence of abuse is found, the child is immediately removed and placed in another foster home. In the ensuing argument between the foster parents and their son, plans are made for him to move out of the home. The parents want to adopt their foster child, and she wants to return to them. However, there will be limits, the worker knows, to the safety that this home can potentially provide, and, once the adoption is final, the agency will no longer be involved. The worker must decide whether the risk to physical safety outweighs the advantages of a loving, permanent home for this little girl.

The second case is also from the child welfare field. The social worker's client, a young girl, is placed in foster care with her younger sibling. Both girls will shortly be available for adoption. The worker is asked to recommend whether the girls should be placed together or separately in an adoptive home. The older sister, the worker's client, is very attached to the younger and wants to remain with her sister. The younger, in foster care with many other children longer than she can remember, is not personally attached to her sister at this time. If a joint adoptive placement is recommended, the younger child's chances for a permanent placement will be affected by the need for finding a family willing to take two children, one of whom, being older, is less "desirable." If separate placements are recommended, the worker's client will suffer another loss in a life already filled with many losses and traumas. Should the worker recommend what she feels to be in the best interest of her client, when this recommendation might not be in the best interests of her client's sister?

The third case presents a renal dialysis patient who has requested that treatment be terminated and that she be allowed to die. She is very ill and depressed but appears competent, and she states that her poor quality of life, and the certainty of her death in the not-too-distant future, makes it impossible for her to continue with dialysis treatments. Her mother, whom the client has named as surrogate decision maker should she no longer be able to make her own decisions, objects, and asks the social worker to help her to stop her daughter from "committing suicide." The social worker finds that she must either support the patient's request, and help her to achieve her goals, or attempt to convince her to continue in treatment and extend her life. The dilemma is suggested as one between the prolongation of biological life and the acceptance of the client's ultimate right to self-determination.

The rights of biological parents form one side of the fourth case presented. A father, currently incarcerated, requests reunification with his 2-year-old daughter, placed almost immediately after birth in a nurturing foster home due to maternal abandonment. The foster family has expressed interest in adoption. The worker must determine appropriate planning for the child (i.e., the child's "best interest"). However, the uncertainty and unpredictability of events as far as twenty years in the future make this decision a particularly difficult one.

In the fifth case, an 18-year-old immigrant, homeless and mentally disabled, is referred by another agency to a community-based agency that specializes in services to the immigrant population. Although her parents live in a neighboring county, the client refuses to live with them, preferring to remain on the streets. She is placed in a home but runs away within a week.

The worker learns that she has been both physically and sexually abused while out on the streets. His genuine concern for her safety is heightened by her mental status, and he feels that she will be unable to protect herself and may face serious harm.

The client wants her freedom to live as she has chosen; the worker is concerned about her safety. What should he do? Should her self-determination take precedence over his obligation to prevent harm? What role does her limited command of the language, her immigrant status, and her mental disability play in the way in which this dilemma must be resolved?

In the sixth case in this section, the worker revisits an old and much discussed issue in the field of adoption. Who, and under what circumstances, should have access to adoption records? How can the potential rights to privacy and confidentiality of each of the parties be respected, while also supporting the potential rights to self-determination and information of each?

The issue is made more complex by the consideration that, in adoption, there are in effect *three* primary clients: the biological family, the adoptee, and the adoptive parents. Should all of their rights be considered equally? What if the rights of one member of the triad conflict with the rights of another? If primary professional obligation is to the client, and there are three of them, how can just and fair decisions be made?

The seventh case focuses on a severely disturbed child with a history of neglect and abuse. Placed in foster care, she reports to the worker that the foster mother has hit her with a belt. She has adjusted well to foster care, in the sense that she has developed an attachment to her foster family, a major achievement.

The worker feels that, should she report the child abuse and terminate the placement, the child would lose the only stability she has had in her life. However, she is obligated by law and professional ethics to report the abuse.

CASE STUDY 1.1

PROTECTING THE BEST INTERESTS OF A MINOR

Abstracted from an unpublished paper by Elena B. Glekas, MSW

PRACTICE CONTEXT AND CASE PRESENTATION

The mission of the sectarian agency where the social worker is placed is to enable people to strengthen and transform their lives by empowering those most in need, by supporting families, and by engaging the broader community in its work. Although the agency believes in the resilience, strength, and healing power of families, it is also fully aware that, under stress, the family support system can break down, endangering children's welfare. In such cases, children are often placed in the agency's Foster Care Program.

Kendra is a 2-year-old female, whose crack cocaine–addicted mother abandoned her with a caretaker at 1 month of age, with no interest in further contacts. The caretaker refused to continue to care for her and was unable to relocate the mother. After CPS intervention, Kendra was placed in the home of Mr. and Mrs. Doe. The foster family and Kendra are supervised by the caseworker through the agency's Foster Care Program.

Kendra has adjusted well to the Does' home, and the Does love her very much. They would like to adopt her, and this is being planned, although parental rights have not yet been terminated. Kendra's mother has not been located, and the agency is initiating termination of parental rights through the court system.

The Does have a 24-year-old son, Tony, residing in their home as well. Tony is schizophrenic and mentally disabled. He desperately wants to leave the Does and live independently, but they feel that he does not have the mental ability to do this successfully and that he continues to need their protection.

Tony recently confessed to the worker that he has sexually abused Kendra. The Does claim that Tony is doing this only because he wants to live independently, hoping that they will ask him to leave the home. However, an investigation by CPS, the Youth Squad, and the police department was immediately begun, and Kendra was taken to a local hospital for examination, where no evidence of abuse was found. She was removed from the Does and placed in a temporary foster home.

Since the sexual abuse issue was revealed, the Does have abandoned their opposition to Tony's leaving. They have participated in planning sessions with Tony and his worker, and Tony has located an appropriate living facility, where some supervision will be provided. He is eager to move and plans to leave in a few days.

The Does would like to continue their plans for adoption, offering Kendra a permanent placement. With them, she would be able to establish secure lifetime relationships with nurturing caregivers. Separation from the only parents she has ever known could have a serious impact. However, placement in a foster home would offer protection from possible physical harm to this little 2-year-old girl. It is difficult if not impossible to foresee events in regards to Tony and his future. Should he fail at independent living, would the Does not take him in, thus possibly placing Kendra at further risk?

(continued)

CASE STUDY 1.1   CONTINUED

The worker must recommend a plan for Kendra. There are several ways in which her dilemma might be phrased. However, she has determined that the most important considerations in making a permanent plan for Kendra are:

Permanency v. Physical Safety

RESEARCH AND RELATED LITERATURE

The family has an enduring impact on the development of the person. The family shapes the child's personality, attitudes, behaviors, and beliefs (Thorman, 1982). There is a recognition that children can suffer severe emotional trauma when they are removed from their parents. Research indicates that children usually do better if they can remain with their own families (Ames & Springen, 1992).

General agreement supports the view that all children need a stable and continuous relationship with a nurturant person or persons in order to develop physically, socially, emotionally, intellectually, and morally (Hess, 1982). Foster children, therefore, are especially vulnerable individuals, prone to become victims unless special care is taken to protect them. Stone and Stone (1983) emphasize that every child needs security in the home environment and that "security" involves both the physical and emotional well-being of the child.

Children entering foster care placement inevitably experience the pain of separation from their family setting, no matter how inadequate that setting has been. Grisby (1994) cites that the loss of an attachment figure arouses anxiety, and actual loss causes sorrow, which, in turn, is likely to arouse anger. Conversely, the maintenance of the bond is experienced as a source of security, and the renewal of a bond is often the source of joy.

It is very important that foster children, already damaged by past experiences, not be further damaged by abrupt procedures (Carbino, 1991). Abrupt removals of children can be damaging to the well-being of both children and foster families. Grisby (1994) adds that the interruption of the attachment relationship may be, in and of itself, detrimental to the child.

Abrupt removal from all persons to whom the child is relating as family, particularly if carried out by persons with whom the child does not have a solid relationship, may well be experienced from the young child's point of view more as kidnapping than protection. Carbino (1991) states that in all instances, abrupt, unplanned removal severely interferes with any sense of permanency and stability.

Whatever the reason for placement, foster children have not had a normal upbringing. By definition, the bonds to a foster child's permanent family have been disrupted. Foster children suffer disproportionately from serious emotional, medical, and psychological disabilities. To compound matters, Ryan (1981) cites that it is well established that foster children are at high risk of further maltreatment while in foster care.

No one knows how many children are abused or neglected while in foster care, but the problem is more widespread than is currently acknowledged. Much mistreatment of foster children goes unreported (Mushlin, 1988). These children may not report the abuse, or, if they do, they may not be believed. Ryan (1981) states that foster children seem particularly vulnerable to sexual abuse. This is a special problem because, by definition, there is no permanent kinship bond in foster care. As a result, the traditional incest taboo does not operate.

Several studies have found that the rate of abuse is much higher for foster children than for children in the general public (Mushlin, 1988). Mushlin further contends that the failure of the foster care programs to follow appropriate minimum standards that would ensure the care and protection of children has led to increased rates of foster care abuse and neglect.

One study reported that the rate of substantiated abuse and neglect in New York City foster family care was more than one and a half times that of children in the general population (Ryan, 1981). There were 49 abused children per 1,000 in the general population, and there were 77 abused children per 1,000 for children in foster family care.

Kaucher and Leon's study of the reasons for child foster care placement (1994) revealed that sexual abuse is a more frequent occurrence in the lives of foster children than is generally indicated. The courts identified sexual abuse in only 5 percent of the cases. Three months later, social workers determined that sexual abuse had been a factor in twice as many cases.

Carbino (1991) cites that the well-being of children is inseparable from the well-being of families of which they are members: Foster family stress resulting from agency responses to an abuse or neglect allegation will be felt by everyone in the family and is harmful to family interactions.

It is a policy of the agency that has placed Kendra that the safety of children who reside in their programs be assured. Consequently, if children state that they have been abused by their foster parent(s), they are immediately removed from the home and placed in another foster home, even if no physical evidence is found. In addition, if prospective foster parents state that they use corporal punishment to discipline their children and will continue to do so with potential foster children, they will not be eligible to be foster parents through the agency.

AUTHOR'S REFLECTIONS, REASONING PROCESS, AND RESOLUTION

Welfare of children, family values, safety, and autonomy are societal values that directly impact on this case. Traditionally, society has placed a high value on the welfare of children and the integrity of families. However, it wasn't until recently that the idea of children's "rights" was generally accepted.

Society has mobilized opinion and developed social institutions to support both children and their families. However, when faced with the abuse and neglect of children by their parents and caregivers, society has been reluctant to address the problems. There is, this worker feels, a paramount need for child protection through legislation, family rehabilitation, and an awareness in the community at large of the need to report such incidences.

The value of family as a unit (in this case composed of Mr. and Mrs. Doe, Tony, and Kendra) is also strongly supported by society. The Does' behavior exemplifies this: Although there have been severe problems and tensions between the Does and Tony,

(continued)

CASE STUDY 1.1   CONTINUED

they have allowed him to remain in the home until he has been able to make permanent plans for himself.

Within the structure of the agency, Kendra is clearly identified as the worker's primary client. The Code of Ethics (Section 1.01) stresses the importance of the worker's obligation to serve the best interests of the client. Therefore, the primacy of Kendra's interests must guide the worker in decision making.

Inherent in the social work profession is the need to respect the rights and dignity of everyone. For Kendra, the worker translates this mandate into two primary obligations: (1) Kendra, as does every other child, has the right to a permanent and stable home; (2) Kendra, and all children, have the right to safety.

Kendra is very attached to the Does and has been secure and happy in their home. Although the Does are not the primary clients, their values also play a role in the worker's understanding of Kendra's dilemma. They are devout in their practice of religion and value family togetherness and responsibility, having demonstrated this over the years by caring for Tony in their home. They love Kendra and have taken her into their home and hearts fully and completely. They demonstrate this by maintaining their desire to adopt Kendra.

The worker has always been a strong advocate of child welfare. She feels that it is very important that children grow up in a loving, nurturing, and safe environment. This is predicated on personal values that include close family relationships, friends, religious values, sincerity, and equality. In terms of the current dilemma, the worker takes a strong protectionist position, firmly believing that children are in need of special protection and that society has an obligation to ensure that protection. She believes that the welfare of all children should be of utmost concern to society.

The ethical dilemma illustrated by this case focuses on the avoidance of two harms: the family's disintegration (notion of permanency) and the potential for Kendra's abuse (notion of safety).

The Does feel obligation to both Tony and Kendra's best interests. For them, these would be served by maintaining the status quo: having both Tony and Kendra in their home, since they do not believe Tony's allegations of sexual abuse. As this is not possible, they have had to examine the situation for a more consequentialist position. This has led them to accept a "least harm" position that allows Tony to move to an independent living situation while adopting Kendra and keeping her at home with them. In advocating for Tony's independence, the worker has also supported this position.

If the worker focuses on a "greatest value" position, she must first determine whom she must consider in her equation. If she includes the Does in her considerations, she might find the greatest value in the return of Kendra to their home; certainly, this would provide immediate happiness for both the Does and Kendra. If, ultimately, she determines that she must consider only Kendra's good, the dilemma resolution is less clear from a theoretical standpoint.

Ethics of care theory is also relevant to this issue. Both Mr. and Mrs. Doe faced conflicts among their caregiving responsibilities: They had to confront Tony about his allegations, deal with the issue between themselves, watch Kendra be removed from their home, adjust to her loss, continue to live in the home with Tony after Kendra's removal, and struggle with the definition of their family.

Though Tony is not the worker's client, the definition of his "best interest" has an impact on the case. The Does define Tony's best interest as remaining with them, where he can be supervised and not be a disturbance to others. Tony defines his best interest as living independently of the Does. The worker is in agreement with Tony's definition, and the impact of her position can affect the family's attempt to address the problem. The ethics of care stresses the importance of promoting positive relationships, a difficult task for the worker in these circumstances. To support this ethic, the worker has arranged for the Does to visit Kendra at school weekly until a permanent plan can be made.

Two primary options present themselves as possibilities to the worker: (1) Kendra can remain at her present (new) placement. The family seems to be providing a safe and nurturing environment. This would maximize safety (potentially) and provide permanency (potentially); (2) Kendra can be returned to live with the Does, with the goal of adoption. This option would provide continuity of care as well as permanency, but leaves open the possibility of abuse by Tony at a later date, when the agency no longer has control over Kendra.

After much deliberation the worker has determined that Kendra's best interests are served by permanency, stability, and security in the only home she has ever known, with the parents who have cared for her and nurtured her thus far. The worker is familiar with the Does and has had a strong, positive relationship with them. It is felt that the values of the Does will support their ensuring the safety of Kendra during future visits with Tony and that the benefits of this placement far outweigh the uncertainties, the potential abuse and neglect, the possible changes in placements, and the lack of identity with parents, which are inherent in the present foster care system.

QUESTIONS FOR THOUGHT AND DISCUSSION

1. The author makes the assumption that, as Kendra's mother is not involved with her planning and care, the Does are, in effect, the "parents" of Kendra and proceeds with her dilemma on that basis. Do you regard them in this manner? If they are considered to be foster parents, as indeed they are, does this change the framing of the dilemma, or does it remain the same?

2. Is there an ethical responsibility on the part of the agency to involve/inform the biological mother of events? Should her status as an addict and abandoner deprive this mother of her parental rights, which she has not legally relinquished?

3. How do you think that the worker's personal values and stance in regard to advocacy for children affects the dilemma? Does it lead to any specific action in this situation?

4. What role do you think the worker's familiarity with the Does, and her respect for them, played in her final determination of placement for Kendra? Do you think this was justified?

5. Might any other steps have been taken to resolve the dilemma in a way that optimizes both permanency and safety?

■ ■ ■ ■ ■ ▬▬▬▬▬▬▬▬▬▬▬▬▬▬▬▬▬▬▬▬▬▬▬▬▬▬▬▬

CASE STUDY 1.2

WHEN "BEST INTERESTS OF CLIENT" HARM A THIRD PARTY

Abstracted from an unpublished paper by
Karen Altenberg Libman, MSW, MBA

PRACTICE CONTEXT AND CASE PRESENTATION

This ethical dilemma takes place in a special education treatment center for emotionally disturbed children, ages 6 through 12 years. Part of the treatment involves individual psychotherapy, and Suzanne, age 7, diagnosed with attachment disorder, has been seeing the caseworker twice weekly since entering the agency program, eight months previously. She lives in a group home with her 3-year-old sister, Cindy, and three other children. The sisters have been in the group home for two years, and parental rights are in the process of being terminated. Alternatives for long-term placement are being explored. Each child has her own worker, and the dilemma presented here is discussed from the perspective of Suzanne's worker.

Both Suzanne and Cindy's workers have been asked to make an independent recommendation regarding priorities: Should the sisters be placed together, or should each sibling be planned for separately? Both workers are aware that a recommendation to maintain the sibling relationship is likely to greatly reduce the adoption chances of the younger sibling: Cindy is a more desirable candidate if she is alone.

The worker faces a primary responsibility to Suzanne, as well as a responsibility to avoid harm to a relevant third party, Cindy. Suzanne's best interest is clearly to have the support of her sibling in the face of multiple family losses, plus an improved chance of adoption because of her connection with a younger, and therefore more desirable (in terms of adoption), sibling. This "best interest" could, however, harm Cindy, who could find an adoptive home more easily independent of Suzanne.

Thus, the dilemma may be specified as:

Best Interests of Client v. Obligation to Nonmaleficence

RESEARCH AND RELATED LITERATURE

Empirical research on the question of preserving the sibling relationship among children in foster care and adoption is limited. Although there is agreement in the literature that sibling relationships are an important part of child development, there is little concrete evidence about the impact of maintaining or separating the sibling subsystem (Hegar, 1988; Staff & Fein, 1992; Timberlake & Hamlin, 1982). Of the research that does exist, most investigators agree that most siblings should be placed together (Staff & Fein, 1992). The Child Welfare League of America's (CWLA) standard for out-of-home care for neglected and abused children clearly states, "siblings should remain together," but acknowledges that in some cases separation is indicated (1989, in Staff & Fein, 1992). The following discussion first presents support for keeping siblings together, then outlines some reasons why separation might be preferable.

According to Ward (1984), sibling bonds may be stronger than parental attachments in families where the parental system is dysfunctional. Siblings provide support to each other in the absence of appropriate parenting. When children are removed from the home, as in this case, the sibling attachment becomes primary because the siblings have been with each other longer than they have been with the parents. In such instances, separation from siblings may be even more stressful than separation from parents.

The sibling relationship provides mutual satisfaction for children in foster care and adoption (Ward, 1984). For the older sibling, the relationship provides an opportunity to "undo" the neglect and abuse from parents through caring for and controlling the younger child. This role can give the older child a sense of purpose and power. Meanwhile, the younger sibling gains a sense of protection and safety from the older sibling (Ward, 1984). Given the reciprocal nature of sibling relationships, children often feel that they have lost a part of themselves when separated from siblings, compounding separation and loss issues associated with foster care (Timberlake & Hamlin, 1982). Maintaining the intact sibling group affords children a natural support network for working through grief and developing a sense of identity (Timberlake & Hamlin, 1982). In the crisis of transitioning from one environment to another, the presence of a sibling provides continuity and predictability in a frightening situation (Ward, 1984). The sibling tie provides an important link to the past and preserves a sense of familial and individual identity (M. Owen, personal communication, 2/23/95; Ward, 1984).

Research suggests that maintaining the sibling relationship reduces the rate of placement disruption (Barth, Berry, Yoshikami, Goodfield, & Carson, 1988; M. Owen, personal communication, 2/23/95; Staff & Fein, 1992). Minimizing disruption of foster care or adoption placements is important for two reasons. First, according to Barth et al. (1988), previous disruptions increase the likelihood of future disruptions, creating a cycle of multiple placements. Second, multiple placements exacerbate and perpetuate the emotional problems of abused and neglected children.

A final point in support of maintaining the sibling relationship, supported by research noted above, indicates that older children have an increased chance of being adopted when they are paired with a younger, more desirable-age sibling (M. Owen, personal communication, 2/23/95).

There is some research that supports separating siblings to further the best interest of each. First, despite the CWLA's strong support for keeping siblings together, the organization acknowledges that in some situations siblings should be separated. Unfortunately, there is disagreement about which circumstances indicate separation (Staff & Fein, 1992). Hegar suggests that "if the relationship is stressful for both (siblings), and if one is the consistent loser in competition for adult affection and approval, then a separate placement for that child may develop self-esteem" (Hegar, 1988, in Staff & Fein, 1992, p. 258).

In the interest of Suzanne, some research indicates that children with attachment difficulties fare better when placed separately from their siblings. The director of the agency shares this view. In his experience, children with attachment problems are better able to attach to new families when only one child is in the home, because of reduced competition for parental affection. According to new evidence coming out of Evergreen, Colorado, a leading treatment center for attachment disordered children, the

(continued)

likelihood of placement disruption is so great among children with attachment difficulties that siblings of these children should be placed separately to protect them from unnecessary multiple placements (M. Owen, personal communication, 3/2/95). These findings have not yet been published, however.

There are a number of reasons why Cindy, the younger sister, would be more "adoptable" if she were alone. First, her age—3 years—makes her more desirable to prospective adoptive parents. Second, she is likely to have fewer emotional problems than the older sister because she has lived in a stable and safe environment for two of her three years. The extent of emotional and developmental damage that was done in the first year of life is unclear, but the two years of stability would likely have mended some wounds. Finally, having lived in a group home for the past two years with three other children besides her sister, the younger child's cognitive awareness and emotional bond to Suzanne as her sister may be only nominal. This is in contrast to Suzanne's more developed understanding of the sibling bond. On the other hand, the younger sister will eventually understand that she has a natural sister, and, at that time, might develop feelings of anger toward "the system" that denied her the opportunity and the right to know her sister. Guilt feelings are also likely to emerge from the knowledge that she was the "chosen" sister, the one selected for adoption while her sister was "rejected" (C. Littman, LCSW-C, personal communication, 3/25/95).

Concern for personal and individual freedom is reflected legally in the increased emphasis on safeguarding the rights of children in juvenile and family court practice (Hegar, 1988). In the legal literature, Reddick (in Hegar, 1988) argues for recognition of a "right of association" for siblings. In divorce and separation cases, where custody is disputed, the courts have shown a preference for keeping siblings together in the same parental home (Hegar, 1988). Generally, the focus is on the best interests of the child, rather than the interests of the parents.

The value of relationship in the field of social work is reflected in the CWLA standard for adoption services, which states, "When there are several children in a family, it is necessary to obtain information about their relationship to one another, in order to decide whether they should be placed together or separately" (CWLA, 1978, in Hegar, 1988, p. 118). Hegar points out that this is the only policy statement concerning sibling placement from a social work standard-setting body. Hegar (1988) summarizes the differences in emphasis between the social work and legal perspectives on sibling placement as needs-focused versus right-focused, respectively.

While the NASW Code of Ethics is explicit in stating that the social worker's primary responsibility is to the client (Sect. 1.01), it is silent on providing guidance on the worker's responsibility to third parties who are affected by decisions made in the interests of the client. Section 1.01 discusses "responsibility to the larger society" and "specific legal obligations" (to report) as situations where the primacy of a client's interest *may* need to be subject to other circumstances but does not address the issue under consideration. Section 1.06d discusses workers who provide services to "two or more persons who have a relationship with each other," but, in this instance, two clients are served by different workers in the same agency.

AUTHOR'S REFLECTIONS, REASONING PROCESS, AND RESOLUTION

Our society values the preservation of families and the right to maintain the family system, without undue intrusion from outside sources. While "family values" are loudly espoused, supporting families is a low priority in the allocation of resources.

The worker's personal values may be hierarchized as friendship, love, family, justice, individual freedom, equality, concern for others, knowledge, truth, and honesty. She has a strong responsibility to consider Suzanne's wishes in this regard and notes that Suzanne consistently expresses her strong tie to her sister and her desire to have a family.

The worker's ethical stance includes a tendency toward applying fundamental principles in a flexible manner based on the unique circumstances of a particular case, thus a preference for evaluating situations on a case-by-case basis rather than adhering to specific rules. Motivation is leaned on as a guiding principle, although outcome is also factored into the decision-making process. Reason is strongly valued as the best method for arriving at a decision.

The worker's values bias her views in this case in at least two ways. First, the orientation toward goodness and rightness of motivation determines the best possible plan. Second, the worker is willing to focus on Suzanne as her primary obligation because there is also a worker advocating for the best interests of Cindy.

One possible approach would apply a deontological theory of "shoulds" or "oughts." Under this type of theory, the focus is on motivation, rather than outcome, in determining "right." Ross presents a deontological theory based on common sense and intuition. He outlines seven obligations that should guide our motives and actions in order for decisions to be moral: nonmaleficence, beneficence, fidelity, reparation, gratitude, self-improvement, and justice. These basic and irreducible moral principles express prima facie obligations, reflecting society's collective knowledge (Beauchamp & Childress, 1994, pp. 103–104). Decisions and actions are considered moral when both the action is "right" and the motive is "good," according to the principles. When two obligations, or principles, are in conflict, then we need to use judgment to evaluate the specific circumstances of a case. In the case at hand, the relevant principles in Ross's theory are nonmaleficence and beneficence, which are in conflict. On one side of the dilemma is the beneficence toward the client, Suzanne, while on the other is the nonmaleficence obligation toward her sister, Cindy. Using Ross's theory, it might seem that the worker's obligation not to harm Cindy outweighs her obligation to the best interests of Suzanne. However, this would place the worker's responsibility to both as equal, which it is not, as Suzanne is the primary client.

Another theoretical approach for evaluating the ethical dilemma in this case is consequentialism, which holds that actions are right or wrong according to the balance of their good and bad consequences (Beauchamp & Childress, 1994, p. 55). The right act is the one that maximizes good, or minimizes bad, thereby producing the best overall result. Utilitarianism follows one universal overarching principle of pursuing the greatest good for the greatest number (Beauchamp & Childress, 1994, p. 55).

In evaluating this case using a utilitarian model, one needs to weigh the goods and harms of each side of the dilemma for each party. Tables presenting the goods and

(continued)

CASE STUDY 1.2   CONTINUED

harms of two decision options follow. As can be seen, the cumulative goods of keeping the siblings together outweigh the cumulative goods of separating them. Additionally, the cumulative harms of separating them outweigh those of keeping them together.

Evaluation of Good and Harm Using a Utilitarian Approach

CLIENT (SUZANNE)	THIRD PARTY (CINDY)
Siblings Remain Together—Good	
1. maintains familial bond and identity	1. maintains familial bond and identity
2. enhances sense of personal identity	
3. avoids another loss in a life filled with losses	
4. increases chances for adoption	
5. may reduce likelihood of placement disruption	
6. may reduce likelihood of multiple placements	
Siblings Remain Together—Harm	
1. may increase likelihood of placement disruption	1. reduces chances for adoption into a permanent home
Siblings Are Separated—Good	
1. increases administrative expediency	1. increases potential adoptive families
2. may improve the attachment process with new family	2. increases likelihood of permanent placement
3. may reduce likelihood of placement disruption	3. adoption may occur more quickly
Siblings Are Separated—Harm	
1. creates loss of familial bond	1. creates loss of familial bond
2. reduces sense of identity	2. creates guilt for being the "chosen" sister
3. may increase the likelihood of placement disruption	3. generates anger toward "the system" for being denied the opportunity to know her sister
4. creates another loss in a life filled with losses	
5. reduces chances for adoption	
6. may inhibit the attachment process	
7. increases feelings of rejection and low self-esteem	

Therefore, the utilitarian model points toward keeping the children together. In this case, act utilitarianism is applied. Rule utilitarianism in the case of foster care and adoption decisions seems less valid, considering the lack of concrete, clear evidence supporting the potential outcome on one side or the other. Additionally, complicating circumstances that are unique to individual cases seem to demand a case-by-case analysis for placement decision making.

Though the final decision is not the worker's, there are three possible recommendations she can make:

1. Actively pursue separate adoptions for the sisters.
2. Keep the siblings together unless or until an adoptive home becomes available for only one sister, then separate the children.
3. Keep the siblings together until a single adoptive home is available for both sisters.

The first alternative enables workers to assist the siblings to address the emotional and psychological issues. The worker's personal value of honesty supports this position. If both girls are considered equally the responsibility of the worker, then a deontological position could support this option as avoiding harm to Cindy.

The second alternative appears to be a nondecision—a postponement of resolution of the ethical dilemma. The illusion of the goal of maintaining the siblings together is preserved, but, in reality, one must acknowledge that an adoptive family will be found more easily for Cindy, and that, therefore, the girls are likely to be separated under this alternative. This alternative assumes that greater harm is done if placement is delayed until a home can be found for both: The younger sister is entitled to a stable, permanent home, despite the implications of this for Suzanne.

Upon reflection, the worker feels that the third alternative, keeping the sisters together, is the preferred choice. It is supported strongly by the utilitarian model, while the application of Ross's theory is affected by the need to determine if Suzanne and her sister should be considered equally the worker's responsibility. Many of the values explored earlier support keeping the siblings together. Societal and legal values reflect family unity, kinship, and preservation. Social work values place relationship and primacy of client interests as the most important values guiding ethical behavior. The client's own value system supports maintaining the sibling bond. The worker's personal values, which stress the importance of family ties, and her emotional bond with Suzanne also lead toward the support of this option. The uncertainty of the outcome that is inherent in this kind of decision making, however, must still be considered.

Although not unambiguous, the research supports the importance of the sibling bond for healthy child development, especially in cases where other family relationships are dysfunctional. In the face of all the losses that the girls have encountered, preserving the sibling tie as a source of continuity, identity, and security seems very important. The worker's motivation has been to benefit both girls, and it is felt that keeping them together would be the best way to do this.

QUESTIONS FOR THOUGHT AND DISCUSSION

1. If obligation to client is considered to be strictly primary, would this change the perception of the dilemma, or even the existence of a dilemma?

2. If this worker were assigned to both siblings, would the reasoning and the outcomes have differed?

3. In laying out the utilitarian calculus, the worker weighs each item in the "goods" and "harms" list equally. Do you feel that this is justified, or do you think that certain items on the list should carry a heavier weight? How would you assign such weights?

4. As Suzanne is older, keeping the siblings together might also realistically mean that adoption might not be possible for either and that they would grow up within the foster care system. What role do you think this consideration should play, if any, in arriving at a decision?

5. The worker's personal hierarchy of values begins with "friendship," "love," "family," and these values appear to have a role in the final resolution of her dilemma. If your personal hierarchy began with "justice" and "equality," might this affect your reasoning? In what way?

■ ■ ■ ■ ■ ▬▬▬▬▬▬▬▬▬▬▬▬▬▬▬▬▬▬▬▬▬▬▬▬▬▬▬▬▬▬▬▬

CASE STUDY 1.3

WHEN LIVING FEELS LIKE DYING: ETHICAL DECISION MAKING WITH A DEPRESSED DIALYSIS PATIENT

Abstracted from an unpublished paper by Mary A. Kardauskas, SHCJ, MSW

PRACTICE CONTEXT AND CASE PRESENTATION

Renal dialysis social workers encounter a variety of ethical issues in their professional practice. Ethical dilemmas frequently center around client self-determination, prolongation of life, confidentiality, resource availability, and hospital/insurance company policies and practices, which may conflict with social work values. The following "composite" case illustrates several of these issues.

The Department of Social Work Services and Utilization Case Management at a major medical center employs two full-time renal dialysis social workers to address the biopsychosocial needs of patients in the inpatient and outpatient dialysis units. Renal social workers provide emotional and concrete support services to patients and families on a long-term basis, addressing patients' adjustment to illness, rights, financial/resource concerns, and social support needs. Renal workers also discuss the issue of Advance Directives with patients and are occasionally called on to interpret patients' wishes when surrogates cannot be reached during a medical crisis.

Mrs. B., a divorced 38-year-old, was diagnosed with end-stage renal disease and juvenile-onset diabetes. She had been a hemodialysis patient since 1986. Forced to leave her job in 1991 due to rapidly declining health, Mrs. B. was soon after faced with desertion by her husband. Her mother, sensing her need and vulnerability, moved in to provide stability and support to her daughter and 8-year-old grandson. Her mother and her son have turned to religion for support.

Over the past year, Mrs. B. has been repeatedly hospitalized, and her intermittent depression has been noted by family and staff. One day during her treatment, she announced to her physician and social worker, "I'm tired of fighting. Living on this machine is worse than dying." She stated she wanted to terminate treatment. Her mother long ago agreed to act as her son's guardian, and she knew he will be well cared for. Mrs. B. had an advance directive that named her mother as her decision maker should she be unable to make decisions herself.

Mrs. B.'s mother was appalled by her daughter's request. She stated that her daughter is "too young to die," and considered her daughter's request suicidal. She stated that Mrs. B.'s giving up like this would set a bad example of coping for her son. Their church holds that all life is sacred, that taking life is a sin, and that "God never gives you more than you can bear." She insisted that the hospital deny Mrs. B.'s request because her depression rendered her incompetent to make medical decisions. She invokes her power as the decision maker named in her daughter's Advance Directive.

In considering Mrs. B.'s request to terminate dialysis, the principal ethical dilemma seems to center on *quality* of life versus prolongation of *biological* life. Related ethical

(continued)

CASE STUDY 1.3   CONTINUED

issues include client self-determination, competency, determining who is the client, welfare of the child, Advance Directives (surrogate's unwillingness to uphold patient wishes), conflicting religious beliefs and values, and physical and psychological definitions of life and death.

The dilemma is specified as:

Quality of Life v. Prolongation of (Biological) Life

RESEARCH AND RELATED LITERATURE

Over the past quarter of a century, dialysis treatment (and near universal health coverage under the 1972 End-Stage Renal Program of Medicare) has saved and extended the lives of literally hundreds of thousands of renal patients. Dialysis prolongs, but does not necessarily ensure quality of, life.

End-stage renal disease (ESRD) affects body function, self-perception, self-image, lifestyle, relationships, vocational function, and financial security and requires ongoing adaptation to illness (Frazier, 1981; Wolcott, 1990). Patients with long-term renal failure and uremia may eventually experience dysfunction in nearly any organ or part of the body. Concurrent illness, such as diabetes or AIDS, may exacerbate the problem (Wolcott, 1990). Depression, the most common psychiatric problem among such patients (Hodroff, 1994; Kimmel, 1994) and an important predictor of mortality (Kimmel, 1994), has been associated with lower quality of life, impaired immunologic function, treatment noncompliance, withdrawal from treatment, and higher suicide rates (Levy, 1991; Sensky, 1993; Wolcott, 1990). Children whose parents are chronically ill may experience fear of abandonment, anger, resentment, guilt, and worry about what will happen to them upon their parent's death.

Requests to terminate dialysis are not unusual, and poor quality of life is a frequently cited reason. Withdrawal from dialysis is now the third most common cause of death among dialysis patients in the United States (Kjellstrand, 1992) and accounted for 8.4 percent of all ESRD deaths in the United States in 1990 (U.S. Renal Data System, 1993). Once dialysis is terminated, death is painless, gradual, but inevitable. Neu and Kjellstrand's (1986) study of 155 renal patients who stopped dialysis found that death occurred in 1 to 28 days, with an average of 8.1 days.

While the concept of the quality of life can be traced back to such ancient philosophers as Aristotle (Ferrans, 1987) and is today often cited as a reason to refuse or withdraw life-sustaining medical treatment, there exists no one standard definition of the term (Ferrans, 1987; Walter & Shannon, 1990). Some common definitions focus on an individual's "social utility," ability to live a normal life, and happiness or satisfaction. Perlman and Jonsen (1990, p. 100) note that many authors use the term to reflect an individual's "subjective satisfaction . . . with his or her own personal life (physical, mental, and social situation)," but that it may alternately refer to an onlooker's (e.g., physician, surrogate) evaluation of another's life situation. An onlooker's view might not match that of the patient, as is evident in the present case.

The sanctity-of-life principle, central to Jewish and Christian religions as well as to secular humanism, maintains that all life is sacred and that the value of physical life is not conditional on an individual's property or characteristics. In so doing, it stands as an important reminder that quality-of-life judgments based on life satisfaction and social utility risk heading down the "slippery slope."

"Sanctity of life," however, has been argued from different perspectives. Absolutists (such as Immanuel Kant) vehemently protest humans' propensity to "play God." Lammers and Verhey (1987, p. 439, emphasis added) illustrate this view: "If withdrawing care results in death, is this really different from more actively aiming at the death of the patient? . . . Death *cannot* be chosen in preference to some lesser evil. . . ." Similarly, Smedes (1987, p. 147) writes:

> (God) gives us the right to stave death off, if we can, with medicine and machines. . . . God alone has the right to take away life, because he is the one who authors it in the first place. . . . If there is a right time for any person to die, God alone may decide what it is.

Meanwhile, others (including Roman Catholic ethicists) distinguish between ordinary and extraordinary treatment. Keyserlingk (1990, p. 43) maintains that preserving a life where there is "excruciating, intractable and prolonged pain and suffering," or where there is "minimal capacity to experience, to relate to other human beings," could be a "dishonouring of the sanctity of life itself," and further suggests that allowing death might be "a demonstration of respect for the individual and for human life in general."

While theologians and others denounce subjective judgments of one's "relative worth" or "social utility," they acknowledge a person's legal/ethical right to make medical decisions. Personalistic quality-of-life judgments involve assessing the benefits and burdens of medical treatment: one's experience of joy, satisfaction, burdens, and suffering; the kind of life possible, given one's prognosis; and the degree to which a condition allows one to live a life that he or she views as worth living (Hastings Center, 1987). Consequentialists also consider the impact on others.

Client self-determination is closely linked to quality-of-life decisions, but serious ethical dilemmas abound. As evidenced by the 1990 U.S. Supreme Court decision in *Cruzan* v. *Director, Missouri Dept. of Health* (Cranford, 1992), the legal system recognizes a competent patient's right to refuse treatment. Similarly, the Patient Self-Determination Act of 1990, enacted to "enhance an individual's control over medical treatment decisions" at hospitals and healthcare institutions (Sabatino, 1993, p. 12), has resulted in guidelines for forgoing life-sustaining treatment. Kidney machines are included among such treatments. If competency is an issue, guidelines specify a psychiatric consultation to determine capacity.

Renal social work colleagues note the intensely personal decision-making process followed by patients who consider terminating dialysis. Issues of competency, however, raise special dilemmas. Patients' abilities to make rational choices may be severely compromised by depression or other psychiatric conditions. Many chronically ill patients experience bouts of depression and confusion (Beauchamp & Childress, 1994). Since termination of treatment inevitably results in death, renal patients' competence to make such decisions must be carefully assessed. Unfortunately, patients whose request is not supported by the wider medical community may be subjected to a psychiatric

CASE STUDY 1.3 CONTINUED

consultation, deemed "incompetent," and their care decisions rendered by surrogates. Thus, a process designed to empower patients may leave some patients feeling depressed and powerless to free themselves from unwanted life-sustaining measures.

While appearing to avoid quality- and sanctity-of-life issues, the NASW Code of Ethics (1996) states that workers "respect and promote the rights of clients to self-determination and assist clients in their efforts to identify and clarify their goals." One might well question how to foster "the rights of clients to self-determination" with a depressed, terminal patient. The position of Mrs. B.'s mother, who is "legally authorized to act on behalf of a client . . . with the client's best interest in mind" must also be considered. "Best interest" tends to be a subjective judgment, relative to the person making it. In this instance, the client's self-determined judgment of her own "best interest" is quite different from that of her mother.

The values set forth by Compton and Galaway (1989) as the bases for social work may also be perceived to be in conflict here. Belief in "client self-determination" could be seen as grounds to support Mrs. B., while supporting the "uniqueness and inherent dignity of the individual" could be read as grounds for upholding her unique, sacred, valuable life.

AUTHOR'S REFLECTIONS, REASONING PROCESS, AND RESOLUTION
Mrs. B.'s request to forgo dialysis is supported by laws and popular opinion concerning quality of life, self-determination and respect for autonomy, personal freedom of choice, and human/legal rights. Her mother's position highlights other societal values: religious belief of sanctity of life, safety ("protecting" her daughter from suicide, shielding her grandson from "poor coping skills"), youth (an obligation to "protect" her daughter), human/legal rights (to legally contest her daughter's competence to make her own decisions), and child welfare (her grandson's needs).

The worker's values (sanctity of life, freedom/autonomy, relationships, safety, and justice) flow from her religious beliefs, which reverence the life and dignity of each person, but she does not subscribe to the preservation of biological life at all costs. Her personal value of freedom and her respect for autonomy enable her to resonate with Mrs. B.'s desire to balance the benefits and burdens of extraordinary treatment, but conflicts with her concern about Mrs. B.'s ability to make such a decision while depressed. The worker values relationships and the commitments they entail, but views Mrs. B.'s decision about treatment as a personal one that she must make in the light of her own situation. The worker's value of safety could potentially spark paternalistic responses to this depressed, terminally ill patient who requests to end her life, but the patient's grim prognosis suggests an advanced disease process where aggressive treatment might stretch the psychosocial reserves of patient and family beyond their limits. The worker's concern for justice causes her to feel committed to advocate for patient self-determination, yet also to understand Mrs. B.'s mother's desire to act justly by preventing a hastened death.

Four key and sometimes conflicting biomedical ethics principles are in evidence in this case: beneficence (balancing benefits against risks and costs); nonmaleficence (avoiding harm); respect for autonomy; and justice (norms for distributing benefits, risks, and costs). Mrs. B. balances the risks and costs of treatment and seeks relief via termination of dialysis; her mother sees no way to balance death against life, and wants to prolong her daughter's life, keep the family together, and "follow God's will." Mrs. B. seeks to avoid the harm of a poor quality of life with death; her mother desires to block the "suicide request" as the greater harm. Mrs. B.'s autonomous decision sets her against her mother's equally autonomous decision. And Mrs. B. sees justice in being able to control her medical care, while her mother sees it in the prevention of a "tragic" suicide.

In support of Mrs. B.'s "poor-quality-of-life" position, several options might be considered. The social worker could call a patient care conference with the patient, renal physician, primary nurse, dietitian, social worker, and members of the family present in order to better identify and address Mrs. B.'s concerns. Options could be explored that might improve her quality of life while preserving her biological life, such as pain management, diabetes and/or renal treatment, and addressing uremia if present. A psychiatric consult might recommend appropriate therapeutic intervention to treat her depression and enhance her coping skills. A support group might assist Mrs. B. in working through some of her feelings about her condition and situation.

It would also be possible to hold the patient care conference but to respect Mrs. B.'s decision to terminate treatment if she still chooses to do so after being informed of all the risks and benefits. The care conference could then be used to address the family's issues, offer support, and provide them with information as well as appropriate referrals. This option respects self-determination and quality-of-life issues, but, by not providing a means to assess Mrs. B.'s "competence," nonmaleficence and sanctity of life might be violated. It would also be possible to accept Mrs. B.'s request for the termination of treatment at face value, without subjecting her to the patient care conference. The worker's role would be to serve both as patient advocate (working with the medical staff, supporting her through her final days, asking her to state her request in writing, helping her to name an alternative surrogate, for example), and as a mediator between patient and family, supporting the family's needs with referrals, legal assistance (for grandson), and so on. This option would also support the values of quality of life and self-determination, but possibly violate nonmaleficence, sanctity of life, and safety by failing to address the competence issue.

In support of the prolongation of biological life, one approach might be to assume that *all* requests to terminate life support warrant a psychiatric evaluation to determine competence. When patients are declared incompetent, surrogates may then override the patients' requests. While this absolutist position upholds the sanctity of life on one level, it also equates patient requests to terminate treatment with "incompetence," invalidates patients' experiences, and thus violates the values of dignity and sanctity it seeks to uphold. It may also violate the principle of nonmaleficence, promote paternalism, and undermine self-determination and justice.

Another possible plan might be to treat Mrs. B. pharmacologically for depression, provide cognitive-behavioral treatment, or logotherapy. As in the first option, the central concern here is who decides incompetence and upon what criteria. If Mrs. B. is judged incompetent only because her choice conflicts with her physician's moral and

(continued)

CASE STUDY 1.3   CONTINUED

ethical position, it might be more appropriate to refer her to another physician rather than subjecting her to interventions against her will. Treatment upholds the values of sanctity of life, nonmaleficence, safety, youth, and quality of life, but potentially can violate self-determination and autonomy, quality-of-life and human/legal rights.

Another possible approach might be to refer the case to the hospital Ethics Committee for review. Competence issues might be discussed more objectively in such an environment. However, recommendations of the ethics committee can still be disregarded, by either Mrs. B. or her mother.

The ethical position chosen by the worker combines elements of both quality-of-life and prolongation of life approaches. It is consequentialist in nature and utilitarian in approach, focusing on the greatest good for the greatest number. It involves several steps: validation, evaluation, collaboration, short-term contracting, and intervention (if agreed on). Preparation, information, and referral for both Mrs. B. and the family would be provided.

Mrs. B.'s request and right to refuse treatment should be immediately validated, and she should be informed that her request is taken seriously. She also should be informed of any standardized procedures for handling such requests, as well as the reasons for such procedures. A psychiatric evaluation to measure her depression, using measures that have proven reliable and valid with the renal population, should be provided immediately. A patient care conference should follow soon after, spelling out her prognosis, the costs and benefits of her options, and what occurs once dialysis is discontinued. Together, the care team and the patient can address the options and alternatives available to her, such as pain management, therapy, and planning to reduce stresses induced by financial condition, strained relationships, or other problems. If Mrs. B. is agreeable, specified services can be contracted for a brief (three- or four-week) period of time. At the end of the contract period, Mrs. B.'s request could be reviewed again and changes in her perceptions and decisions discussed.

If Mrs. B. continues to request the termination of treatment, this request should be honored. She should be allowed to choose the date she wishes to discontinue treatment, as well as the place she wishes to spend her final days. Clergy, legal counsel, and changes in designated surrogate could be offered.

The social worker should meet with the family to provide information and support, and referrals to the Ethics Committee and/or outside resources can be offered. They should be assisted in saying their goodbyes and be supported upon Mrs. B.'s death.

The resolution suggested here is both absolutist (in suggesting a protocol) and relativist (in its sensitivity to Mrs. B.'s particular case). The sense of duty to protect life is deontological, while its efforts to offer "the greatest good" is teleological. It upholds the biomedical ethical principles of nonmaleficence in preventing passive, voluntary euthanasia chosen because of depression; of beneficence, by clearly spelling out risks and benefits; of autonomy in upholding Mrs. B.'s right to self-determination; and of justice in proposing the development and use of a protocol. It upholds societal, professional, client and worker values of quality of life, as well as sanctity of life, religious belief, self-determination, family relationships, safety, and justice. It passes Loewenberg and

Dolgoff's (1992) Ethical Principles Screen: protecting life, yet also balancing risks and benefits; evidencing equality, reverencing autonomy and independence, causing least harm, attending to quality-of-life issues, and incorporating truthfulness and full disclosure.

In facilitating communication between the patient/family unit and the healthcare team, providing information and support to patient and family, advocating for patient rights, and providing comfort and support to the family, social workers who work with cases such as this one can enable individuals and families to face difficult and final decisions with sensitivity and dignity.

QUESTIONS FOR THOUGHT AND DISCUSSION

1. Does the phrasing of the dilemma as simply "quality of life" adequately and clearly represent what is at issue here? Is there another way that it might be stated?

2. Dialysis also presents the possibility of a distributive issue. There is another patient in need of dialysis who wants to live and who could use Mrs. B.'s time slot for treatment. Should this be a factor in your decision?

3. If a patient has given decision-making rights to another individual, and then disagrees with the individual, how would you decide which position has the greater strength? Should a patient whose decision runs contrary to your own, the physician's, or a multidisiplinary team's values be deemed "incompetent"?

4. There are several ways in which quality of life may be evaluated, each of them subjective: The person may be considered the only valid judge of life quality; the family may judge based on their knowledge and experience with the person; a professional may judge based on experience with similar situations, knowledge of medical and psychological processes, and so on; a group, such as an Ethics Committee, may judge based on their collective impressions. In cases where assessments do not agree, whose assessment do you feel is most valid?

5. What is (or should be) the ethical responsibility of the caregivers who would be responsible for putting any choices made by any of the persons suggested in question 4 into effect? Whose recommendations, if any, are they obligated to follow? What if their personal ethical position differs from these recommendations?

CASE STUDY 1.4

READING THE FUTURE: WHEN "BEST INTEREST" MUST LAST TWENTY YEARS

Abstracted from an unpublished paper by Amy Craig-Van Grack, MSW

PRACTICE CONTEXT AND CASE PRESENTATION

The Out-of-Home Unit provides services to families with children who have been removed from their homes, usually due to substantiated abuse or neglect. Services are provided to the family and child by the assigned social worker on a loosely defined case management basis; that is, the worker (a) assesses the needs of the family; (b) develops a case plan and service contract; (c) delivers or refers, coordinates and monitors service provision (i.e., drug treatment, therapy, job training); and (d) works with the family and child until case plan goals are achieved. Permanency plans for these children range from reunification with biological parent(s), custodial placement with extended family, adoption, long-term foster care, and/or preparation for independent living. Oversight of the caseworker's activities is provided routinely through supervision, administrative review, and court review of each case.

Tonya Morris was born fifteen days after her father, Terence Calvert, was incarcerated due to his conviction on drug possession and distribution charges. The next day, her mother, Paula Morris, left Tonya with an "unwilling caregiver" and never returned to reclaim her. Tonya was placed in foster care with Beverly Becker where she remains today—nearly nineteen months later. Tonya's mother is a long-time drug user, and Tonya apparently suffered exposure to drugs *in utero*. Since Tonya's placement in foster care, the agency has been unable to locate her. Mr. Calvert would like to care for Tonya. However, she would likely be 2 years old before reunification could feasibly be initiated.

Tonya is obviously very bonded to and well-loved by her foster mother and foster sister. Her foster mother has expressed a desire to adopt Tonya on several occasions. Hers is the only home Tonya has known, and she is happy and secure in this placement.

The worker faces the dilemma of:

Best Interests of Child v. Parental Rights

RESEARCH AND RELATED LITERATURE

What Do Children Need? Abraham Maslow delineated a pyramid of "needs and values which are related to one another in order of their strength and priority, in a manner which is both hierarchical and developmental" (Longres, 1990, p. 356). These needs, in descending order of significance, are (1) basic physiological need, (2) personal safety needs, (3) belongingness and love needs, (4) esteem needs (self and others), and (5) self-actualization needs (Longres, 1990). Similarly, Erik Erikson advanced a theory of psychosocial development "derived from the . . . principle of epigenesis, or the idea that each stage depends on resolutions of the experiences of prior stages" (Greene & Ephross, 1991, p. 84). Erikson used the concept of an expanding "radius of significant relationships" to describe the child's experience of human relationships throughout the life cycle. Thus, the child's needs must be assessed on a number of levels—physical, cognitive, emotional, and social. Moreover, these needs must be considered on a vertical axis (signifying priority) and on a horizontal axis (signifying time).

Most developmental theorists identify interpersonal difficulties in adulthood as reverberations of childhood relationship and attachment issues. For children in foster care, the issue of attachment is particularly germane as it may circumscribe development and adult functioning: "[F]oster children in clinical settings have been characterized as lacking the ability to form relationships, having inadequate parental images (either glorified or denigrated) to serve as a basis for socialization, and being confused about their identities. . . ." (Fein, 1991b, pp. 578–579). Additionally, there is "evidence that many foster children have serious educational deficits, are in poorer health, and are more likely than other children to suffer developmental and emotional problems and to have limited access to appropriate health and mental health care" (Allen, 1991, p. 613).

Goldstein, Freud, and Solnit (1973) substantiate "the need of every child for unbroken continuity of affection and stimulating relationships with an adult" (Goldstein, Freud, & Solnit, 1973, p. 6). They define and differentiate the concepts of the "wanted child," the "psychological parent," and the "biological parent." They advance a number of principles regarding child development—namely, that the child's development unfolds in response to environmental influence; that children have innate characteristics that influence their interaction; that during childhood, children change constantly, whereas adults are more or less psychically fixed; that the child's needs are not stable; that children have a different sense of time than adults; that children lack reason to interpret events; and that "children have no psychological conception of relationship by blood tie until quite late in their development" (Goldstein et al., 1973, p. 12). The integration of these principles lead the authors to conclude that "[c]ontinuity of relationships, surroundings, and environmental influence are essential for a child's normal development" (Goldstein et al., 1973, p. 31).

What Are Parents' Rights with Respect to Their Children? Children have historically been viewed as chattel, the property of the father, who retained complete control over their well-being, care, and all other aspects of their lives. However, in the late 1800s, "there was a dramatic shift away from fathers' common law rights to custody and control of their children toward a modern emphasis on the best interests of the child . . ." (Mason, 1994, xiii). Currently, when the family breaks down, due to death, divorce, parental abuse or neglect, the state asserts itself as the arbiter of the child's best interests. At this point, issues of child custody and best interests become considerably more complicated. Nonetheless, "[t]he basic right of biological parents to the custody of their children has not appreciably diminished" (Derdeyn, 1977a, p. 377).

Freedom and privacy are first-order principles in the United States, espoused in the Constitution and the Bill of Rights. Rights apply to families as well as to individuals. "Family privacy, freedom from government interference, and the right to raise children according to individual beliefs are among the fundamental rights secured by the

(continued)

CASE STUDY 1.4   CONTINUED

Constitution" (Huxtable, 1994, p. 60). Thus, parents have a right to privacy and to freedom to maintain their families as they choose insofar as their actions do not compromise their children's physical safety and general well-being.

When a report of abuse or neglect (or, in this case, abandonment) is made, family freedom and privacy are necessarily reduced as the state exercises its duty to protect the child from harm (Stein, 1991). If a report is substantiated, the family (parent *and* child) has a statutory right to "reasonable efforts" to preserve the family and prevent placement of the child in alternative care. In fact, state agencies are required to demonstrate reasonable efforts to the courts prior to removing a child. If a child is removed, the family has a right to "reasonable efforts" to reunify the family. Thus, if a report is made and substantiated, the parents and child have a right to services designed to mitigate the conditions deemed harmful to the child. It can be further argued that the right to services includes a presumption of timeliness and efficacy of those services.

The parent has a right to visitation unless visitation is deemed to be harmful to the child. Further, the agency is required to promote and facilitate visitation, including transporting participants and supervising visits if necessary. Finally, a parent is guaranteed due process prior to removal of his or her children and prior to termination of his or her parental rights.

Where Does the Law Stand? Child welfare and the law in the United States have become more deeply and inextricably linked during the latter half of the twentieth century. Moreover, "[i]n the legal arena, superimposed upon the essentially immutable tradition of a biological parent's proprietary interest in his children, there is a growing awareness of the emotional needs of children" (Derdeyn, 1977b, p. 611). Hence, the legislative and judicial domains are increasingly prescriptive and proscriptive regarding service delivery to families and children. Federal policy concerning children in out-of-home placement is primarily contained in Public Law 96-272, the Adoption Assistance and Child Welfare Act of 1980.

That legislation was designed to end the drift of children in foster care by encouraging planning for permanency for each child within a hierarchy of desirable options, ranging from returning the child to his or her biological parents, through adoption, to long-term foster care. It was also meant to provide for oversight to move cases through the child welfare system and to develop preventive services to avert the family breakdown that removal of children from the home entails (Fein, 1991a, p. 576). States, including the District of Columbia, enact legislation that complies, for the most part, with federal legislation in order to secure funds to deliver services to families with children in out-of-home placements.

In the child welfare arena, children have the right to protection from harm and to reasonable efforts to preserve and/or reunify their families. However, in cases involving conflict over custody, children do not necessarily have the right to choose. Nonetheless, they do have a right to the representation of a *guardian ad litem* who has no conflict of interest or obligation and advises the decision-making body regarding the child's best interest. Also, while professionals across the spectrum concur that a child needs permanence and stability, these cannot be legislated as rights. It is apparent from the often vague or undefined terms in legislation (i.e., "reasonable efforts" and "best interests") that legislators have similarly struggled to strike a balance between the best interests of children and the rights of parents.

Further, with regard to visitation, "[s]tates and federal statutes recognize the importance of parental visiting. Some states require agency staff to promote visiting. Others allow failure to visit to be used as a basis for termination of parental rights . . ." (Proch & Howard, 1984, p. 140). In addition to legislation, court rulings impact parent-child relationships. With regard to this particular case, "incarcerated parents have a constitutionally protected right to visits with their children" and "efforts of an incarcerated parent to continue contact with her or his children must be considered in relation to the limits that imprisonment places on parents" (Stein, 1991, p. 74).

Finally, however, if reunification with the biological parent is deemed contrary to the child's best interest, the parent has the right to due process prior to termination of his or her parental rights. Nonetheless, "[t]he conditions that serve to justify removing a child from an unsafe environment are not necessarily sufficient to justify severing parental ties. . . . [T]he state must show that the consequences of allowing the parent-child relationship to continue are more severe than the consequences of termination" (Stein, 1991, p. 71). Again, with respect to the facts of this specific case, "imprisonment alone is not sufficient grounds to terminate parental rights" (Stein, 1991, p. 74). However, a New York court ruled that "an imprisoned parent's consent to adoption was not necessary and that termination without his consent did not violate his due process rights if there was clear and convincing evidence that adoption was in the child's best interests" (Stein, 1991, p. 74).

Where Does Agency Policy Stand? Legislation and judicial decisions often dictate agency policy. Agency regulations are written and implemented to comply with the law. In child welfare, this can be an onerous task. Nonetheless, the agency attempts to conform with the bulk of the law reviewed above.

In terms of the value-base of the agency, its mission statement makes these clear: "The mission . . . is to support the development of healthy families; to assist families and children in need; to protect abused and neglected children; and to provide a permanent home for all children. This mission is accomplished . . . through a service delivery system which recognizes the value of cultural diversity and family strengths . . ." (Family Services Administration, 1995). Seven principles are delineated to provide guidance for the agency worker: (1) Children need families; (2) safety is the first concern; (3) a crisis is an opportunity for change; (4) not all problems need to be addressed; (5) most families do care about each other; (6) everyone is doing the best he or she can at the time; and (7) power for change resides within the family. In order of preference, the agency supports: (1) reunification with biological parents; (2) return to a relative; (3) adoption; (4) independent living; and (5) long-term foster care.

NASW Code of Ethics. Among the Ethical Principles that apply to this dilemma, under the value of Social Justice, is the statement that social workers "strive to ensure

(continued)

CASE STUDY 1.4   CONTINUED

equality of opportunity. . . ." As a parent, Mr. Calvert is entitled to be able to maintain a relationship with his daughter. Under the value of Dignity and Worth of the Person, it is noted that workers should treat each client in a "caring and respectful manner" and "promote client's socially responsible self-determination." Additionally, under the value of Importance of Human Relationships, it states, "Social workers seek to strengthen relationships among people in a purposeful effort to promote, restore, maintain, and enhance the well-being of individuals, families, social groups . . ." (NASW Code of Ethics, 1996).

Certainly, these sections of the Code support the consideration of the rights of Mr. Calvert and the value and importance of family relationships.

Additionally, in the Ethical Standards section of the Code (6.04b), it is stated, "Social workers should act to expand choice and opportunity for all people, with special regard for vulnerable, disadvantaged, oppressed and exploited people and groups." In his state of incarceration, Mr. Calvert is certainly vulnerable and disadvantaged. It is uncertain whether the reasons for his incarceration, drug possession and distribution, are related to oppression. Section 6.04d states, "Social workers should act to prevent and eliminate" domination, exploitation, and discrimination. To impede the exercise of Mr. Calvert's parental rights would seem to violate this obligation by denying him parental rights due to his incarceration. He is following the laws, accepting punishment, and wants to be a parent to Tonya.

However, Tonya is the worker's primary client, and her obligation, clearly, is to her (Sect. 1.01). As a minor, Tonya lacks full decision-making capacity, and the social worker must act in her behalf. Section 1.14 states, "When social workers act on behalf of clients who lack the capacity to make informed decisions, social workers should take reasonable steps to safeguard the interests and rights of those clients." It is the worker's responsibility to ensure that Tonya's interests are protected. This might support her remaining with her secure and nurturing foster family.

AUTHOR'S REFLECTIONS, REASONING PROCESS, AND RESOLUTION
The worker believes in the determinative nature of childhood experience and values responsible, loving parenting. This position is confirmed by societal values, which, however, place biological ties above other concerns. Translated into agency policy and child welfare laws, the hierarchy supports: (1) the primacy of biological ties, (2) the child's well-being, (3) freedom and self-determination, (4) privacy, and (5) the importance of family. It may be assumed that this case remains open at the agency due to society's stronger emphasis on biological ties. (Otherwise, it would have been moved to adoption.) Tonya's age at the time of her placement (20 days old) and the duration of her placement (possibly as long as two years) distinguish this case, for the worker, from similar cases.

Two possible courses of action include (1) continuing efforts for and ultimately reunifying Tonya with her biological father or (2) seeking administrative and court approval of a change in goal from reunification to adoption or long-term foster care. The first option would preserve Mr. Calvert's rights as Tonya's biological father to regain custody. The second option would enhance Tonya's chances for permanence and stability as it is fairly certain that a change in goals would ensure Tonya's continuing long-term care by Ms. Becker. However, a goal of adoption would require that the agency seek to terminate Mr. Calvert's parental rights. Considering the circumstances of this case and the research elaborated above, it seems plausible that a court would allow a termination in the "best interests of the child." A goal of long-term foster care would *not* require a termination of parental rights.

Research cites foster care reentry rates of close to 33 percent for children following reunification (Fein & Staff, 1993; Hess & Folaron, 1991). Further, "the most frequent contributor to placement reentry [is] the fact that the problems of the parents that precipitated placement [are] not resolved. The number and severity of the parents' problems also contribute to reentry . . ." (Hess & Folaron, 1991, p. 408). Other factors that contribute to a poor prognosis for successful reunification in this case include Mr. Calvert's history with drugs, his criminal record, lack of a high school degree or GED, apparent lack of an informal support system, lack of a home or prospective employment, and lack of knowledge and experience in child-rearing. Reunification with Mr. Calvert would, therefore, be considered very "high risk." Additionally, none of these factors addresses a lack of strong relationship between Tonya and Mr. Calvert.

On the other hand, a change in goal to adoption or long-term foster care would almost certainly ensure that Tonya would remain with her psychological family, maintain her affective ties and give her the best chance for optimal personal development—all of which are advocated by Goldstein et al. (1973). Her placement with Ms. Becker, who has demonstrated her care to be very loving and comprehensive and is extremely unlikely to withdraw from her current charge as Tonya's primary caregiver, can be considered "low risk." Moreover, remaining with Ms. Becker would not preclude Tonya from establishing and maintaining a relationship with her biological father, regardless of whether his parental rights are terminated.

There are a number of principles to be found in ethical theory that direct the decision-making process. These principles include "nonmaleficence," the "greatest good for the greatest number," "least harm," "substituted judgment," "best interests," and "quality of life." The concept of nonmaleficence might lead one to avoid abrogating the biological relationship. However, it might also discourage interrupting the psychological relationship. All of the other ethical principles weigh heavily in favor of the second option of changing Tonya's goal from reunification to adoption or long-term foster care. For example, in attempting to allow Tonya self-determination regarding her living situation and by recognizing a child's limited understanding of blood ties (Goldstein et al., 1973), one might "substitute" a judgment that she would prefer to remain in Ms. Becker's care until such time as she was old enough to understand her incontrovertible relationship with Mr. Calvert and choose otherwise.

The values hierarchy pits the importance of biological ties vis-à-vis the child's well-being. The practice issues cited above, however, require that one evaluate the high risk to Tonya's well-being of preservation of Mr. Calvert's biological ties to the full extent (i.e., through reunification). Nevertheless, it must be recognized that *custody is not the categorical imperative of an intact biological relationship,* nor even of a psychological relationship, between a parent and child. Thus, the decision for action and its

(*continued*)

CASE STUDY 1.4   CONTINUED

justification take into account all of the social values deemed relevant to Tonya's case and contemplate their maximal fulfillment. Thus, the worker would choose to change Tonya's goal from reunification to adoption under the assumption that Ms. Becker would seek and be approved for her adoption.

QUESTIONS FOR THOUGHT AND DISCUSSION

1. Tonya, age 2, has little say in determining her future. How might a social worker consider the wishes in this regard of an 8-year-old? A 12-year-old? A 16-year-old?
2. Biological ties are highly valued in society, as demonstrated by court cases like Baby Jessica. This alludes to the nature–nurture debate. What position, if any, do you feel best reflects the values of the social work profession?
3. The worker in this case appears to have the authority to take certain actions and espouse certain positions based on her assessment and judgment of the situation and of Tonya's best interests. Do you feel that these kinds of decisions are best made by the child's worker, a professional team, the courts, or another decision maker? What are the advantages and disadvantages of each option?
4. Mr. Calvert, Tonya's biological father, is currently incarcerated. Do you think that, when he is released, his "debt to society" is paid and his record should not be considered in making a decision about Tonya? If you do not agree, how would you take his incarceration into consideration?
5. Considering society's accepted primacy of biological rights, which are demonstrated through the family preservation and reunification policies, what do you feel are justifiable reasons for setting these aside?

■ ■ ■ ■ ■

CASE STUDY 1.5

IN THE CLIENT'S INTEREST: SELF-DETERMINATION AND MENTAL DISABILITY

Abstracted from an unpublished paper by Jose Carlos Vera, MSW

PRACTICE CONTEXT AND CASE PRESENTATION

An urban, community-based organization provides services specifically targeted at an immigrant minority population. These services include case management, team parenting, alcohol and drug treatment, advocacy, and housing.

Another client of the agency refers Luisa for services, and she is assigned to this caseworker. She is 18 years old, homeless, and mentally disabled. Though her family resides in a nearby county, she refuses contact with them, preferring to live independently on the city streets. Luisa is placed in a home, but she runs away, presumably returning to the unsafe neighborhood where she had been living. The worker loses contact with her.

A week later, through the client who originally referred her, the worker learns that Luisa has been sexually and physically abused. The worker is concerned about her safety, fearing further rape, murder, and violence if this young woman continues to live on the streets. He feels that Luisa does not have the mental capacity to look out for herself and take even elementary precautions to prevent harm.

When he contacts her on the street, Luisa is adamant. She desires to remain in the neighborhood, which she has come to know. She does not desire agency involvement, housing, or other services. All that she asks is that she be left alone to live as she wishes. She is not harming or disturbing anyone and wishes to live as she chooses.

The worker respects Luisa's right of self-determination—her right to determine what is best for her. Her mental status in terms of her disability has not been legally determined, so the presumption must be that she is competent. However, her mental limitations are immediately apparent, and Luisa is at risk of harm if she continues to live on the street. It would seem to be in her best interest to offer her protection from harm.

The worker finds himself caught in a dilemma that may be defined as:

Client Self-Determination v. Obligation to Prevent Harm

RESEARCH AND RELATED LITERATURE

Self-Determination. The Supreme Court upholds self-determination as a fundamental right that is protected by the Ninth and Fourteenth Amendments. The NASW Code of Ethics strongly supports client self-determination. In the United States, people are presumed competent, and thus able to self-determine, unless incompetence has been proven.

Often, however, this fundamental right is divested from mentally disabled citizens and assigned to persons appointed as their guardians. Mentally disabled citizens

(continued)

CASE STUDY 1.5   CONTINUED

are regarded as incompetent to make decisions or to manage their affairs. In order to protect the rights of these citizens, legal resources are available. Although the agency strongly supports self-determination, experience with mentally disabled clients in this inner-city community has demonstrated that they are often unable to make decisions that are in their best interests in terms of safety and protection.

Beauchamp and Childress (1994) state that "Persons incompetent by virtue of dementia, alcoholism, immaturity and mental retardation present radically different types and problems of incompetence" (p. 135). One may also be incompetent to make certain kinds of decisions, but not others. The capacity to understand the choices and issues, to reason and reflect, to communicate the choice and explain the reasoning may vary according to circumstance. Thus, Luisa may be competent to make some choices about her life, but not others.

Legally, Luisa is competent. Assessing her in order to establish incompetence is difficult due to communication problems and to her homeless lifestyle. She also demonstrates a reluctance to develop a relationship with the worker. She is not harming anyone (except for exposing herself to risk), and it would be difficult to force a competency evaluation upon her. Thus, from a legal perspective, she remains competent and able to make her own decisions.

Obligation to Prevent Harm.   According to Frankena (1973), "We ought to do good and prevent harm." Beneficence, doing good, and nonmaleficence, the prevention of harm, often are considered together as obligations. John Stuart Mill considered beneficence praiseworthy and virtuous, and the "greatest happiness" principle supports always producing the greatest good for the greatest number, or a net balance of good over bad consequences. Immanuel Kant considered beneficence an imperfect duty, for, he states, one has some choice about the occasions in which to do good. However, he states that it is certainly wrong to ever inflict harm on someone. Thus, it would seem justifiable to intervene if an individual's activities present serious harm to another or to that individual (Frankena, 1973).

The debate concerning obligation to prevent an individual from harming him- or herself is an ancient one. On one side, arguments that support self-determination would give the individual the right to choose activities that might result in harm to that individual. On the other, one can argue that members of a society have the obligation to protect one another from self-destructive behavior, and that it is sometimes necessary to interfere with an individual's self-determination to prevent harm.

Not enough is currently known about Luisa's level of mental disability to enable a clear determination of competence. Inaccessibility, lack of cooperation, and communication difficulties render such a determination difficult. Thus, she continues to have the legal rights of competency.

Section 1.14 of the NASW Code of Ethics (1996) addresses clients who lack decision-making capacity, stating that in these cases "social workers should take reasonable steps to safeguard the interests and rights of those clients."

The Code also supports the social worker's responsibility for promoting the general welfare of society (Sect. 6.01), which may be interpreted as the obligation to support the welfare of each of the members of the society as well.

Research. Luisa appears to be a homeless person at high risk: She has already been raped and abused; she does not speak the language; she is mentally disabled; and she is a woman. A study of this population found that programs must be tailored specifically to women (Hagen & Ivanoff, 1988). Padgett and Struening (1992) found that risk is a constant in the lives of homeless women, particularly risks of physical assault and abuse. They noted a correlation between mental and substance abuse problems and violence encountered by women on the streets. For this population, the struggle is not only for survival, but also for safety. It is unclear due to Luisa's language difficulties and mental disability if she is even aware enough to "struggle" for her own safety.

Dunn-Strohecker (1987) noted that the population of homeless mentally disabled persons is growing and that there is a lack of success in using traditional methods of treatment and services to this population. This population is in need of innovative services that will include outreach and a variety of possible resources to meet individual needs. It is possible that the current resources in the community are not meeting Luisa's needs.

A descriptive study by Mercier and Racine (1995) of case management with homeless women found that a high frequency of contacts (four a week) and the provision of concrete services were the primary activities. They emphasize the amount of worker time and effort that is required in order to develop a relationship with the women. In Luisa's case, this would be made more difficult by the language barrier.

AUTHOR'S REFLECTIONS, REASONING PROCESS, AND RESOLUTION
The worker must consider various obligations and responsibilities in arriving at a decision regarding whether or not intervention to protect Luisa's well-being is justified. Some of the issues that need to be balanced are

1. The profession's responsibility to the general welfare of society.
2. The importance of treating all persons with dignity and respect, acceptance, and a nonjudgmental attitude.
3. The worker's obligation to ensure that "all persons have access to the resources, employment, services, and opportunities they require in order to meet their basic human needs and to develop fully" (NASW Code of Ethics, 1996, Sect. 6.04a). Services were provided to Luisa, but she refused them. She does not "require" services—can they be imposed on her?
4. The obligation to protect life, an obligation that can be interpreted as protecting her safety and security, or as not obstructing her right to make life choices despite her retardation.
5. The professional commitment to self-determination, autonomy, and freedom, which may come second to the obligation to protect Luisa from harm.
6. A consideration of Luisa's values: her desire to live independently of her family and/or others and her desire for an education, which she has expressed to the worker.

(*continued*)

CASE STUDY 1.5   CONTINUED

The worker's personal values strongly support freedom and the right to make personal choices and decisions—pursuing our own good in our own way, as stated by Varga (1978). However, this population challenges the worker to consider other important issues as well. In particular, the worker perceives a moral obligation as Luisa's social worker to prevent potential harm to her and risks that he is able to assess, and she is not.

In determining a course of action, the worker recognizes that the obligation to prevent harm must be primary, and thus supersedes Luisa's right to self-determination in this instance. The Code of Ethics supports serving the client with maximum professional skills and competence. Thus, the worker will assist Luisa to obtain the services that are needed, being careful to maximize opportunities for self-determination within these. For example, Luisa can be encouraged to pursue an education in a field that is meaningful to her, at a school she selects. She can be given choices regarding living arrangements, so that she can select those that are most comfortable to her. Employment and training can also be explored. Luisa's English skills can be enhanced through instruction as well. From a legal perspective, the worker can also refer Luisa to specialized resources for people with mental retardation to ensure that her rights are protected, and/or initiate guardianship proceedings on her behalf so that she will have someone "looking out" for her best interests.

The worker believes that Luisa's desire for self-determination, and the form in which this has manifested itself thus far, may also be influenced by her status as a recent immigrant with a limited command of the English language. Thus, Luisa may see homelessness as an optimal choice because it provides her with maximum immediate freedom. It is the responsibility of the worker to expand Luisa's choices by providing her with services that will enable her to more meaningfully "take charge" of her own life. This supports her self-determination, as well as the worker's obligation to prevent harm for this client.

QUESTIONS FOR THOUGHT AND DISCUSSION

1. One of the difficult issues in working with the homeless population involves defining when a person becomes a client. If one is doing outreach, providing a bus token, a sandwich, a coat, to a homeless person, can that person be considered a client? Can one justify that there is any kind of "contract," however minimal, between the worker and the person who accepts an occasional snack or a pair of gloves when it is cold?

2. If one cannot say that such a person is indeed a client, can a worker justify intervention on behalf of that client on ethical grounds without an appeal to the courts?

3. Much attention has been focused recently on the "rights" of the homeless—to shelter and food, to support services, and so on. Does an individual have the "right" to refuse such "rights"?

4. When a homeless person refuses services and continues to live on the street, members of society can, and often do, express their "rights" not to have access or passage

through public areas restricted; not to be exposed to unpleasant or offensive sights, sounds, or smells, and to have clean and orderly streets; not to be approached, sometimes aggressively and/or threateningly, for money; and thus the right to have such persons removed. How would you balance the rights and claims of individuals against those of society?

5. Traditionally, society has drawn a line between the "deserving poor" and the "non-deserving poor," a line that has been repeatedly challenged, yet seems to persist in public forums and debates. For example, a family that is homeless because the principal wage earner has been laid off and is unable to secure alternative employment is often viewed differently from a family where parents are long-term substance abusers and have been homeless even after several generations of welfare support. This line can affect access to services and programs, eligibility for housing, private charitable support, and public attitudes. Do you feel that such a distinction is justified? What criteria would you use in making the distinction?

■ ■ ■ ■ ■ ▬▬▬▬▬▬▬▬▬▬▬▬▬▬▬▬▬▬▬▬▬▬▬▬▬▬▬▬▬▬▬▬

CASE STUDY 1.6

THE ADOPTION RECORDS CONTROVERSY: THREE PRIMARY CLIENTS WHOSE INTERESTS MAY CONFLICT

Abstracted from an unpublished paper by Sarah M. Russell, MSW

PRACTICE CONTEXT AND CASE PRESENTATION

Adoption is not just a program for children. Adoption creates a legal family for children when the birth family is unable or unwilling to parent. It expands existing families and engages adoptive parents in the priceless experience of parenting. Birth parents who voluntarily place their child with adoptive parents may also benefit from adoption. It frees them from the parenting role, which they may feel unready to assume. Adoption also offers birth parents the hope for a better life for their child. At its best, adoption meets the hopes of the child, the adoptive parents, and the birth parents. U.S. adoption law and practice have developed to address the needs of this adoption triangle (Pannor & Baran, 1984).

Beginning in the early to mid 1970s, adoptees in increasing numbers have been demanding information about their biological parents and their medical history. Initially, adoptive parents and mental health professionals saw this quest as a failure in the adoption or as a sign of pathology in the adoptee. Now, the adoptee's need to know about birth origins is seen increasingly as a legitimate need, and reunions between adoptees and their birth parents are becoming more commonplace. Adoptees are also joining together in an effort to reform adoption practice (Campbell, Silverman, & Patti, 1994).

The movement toward more open adoptions and reunions of adoptees with their birth parent(s) presents a serious ethical dilemma for all social workers. This dilemma focuses on the adoption triad that includes the adoptee, the birth parents, and the adoptive parents. Each practitioner must address the dilemma of the right of any member of the adoption triad to access information regarding the adoption *versus* the right of other triad members to confidentiality and anonymity.

It can also be stated as:

Right to Confidentiality v. Autonomy

for each member of the adoption triad.

RESEARCH AND RELATED LITERATURE

Abramson (1989) defines autonomy as a form of personal liberty by which one decides one's own course of action according to a plan chosen by oneself. She further conceptualizes four criteria by which to assess autonomy, all helpful in looking at the various members of the adoption triad. The first criterion is autonomy as *free action*. In other words, autonomy is both voluntary and intentional and not the result of coercion or any undue influence including either internal or external constraints. Next, there is a component of *authenticity* by which an action is consistent with the attitudes, values, dispositions, and life plans that are characteristic of an individual. A third criterion is one of *effective deliberation* that entails a problem-solving process *leading to an action.* Last, the criterion of *moral reflection* explores whether a person has thought about and accepted the values on which the action is based.

The early literature on unsealing adoption records generally contends that adoptive parents would feel threatened by such a policy (Burke, 1975; Lifton, 1979; Pannor & Nerlove, 1984; Sorsky, Baran, & Pannor, 1978). They fear the loss of love and loyalty of their adopted children if origins are learned or reunion is established with biological parents. These early studies are largely impressionistic or discursive in nature and are based on small samples of volunteers or participants handpicked by social service agencies (Sachdev, 1991).

Adoptive parents state concern that openness in adoption might cause confrontation with the biological mother and interference with the adoptive relationship. On the other hand, they may be faced with a need for medical or developmental information for more appropriate parenting. Birth parents are not disinterested parties to the adoptive family (Feigelman & Silverman, 1983).

Biological mothers are afraid that access to adoption files might result in unwanted intrusion in their newly formed lives by disgruntled adoptees and, thus, would open old and forgotten wounds. Sorsky et al. (1978) contended that discovery of genealogical facts could prove embarrassing to adoptees, and the opportunity to regain contact with biological parents could disrupt their identification with their adoptive family. On the other hand, Sachdev (1989) found that 88 percent of biological mothers supported releasing information about their identity to adoptees. Their agreement was also conditional, wanting to be assured that the adoptee's decision was not precipitous or motivated by vengeance or resentment. More than 75 percent of these women were afraid that the adoptee might make an indiscreet and unwanted appearance, and favored the requirement of their consent before identifying information was released.

A study of the role of biological mothers in the adoptive parent–adoptee relationship revealed that biological mothers lacked the initiative to undertake contact with the child. The reasons they give for this include the dilemma about their own rights, concern for the adoptive parents, concern for the adopted child, effects on their own emotional state, effects on their own family relationship, uncertainty of the mechanism for contact, and fear of the child's negative reaction (Silverman, Campbell, Patti, & Style, 1988).

Raynor (1990) reported that adoptees displayed considerable reticence (only 57 percent approved) in their support for the policy allowing the release of their identity to biological mothers, although 80 percent supported the policy on the condition that their prior consent be obtained. They were afraid that the biological mother might disrupt their happy home life or harass them. Adoptees who were opposed to the release of their identifying information were either not convinced about the reasons why a biological mother would have interest in the child she relinquished, or they were afraid of an unwanted intrusion in their lives (Marcus, 1981).

(continued)

CASE STUDY 1.6   CONTINUED

The issue of the right to information also centers around different issues for each member of the adoption triad. Any member in the adoption triad may have a legitimate reason for conducting a search. The adoptive parents may feel they need more information to deal with an adoptee's specific developmental needs, especially if they are atypical or pathological. Birth mothers often mourn the loss of natural children and want information about them. The greatest amount of literature has addressed adoptees and their reasons for needing to search. Broadzinsky, Schechter, and Henig (1992) claim that all adoptees engage in an internal search process. This universal search begins during the early school years and continues, in fantasy or reality, throughout life, especially at times of transitions such as marriage, birth of a child, and so on. This search often centers on the need of adolescents to solve the identity crisis identified by Erik Erikson. During this stage many teenagers begin to actively imagine what their birth parents look like, as a source of clues about how they will look when they grow up. It is also the task of late adolescence to want to separate from the family. Thinking about one's birth parents, and imagining who they are, is almost universal for adopted adolescents who have two families from which to separate, although one of those is only vaguely identifiable (Silin, 1996).

In a study by Geissinger (1994), the data revealed that a significant majority of all adoptive parents expressed their support for a disclosure policy. Support was stronger among younger parents compared with older parents. However, probe questions revealed that the adoptive parents' support was more apparent than real. They acknowledged the rights of adopted persons to information about, and reunion with, biological parents when questioned on an impersonal level and in the context of social justice. They tended to manifest underlying apprehension and reservation once the issue was brought closer to home—that is, when they were asked to view the disclosure policy in relation to their own adopted children (Sachdev, 1989).

Geissinger (1994) reaffirmed these findings. Adoptive parents wanted the disclosure to be contingent on the criteria that the adoptees' desire for information stemmed from genuine need for identity formation and not from idle curiosity, that the desire was not an evanescent phase or a developmental crisis but represented a sustained psychological and emotional distress, that the adoptees' motives were positive and not driven by the need to express negative feelings or to cause harm to the biological parent, and that adoptees had the emotional strength to be able to cope with the experience.

Adoptive parents need to be prepared to meet the special needs of their adopted children. If they know from the beginning that the fact that they did not give birth to their child will be an issue for the child as he or she grows, they can be prepared to deal with this reality (Pannor & Baran, 1984). Preparation might also prevent some of the negative effects reunions have on some families.

In general, biological mothers felt a sense of gratitude for the care the children received from the adoptive parents. They regarded them as real parents whose rights to the children superseded their own need to be reunited with the children. Nevertheless, biological mothers revealed their loss and the need for information about the relinquished children, as well as the possibility for reunion when the children became adults.

Because they wanted to avoid any impression of surreptitious involvement in the children's lives, they favored mandatory parental consent for releasing identity of minor adoptees. Many also favored informing the adoptive parents of their intent, as a courtesy (Lifton, 1979).

Campbell, Silverman, and Patti (1991) found that adoptees' motivations for searching for their biological parents and what they hoped would result from a reunion were intertwined. Four types of motives emerged from their data: first, life cycle transitions, such as the birth of a baby, which made them aware of the birth mothers and their feelings, and second, the desire for information concerning medical conditions or specific information about why they were adopted. The other reasons include the hope for a relationship with the birth parent and the desire to better understand themselves.

Rosenberg and Horner (1991) found that their data did not support others' findings that dissatisfaction with adoptive families was a factor in the decision to search. They did find that it may be easier to search when the adoptive family is supportive. The adoptees in their study seemed to be looking for ways to build an extended nuclear family, not to replace their adopted family. They seemed to need to bring the two parts of themselves together so that they could build a sense of self that felt complete to them. In their view, it was important that meeting this need not jeopardize the integrity of the adoptive family or the adoptee's relationship with that family.

Some of these studies support the earlier authors' observations that fears and suspicions may run deep among members of the adoption triad about each other's motives. All may perceive the other parties as being insensitive to their feelings and needs. However, the studies on reunions show that these assumptions and perceptions are unrealistic. Additionally, these studies provide ample evidence that each triad member shows a considerable concern for the other parties' interests and feelings (Sachdev, 1991).

**AUTHOR'S REFLECTIONS, REASONING PROCESS,
AND RESOLUTION**
Our general societal values include freedom, justice, equality, autonomy, privacy, and well-being. Those that seem particularly relevant here are freedom, autonomy, and privacy. Loewenberg and Dolgoff's Ethical Principles Screen (1992) suggests that the *Principle of Autonomy and Freedom* is applicable to this dilemma, as is the *Principle of Privacy and Confidentiality*. A third ethical principle, listed last is the *Principle of Truthfulness and Full Disclosure*.

The National Association of Social Workers' (NASW) Code of Ethics (1996) provides guidance on this dilemma in Section 1.02, Self-Determination. It is appropriate to encourage a client's right to self-determination and to assist him or her in efforts to identify and clarify goals. This must be balanced with the caveat that if the clients' actions could pose a serious, foreseeable, and imminent risk to themselves or others, the social worker has an obligation to help clients limit their goals (NASW, 1996). Additional guidance is provided in Section 1.07, Privacy and Confidentiality: Clients. Specifically, social workers should protect the confidentiality of all information obtained in the course of professional service, except for compelling professional reasons (imminent harm, legal proceedings, etc.).

(continued)

CASE STUDY 1.6   CONTINUED

> The writer's personal values also influence her view of the dilemma. These include self-actualization, balance of mind/body/spirit, human relationships, social justice, the dignity and worth of all humans, self-determination, autonomy, truth, honesty, sincerity, responsibility, thoughtfulness, consistency, humility, and kindness.
>
> After considering various options, including maintenance of sealed records only, sealed records with nonidentifying information only available, a court decision by a judge following petition by a triad member, a mutual consent adoption registry (adoptee must be of legal age), and open adoption, the writer believes that the mutual consent adoption registry appears to offer maximum benefits to each member of the triad. This position ensures the values of freedom, autonomy, and privacy as well as self-actualization and self-determination for all parties in the adoption triad. It also provides necessary protection for those who do not wish to participate.

QUESTIONS FOR THOUGHT AND DISCUSSION

1. The author of this article makes the assumption that all three members of the adoption triad—biological parents, adoptive parents, and child—should be considered equally regarding rights to privacy and confidentiality as well as rights to information. Do you feel that this is a valid premise? Are the rights of adoptive parents to information, for example, the same as those of the adoptive child? Do they have the same right to confidentiality and privacy as the biological parents?
2. If you think that there are differences in the rights and obligations of members of the triad, would that affect the way that you might state the dilemma?
3. If a mutual consent adoption registry were to be established, how would it be funded? Under whose auspices would the registry be maintained, and how would the information it contained be safeguarded? In order for it to function appropriately, all members of all adoption triads would need to be aware of its existence. Would this be a justifiable use of public funds?
4. Would there be certain kinds of situations where the confidentiality and privacy of the mutual consent registry could justifiably be violated or suspended? What conditions might justify such suspension?
5. Much attention has been focused lately on the finality of a surrender of a child for adoption, and adopted children have been returned to their biological parent(s) in certain circumstances. What do you see as the major issues that must be addressed here? The irrevocability of decision making? The rights of an absent or unaware parent? Who should make such decisions? Should there be national policies to define the "rights" of each member of the triad, or are these best decided on a case-by-case basis?

■ ■ ■ ■ ■ ■

CASE STUDY 1.7

BELIEVING AN EMOTIONALLY DISTURBED CHILD:
ABUSED OR CONFUSED?

Abstracted from an unpublished paper by Shahla R. Adam, MSW

PRACTICE CONTEXT AND CASE PRESENTATION

Mary, a 7-year-old girl, has been referred to an outpatient mental health facility for children and families with emotional disorders. Her history includes neglect and sexual and physical abuse. Her situation is chaotic at best: She is verbally and physically aggressive toward her peers, lies, and purposefully hurts infants and animals. Her preliminary diagnosis is Post-Traumatic Stress Disorder, Attachment Disorder, and borderline traits. She is currently placed in foster care, and the foster mother has repeatedly expressed her frustrations with Mary's unmanageable behavior, stating that, if the behavior continues, she would ask for her removal from the home, as she finds it nearly impossible to manage Mary.

Mary has made solid progress in attachment to this foster family, a monumental gain. During a psychological evaluation, Mary reveals that her foster mother has hit her with a belt. Given the history, the evaluating psychologist chooses not to disclose the client's allegations to Protective Services but, instead, informs the social worker.

Several dilemmas present themselves to the worker: (1) her duty to report the alleged child abuse versus her obligation to respect a colleague's opinion and judgment; (2) her duty to report versus the maintenance of the stability of the current placement; and (3) should the foster mother request Mary's removal, as the worker believes might occur, the stability of the child's placement versus the foster mother's right to self-determination.

The worker determines that the salient dilemma is the second, the:

Duty to Report v. Maintenance of Stability for Child

RESEARCH AND RELATED LITERATURE

It is imperative that practitioners who provide services to families and children be knowledgeable regarding what constitutes abuse/maltreatment and the conditions that require reporting.

Child abuse may be defined as the sustaining of physical injury by a child, which occurs as a result of inhumane or cruel treatment, or as the result of a malicious act. Persons acting in a professional capacity are mandated to report suspected child abuse. These include psychologists, social workers, counselors, teachers, psychiatrists, and medical professionals.

Those who fail to report place themselves at risk for legal and professional sanctions. This may cause professionals to tend to err on the conservative side. Legal representatives espouse that "direct disclosure of maltreatment invariably constitutes

(continued)

CASE STUDY 1.7   CONTINUED

reasonable suspicion of child abuse and surpasses the reporting threshold of most mandated reporters" (Kalichman, 1993, p. 88).

The law does not permit professionals to engage in decision making when faced with reasonable suspicion of abuse. Kalichman (1993) warns professionals not to dilute their professional role by trespassing into an investigative role. Role conflicts occur as a result of incompatible role expectations (mandated reporter v. keeper of secrets).

Smith (1986) provides further evidence for social workers' duty to report, finding that it is critical that professionals not convey disbelief in the child's allegations. The social worker communicates to the child a belief in the child's statement when he or she reports the abuse and attempts to assure the child's immediate safety. Crenshaw, Bartell, and Lichtenberg (1994) support mandatory reporting for all cases of suspected abuse and suggest involving the family in the process.

On the one hand, the worker's agency closely follows a policy of adherence to mandatory reporting laws and of safeguarding a child's immediate safety. On the other hand, situations are often not as clear or straightforward as the duty-to-report position proposes. Workers acknowledge competing concerns such as the damaging of the stability of a child's placement (Rothery & Cameron, 1990). Concerns about the child's immediate welfare and the repercussions of reporting inhibits some professionals (Kalichman, 1993).

Whether or not the abuse is substantiated, reporting Mary's allegations may nonetheless trigger a chain of events that would lead to her removal from her current foster home, especially given the foster mother's oft-repeated frustrations with Mary.

Limited literature is available supporting the higher significance of a child's current placement in this dilemma. Proof, for the most part, exists in evidence maintaining the importance of a child's attachment, which is strongly threatened by multidisplacements (Miller, Mackey, & Maginn, 1981), and Rossman (1985) notes that a child's repeated separation from a current placement further traumatizes the maladjusted child, possibly leading to antisocial behavior, developmental lags in speech, weak ego formation, heightened rage, and self-destructive tendencies.

Studies indicate that a child who lacks a history of stable placements experiences difficulty in negotiating boundaries with others given his or her ambivalence with interpersonal relationships (Rossman, 1985). Such children tend to reject others before allowing themselves to be vulnerable to the pain of future separation and loss (Miller et al., 1981). Miller et al. note that a child often behaves in ways that lead to rejection in order to manage the anxiety regarding the perceived *threat* of rejection by the caregiver. This appears to be the case with Mary.

The dilemma is heightened by the possibility that either Mary's allegations are false, given her tendency to lie, or that physical abuse is possible given the foster mother's frustrations with raising Mary. DeYoung (1988) and Bernet (1993) encourage practitioners to assess the degree of truthfulness in a child's allegations prior to reporting suspected abuse.

Thus, inadvertently, a child reporting abuse may be removed from a nurturing home, impacting on his or her sense of safety, well-being, and attachment. It is also critical to note that the clinician's decision not to report certain circumstances has been identified by some professionals as a higher ethical standard as compared to mandatory reporting laws (Kalichman, 1993).

The worker also consulted with an attorney on Mary's behalf. The attorney expressed a firm belief that Mary should remain with her family, feeling that leaving a child in the hands of "the system" is often more disruptive and traumatizing to the child than leaving him or her in a potentially abusive home.

The profession of social work has always had a strong commitment to the protection of, and advocacy for, vulnerable populations such as children. This client's vulnerability is especially great: Her history of abuse and neglect, her diagnosis of Post-Traumatic Stress Disorder, Attachment Disorder, and borderline traits, and her placement in foster care make the worker's obligation to her safety and best interest a primary concern. The Code of Ethics, in subsection 1.1, supports the worker's legal obligation to report suspected child abuse. As a child, Mary also fits into the category of "clients who lack decisional capacity." The Code clearly states that "workers should take reasonable steps to safeguard the interests and rights of those clients" (1.14).

AUTHOR'S REFLECTIONS, REASONING PROCESS, AND RESOLUTION

Reasonable suspicion, rather than confirmed knowledge, is adequate grounds for reporting abuse or neglect. This nebulous term tends to leave the decision whether to report to the individual's discretion (Campbell, 1995).

The duty to report is clearly supported by deontological theories, where the motive of an action makes it morally right. Reporting could have as a motive the safety and protection of vulnerable members of society, the obligation to follow the law, or the duty to adhere to agency policy. Using the *motive* as the point of moral value in decision making, the worker would be obligated to report abuse and neglect.

Teleological, or consequentialist, theories place the moral value of an action on the end that is achieved. Such theories would consider what measures, in fact, would best ensure the safety of the child and act upon these. It is clear that potentially different results might be obtained depending upon which theory is selected as a foundation for decision making.

Additionally, consideration must be given to Mary's history of child abuse, unstable placements, failed attachments, crying, and manipulative behavior in assessing whether her allegations or child abuse should be acted on by the worker. Acting on them without considering the possibility that Mary may not be telling the truth may place Mary at additional risk by necessitating another placement for this already disturbed and vulnerable child.

Societal values supporting reporting of the suspected abuse include the principle of the value of protecting a life, the value of safety, and the legal rights of children. Society supports childrearing practices that denounce the use of corporal punishment. Adults outside of a child's home are included among those society holds responsible for a child's well-being. Values supporting maintaining the stability of placement include well-being, mental health, family integrity, individual potential for improvement, quality of life, and least harm. Least harm implies that the possibility of physical injury may

(continued)

CASE STUDY 1.7   CONTINUED

not in all instances be as detrimental as the threat of damage to the child's mental health and stability.

The worker recognizes that her personal values impact on the dilemma as well. She values the child's safety, as well as her mental health. She also values her professional obligation, clearly stated in the Code of Ethics, to follow the laws of reporting. Personal values include health, safety, knowledge and truth, and proper disciplining of children. She does not subscribe to the use of corporal punishment, and this tends to bias her toward the reporting side of the dilemma.

The possible options suggested by the research, ethical principles, and theories relevant to this case include: (1) abiding by the reporting law and reporting the abuse; (2) choosing not to report the abuse in the interest of maintaining the stability of the placement; (3) contacting the foster mother prior to the report and exploring plausible options (taking on an investigative role); and (4) reporting the abuse with qualifiers of the child's history and current problems, notifying the foster mother of the report and attempting to salvage the placement by offering professional support and advice.

After much reflection, the social worker elects to follow the fourth option: to notify Protective Services, noting Mary's loose reality testing and working with the foster mother to reduce the possibility that she will request the removal of Mary from her home.

While adherence to mandatory reporting laws alone was not, for this worker, sufficient rationale for the ultimate decision, taken with values that are maximized by this resolution, such as truth, protection, and legal rights of Mary, potential for improvement in the family, and Mary's mental well-being, this option appears optimal in this circumstance. Failure to report could jeopardize the child's safety and the social worker's license, could lead to the later removal of the child from the home, and could, at worst, lead to Mary's death. Furthermore, failure to listen to a child's report of abuse, regardless of its truthfulness, conveys a negative message to the child, damaging mental health, trust in others, sense of well-being, and attachments. In fact, the worker's support of the family in this option may maximize their ability to manage the family situation, and thus better ensure the stability of the child's placement.

QUESTIONS FOR THOUGHT AND DISCUSSION

1. The use of corporal punishment in the disciplining and training of a child varies in different cultures. Should corporal punishment be acceptable when it is a part of a comprehensive, accepted cultural practice?
2. Corporal punishment and other forms of discipline also vary by time period and were acceptable early in this century. What makes such punishment acceptable or not acceptable? Are these absolute standards?
3. The worker might have chosen one of her other options: that of exploring, with the foster mother, Mary's allegations of abuse prior to determining whether to report. In that instance, Mary's foster mother might have completely denied all of the allega-

tions. How would the worker then determine credibility and establish a course of action? Do you think that this was a viable option?

4. In cases where choices must be made between a child's potential physical safety and a child's potential mental and emotional well-being, where would you place your priorities?

5. Should a higher standard of parenting be demanded of foster parents than of biological parents? If so, on what grounds do you take that position?

REFERENCES AND BIBLIOGRAPHY

Case Study 1.1

Ames, K., & Springen, K. (1992, June). Fostering the family. *Newsweek,* 64–65.

Carbino, R. (1991). Advocacy for foster families in the United States facing child abuse and neglect allegations: How social agencies and foster families are responding to the problem. *Child Welfare, 70*(2), 131–149.

Grisby, R. K. (1994, May). Maintaining attachment relationships among children in foster care. *Families in Society: The Journal of Contemporary Human Services, 75*(5), 269–276.

Hess, P. (1982, January). Parent-child attachment concept: critical for permanency planning. *Social Casework: The Journal of Contemporary Social Work,* 46–53.

Kaucher, C., Leon, R. (Eds.). (1994, September). Why are so many kids in foster care? (Available from the Metropolitan Washington Council of Governments, Washington, DC.)

Mushlin, C. (1988). Unsafe havens: The case for constitutional protection of foster children from abuse and neglect. *Harvard Civil Rights and Civil Liberties Law Review, 23,* 205–207.

Ryan, P. (1981, February). *Foster home child protection* (pp. 31–32). New York: Vera Institute of Justice.

Stone, N. M., & Stone, S. F. (1983). The prediction of successful foster placement. *Social Casework, 64,* 11–17.

Thorman, G. (1982). *Helping troubled families.* New York: Aldine Publishing Co.

Case Study 1.2

Barth, R. P., Berry, M., Yoshikami, R., Goodfield, R. K., & Carson, M. L. (1988). Predicting adoption disruption. *Social Work, 33*(3), 227–233.

Beauchamp, T. L., & Childress, J. F. (1994). *Principles of biomedical ethics* (4th ed.). New York: Oxford University Press.

Hegar, R. L. (1988). Legal and social work approaches to sibling separation in foster care. *Child Welfare, 67*(2), 113–121.

Littman, C., LCSW-C, personal communication.

Loewenberg, F. M., & Dolgoff, R. (1992). *Ethical decisions for social work practice* (4th ed.). Itasca, IL: F. E. Peacock.

National Association of Social Workers. (1996). *NASW Code of Ethics.* Washington, DC: Author.

Owen, M., professor, National Catholic School for Social Service, personal communication.

Staff, I., & Fein, E. (1992). Together or separate: A study of siblings in foster care. *Child Welfare, 71*(3), 257–270.

Timberlake, E. M., & Hamlin, E. R. (1982). The sibling group: A neglected dimension of placement. *Child Welfare, 61*(8), 545–552.

Ward, M. (1984). Sibling ties in foster care and adoption planning. *Child Welfare, 63*(4), 321–332.

Case Study 1.3

Beauchamp, T. L., & Childress, J. F. (1994). *Principles of biomedical ethics* (4th ed.). New York: Oxford University Press.

Bishops' Committee of the Confraternity of Christian Doctrine. (Eds.). (1970). *New American Bible*. New York: Catholic Book Pub. Co.

Bowles, A. L., Sr. (1992). Commentary. *Hastings Center Report, 22*(6), 28.

Compton, B. R., & Galaway, B. (1989). *Social work processes* (4th ed.). Belmont, CA: Wadsworth.

Cranford, R. (1992). Legal aspects of stopping dialysis. In C. M. Kjellstrand & J. B. Dossetor (Eds.), *Ethical problems in dialysis and transplantation* (pp. 127–142). Boston: Kluwer Academic.

Ferrans, C. E. (1987). Quality of life as a criterion for allocation of life-sustaining treatment: The case of hemodialysis. In *Health care ethics: A guide for decision makers* (pp. 109–124). Rockville, MD: Aspen.

Frazier, C. L. (1981). Renal disease. *Health and social work, 6* (4S–supplement), 75S–82S.

Hastings Center. (1987). *Guidelines on the termination of life-sustaining treatment and the care of the dying*. Bloomington, IN: Indiana University Press.

Hodroff, K. (1994). Depression and the kidney patient: A nursing perspective. *Clinical Strategies: The AKF Newsletter for Nephrology Professionals, 1*(1), 1–4.

Kaye, M. (1992). Religious aspects of stopping treatment. In C. M. Kjellstrand & J. B. Dossetor (Eds.), *Ethical problems in dialysis and transplantation* (pp. 117–125). Boston: Kluwer Academic.

Keyserlingk, E. W. (1990). The quality of life and death. In J. J. Walter & T. A. Shannon (Eds.), *Quality of life: The new medical dilemma* (pp. 35–53). New York: Paulist.

Kimmel, P. L. (1994). Depression and mortality in ESRD patients. *Clinical Strategies: The AKF Newsletter of Nephrology Professionals, 1*(1), 1–3.

Kjellstrand, C. M. (1992). Practical aspects of stopping dialysis and cultural differences. In C. M. Kjellstrand & J. B. Dossetor (Eds.), *Ethical problems in dialysis and transplantation* (pp. 103–116). Boston: Kluwer Academic.

Lammers, S. E., & Verhey, A. (Eds.). (1987). *On moral medicine: Theological perspectives in medical ethics*. Grand Rapids, MI: William B. Eerdmans.

Levy, N. B. (1991). Psychiatric aspects of renal care. In D. Z. Levine (Ed.), *Care of the renal patient* (2nd ed., pp. 181–186). Philadelphia: W. B. Saunders.

Loewenberg, F. M., & Dolgoff, R. (1992). *Ethical decisions for social work practice* (4th ed.). Itasca, IL: F. E. Peacock.

Medical Center. (1993). Unpublished manual (name withheld).

National Association of Social Workers. (1996). *NASW Code of Ethics*. Washington, DC: Author.

Neu, S., & Kjellstrand, C. M. (1986). Stopping long-term dialysis: An empirical study of life-support treatment. *New England Journal of Medicine, 314,* 14–20.

Perlman, R. A., & Jonsen, A. (1990). The use of quality of life considerations in medical decision making. In J. J. Walter & T. A. Shannon (Eds.), *Quality of life: The new medical dilemma* (pp. 93–103). New York: Paulist Press.

Sabatino, C. P. (1993). Surely the wizard will help us, Toto? Implementing the patient self-determination act. *Hastings Center Report, 23*(1), 12–16.

Sensky, T. (1993). Psychosomatic aspects of end-stage renal failure. *Psychotherapy and Psychosomatics, 59,* 56–68.

Smedes, L. B. (1987). Respect for human life: "Thou shalt not kill." In S. E. Lammers & A. Verhey (Eds.), *On moral medicine: Theological perspectives in medical ethics* (pp. 143–149). Grand Rapids, MI: William B. Eerdmans.

Starck, P. L. (Ed.). (1992). *The hidden dimension of illness: Human suffering* (pp. 25–42). New York: National League for Nursing Press.

U.S. Renal Data System. (1993). *1993 annual report.* Washington, DC: U.S. Government Printing Office.

U.S. Supreme Court. (1990). *Cruzan v. Director, Missouri Department of Health,* 110 C. Ct. 2841. Washington, DC: Author.

Valdez, R., & Rosenblum, A. (1994). Voluntary termination of dialysis: When your patient says, "Enough is enough!" *Dialysis and Transplantation, 23*(10), 566–570.

Walter, J. J., & Shannon, T. A. (Eds.). (1990). Introduction. In J. J. Walter & T. A. Shannon (Eds.), *Quality of life: The new medical dilemma* (pp. 7–8). New York: Paulist Press.

Wight, J. (1993). On discontinuing dialysis. *Journal of Medical Ethics, 19*(2), 77–81.

Wolcott, D. L. (1990). Psychosocial adaptation of chronic dialysis patients. In A. R. Nisserson, R. N. Fine, & D. E. Gentile (Eds.), *Clinical dialysis* (2nd ed.; pp. 735–746). Norwalk, CT: Appleton & Lange.

Case Study 1.4

Allen, M. (1991). Crafting a federal legislative framework for child welfare reform. *American Journal of Orthopsychiatry, 61*(4), 610–623.

Derdeyn, A. P. (1977a, July). Child abuse and neglect: The rights of parents and the needs of their children. *American Journal of Orthopsychiatry, 47*(3), 377–387.

Derdeyn, A. P. (1977, October). A case for permanent foster placement of dependent, neglected, and abused children. *American Journal of Orthopsychiatry, 47*(4), 604–614.

Family Services Administration Child and Family Services Division. (1995, March 3). *Policy handbook.* Washington, DC: Author.

Fein, E. (1991a). The elusive search for certainty in child welfare: Introduction. *American Journal of Orthopsychiatry, 61*(4), 576–577.

Fein, E. (1991b). Issues in foster family care: Where do we stand? *American Journal of Orthopsychiatry, 61*(4), 578–583.

Fein, E., & Staff, I. (1993). Last best chance: Findings from a reunification services program. *Child Welfare, 72*(1), 25–40.

Goldstein, J., Freud, A., & Solnit, A. J. (1973). *Beyond the best interests of the child.* New York: The Free Press.

Greene, R. R., & Ephross, P. H. (1991). *Human behavior theory and social work practice.* New York: Aldine de Gruyter.

Hess, P. M., & Folaron, G. (1991). Ambivalences: A challenge to permanency for children. *Child Welfare, 70*(4), 403–424.

The Holy Bible, Revised Standard Version (2nd ed.). Nashville: Thomas Nelson.

Huxtable, M. (1994). Child protection: With liberty and justice for all. *Social Work, 39*(1), 60–66.

Janis, I. J., & Mann, L. (1977). *Decision making: A psychological analysis of conflict, choice, and commitment.* New York: The Free Press.

Kadushin, A. (1977). Myths and dilemmas in child welfare. *Child Welfare, 56*(3), 141–153.

Loewenberg, F. M., & Dolgoff, R. (1992). *Ethical decisions for social work practice.* Itasca, IL: F. E. Peacock.

Longres, J. F. (1990). *Human behavior in the social environment.* Itasca, IL: F. E. Peacock.

Mason, M. A. (1994). *From father's property to children's rights: The history of child custody in the United States.* New York: Columbia University Press.

Murray, C. (1993, October 29). The coming white underclass. *The Wall Street Journal,* p. A31.

National Association of Social Workers. (1996). *NASW Code of Ethics.* Washington, DC: Author.

Proch, K., & Howard, J. (1984). Parental visiting in foster care: Law and practice. *Child Welfare, 58*(2), 139–147.

Reamer, F. G. (1990). *Ethical dilemmas in social service.* New York: Columbia University Press.

Stein, T. J. (1991). *Child welfare and the law.* New York: Longman.

Williams, C. C. (1991). Expanding the options in the quest for permanence. In J. E. Everett, S. S. Chipungu, & B. R. Leashore (Eds.), *Child welfare: An Africentric perspective* (pp. 266–289). New Brunswick, NJ: Rutgers University Press.

Case Study 1.5

Abramson, M. (1989). Autonomy vs. paternalistic beneficence: Practice strategies. *The Journal of Contemporary Social Work, 70*(2), 101–105.

Beauchamp, T. L., & Childress, J. F. (1994). *Principles of biomedical ethics.* New York: Oxford University Press.

Burgdorf, R., Jr. (1980). *The legal rights of handicapped persons: Cases, materials, and text.* Baltimore: Paul D. Brookes.

Dunn-Strohecker, M. (1987). *From street to treatment: An examination of five demonstration programs for persons who are homeless and mentally disabled.* Unpublished Ph.D. dissertation, Brandeis University.

Frankena, W. K. (1973). *Ethics.* Englewood Cliffs, NJ: Prentice-Hall.

Hagen, J. L., & Ivanoff, A. M. (1988). Homeless women: A high risk population. *Journal of Women and Social Work 3*(1), 19–33.

Hepworth, D., & Larsen, A. (1992). *Direct social work practice.* Belmont, CA: Wadsworth.

Loewenberg, F., & Dolgoff, R. (1992). *Ethical decisions for social work practice.* Itasca, IL: F. E. Peacock.

Mercier, C., & Racine, G. (1995). Case management with homeless women: A descriptive study. *Community Mental Health Journal 31*(1), 25–37.

National Association of Social Workers. (1996). *NASW Code of Ethics.* Washington, DC: Author.

Padgett, D. K., & Struening, E. L. (1992, October). Victimization and traumatic injuries among the homeless: Associations with alcohol, drug, and mental problems. *American Journal of Orthopsychiatry, 62*(4), 525–534.

Reamer, F. (1990). *Ethical dilemmas in social service.* New York: Columbia University Press.

Saltzman, A., & Proch, K. (1990). *Law in social work practice.* Chicago: Nelson Hall.

Varga, A. C. (1978). *On being human: Principles of ethics.* New York: Paulist Press.

Case Study 1.6

Abramson, M. (1989). Autonomy vs. paternalistic beneficence: practice strategies. *Social Casework: The Journal of Contemporary Social Work, 70*(2), 101–105.

Barth, R. P., (1995). Adoption. In *The social work encyclopedia* (19th ed., Vol. 1). Washington, DC: NASW Press.

Bill of Rights: The First Ten Amendments to the U.S. Constitution. (1791).

Broadzinsky, D., Schechter, M., & Henig, R. M. (1992). *Being adopted, the lifelong search for self.* New York: Doubleday.

Burke, C. (1975). The adoptee's constitutional right to know his origins. *Southern California Law Review, 48*(5), 1196–1220.

Campbell, L. H., Silverman, P. R., & Patti, P. B. (1991). Reunions between adoptees and birth parents: The adoptees' experience. *Social Work, 36*(4), 329–335.

Campbell, L., Silverman, P. R., & Patti, P. (1994). Reunions between adoptees and birth parents: the adoptive parents' view. *Social Work, 39*(5), 542–549.

Feigelman, W., & Silverman, A. R. (1983). *Chosen children: New patterns of adoptive relationships.* New York: Praeger.

Geissinger, S. (1994). Adoptive parents' attitudes toward open birth records. *Family Relations, 33*(4), 579–585.

Lifton, B. J. (1979). *Lost and found: The adoption experience.* New York: Dial Rose.

Loewenberg, F. M., & Dolgoff, R. (1992). *Ethical decisions for social work practice.* Itasca, IL: F. E. Peacock.

Marcus, C. (1981). *Who is my mother?* Toronto: MacMillan of Canada.

National Association of Social Workers. (1996). *NASW Code of Ethics.* Washington, DC: Author.

Pannor, R., & Baran, A., (1984). Open adoption as a standard practice. *Child Welfare, 63,* 245–250.

Pannor, R., & Nerlove, E. A. (1984). Fostering understanding between adolescents and adoptive parents through group experience. *Child Welfare, 16*(8), 537–544.

Raynor, L. (1990). *The adopted child comes of age.* London: George Allan and Unwin.

Rosenberg, E. B,. & Horner, T. M. (1991). Birthparent romances and identity formation in adopted children. *American Journal of Orthopsychiatry, 61*(1), 70–77.

Sachdev, P. (1989). *Unlocking the adoption files.* Lexington, MA: Lexington Books.

Sachdev, P. (1991, March). The birth father: A neglected element in the adoption equation. *Families in Society: The Journal of Contemporary Human Services.*

Silin, M. W. (1996). The vicissitudes of adoption for parents and children. *Child and Adolescent Social Work Journal, 13*(3), 255–269.

Silverman, P. R., Campbell, L., Patti, P., & Style, C. B. (1988). Reunions between adoptees and birth parents: The birth parents' experience. *Social Work, 33,* 523–528.

Sorsky, B., Baran, A., & Pannor, R. (1978). *The adoption triangle: The effect of sealed records on adoptees, birth parents, and adoptive parents.* Garden City, NY: Anchor/Doubleday.

Case Study 1.7

Beauchamp, T. L., & Childress, J. F. (1994). *Principles of biomedical ethics.* New York: Oxford University Press.

Bernet, W. (1993). False statements and the differential diagnosis of abuse allegations. *Journal of the American Academy of Child and Adolescent Psychiatry, 32*(5), 903–910.

Campbell, J. C. (1995). *Assessing dangerousness: Violence by sexual offenders, batterers, and child abusers.* London: Sage Publications.

Crenshaw, W. B., Bartell, P. A., & Lichtenberg, J. W. (1994). Proposed revisions to mandatory reporting laws: An exploration survey of the child protective service agencies. *Child Welfare, 73*(10), 15–27.

DeYoung, M. (1988). A conceptual model for judging the truthfulness of a young child's allegations of sexual abuse. *American Journal of Orthopsychiatry, 56*(4), 550–559.

Kalichman, S. (1993). *Mandated reporting of suspected child abuse: Ethics, law, and policy.* Washington, DC: American Psychological Association.

Loewenberg, F. M., & Dolgoff, R. (1992). *Ethical decisions for social work practice.* Itasca, IL: F. E. Peacock.

Miller, F. B., Mackey, W., & Maginn, V. J. (1981). The modern displaced child: The repetitive foster child. *Journal of Clinical Child Psychology, 12,* 21–26.

National Association of Social Workers. (1996). *NASW Code of Ethics.* Washington, DC: Author.

Rossman, P. (1985). The aftermath of abuse and abandonment. *Journal of the American Academy of Child Psychiatry, 24*(3), 345–352.

Rothery, M., & Cameron, G. (1990). *Child maltreatment: Expanding our concept of helping.* Hillsdale, NJ: Lawrence Erlbaum Associates.

Smith, G. (1986). Child sexual abuse. *Adoption and Fostering, 10*(3), 13–18.

CHAPTER TWO

NASW ETHICAL STANDARD TWO

Social Workers' Ethical
Responsibilities to Colleagues

INTRODUCTION

Provisions of Code

As colleagues and co-workers, supervisors and supervisees, students and field instructors, employers and employees, most social workers interact with their fellow professionals on a daily basis. Section 2 of the Code of Ethics addresses ethical standards that should be observed by all parties regarding such relationships.

The very first statement (2.01a) obligates social workers to treat colleagues with respect and to represent qualifications, views, and obligations of colleagues in a fair manner by avoiding "unwarranted negative criticism," particularly in reference to competence or individual attributes (2.01b). This first section also asks that social workers cooperate with colleagues of their own and other disciplines on behalf of client well-being (2.01c).

Specific guidelines follow this broad statement. Social workers are obligated to respect confidential information shared by colleagues in the context of professional relationships (2.02). They also are obligated to the work of interdisciplinary teams of which they are members (2.03a). When ethical issues for the worker arise from the actions or decisions of an interdisciplinary team, workers should use appropriate channels to try to revise them (2.03a). If this is not possible, other avenues should be pursued consistent with the well-being of the client (2.03b). Where a worker is aware of a dispute between colleagues or colleague and employer, the worker should be careful not to exploit the situation (2.04).

Social workers use consultation with colleagues on a frequent basis, and guidelines for such consultation are addressed as well. They are encouraged to seek the advice of knowledgeable and competent colleagues for the benefit of their clients but, in the course of such a consultation, should disclose "the least amount of information necessary" (2.05). In addition to consultation, social workers should utilize referral to other professionals when this is beneficial to the client's interests. They are prohibited from "giving or receiving payment" for such a referral (2.06).

The major problematic areas addressed include sexual relationships, which are proscribed in the supervisor–supervisee, student–trainee relationships and should be avoided between colleagues (2.07); the proscription against sexual harassment (2.08); the obligation to address the impairment of a colleague, first with the colleague and then, if unsuccessful, with appropriate channels (2.09); and the very similar procedure in the case of the incompetence of a colleague (2.10).

An important subsection addresses the unethical conduct of colleagues, obligating social workers to "take adequate measures" to discourage, prevent, and/or expose such behavior (2.11a), and to be knowledgeable about policies and procedures for handling ethical complaints.

Where a social worker believes that a colleague has acted unethically, the worker should follow procedures similar to those listed above for incompetent and impaired social workers. He or she should first discuss his or her concern with the colleague, and, if the concern is legitimate and cannot be rectified by the colleague, action through formal channels is required (2.11c,d).

Social workers also have a clear obligation to assist colleagues who are being unjustly accused of unethical conduct (2.11e).

The Cases

While there is surely no dearth of issues surrounding colleagues, and while students were very well aware of these, the particular vulnerability that attaches to student status prevented most from choosing to address these issues. There seem to be several reasons for this: Students were uncomfortable about addressing ethical issues relating to presumably much more experienced colleagues; they were unwilling to place their grades and education at risk by openly attempting to address an ethical issue regarding a colleague; they were afraid that they would offend a colleague; they were concerned that addressing collegial issues in so public a forum would cause loss of anonymity to both student and colleague; and they were unsure of where their personal and professional responsibilities lay.

Thus, only three cases are included in this section. It is hoped that, with these, and the specific guidelines in the Code of Ethics, both students and colleagues will feel more comfortable in expressing ethical concerns related to colleagues.

The first case presented involves an indirect responsibility of a worker to colleagues: the obligation to enable, assist, and support other social workers in obtaining the highest degree of competence and skill and the most thorough knowledge base. The worker in this case finds herself immersed in a dilemma when her obligation to colleagues in this regard violates client confidentiality and informed consent, thus compromising client self-determination, trust, privacy, and freedom.

The staff of this agency, with a high commitment to competence and skill development, utilizes an educational method of group supervision around video recordings. Members of the staff are asked to take turns providing such recordings for viewing by the group, and there is strong pressure to participate in this manner. However, the informed consent for video recording signed by clients does not allude to the recording being used specifically for educational purposes. The worker's concern for confidentiality and privacy for clients leads her to question her own willingness to contribute a recording to the group, while her colleagues' expectations would seem to require her participation.

In the second case, a first-year intern one month into her field placement is confronted with blatant professional misconduct by a newly hired MSW social worker. Her problem is greatly exacerbated because she and this social worker are the only two social workers at her placement; her field supervision is contracted through another agency. Thus, she is the only person who is aware of the misconduct. Should she risk the goodwill of this colleague and others at her agency by reporting the unprofessional behavior? Alone and feeling very vulnerable, she struggles between her own right to self-determination, which she views as protecting herself from possible retaliation, loss of internship placement, or poor grades, and her obligation to follow the Code of Ethics and report her colleague's misconduct.

In the third case, a worker is faced with a not uncommon dilemma. The agency has a beautifully written policy that it includes mission, services, and goals for clients. However, it is written generally and provides little guidance in specific situations. Thus, the director of the program has determined how the policy will be interpreted and administered and has set conditions for acceptance into the agency's program that, in her experience and estimation, best utilize this scarce resource. There is a long waiting list, and the program director's cutoffs make the process easier to administer.

The worker's client needs transitional housing, and the worker is advocating on her behalf with the director of the transitional housing program. However, in the process, she is told by the client that she (the client) has had contact with the abusive father of her children, recently in jail. The worker knows that one of the program director's cutoff points, "undesirable interpersonal relationships," applies to this one.

Both workers and colleagues expect loyalty, honesty, trust, and to be treated professionally, with dignity and respect. However, if the worker shares this information with the director of the program, her client will lose her opportunity for self-sufficiency via transitional housing. If the worker does not share the information, she undermines professional work relationships and the ethics and value base of the profession as a whole.

CASE STUDY 2.1

SHARE AND SHARE ALIKE: A DILEMMA IN PROFESSIONAL EDUCATIONAL DEVELOPMENT

Abstracted from an unpublished paper by Karen A. Wilson, MSW

PRACTICE CONTEXT AND CASE PRESENTATION

The mission of a youth services agency is to provide at-risk children with a better opportunity to complete school, obtain skills that lead to employment or additional education, and lead mentally and physically healthy, drug-free lives through services such as individual and family counseling, medical services, therapeutic groups, educational activities, employment groups, cultural enrichment, recreation, and services for parents. Supervision is provided both on the individual and group level. Video recording of sessions is encouraged to promote learning and skill development, and an informed consent form is routinely obtained from the youths and families served. This form specifies that "tapes are reviewed by the counselor to more effectively plan a course of treatment. Tapes are also available for viewing by the family—a process often useful to the progress of counseling." It does not indicate that videos could also be used in group supervision, which would entail viewing of the videos and discussion by the youth services staff of approximately twenty workers.

Workers may verbally provide additional information to clients regarding video recording, but workers have not seen a policy that addresses this issue, and the specific contexts in which such recordings may be used is not clearly defined. Therefore, any additional information provided depends on the individual worker, who must be guided by his or her own experience and judgment, rather than by an organized, consistent, and equitably applied agency policy.

Agency staff and administration have a strong commitment to professional development and growth and see video recording as an effective mechanism for the achievement of this goal. Competent, skilled workers, it is felt, provide the best possible services to clients. Group supervision enables appropriate sharing of knowledge base and skills between colleagues, enhancing the professional ability of each worker. Participation by each member of the staff in the group supervision process through the use of a video-recorded interview is viewed as a part of a worker's responsibility as a colleague. Thus, each worker is expected to contribute to the overall professional growth of the whole staff. Abrogation of this obligation may be interpreted as an unwillingness on the part of a worker to assist and enable the jointly held staff goal of optimal professional development. Workers take turns bringing a video recording to group supervision sessions, and they share in the discussion that the video recording engenders.

The worker recognizes the value of professional education and growth and, indeed, holds such growth as an important personal value. However, she feels a strong commitment to her clients and views the clients' interests as primary. She is uncertain that this use of client recordings, which includes visual as well as auditory information,

(continued)

CASE STUDY 2.1 CONTINUED

and thus precludes any confidentiality, is really in the interest of her clients at all. Furthermore, she believes that the "informed consent" that has been obtained from the clients does not specifically inform them about this breach in confidentiality.

She has, in truth, obtained consent for video recording "for educational purposes" from her clients. However, as they know that she is a student, she believes that the clients' understanding is that the videotapes will be viewed by the field instructor only, in order to better train the worker. The clients have accepted this use. While "educational purposes" might fit the broader purpose as well, that was not the understanding held by the clients.

Week after week, the worker has been giving the assembled staff excuses for not bringing a client video recording to share, while not voicing her ethical concerns. There is pressure placed on her by the rest of the staff, which has grown unbearable and is beginning to impact strongly on her relationship with her colleagues. Should she ask one of her clients for a broader informed consent? Should she bring in a video recording without specific client consent? Should she continue her delaying tactics? Should she confront the group with her concerns?

The dilemma may thus be stated as:

Confidentiality v. Obligation to Professional Educational Development

RESEARCH AND RELATED LITERATURE
Confidentiality. Koestler (as cited in Wilson, 1978) defines confidential information as

> those personal facts or conditions pertaining to the client's life which he has communicated to the agency for definite purposes related to the service he is requesting or receiving from the agency. It is the client's right and expectation that such information will be respected and safeguarded by the agency and all of its personnel: professional, administrative, secretarial, and clerical staff; field-work students, volunteers. (p. 1)

However, such a definition is not always made clear to the client. First of all, the client is usually not aware that there are two kinds of confidentiality: (1) absolute, where "data learned or observed by the social worker stay with that individual and are never passed on to anyone or anything" (Wilson, 1978, p. 5), and (2) relative, where "much of the communication between the client and social worker is shared with others in the system as part of the service-delivery process" (Wilson, 1978, p. 5). In many instances, the client believes or is sometimes misled to believe that the issue of confidentiality is absolute.

The client may also be unaware that social work counselor–client communications do not have legal protection in some states. "Thus, while the profession recognizes the importance of confidentiality, such awareness is no guarantee that attorneys and courts cannot gain access to sensitive information" (Wilson, 1978, p. 2).

The effects of breaching confidentiality can be devastating to the client, social worker, and agency. The National Social Welfare Assembly, Inc. (1958), states, "In social work, confidentiality is a basic, lasting concept. Without mutual trust and a strong sense of responsibility on the part of the agency for the person needing its services, a productive relationship cannot be built" (p. 40). A breach of confidentiality by the social worker and/or the agency is considered a breach of professional ethics. The NASW Code of Ethics (1996), Section 1.07c, states:

> Social workers should protect the confidentiality of all information obtained in the course of professional service, except for *compelling* [author's emphasis] professional reasons. The general expectation that social workers will keep information confidential does not apply when disclosure is necessary to prevent serious, forseeable, and imminent harm to a client or other identifiable person.

Section 1.07e states:

> Social workers should discuss with clients and other interested parties the nature of confidentiality and limitations of client's right to confidentiality. . . . This discussion should occur as soon as possible in the social worker–client relationship and as needed throughout the course of the relationship.

Section 1.07p states:

> Social workers should not disclose identifying information when discussing clients for teaching or training purposes unless the client has consented to disclosure of confidential information.

Section 2.01c stresses cooperation, but limits it to purposes of client well-being:

> Social workers should cooperate with social work colleagues and with colleagues of other professions when such cooperation serves the well-being of the client.

And in Section 2.02:

> Social workers should ensure that such colleagues [with whom information is shared] understand social workers' obligation to respect confidentiality and any exceptions related to it.

> In considering basic harms, Gewirth (1990) states:

> rules against basic harms to the necessary preconditions of actions (such as life, health, food, shelter, mental equilibrium) take precedence over rules against harms such as lying or revealing confidential information or threats to additive goods such as recreations, education, and wealth. (p. 62)

Breach of confidentiality and trust presents a risk of affecting mental equilibrium, which, according to Gewirth, must take precedence over the staff's professional educational development.

Gewirth (1990) also states that "individuals' rights to well-being may override laws, rules, regulations, and arrangements of voluntary associations in cases of conflict," further supporting confidentiality.

(continued)

CASE STUDY 2.1   CONTINUED

Professional Educational Development. Video recording improves counseling skills and also allows for consultation that could result in a more effective course of treatment for clients. Kaslow (1986) states, "Only by observing someone in action does a supervisor ever really know what it is that their supervisee does" (p. 156). Video recording is one method used for observation.

Ryan (1969) lists some advantages of video aids in practicum supervision:

(1) Videotaping does permit instantaneous analysis of non-verbal material in counselor education practicum and classes. The video picture makes the counseling session real for the student; (2) large classes can watch, react, and interact with what they see and hear; and (3) the client can view his tape immediately after the session if this is deemed advisable by the supervisor. (p. 128)

Also, when appropriate, supervisors will suggest readings that will help the counselor learn alternate ways of coping with the material. Still, another use of recording is "to provide firsthand feedback to clients by having them listen to or view their actual behavior in live sessions" (Hepworth & Larson, 1993).

Carkhuff (1966), however, cautions that

recording is used for many purposes—supervision, consultation, research—but some aspects of this are intolerable even though heard only by professional colleagues. Whether taped or not, the counselor serves for purposes of the client and must be shaped by what is effective for the client, not what is effective for his colleagues. He must have full awareness of the effect of the tape recording upon both himself and the client. (p. 471)

Video recording clients can be extremely revealing. Hepworth and Larson (1993) state that video-recorded sessions with clients

should be guarded with utmost caution to assure that copies cannot be made and that unauthorized persons do not have access to them. When they have served their designated purpose, tapes should be promptly erased. Failure to heed these guidelines constitutes a breach of professional ethics. (p. 80)

The *Clinical Social Work Journal,* Vol. 2, Winter 1974 (as cited in Wilson, 1978), states, "When confidential information is to be used for professional educative purposes, every effort should be made to conceal the true identity of the individuals discussed" (p. 42). Wilson (1978) states, "When it comes to a choice between presenting accurate recordings in the classroom and preserving the privacy and confidentiality of the consumers served, the client's needs must take priority" (p. 36). Wilson suggests that violations can be minimized if

(1) the client is informed that this process is occurring and how the results will be used; (2) his written permission (informed consent) is secured in making the recording; (3) his specific written consent is obtained each time the material is released to other persons; (4) his identity is disguised (unless the client gives specific written permission to use the material as is); (5) he has the right to see or hear the finished product to either approve it for use or make corrections and deletions; (6) permission for recording and use of the

material is also obtained from the interviewer or other involved staff members; and (7) tapes are stored securely. Tapes should also be erased as soon as they are no longer useful so they cannot become the subject of a subpoena or other action that might not work to the client's benefit. (p. 42)

The client should also be provided the right to decline.

The NASW Code of Ethics addresses continuing education and staff development in subsection 3.08. It states:

Social work administrators and supervisors should take reasonable steps to provide or arrange for continuing education and staff development for all staff for whom they are responsible. Continuing education and staff development should address current knowledge and emerging developments related to social work practice and ethics.

In this case, administration is aware that supervisors are providing in-service education through the use of videotaped client interviews. They are committed to staff development and have determined that the peer process provides optimal opportunities for ongoing learning. They have not found this ethically objectionable.

AUTHOR'S REFLECTIONS, REASONING PROCESS, AND RESOLUTION

Our society treasures freedom, justice, respect, happiness, honesty, trust, right to privacy, education, self-determination, and individualization. All but education would seem to support the maintenance of confidentiality, or, at least, full, informed consent. According to Loewenberg and Dolgoff (1992), "Societal values usually, but not always, provide guidelines for professional ethical behavior." Professional values such as honesty, confidentiality, personal and educational growth, individualization, and self-determination clearly mirror those of society and are reflected in the NASW Code of Ethics. However, the Code also includes clear obligations toward skill and competence for workers and colleagues:

Some of the principles supported by societal and professional ethics are as follows:
People should always tell the truth.
People should always be honest.
People should be afforded the right to privacy.
People should always seek ways to better themselves.
All people should have the right to freedom and justice as long as it is not hurting anyone else or themselves.
No one has the right to use another for personal exploitation.

Personal values also influence professionals' consideration of dilemmas. The worker values knowledge of self, family, happiness, respect, honesty, trust, confidentiality and privacy, self-determination, individualization, and personal and professional growth, which integrate well with both professional and societal values.

Several choices of action must be considered: (1) to inform the client and family that video recordings are viewed by staff members beyond the worker's immediate supervisor; (2) to inform as in number 1, but also present the overall risks of such use

(continued)

CASE STUDY 2.1   CONTINUED

of recordings; (3) to inform as in number 1, present overall risks and also worker's assessment of risks inherent in each client's unique situation; (4) to inform as in number 1 but, in video recording, shield the client's identity as much as possible, thus maximizing confidentiality but also losing the client's nonverbal cues, which may compromise both learning and consultation; (5) to inform as in number 1, but have the client view each recording and determine whether it can be viewed by other staff members; if not, view with supervisor and erase video; (6) to inform the client that video recordings are a part of the agency's commitment to professional education, can benefit them personally through consultation, and that agreeing to the participation in such recording is a condition of agency service; (7) to inform client as in number 1, but state that the videos will be retained by the agency for two days only and then be erased; (8) to refuse to participate in video recording of clients.

Reflecting on the most salient values and principles, the worker determines that a client may be asked to have a session recorded, provided that he/she/they can be adequately informed regarding the purpose of the recording, how it will be used, who will view it, and the disposition of the film. This would support the highest level of client self-determination, and preserve trust, honesty, privacy, and respect, while also enabling professional growth, education, and competence, as well as consultation on behalf of the client(s). It would also support the NASW Code of Ethics fully in all of its parts, and would resolve the dilemma by supporting the values that undergird each side.

QUESTIONS FOR THOUGHT AND DISCUSSION

1. The balance between client's right to privacy and confidentiality and the educational needs of professionals is delicate and difficult to define. The traditional structure of the profession itself, which defines the need for supervision and consultation for each worker, limits the possibility of confidentiality. Do you feel that this structure is necessary to the responsible and ethical practice of social work?

2. There is a sense in which this dilemma pits the privacy, trust, and possibly the welfare of the present client against the possible benefits of increased competence and skill to future clients. Is it justifiable to compromise the confidentiality of a present client in the interest of future clients?

3. Should policies about video recording apply to all clients of an agency equally, or should the particular issues, problems, and feelings of each client determine decisions regarding the use of video recording? The former supports equality; the latter, need.

4. Workers in agencies are justifiably interested in increasing their professional knowledge and skills. Are the agencies themselves the preferred venues for such learning activities, or might other resources be utilized? How can agencies support the use of such resources?

5. What would constitute a valid informed consent for video recording at this agency? Design a consent form that supports both maximal client self-determination and professional skill development through recording use.

CASE STUDY 2.2

COLLEAGUE MISCONDUCT: WHAT'S AN INTERN TO DO?

Abstracted from an unpublished paper by Jeanine Castilho da Silva, MSW

PRACTICE CONTEXT AND CASE PRESENTATION

A nonprofit, community-based Catholic agency's mission is the provision of crisis intervention to underserved populations, particularly uninsured and undocumented immigrants, through direct, short-term, and emergency assistance. The majority of clients are low-income Central American immigrants. The agency is divided into two departments: a Medical Clinic and Social Services. Each department has a coordinator and runs separate, distinct programs. Social Services clients can also receive immigration and employment assistance through the agency, while the Medical Clinic also provides mental health services through a family therapist and a psychiatrist.

Social Services is staffed by one full-time religious as coordinator, one immigration worker, and one employment specialist. The academic year during which the dilemma occurred was the first time social work interns were placed at the agency, and supervision was contracted out. As the agency did not have a social work focus, or experience in working with social work interns, it was a challenge to define an appropriate role, especially for a first-year intern. One month after the internship began, the agency hired Brenda, an MSW social worker who was not licensed and had not received supervision upon receiving her MSW degree. The coordinator was apparently not familiar with the importance of hiring a licensed social worker and assumed Brenda was able to perform the needed clinical social work services. However, her inability to provide these services was obvious to the intern, who was the only other social work–oriented person on the staff of the agency. As an example, the social worker failed repeatedly to respect privacy, thereby violating NASW article 1.07(a) in the Ethical Code, potentially placing clients and other members of the community at risk and violating their trust. Determining that a social worker is representing herself unfairly can be a complex task—all the more complex for an intern just beginning to learn about professional codes and practices.

The ethical issue revolves around social workers' responsibility to report misconduct by professional colleagues. While both social workers and social work interns have this responsibility, interns are especially vulnerable, and there is often a reasonable fear of confrontation or retaliation that may negatively impact the internship and the student in a number of ways. The possibility of poor grades, conflict, termination, isolation, and other behaviors on the part of colleagues and agency staff make reporting professional misconduct difficult for interns, and the self-determined need for self-protection may limit reporting.

One side of the dilemma is the intern's right to self-determination in not reporting and thus maintaining an appropriate working environment to support her goals of achieving of professional education. The intern had devoted a great deal of personal

(continued)

CASE STUDY 2.2   CONTINUED

time and effort in preparing for and entering the MSW program, and a positive internship experience in a good learning environment was extremely important to her. The risk of reporting, she felt, could severely damage the good rapport that the intern had established with the staff in the month prior to Brenda's arrival. Further, it was intimidating to consider confronting someone who was already an MSW and obviously more experienced in the field. It is also important to note that it is difficult to challenge a social work colleague once one is an MSW or LCSW, as it can severely impact the work relationship, the work environment, and even threaten job security.

On the other hand, one of the marks of a profession is self-monitoring, and there is a clear obligation to report misconduct by colleagues. Poor representation of the profession's ethical codes, mission, goals, and standards compromises its status as a whole. Perhaps most importantly, the welfare of vulnerable clients may be at stake. The NASW's Code of Ethics clearly states that a social worker is first and foremost responsible for the safety and well-being of clients. Students are responsible for adhering to the tenets of the Code of Ethics from the moment they enter a professional social work program.

The dilemma may be phrased as:

Obligation to Report Colleague's Misconduct v. Self-Determination

RESEARCH AND RELATED LITERATURE

Relatively little research was available regarding issues raised by this dilemma. The rights of individual social workers to self-determination has not been addressed, and there is relatively little information on social workers' attitudes toward and experiences with reporting colleagues. It is hoped that this presentation will focus professional interest on this important ethical issue.

The Right to Self-Determination. The respect for the client's right to self-determination is one of the first things taught in MSW programs. It is the first standard of practice addressed in the NASW Code of Ethics. However, it is interesting to observe the limited information available for the social worker about his or her *own* right to self-determination. Working with a social work colleague who is violating the Code of Ethics, such as Brenda, is challenging both personally and professionally.

The intern's agency provided both a verbal and a written protection for students in training through extensive provision of supervision. The agency's policy manual states, ". . . an agreement is drawn up between the school and agency specifying the conditions and the limitations of the services provided by the students. Students will be appropriately supervised and supported according to the agreement." Both the outside, contracted MSW supervision and agency staff, in adhering to this policy, frequently requested feedback regarding interns' academic learning and professional development at the agency, providing support and validating interns' abilities to reason and function professionally.

Obligation to Report Colleague Misconduct. The NASW Code of Ethics defines so-cial workers' responsibilities to the profession. In section 2.11 it states, "Social work-ers should take adequate measures to discourage, prevent, expose, and correct the unethical conduct of colleagues" (NASW Code of Ethics, 1996, p. 18). Quite clearly, we are directed to report misconduct of our social work colleagues. In section 2.10(a), the Code states that the first step one should take is to address the colleague's incom-petence with him or her and "assist in taking remedial action" (NASW Code of Ethics, 1996, p. 18). Second, if the colleague does not take adequate steps to improve his or her incompetence, then one should go through the appropriate channels of supervisors, agencies, NASW, licensing and regulatory bodies, and other professional organiza-tions (NASW Code of Ethics, 2.10(b), p. 18). Article 3.09, part C, states, "Social work-ers should take steps to ensure that employers are aware of social workers' ethical obligations as set forth in the NASW Code of Ethics" (1996, p. 21).

Additionally, the Code of Ethics outlines ethical responsibilities to society. Arti-cle 6.01 states, "Social workers should promote the general welfare of society, from local to global levels, and the development of people, their communities, and their en-vironments" (NASW Code of Ethics, 1996, p. 26). Therefore, we first have a responsi-bility to our clients, then to our agencies, profession, and society.

When issues of professional misconduct arise, NASW has a specific process by which the complaint is brought to a Chapter Committee on Inquiry (COI), the National Committee on Inquiry (NCOI), and the Board of Directors. If violations of the code are found after a review, the social worker will be given a reprimand or censure, or supervi-sion of the member's practice by an authorized person will be required. Action at the na-tional level is required to suspend NASW or Academy of Certified Social Workers membership or to make public a report of professional misconduct (Berliner, 1989, p. 70).

In a study of social worker misconduct, Levy states, ". . . staff members must feel ethically responsible to prevent, forestall, discourage, and stop the malevolent acts of colleagues" (1979, p. 280). These research findings see reporting misconduct as integral to maintaining professional standards within the profession of social work. The protec-tion of the client, who is vulnerable and can be damaged by unprofessional behavior, is the primary reason for reporting misconduct. Either direct observation of misconduct or simply awareness of misconduct are grounds for reporting colleagues. Social work-ers' responsibility in this regard is owed to clients, to the profession, and to society as a whole (Berliner, 1989, p. 69; Levy, 1979, p. 280; NASW Code of Ethics, 1996, pp. 26–27; Pharis, 1987, p. 190; Rhodes, 1992, p. 44).

The agency's policy and procedures manual clearly states that staff must work within the established policies and mission of the organization to assist people and work toward "the well-being of the clients and communities" served by the agency. This would seem to imply a policy obligation to expose a colleague performing unpro-fessionally as well.

AUTHOR'S REFLECTION, REASONING PROCESS, AND RESOLUTION

One of the key values in our society is freedom and the right to speak one's mind and make decisions for oneself. This value supports self-determination and would seem to

(continued)

CASE STUDY 2.2   CONTINUED

support a social worker's right to determine what he or she will do about misconduct in a colleague. While valuing freedom, however, we also value safety, and we believe that all people have a basic right to be free of harm. Our laws support both of these values, and nonadherence can result in a variety of sanctions, including incarceration. Societal values can be used to support either alternative: A social worker who witnesses misconduct and fears retribution for reporting has the right to feel safe in her place of employment; the client, profession, and the overall society also have the right to safety.

The utilitarian principle, which values the greatest good for the greatest number, is integral to our society. The NASW Code of Ethics lists social justice as one of its guiding principles, along with recognition of the importance of human relationships. These would seem to support the obligation to report over the worker's right to self-determination. In other words, according to our societal values and principles, we place more importance on preventing a social worker from harming others in society than on the social worker's right to determine whether to report the misconduct for personal reasons. Where collective harms may occur, individual rights may take a secondary role. This position seems to be supported by the NASW Code of Ethics, which clearly states professional obligations to report misconduct as important to clients, agencies, the profession, and society.

Most of the agency's clients were low-income, underserved, and undocumented immigrants from Central America. Based on their cultural values and experience in emigrating to the United States, they strongly value privacy and confidentiality—particularly with family-related problems. Brenda's privacy violations clearly violated cultural as well as professional standards. In this situation, of utmost importance is that safety be the first value to consider when making decisions regarding the dilemma, and the protection of vulnerable clients is paramount. Privacy supports safety and is essential to the development of client trust. When a social worker shares client problems inappropriately with others and with the public at large, as Brenda did, many people can be harmed, and the trust in the profession as a whole can be in jeopardy. Freedom and the right to self-determination is ranked third because it is felt that people must first feel safe; second, must believe their problems will be kept confidential; and only after these, have the right to self-determination. This would support subsuming the worker's right to self-determination to the primary rights of her clients.

This intern's personal values hierarchy includes safety, truth, personal growth and self-actualization, and responsibility to others. A Catholic tradition that supports equality, fairness, and beneficence, as well as personal experiences in a low-income, single-parent family where truth, care, and responsibility for others were highly valued, support reporting misconduct despite potential negative personal effects. Personal safety in potentially losing a good internship seemed outweighed by the potential harm that could be done to clients. However, fear and concern about repercussions gave strength to the self-determination position.

Several options were considered in resolving this dilemma. A social worker, like every other person, has a right to self-determination and may choose to remain silent about the misconduct to protect her or his position in the internship. One of the few articles on this subject says that the agency has an ethical responsibility to ensure that its staff members grow and develop professionally (Levy, 1979, p. 281). Remaining silent will support this worker's learning and professional growth in a positive ambiance. It is, arguably, the agency's responsibility, not the interns, to be aware of staff performance and detect misconduct. Our societal values of freedom and privacy support self-determination by giving the social worker the liberty to choose not to report.

A second option in favor of self-determination is to leave the placement, giving a non-related, acceptable reason for requesting a change. Our societal rights to freedom would support this position, suggesting that each person has the right to determine his or her own course of action. A third option would be to confide in one person, either at the field placement or at school, swearing them to secrecy and asking for help and advice. However, informing another person will involve that person's own ethics and professional obligations in decision making and could also place the person in a difficult position by not enabling him or her to take the actions he or she may feel professionally bound to take. Also, the person chosen for the confidence may refuse to be bound by secrecy.

In support of the obligation to report misconduct, the first option is to confront Brenda in a nonthreatening manner and determine whether her behavior improves after this discussion. This is clearly stated in the NASW's Code of Ethics, in articles 2.10 (a) and (b), where social workers are directed to confront colleagues regarding their incompetence. This option is in line with the societal value of safety, in that social workers have a responsibility to protect and ensure that all people are safe from harm.

A second option would involve sharing Brenda's behavior with a professional at the school or agency without swearing this person to secrecy. The NASW's Code of Ethics and some of the research directs a social worker to go through the "proper channels" in reporting misconduct (NASW Code of Ethics, 1996, p. 18). A third option is to contact relevant state licensing boards and the National Association for Social Workers and file a formal report. All three of these options put the values of client safety and privacy ahead of a social worker's right to freedom to choose to report.

The course of action selected was based on personal ethical beliefs and commitment to the profession of social work and clients and was grounded in both societal and personal values: to report the misconduct as the NASW Code, article 2.11, recommends, which is "to take action through the appropriate formal channels" (NASW's Code of Ethics, 1996, p. 18). The theoretical arguments in favor of this decision are based on the utilitarian idea of providing the greatest good for the greatest number of people. To support this position, it may be necessary at times to subordinate one's personal interest and safety to the greater good. Professional relationships with clients require that they be able to trust that they will be safe and that their privacy will be respected. The decision was made to report Brenda's behavior to both school and agency professionals.

While any intern may be wary of reporting the misconduct of other professionals and concerned about the effect this might have on learning, grades, and the internship experience as a whole, it would seem to this writer that to avoid challenging and potentially difficult situations limits the kind of personal growth and learning that are vital to competent professional development. Being a social worker is often challenging in many ways and involves making ethical decisions that impact many people's lives. A

(continued)

CASE STUDY 2.2   CONTINUED

part of this may be learning to take personal risks and, at times, to make personal sacrifices in the interests of vulnerable clients.

To summarize, these questions were considered in resolving this ethical dilemma: (1) Who will suffer the greatest harm? (2) How can the least harm to the least number of people be promoted (utilitarianism)? and (3) How can a decision be made that incorporates both individual and client values? The most essential societal and personal value seemed to be safety; the second, trusting that social workers will act ethically, a personal value; and third, the societal value of privacy, which demands confidentiality. Freedom, while still very important, is last in the hierarchy because it is contingent first on the values of safety, trust, privacy, and responsibility to others.

In a sense, this intern's decision has resolved her dilemma in a unique manner. By reporting client misconduct, she *is* in fact exercising her right to self-determination. Self-determination does not always mean self-protection and self-interest; the distinction is an important one to consider. Additionally, during this past academic year a professor had a wonderful saying that seemed applicable to this particular dilemma: "Do not ask your clients to do something that you are not willing to do yourself." It would be impossible for the intern to encourage clients to honor ethical codes while violating them herself.

QUESTIONS FOR THOUGHT AND DISCUSSION

1. Colleague misconduct in regard to client privacy is only one of the situations students may encounter in their field work placement. What other kinds of colleague misconduct occur in social agencies? If you have observed misconduct, what have you done? What have other professionals done? In the context of the NASW Code of Ethics, do you feel that appropriate actions were taken?

2. Working with a group of students, design a comprehensive agency policy which defines expectations of professionals, and actions that will be taken should these be violated. What kinds of behaviors would you include? How will you monitor violations?

3. In the context of your own agency setting, develop a plan for actions you would take if you observe professional misconduct. On what basis would you decide to take action or not to take action? Who would you approach? What steps would you take?

4. The writer raises an important issue that is not discussed frequently in the profession: Where do the "rights" and "self-interest" of individual professionals come in? Must workers always subsume individual interests to client interests? What about your family's interest? Your partner's interest? Your outside obligations and responsibilities?

5. Consequentialist theories that focus on action and effect hold professionals responsible for any actions that harm clients or are professionally inappropriate. Deontological theories state that motives are vital in determining misconduct: If the intent was good, but a client was inadvertently harmed, one should consider the motive and not the result. Which position do you feel should be used in judging professional misconduct? Why?

CASE STUDY 2.3

WHEN A COLLEAGUE "DEFINES" POLICY—AND YOU DON'T AGREE!

Abstracted from an unpublished paper by Linda K. Lopez, MSW

PRACTICE CONTEXT AND CASE PRESENTATION

Karen, a 20-year-old single mother of two young boys, ages 3 months and 2 years, has been living in a homeless shelter with her children for three months. She is a good prospective candidate for a transitional housing program, because she has a high school diploma and has completed one year of college. She presents herself as a competent young woman—alert, communicative, able to maintain eye contact when speaking— and she generally has a high level of interpersonal social functioning, all valuable skills for future employment.

There is a history of alcoholism and abuse in her family of origin. The father of her boys was known to have gone to jail for auto theft and assault before the birth of Karen's first baby. She has not heard from him for about six months and was not living with him prior to her homelessness. She expresses sadness that he has not seen his baby. She also said he "had a bad temper and had hit her a few times."

The social worker is seeing Karen through the Emergency Services Department of the Department of Social Services (DSS). A two-bedroom apartment is about to become available in the Transitional Housing Program, another service of DSS, and the social worker wants to advocate for Karen and her family. A treatment team meeting is scheduled to discuss her case. The day before the meeting, the social worker has an appointment with Karen. During the meeting, Karen confides in the worker that she has met with the father of her children "just so he could see his kids. I know we can't be together." When the worker tells her this could harm her chances for transitional housing, due to his history, she asks the worker to please keep it a secret. Without answering this directly, the worker says, "I will do what I can to help get you into transitional housing."

The social worker knows that during the treatment team meeting, there will be questions about whether Karen has had any contact with the father of her children. In order to be placed in transitional housing, a client must be likely to achieve self-sufficiency, according to agency policy. The staff member in charge of the program has interpreted this to mean the client should not be involved in undesirable interpersonal relationships, even with the father of her children. She believes that such relationships compromise the client's ability to become successfully self-sufficient and that expediency, and maximal utilization of resources, supports her exclusion of such clients from the program. If the worker reveals Karen's brief contact with the father, the program director will immediately exclude her from consideration.

The worker has an obligation to the best interests of her client. She also has an obligation to treat colleagues with dignity, honesty, and respect. The program director expects loyalty from the worker, and the worker's support in ensuring the success of the transitional housing program.

(continued)

CASE STUDY 2.3   CONTINUED

There are several aspects to this dilemma. The worker finds the one most ethically difficult for her involves deciding whether to protect what she perceives to be the best interest of her client as opposed to supporting her colleague's position and expertise as she is professionally obligated to do, although she does not agree with her interpretation of the agency's policy toward "undesirable interpersonal relationships."

The dilemma may be stated as:

Best Interests of Client v. Obligation to Colleague

RESEARCH AND RELATED LITERATURE

Actual Agency Policy. The stated mission of the Department of Social Services is to provide eligible clients the means for meeting the basic needs of food, shelter, clothing, and protection, as well as provide opportunities for clients to reach the highest possible level of self-sufficiency. The agency vision is to "help clients reach their maximum potential as independent and self-sufficient members of the community" (Agency Policy Statement).

The purpose of the Emergency Services Program is to provide a full continuum of services to homeless families and adults and those who are experiencing crises. The program offers preventive, crisis intervention, and transitional/supportive casework services in order to resolve the crises and prevent their recurrence. The policy states that the target populations with highest priority are homeless families. One of the goals of the program is "to enhance stabilization and prevent recurrence of emergencies through the provision of transitional services." The policy includes three eligibility requirements: (1) Clients must have a historical pattern of residency in the county, (2) clients must not have sufficient personal resources to resolve the emergency, and (3) assistance will only be provided as part of a casework plan that will resolve the emergency and contribute to a manageable ongoing financial and social situation (Agency Policy Statement).

In practice, this global definition of eligibility allows broad latitude for judgment. In fact, the number of clients awaiting services and living in homeless shelters has grown in the past few years, allowing social workers to choose the most desirable clients to receive certain services. "Desirable" can be translated to mean most likely to succeed and become self-sufficient. The program's director has noted that a pattern of destructive interpersonal relationships is a negative attribute.

Agency Policy Literature Rev

iew. According to Loewenberg and Dolgoff (1992), the goals and objectives of many organizations are not always congruent with the objectives of the profession of social work. Sometimes there are rules that conflict with social workers' professional obligations to give priority to their clients' interests. This was especially noted in the case of advocacy responsibilities.

Levy (as cited in Reamer, 1990) has written that the social worker owes certain ethical responsibilities to the employing agency and that foremost among these is the obligation to act for and represent the agency loyally and unequivocally. In his view, if the social worker cannot stand on the side of the agency policy, then it is time to leave the agency. Reamer (1990) offers the viewpoint that this obligation could be overridden by a situation in which the client's right to basic preservation of life was at stake (in the case of a suicidal client).

A comparative study of ethical decision making was done by Walden, Wolock, and Demone (1990), using case vignettes to propose ethical dilemmas. The results showed that advocating for clients without violating agency policy was the response of choice. This allowed the social worker to be ethically responsive within a context of conflicting demands and pressures. An interesting finding was that client behavior appeared to affect the worker's decisions: If a client was doing something illegal or unacceptable, the worker tended to lean toward the system-oriented response. In other words, workers were more client-oriented when clients were seen as nondeviant.

Linzer (1992) conducted an analysis of the process an agency went through in defining its policy regarding sexual behavior of developmentally disabled residents of a group home. State law guaranteed the rights of group residents to sexual expression. Social workers supported the value of client self-determination, but parents preferred that the group home provide sexual limits. The sectarian agency also had to consider the input of the members of the community. This group had values similar to the parents; they supported a strict limitation on sexual activity outside of marriage. The agency decided on a compromise between these three groups for the policy: Sexual expression was to be permitted or restricted on an individual basis, and sexual intercourse was not permitted on agency property between unmarried persons.

Ethical Responsibilities. Joseph (1983) addresses the concept of the ethical responsibilities of organizations. The question of whether the organization itself is obligated to behave ethically or whether the ethical obligation should apply only to the individuals who make up the organization is one that needs to be addressed. Historically, organizations have used a rational decision-making model that tends to be utilitarian (the end justifies the means). An example: A supervisor in a mental institution instructs a worker to present a client's case in a "very favorable" way, so as not to jeopardize the discharge plan. In this view, the organizational decision is governed by rules of rational efficiency (utility), while the decision of the individual is governed by ethical responsibility. An alternative position to this view is that an organization, as well as an individual, is a moral agent, ethically responsible for its actions. Joseph (1983) concludes that ethical decision-making models are needed in conjunction with rational problem-solving models. Many social service organizations experience a dilemma between an ethic of utility and one of humanitarian service.

In this instance, however, the director of the program has chosen to define agency policy in a way that is not explicitly stated. Her motivation—optimal successful utilization of the transitional housing units—appears congruent with social work values and responsibility to society. However, utilizing this interpretation may, at times, compromise

(*continued*)

CASE STUDY 2.3   CONTINUED

the opportunities of clients such as Karen through a restriction not explicitly stated in the policy.

The NASW Code of Ethics (Sect. 3.07b) states:

> Social workers should advocate for resource allocation procedures that are open and fair. When not all clients' needs can be met, an allocation procedure should be developed that is nondiscriminatory and based on appropriate and consistently applied principles. (1996, pp. 20–21)

Ethical Responsibility to Colleagues. The worker has an obligation to support her colleague. Section 2 of the NASW Code of Ethics addresses a worker's responsibility toward colleagues, including treating colleagues with "respect" (2.01a), and "cooperat[ing]" with them (2.01c). If the worker does not share information regarding Karen with the program's director, the worker may be impeding the director's ethical and competent performance of her professional responsibilities.

Furthermore, the worker has specifically defined responsibilities in regard to the "unethical" conduct of colleagues, if indeed she perceives the program director's actions and position in this manner. Subsection 2.11a of the NASW Code of Ethics states, "Social workers should take adequate measures to discourage, prevent, expose, and correct unethical conduct of colleagues."

Workers should seek resolution when they believe a colleague is acting unethically by discussion with the colleague (2.11c). If this is unsuccessful, the worker should "take action through appropriate formal channels" (2.11d).

AUTHOR'S REFLECTIONS, REASONING PROCESS, AND RESOLUTION

This client is currently in need of assistance so that she can become self-sufficient. Providing such assistance does not necessitate depriving the client of the freedom to use her own judgment concerning where to live and with whom to associate. Self-sufficiency is a value the agency chose to put in its mission statement, without qualification as to circumstances. The program director's position could be interpreted as an invasion of the client's privacy as well.

Trustworthiness is an important aspect of the client–worker relationship, as well as of the colleague relationship. It is expected of both: The client expects the worker to maintain her confidences if violating them could be harmful to the client's goals. She also expects that the worker will act in her best interest. The program director values the worker's trustworthiness as well. She has limited spaces in the transitional housing program and is concerned that these will be distributed in a way that maximizes their usefulness. She trusts the worker to share any information that might limit the success of a client in transitional housing, and she has determined from her experience that "undesirable interpersonal relationships" tend to do just that.

Ethical principles that can be used to judge possible options in this case include the commitment of the social worker to represent the agency and preserve its policies, the obligation to treat colleagues professionally, the right of the client to self-determination (choosing to see the father at all), and her right to confidentiality. Values that seem relevant to this dilemma include self-sufficiency, self-determination, trustworthiness, responsibility, justice, and freedom.

The director of the program, it would seem, has taken a rule utilitarian position regarding admission to transitional housing. She has determined that, *as a rule,* clients do better when they do not have negative interpersonal relationships. For the sake of economy and efficiency, and for ensuring the best chances of success, she has made this a rule for the program. Unfortunately, rule utilitarianism sacrifices the individual, who cannot be considered separately. If each case could be considered unique, act utilitarianism would be applied and each situation's potential for success be evaluated individually. This would maximize justice, but sacrifice efficiency and economy. Karen's contact with the father of her children would then be viewed, not as the determining factor, but as one of many factors to be considered in evaluating her chances for success in the program.

Although the worker wishes it were so, she does not think it is possible to have strictly normative ethics. "Oughts" can always be challenged by a difficult situation. The worker must begin with a deontological outlook, based on religious beliefs and the ideal of love. This can be love of self, love of another, or love of many others, depending on the situation. Love is the absolute ethical good and the actual expression of the divine in man, but each situation must be considered in a subjective, intuitive way in order to see how to apply this ideal into action. The worker believes that the good is not in the end, but in the means, and especially the motive. If one truly acts out of love, then one is acting ethically. The end is really out of any individual's hands.

In consideration of all of the above, the worker recognizes that she must tell the truth, explain the client's well-intended motives, and leave the end to take its natural course. The choice of withholding the truth about the client's seeing the father of her children suggested a feeling of negative awareness of self to the worker. It violates the ethical code that binds colleagues in sharing common work and goals on behalf of society, possibly compromises other clients, and erodes the commonly held value base of the profession.

However, the worker recognizes her own discomfort with the program director's interpretation of the agency's policy regarding transitional housing. Within the boundaries of the colleague relationship, she will ask for supporting documentation and rationale, discuss her position with the program director, and advocate for change in the interpretation if, after further information is gathered, she feels that this interpretation is unjust.

QUESTIONS FOR THOUGHT AND DISCUSSION

1. Policies are often written in generalities, yet must be applied specifically. How might a worker approach an attempt to understand the intent of a policy in a particular situation?
2. Agencies and workers often find themselves caught between the efficiency and economy of rule utilitarians and the justice of act utilitarians. If you were the program

director of the transitional housing program, which would you feel would best contribute to the stated mission of the agency and the program?

3. Lack of information limits the ability to make reasonable choices regarding eligibility and suitability of a client for a program. Providing the information may violate client confidentiality, compromise loyalty and trust, and place the interests of the program above those of your client. If you were Karen's worker, what would you have done?

4. If a colleague, such as the program director, interprets an agency policy in a way that you feel belies and perhaps hinders its intent, what do you feel is your ethical responsibility, if any? How can you minimize harm to the colleague, the program, the agency, and yourself?

5. The worker did not appear to utilize supervision in determining a course of action to resolve her dilemma. What ethical dimensions are added if a supervisor is introduced into the situation? For the worker? The supervisor? The colleague? The client?

REFERENCES AND BIBLIOGRAPHY

Case Study 2.1

Carkhuff, R. R. (1966). Counseling research, theory, and practice. *Journal of Counseling Psychology, 13*(4), 467–480.

Gewirth, A. (1990). A guide to ethical decisions. In F. G. Reamer (Ed.), *Ethical dilemmas in social service* (2nd ed.). New York: Columbia University.

Hepworth, D. H., & Larson, J. A. (1993). Operationalizing the cardinal social work values. In *Direct social work practice* (pp. 52–89). Pacific Grove, CA: Brooks/Cole.

Kant, I. (1990). Truth-telling and competing interests. In F. G. Reamer (Ed.), *Ethical dilemmas in social service* (2nd ed.). New York: Columbia University.

Kaslow, F. W. (1986). *Supervision and training: Models, dilemmas, and challenges.* New York: Haworth Press.

Loewenberg, F. M., & Dolgoff, R. (1992). *Ethical decisions for social work practice.* Itasca, IL: F. E. Peacock.

National Association of Social workers. (1996). *NASW Code of Ethics.* Washington, DC: Author.

National Social Welfare Assembly. (1958, April). *Confidentiality in social services to individuals.* New York: Author.

Ryan, C. W. (1969). Video aids in practicum supervision. *Counselor Education and Supervision, 8,* 125–129.

Wilson, S. J. (1978). *Confidentiality in social work.* New York: Macmillan.

Case Study 2.2

Berliner, A. K. (1989, January). Misconduct in social work practice. *Social Work, 69–72.*

Levy, C. S. (1979). The ethics of management. *Administration in Social Work, 3*(3), 277–288.

Loewenberg, F. M. & Dolgoff, R. (1996). *Ethical decisions for social work practice.* Itasca, IL: F. E. Peacock.

National Association of Social Workers. (1996). *NASW Code of Ethics.* Washington, DC: Author.

Perlman, G. L. (1988, September/October). Mastering the law of privileged communication: A guide for social workers. *Social Work, 425–429.*

Pharis, M. E. (1987). Right on! Comment on the revised code of ethics of the National Federation of Societies for Clinical Social Work Practice. *Clinical Social Work Journal, 15*(2), 188–191.

Reamer, F. G. (1990). *Ethical dilemmas in social service: A guide for social workers* (2nd ed.). New York: Columbia University Press.

Rhodes, M. L. (1992, January). Social work challenges: The boundaries of ethics. *Families in Society: The Journal of Contemporary Human Services, 40–47.*

Case Study 2.3

Albers, D. A., & Morris, R. J. (1990). Conceptual problems in studying social workers' management of confidentiality. *Social Work, 35*(4), 361–362.

Biestek, F. (1975). *The casework relationship.* Chicago: Loyola University Press.

Joseph, M. V. (1983). The ethics of organizations: Shifting values and ethical dilemmas. *Administration in Social Work, 7*(3/4), 47–57.

Linzer, N. (1992). The role of values in determining agency policy. *Families in Society: The Journal of Contemporary Human Services, 73*(9), 301–309, 553–558.

Loewenberg, F. M., & Dolgoff, R. (1992). *Ethical decisions for social work practice.* Itasca, IL: F. E. Peacock.

Moore-Kirkland, J., & Irey, K. V. (1981). A reappraisal of confidentiality. *Social Work, 5,* 319–322.

National Association of Social Workers. (1996). *NASW Code of Ethics.* Washington, DC: Author.

Reamer, F. G. (1990). *Ethical dilemmas in social service.* New York: Columbia University Press.

Walden, T., Wolock, I., & Demone, H. W. (1990). Ethical decision making in human services: A comparative study. *Families in Society: The Journal of Contemporary Human Services, 71*(2), 67–75.

CHAPTER THREE

NASW ETHICAL STANDARD THREE
Social Workers' Ethical Responsibilities to Practice Settings

INTRODUCTION

Provisions of Code

When a professional social worker is hired by an organization, there are generally both explicit and implicit terms to which both parties agree. On the part of the worker, these might include loyalty and fidelity to the mission and purposes of the organization, the responsible use of resources, including one's own time and expertise, and adherence to the policies and procedures of the practice setting. The worker should also seek to prevent and eliminate discrimination and improve policies, procedures, and services as needed in an appropriate manner.

This section of the Code calls for particularly careful and reflective consideration. Because workers are generally very dedicated to the interests of their clients, there is often an assumption that these interests take priority over obligations to the agency when the two appear to conflict. Common examples include the client who violates an agency policy: the patient who disregards the rules of the residential treatment center, the mandated client who misses appointments, the TANF mother with an outside, unreported job or other source of income, the student who cheats on an exam, the drug rehabilitation program client who continues to abuse drugs "occasionally." In each of these cases, the client can present a strong argument in support of his or her action, an argument that the worker finds plausible and with which he or she can empathize. Additionally, the client often has confided this information to the worker with the presumption that confidentiality will be observed.

The practice setting is the "big guy," and the client the "little guy." What can a little infraction do to the agency, the worker reasons? Not much. The client's benefit can outweigh it! Besides, there are those sticky issues of trust, confidentiality, and building relationships.

However, the employer has given the worker a position of trust, in the expectation that this trust will not be violated. Additionally, such behavior can seriously injure the organization. Nonadherence to policy often violates funding criteria. It uses resources inappropriately, thus deflecting the accomplishment of the agency's mission. It may also affect the availability of service to future clients. Additionally, policies may reflect years of experience and careful reflection and are usually designed specifically to meet the stated mission and purpose of that particular setting. Do practice settings, as well as individuals, have a right to self-determination within certain parameters?

Siding with the client against the practice setting also affects the client's perception of self, worker, and agency. The client sees the worker colluding with him or her against the practice setting; thus, the organization, the source of help to which the client originally came, the very meeting ground that has brought client and worker together, is seen as the enemy. The client observes that the proscribed behavior is condoned by the worker, which can serve either to reinforce it or cause the client to lose respect for the worker. In violating agency policy, the worker is modeling for the client behavior that is contrary to the ideals of honesty and integrity, and that is not condoned by society.

There are other ethical issues in the relationship between a social worker and his or her agency that may create conflicts as well. The problems suggested above involve ethical issues between an agency and a client, with the worker caught in the middle. Other scenarios may relate primarily to the relationship between the worker and the employing agency. Many of these problems between worker and employer are related to policies with which the worker may disagree, or question. Out of concern for clients, workers often have difficulty with policies that compromise what may be viewed as the client's rights and interests on behalf of organizational efficiency, funding needs, or expediency.

In such cases, workers have several choices: They may privately disregard agency policies and procedures, thus violating their employment contract; they may publicly disregard them, thus undermining the authority and legitimacy of the agency; they may follow them, thus violating their own personal standards of ethics and justice, and possibly compromising clients' welfare; or they may follow them while advocating for change through the agency's own system, possibly compromising present clients but seeking to prevent the effect of such policies and procedures on future clients.

Social workers also have the choice of going outside the agency to government bodies, licensing and/or funding sources, or to the general public in attempting to address issues of vital concern. They may also terminate their employment with the agency, thus releasing themselves from a "contract" that conflicts with personal values and worldview.

Section 3 of the Code of Ethics addresses the relationship between the social worker and the practice setting specifically. Because supervision and consultation are an integral part of the functioning of the profession as a whole, the first subsection addresses these. It obligates supervisors and consultants to act only within their areas of expertise (3.01a), to maintain "clear and sensitive boundaries" (3.01b); it proscribes dual or multiple relationships where there is risk of harm to the supervisee (3.01c); and it requires that supervisee evaluations be "fair and respectful"(3.01d), on the basis of "clearly stated criteria" (3.03).

Education and training is a particularly delicate area within practice settings. Field instruction is a vital part of social work education, enabling students to experience and learn from actual client contact within a practice setting. The Code addresses competence and fairness of educators and field instructors (3.02a and b), proscribes dual or multiple relationships (3.02d), and asks that clients be routinely informed when a student provides services (3.02c).

Subsections 3.04a through d set guidelines for client records that support accuracy, timeliness, privacy, and storage that promote both the efficiency of the practice setting and a concern for the privacy and dignity of clients. Billing practices should "accurately reflect the nature and extent of services" (3.05).

A concern for the client is also reflected in subsection 3.06, which addresses transfers of clients, suggesting that workers consider and discuss with clients the appropriateness of the transfer (3.06a). When a worker finds that a client has previously been served by another organization or colleague, the worker must discuss with the client "whether consultation with the previous service provider is in the client's best interest" (3.06b).

Administrative issues are also addressed. Administrators have responsibility for (1) advocating for funds adequate to the clients' needs (3.07a) and ensuring that they are distributed within the agency in a nondiscriminatory manner (3.07b), (2) setting aside funds for adequate staff supervision (3.07c), and (3) staff development and continuing education (3.08). Administrators are also responsible for ensuring that their organization is in compliance with the NASW Code of Ethics (3.07d).

Subsection 3.09 addresses the worker's commitment to the agency, stating that workers should generally adhere to commitments (3.09a) and work to improve "policies and procedures" and the "efficiency and effectiveness" of services (3.09b). Social workers must ensure that employers are aware of the NASW Code of Ethics and their ethical obligations (3.09c) and not allow organizational policies to interfere with ethical practice (3.09d). This obligation would support the following one: preventing and eliminating discrimination (3.09e). During labor-management disputes, workers should "be guided by the profession's values, ethical principles, and ethical standards" (3.10b).

Ethical principles in the practice setting should also be considered when employment or field placement is planned (3.09f). Last, but surely not least, workers are obligated to be careful stewards of the resources of their organizations (3.09g).

The Cases

The first case presented in this chapter addresses the issue of informed consent. The worker, employed by a mental health outpatient center, is confronted by an upset client, who claims that the consent form used by the agency is so broad and so general that she is left unaware of the implications of signing. She states that she would not have signed the form had she known of its potential applications. Initially agreeing with the client, the worker undertakes to examine agency policy in regard to informed consent, relating it to agency mission, clientele served, efficiency, and effectiveness. She then assumes a position of advocacy for change using the agency's structure for policy considerations.

The second case relates to a common problem in the social work setting in this age of modern technologies: the appropriate use of computerized files and demographic information. In the interests of efficiency, and to facilitate accountability to third-party payers and government agencies, the worker's agency has decided to place previously confidential information on the computer. As the agency has no policy for controlling access to the data, the worker is concerned with the potential for violations of client privacy and confidentiality. She must determine whether she, individually, will cooperate with the agency's requests that she computerize her client recordkeeping. Realizing that her ethical problem is wider than her own client population, she assumes an instrumental role in advocating for measures to ensure client confidentiality of records through the use of codes and controlled access.

Many social agencies work with ethnically and culturally diverse populations, and "sensitive" practice is an obligation of the worker, whose primary concern is the well-being of the client. The agency also purports to be concerned with the well-being of the client. The difficulty occurs when the client's perception of "well-being" is defined by a cultural perspective that differs from that espoused by the agency in defining this same "well-being." With obligations to both agency and client, how can a worker balance the two in order to provide service that both meets the needs of the client and fulfills the mission, policy, and program of the agency?

This ethical dilemma is clearly evident in the third case presented in this section. A Cambodian family, living in public housing, resists obtaining the education and language skills necessary for the achievement of the independence that is the goal of the program, in favor of traditional values of family unity and responsibility of children to parents, which it sees as primary. The family sees its "best interest" and strength as upholding the traditional Cambodian cultural values. The agency sees the family's "best interest" in achieving financial independence, learning the language of the new country, and, eventually, leaving the housing program—all Euro-American, "Western" goals established by the dominant societal system. The agency has structured its services to support and encourage these goals. How can the worker meet the needs of both client and agency?

In the fourth case presented, a special school setting's policy reflects the school's belief that openness and sharing information about students that would be helpful to other professionals working with the students is expected. However, social workers have a clear obligation to maintain the confidentiality of clients. The circumstances are further complicated by concerns about sharing information with parents and questions about obtaining parental consent for information sharing. Children who are severely mentally disturbed, such as those in the school, may be less able than other children to be involved in decisions regarding sharing information. The author struggles with conflicting obligations and responsibilities to try to define a clear and consistent course of action.

In the fifth case, a worker in an employee assistance program finds herself with a severe conflict of loyalties. She has been hired specifically to provide services that will enhance employees' work performances. She begins to work with a self-referred employee who is depressed and whose work performance is poor, but who tells her that her job is the only stability in her life, necessary to her support as well as her general functioning. Despite efforts on her part and on that of the employee, performance does not improve with intervention. The worker realizes that her obligation to her employer demands that, if she is unable to assist her client's performance to improve, she should bring the matter to the employee's supervisor to request help. However, she also knows that this action will call attention to the employee's problems and place her job in jeopardy. Whose interests must the worker consider primary?

Managed care has presented complex and challenging problems to social workers, both individually and to the profession. Efficiency and cost-effectiveness are often difficult to measure in the context of social services. In the sixth case, an intern who is serving as intake worker at a mental health agency that serves HIV/AIDS clients must determine whether group or individual therapy is appropriate for each client. Clients generally request individual therapy, and there are strong arguments in support of individual therapy for this special needs population. However, the agency is experiencing serious fiscal problems: Services are underfunded and understaffed, and the demand for them is growing. There has been a distinct shift to a managed care model of service provision to increase efficient use of limited resources. Reimbursement is based on the number of clients served. To address client needs in the context of available resources, the agency is focusing on group rather than individual therapy. While recognizing the importance of funding and fiscal viability, the worker is concerned about the individual clients he sees, who may not receive the services needed in a group therapy setting.

■ ■ ■ ■ ■

CASE STUDY 3.1

CAN LIMITATION OF INFORMED CONSENT BY AN AGENCY EVER BE JUSTIFIED?

Abstracted from an unpublished paper by Diane Inselberg Spirer, MSW, M.S.

PRACTICE CONTEXT AND CASE PRESENTATION

A partial hospitalization program provides intensive treatment for adults whose problems call for less than full hospitalization. The goal of the program is to assist individuals in attaining their optimal level of functioning in the community through the use of structured, intensive outpatient treatment. The program utilizes treatment modalities offered in inpatient settings, but in an environment that permits patients to interact more fully and effectively with family and community. Psychoeducation and expressive therapies help patients set goals, practice new behaviors, and learn new skills.

Treatment is provided by a multidisciplinary staff including psychiatrists, nurses, social workers, and expressive therapists. Goal-specific, individualized treatment plans are approved by a physician and include assessment and diagnosis; individual, group, and family therapy; expressive therapies; pharmacotherapy; psychoeducation; and chemical dependency deprogramming.

Agency policy requires that clients have a therapist outside the program who will continue with them at the conclusion of their treatment with the agency. Close collaboration with the patient's outside therapist is an integral part of the program, and it provides a smooth transition to conventional outpatient treatment. Patients are informed prior to admission to the program verbally or in writing that collaboration with community therapists is an integral feature of the program. The staff will refer to outpatient practitioners those patients who do not already have such a relationship. The patient is requested to sign a consent to the release of information to the outside therapist on the first day of treatment. If the patient refuses to sign the form, or declines contact with an outside therapist, admission to the program is denied.

The consent to release information is a limited consent form. The purpose of the disclosure to the outside professional, as written on the form, is "to facilitate treatment involvement and communication." The form indicates that the type of information to be disclosed consists of "information on patient progress, treatment and discharge planning, psychological evaluation."

A patient who has been in the program for six months expresses significant distress with the frequency and content of the agency's contact with her outside therapist. She stated that the form she signed was not detailed and that she had not realized that the contact was at the total discretion of the treatment team.

The worker became concerned with considering how the agency should craft its outside therapist consent form so as best to meet its mission of providing successful treatment. Could this best be achieved by providing clients with a full-informed consent form, which details all situations in which an outside therapist will be notified, or by

(continued)

CASE STUDY 3.1   CONTINUED

having a limited informed consent form, which preserves the agency's flexibility in providing treatment?

From the client's perspective, full-informed consent might be viewed as empowering and upholding autonomy and furthering self-determination. It provides clear guidance and structure to the agency in the contacting of outside therapists. However, it limits agency flexibility. Thus, full-informed consent empowers the patient but may impede successful treatment; limited-informed consent empowers the therapist in treatment, but may limit the patient's autonomy.

Informed Consent v. Optimal Fulfillment of Agency Mission

RESEARCH AND RELATED LITERATURE

The literature of social work remains sparse as to the circumstances in which client consent is required (Reamer, 1987). Confusion over these issues tends to persist both within and among professional groups (Lindenthal & Thomas, 1984).

In the late eighteenth century, Western physicians and scientists began to develop traditions that encouraged professionals to share information and decision making with their clients (Reamer, 1987). In 1914, the first major judicial ruling, *Schloendorff* v. *Society of New York Hospital,* upheld that right to self-determination in regard to one's own body (Reamer, 1987).

However, in support of the agency's limited-consent position, the competence of clients affects their capability of giving informed consent. Clients must be able to make choices, understand factual issues and their own situation, and manipulate information (Reamer, 1987). These capabilities may be seriously impaired in a severely disturbed individual because cognitive faculties are influenced by the disturbed emotional state (Sehdev, 1976). Although an advance directive may provide a means for avoiding competency issues, it may be assumed that few such directives specifically deal with mental health treatment and the flexibility allowed to caregivers in making disclosures to outside therapists (Spirer, personal communication, 1995).

It is possible to question whether all clients are prepared to assume full responsibility for self-direction. Individuals may have differing amounts of experience, physical or mental abilities, and ability to cope with frustration and disruption (Rothman, 1989). Thus, one may question whether self-determination should not be superseded by a responsibility to prevent suffering. However, mental illness is still a poorly understood phenomenon (McGough & Carmichael, 1977).

Exceptions to the obligation of informed consent have centered on duty-to-warn cases, where there was a danger to a third party. Such legal cases include *Tarasoff* v. *Regents of the University of California, Lipari* v. *Sears, Roebuck & Co., Brady* v. *Hopper, Thompson* v. *County of Alameda, Jablonski by Pahls* v. *United States,* and *Shaw* v. *Glickman,* the last of which takes the opposing position and upholds confidentiality. Less clear is the obligation to violate informed consent for the sake of preventing injury to the person whose consent is violated, where the general safety of the public is not an issue. In any case, it is probably unlikely that all violations of full-informed consent in this practice setting involve actual danger to the clients served.

Self-determination connotes free choice or self-direction on the part of the beneficiaries of professional helping services (Rothman, 1989), and it has been related to informed consent. It can be viewed as a basic human right, a vehicle for client improvement, an opportunity for learning coping skills, and a way of keeping public assistance agencies out of inappropriate areas of a client's life (Rothman, 1989). It has been seen as basic to human development, dignity, and freedom (Perlman, 1965).

The Constitution affords protection of self-determination and bodily integrity, through judicial interpretation and application. Personal autonomy is seen as the fundamental right of each citizen to select and abide by his or her own values so long as he or she does not infringe on the rights of others (McGough & Carmichael, 1977).

Social workers' orientations to confidentiality management and the likelihood of breaking confidences in particular may relate to the nature of their professional role, which is relatively more vulnerable and probably more ambiguous than that of psychiatrists and psychologists. Thus, they might err in a conservative direction by disclosing information as a defensive strategy in response to an increasing number of legal decisions obligating disclosure. This role ambiguity and lack of legal knowledge regarding this issue possibly contributes to social workers' breaching of confidences in clinical situations (Lindenthal & Thomas, 1984).

The NASW Code of Ethics supports informed consent, based on the values of dignity and worth of the person, the importance of human relationships, and integrity, which further supports the ethical principle of trustworthiness for social workers. In terms of standards, obligations to clients are addressed in the first subsection of the first section of the Code, thereby giving them a place of vital importance in guiding social workers' practice. Subsection 1.01 obligates workers to their clients as their primary responsibilities, while 1.02 defines the obligation "to promote the rights of clients to self-determination."

There are five parts in the subsection on informed consent, which immediately follow. Subsections 1.03a and 1.03c are applicable to this dilemma and are thus quoted below in their entirety.

> Social workers should provide services to clients only in the context of a professional relationship based, when appropriate, on valid informed consent. Social workers should use clear and understandable language to inform clients of the purpose of the service, risks related to the service, limits to services because of the requirements of a third-party payer, relevant costs, reasonable alternatives, clients' right to refuse or withdraw consent, and the time frame covered by the consent. Social workers should provide clients with an opportunity to ask questions. (1.03a)
>
> In instances when clients lack the capacity to provide informed consent, social workers should protect clients' interests by seeking permission from an appropriate third party, informing clients consistent with the clients' level of understanding. In such instances social workers should seek to ensure that the third party acts in a manner consistent with clients' wishes and interests. Social workers should take reasonable steps to enhance such clients' ability to give informed consent. (1.03c)

(continued)

CASE STUDY 3.1 CONTINUED

Additional guidelines for privacy and confidentiality are specified in subsection 1.07 of the Code of Ethics:

Social workers should respect clients' right to privacy. (1.07a)
Social workers may disclose confidential information when appropriate with a valid consent from a client or a person legally authorized to consent on behalf of a client. (1.07b)
Social workers should protect the confidentiality of all information obtained in the course of professional service, except for compelling professional reasons. . . . does not apply when disclosure is necessary to prevent serious, forseeable, and imminent harm . . . social workers should disclose the least amount of confidential information necessary. (1.07c)
Social workers should inform clients, to the extent possible, about the disclosure . . . and the potential consequences, when feasible before the disclosure is made. (1.07d)

These statements appear to strongly support a full-informed consent and/or a maintenance of confidentiality. The client is not in "clear, forseeable, imminent danger" of harm in the extreme sense that appears to be alluded to in the Code. She has not been deemed incompetent and thus has a right to act in her own behalf in terms of informed consent. However, a social worker's first ethical obligation is to service and to the client's best interests. These may be better furthered by providing information to her therapist, which will enable provision of appropriate therapeutic services.

AUTHOR'S REFLECTIONS, REASONING PROCESS, AND RESOLUTION
Professional values emphasize the primacy of the client's interests. However, competency issues also are recognized to affect how a social worker should appropriately respond to a client with mental illness and possible impairment in competence. Though the client signed the consent form the agency required, she did not fully understand all the implications of what she was signing. Whether this was due to her mental disability or to ambiguity in the form and explanations offered is not clear. "Primacy of client interest" can be seen to support both sides of the dilemma: If getting well is the primary interest, an argument could be made for the looser, more limited form. If self-determination and autonomy is the primary interest, a full-consent form would be required.

It is important to consider the societal values that might impact on this dilemma. These include self-determination and independence, autonomy and self-respect, trust in others and in oneself, and honesty. Thus, they would seem to support the "informed consent" side of the dilemma. However, one could say that, for the client population served, these could best be achieved by optimal treatment, which includes the flexibility on the part of the agency to maintain appropriate contact with the client's outside therapist.

This client, and probably the majority of the clients treated in the program, does value self-determination and autonomy very highly. She has established her treatment goals. She has, however, also chosen the program, read the information about the program, and signed the release of information consent form.

The worker's personal values also are recognized to impact on the dilemma. Trust, truthfulness, acceptance, loyalty, sincerity, patience, wisdom, and knowledge as values caused the worker initially to favor a full-informed consent for all agency clients.

The worker found two additional sources of ethical guidance useful in developing a resolution to this dilemma: the Bible and the Declaration of Independence. The Bible tells us to do unto others as we would have others do unto us. This brings the worker into the dilemma in a much more direct fashion: She needs to address for herself which she would prefer, were she in the position of this client. This process of self-reflection can be helpful in understanding the client more fully. The Declaration of Independence includes this vital and basic statement: "[A]ll men are created equal, and are endowed by their Creator with certain unalienable rights: among these are life, liberty, and the pursuit of happiness." While these seem to support the self-determination position at first, later reflection on "the pursuit of happiness" might lead one to consider if optimal mental health would be a great asset in this regard.

Aristotle saw the goal of human life as the achievement of happiness. We achieve happiness, he believed, through the fulfillment of our natural function, living a life with reason and moving always toward self-actualization. Following this line of thought does not provide much guidance either, however, for it is still unclear whether happiness can best be achieved, in this dilemma, by full-informed consent and the opportunity to refuse the help of the program, or by a limited-informed consent and the benefits the program can provide in terms of mental health.

The agency has integrated the use of an outside therapist as a necessary part of its program, and a condition of acceptance into the program is the signing of a consent form that allows the treatment team to share information with the outside therapist. The agency has determined that this is necessary to the fulfillment of its mission and goals: to assist clients to become independent and well-functioning members of society.

The use of a full consent form, which specifies all of the circumstances under which the agency may contact the outside therapist, supports the client's right to participate in determining when the intervention of the outside therapist would be useful. Full-informed consent supports autonomy and self-determination and helps clarify the client's values, beliefs, and priorities. It assists in the development of a mutually supportive and trusting relationship between client and agency based on full knowledge and participation in all aspects of treatment.

The limited form currently in use acknowledges that the client may not be able to evaluate the need for outside intervention by the very reason that the client is seeking treatment: a disturbed emotional state. It can protect the client from harm in some circumstances and provide the information needed by an outside therapist, so that the best service can be rendered after the client's participation in the program is terminated. It preserves some self-determination in that the client has the right to refuse to sign the form as offered and thus refuse treatment with the program.

In trying to balance these competing positions and priorities, the worker would recommend the continuation of the use of a limited-consent form, with an additional statement added that defines the two instances in which the outside therapist may be contacted as assistance in treatment and notification of a threat to client or third party; stipulates that when possible, client will be informed in advance of the contact; changes

(continued)

CASE STUDY 3.1 CONTINUED

program policy to require that a reasonable effort to notify clients in advance of the contacting of the outside therapist be made; stresses the importance of the outside therapist to the treatment process.

This resolution was chosen because it was felt that full-informed consent might be difficult for some clients to comprehend. A limited form would allow greater freedom and flexibility in tailoring the actions taken upon the needs of each individual client. However, the changes incorporated into the form would also serve to maximize self-determination as much as possible.

QUESTIONS FOR THOUGHT AND DISCUSSION

1. Do you think it is possible to have a form that would cover "full-informed consent"? What might it include?
2. The "full consent" issue the author focuses on addresses the sharing of information with an outside therapist exclusively. Are there other issues in a program such as this one that you think might require informed consent?
3. Understanding confidentiality and determining the circumstances when it might be breached are basic issues to professional functioning. What limits would you place on confidentiality? Would they differ if you were dealing with a child? An adolescent? A family? An emotionally disturbed client? A mentally disabled client?
4. What is the relationship between your perception of the obligation to confidentiality and your client's ability to grasp the concept of confidentiality and informed consent? Are you obligated to maintain the confidentiality of someone who cannot comprehend what this means?
5. How might you design a consent form that might be appropriate to this agency's mission, program, and clientele?

■ ■ ■ ■ ■

CASE STUDY 3.2

COMPUTERIZED RECORD KEEPING: AGENCY EFFICIENCY VERSUS CLIENT PRIVACY

Abstracted from an unpublished paper by Aimee H. Mclain, MSW

PRACTICE CONTEXT AND CASE PRESENTATION

A mental health center, located in a major urban center, offers psychotherapy to approximately 500 clients at rates that the economically disadvantaged can afford. Recently, a quality assurance director was hired to formulate and implement new procedures for recordkeeping and oversight.

The clinic receives the majority of its funding from Medical Assistance. Therefore, the current recordkeeping procedures are designed to pass an audit by insurance regulators. Patient files record demographic, diagnostic, and therapeutic information as prescribed by code. Records are kept by hand, in notebooks, and there is no centralized listing of clients, diagnoses, treatment, or other information.

In order to increase the efficiency of the agency and optimally utilize the staff to provide services, the quality assurance director wishes to utilize a computer system to manage client data, which would be available through three computer terminals. Efficiency and effectiveness of service delivery systems through computerization potentially increase both the quality and the quantity of services provided, as well as the number of clients that the agency can serve. It makes maximum use of available funding.

Such procedures, while maximizing efficiency, could compromise client privacy and confidentiality. Easy access and availability of sensitive information could compromise one of the basic elements in the therapeutic relationship—trust.

The dilemma addressed can be stated as:

Efficient and Effective Agency Service v. Client Privacy and Confidentiality

RESEARCH AND RELATED LITERATURE

Legislation on both sides of the issue reflects this dilemma. Nye (1980) points out that "the United States Supreme Court and the several District Courts have iterated and reiterated the constitutional basis of privacy as a fundamental right" (*Doe* v. *Roe*. 1977. N.Y. Law J [Nov. 25]; *Friendship Medical Center, Ltd.* v. *Chicago Board of Health.* 1974. 505F. 2d 114 [7th circuit 1974]; *Planned Parenthood Association* v. *Danforth.* 1976. 428 U.S. 52; *Roe* v. *Ingraham.* 1975. 403 F. Supp. 931. 2nd Dist. of N.Y.; *Whelan* v. *Roe.* 1977. 429 U.S. 589, 97 S.Ct.869). At the same time, both legal and clinical professionals recognize that there are instances in which an individual's right to privacy must be balanced against legitimate societal interests (Nye, 1980, p. 649). Nye also points out that the Federal Privacy Act of 1974 "establishes as a basic philosophy 'good information management practices,' requiring government agencies to "establish appropriate administrative, technical and physical safeguards to insure the security and

(continued)

CASE STUDY 3.2   CONTINUED

confidentiality of records'" (p. 650). Schrier (1980) adds "the Federal Privacy Act applies only to the federal government, but in civil actions alleging negligence for wrongful disclosure, agencies may be held to the standards established in the act" (p. 452).

Lanman (1980) also discusses the legislation governing the confidentiality of alcohol and drug-abuse patients' records and suggests that there is a need for similar legislation with regard to mental health records, as the public stigma of mental illness could contribute to a deprivation of liberty.

However, the need for oversight and regulation of mental healthcare providers must also be recognized. Federal, state, and local codes require that demographic as well as diagnostic information be kept in a patient's file and that regular notes be entered regarding a patient's therapeutic progress. Regulators routinely audit agency files to ensure compliance. "Most of these mandatory exposures of individual data reflect the concerns of society, concretized in the form of legislation and regulations. It is clear that medical and other health and social services records cannot be solely controlled by the consumer and provider" (Schuchman, 1980).

"Information technology can be a powerful tool for developing efficient, accurate, and comprehensive patient records" (Mutschler, 1990, p. 191). Clinical social workers spend hours on documentation to ensure suitability of treatment. This time could be greatly reduced through the use of computers. Mutschler (1990) studied the implementation of a prototype information system for hospital social workers that collected data similar to that collected by the mental health center under discussion and found that "based on user assessment, the most immediate benefits of the information system were in the increased efficiency of the structured tasks and the considerable time savings in generating monthly reports" (p. 194). Improving the ease and efficiency of data collection could have valuable benefits for progress monitoring as well.

An additional use of computer records that benefits patients and therapists was implemented at the Ozark Guidance Center. A computerized recordkeeping and message system that could be staffed by a single worker was developed, so that after-hour emergencies could be handled in an appropriate manner (Brod, 1987). This use could be expanded to facilitate coordination of services between several different systems, such as family counseling, individual counseling, support groups, and so on. As more agencies adopt the managed healthcare model, such a recordkeeping and message facility could vastly increase the efficiency of communication. Computers can also facilitate and ease the generation of documentation and justification for services increasingly required by insurance companies, thus ensuring continued funding (Nurius & Hudson, 1988).

Although there are clearly many advantages to the use of computerized recordkeeping, there are potential dangers as well. The ease of access to records can lead to fears that sensitive client information could be released to inappropriate persons.

Examination of the Code of Ethics reveals conflicting directives to social workers. On the one hand, workers are obligated to respect the privacy of clients and hold information in confidence (1.07). On the other, workers are also obligated to improve the employing agencies' policies and procedures to increase effectiveness and efficiency.

Subsection 3.09a obligated workers to "adhere to commitments made to employers and employing organizations."

Subsection 3.09b states: "Social workers should work to improve employing agencies' policies and procedures and the efficiency and effectiveness of their services."

On the other hand, however, subsection 3.09d obligates workers in a different direction:

> Social workers should not allow an employing organization's policies, procedures, regulations, or administrative orders to interfere with their ethical practice of social work. Social workers should take reasonable steps to ensure that their employing organization's practices are consistent with the *NASW Code of Ethics*.

In Section 1 of the Code of Ethics, electronic records are addressed specifically:

> Social workers should protect the confidentiality of clients' written and electronic records and other sensitive information. Social workers should take reasonable steps to ensure that records are stored in a secure location and that clients' records are not available to others who are not authorized to have access. (1.07l)
>
> Social workers should take precautions to ensure and maintain the confidentiality of information transmitted to other parties through the use of computers, electronic mail, facsimile machines, telephones and telephone answering machines, and other electronic or computer technology. Disclosure of identifying information should be avoided whenever possible. (1.07m)

AUTHOR'S REFLECTIONS, REASONING PROCESS, AND RESOLUTION

W. D. Ross's propositions (cited in Beauchamp & Childress, 1994, pp. 103–106) regarding intuition and common sense could be applied to this dilemma. If the principle of nonmaleficence is considered to be the highest value, the maintenance of privacy and confidentiality must take priority over agency efficiency. In this case, the avoidance of a possible harm takes precedence over the promotion of possible good. If beneficence is considered most highly, it is possible to argue in favor of the use of computerized recordkeeping in that this would promote the most efficient use of all agency resources, thus benefiting the most people.

Gewirth (1978) begins with the concept that all human beings have a basic right to freedom and well-being. It could be assumed that possible abuse of private and confidential information could inhibit these rights. Because these basic rights take precedence over additive rights, the possible benefits of computer use must give precedence to them.

However, if the summum bonum (greatest good) is held as the primary principle, and the theory is the utilitarian position of the greatest good for the greatest number, one would have to support the use of computerized recordkeeping as contributing to the good of all clients and potential clients in maximizing the efficiency of agency services. The issue of the general threat of loss of privacy, however, might serve to temper this conclusion.

As a society, Americans value the right to privacy very highly, but also value efficiency. In practice, the argument can be made that efficiency overbalances privacy.

(*continued*)

CASE STUDY 3.2   CONTINUED

An example of this might be the violation of privacy supported by mandatory drug testing, which favors the efficiency of drug-free workers and athletes over their individual rights to privacy.

The social work profession seems to lean toward the primacy of individual rights, including the right to privacy. More frequent references are made in the Code of Ethics to individual client rights than to efficiency and effectiveness of services, and there are specific provisions regarding client information stored on computers.

The author's own values tend to support efficiency and effectiveness of services. Confidence in the legal system and in societal values allows the author to feel that injury to clients resulting from computerized recordkeeping could be minimized and justified in the interests of effective agency functioning. Clients, it would seem, have a stake in both positions. Many clients complain of waiting a long time for therapy and of the inefficiency of recordkeeping. On the other hand, the potential stigma derived from more public knowledge of mental and emotional difficulties could also damage access to employment or services.

The individual worker has two options: She may refuse to participate in information gathering, thus possibly risking her job and affecting her client or she may participate fully in the agency's decision to computerize records with the goal of the efficiency of service.

The first option is most clearly supported by the principle of nonmaleficence, as participating in computerizing agency files could lead to breaches of privacy and confidentiality. The freedom and well-being of the worker's current clients can be served through this option, although the unnecessary problems and delays that the lack of computerization causes can also affect clients negatively.

The worker elects the second option in resolving this dilemma. This option is supported by the principle of beneficence, of summum bonum, doing the greatest good for the greatest number by utilizing the agency's resources most appropriately. Though this choice contains the possibility of problems, the worker makes a commitment to minimize these by mobilizing the staff of the agency toward the development of an adequate client protection system, such as a code system for files that are accessible in a very limited manner to staff. This would maximize efficiency and also reduce the risk of violating an individual client's privacy and confidentiality.

QUESTIONS FOR THOUGHT AND DISCUSSION

1. In order to reconcile clients' rights and the requirements of agency efficiency and regulatory bodies, some workers carefully monitor, edit, and phrase the material entered into client records, withholding information at times when it is deemed potentially harmful to the client. Do you feel that this is an ethically justifiable approach to this issue?

2. What information, if any, do you think clients should be given about the limits of privacy and confidentiality of records? How does this interface with your position in question 1, above?

3. Is it, or should it be, the responsibility of an agency to safeguard the use made by third parties and/or regulatory agencies of information contained in patient records? Is the agency responsible for the confidentiality and privacy of this information once it leaves their premises in the hands of an insurer or regulatory body? If you feel that it is, how might an agency protect clients from abuse by third parties of confidential information?

4. Is a worker ever justified in refusing to adhere to the policy of the agency that employs him or her? In other words, does the author's option of nonadherence to computerization requirements violate the explicit or implicit contract between employee and employing organization? Is the agency justified in terminating or taking disciplinary action against such an employee?

5. One of the sources cited in this article states that access to records cannot be limited only to consumers and providers of services. Do you agree with this position? Why or why not?

■ ■ ■ ■ ■ ▬▬▬▬▬▬▬▬▬▬▬▬▬▬▬▬▬▬▬▬▬▬▬▬▬▬▬▬▬▬

CASE STUDY 3.3

MEETING THE NEEDS OF IMMIGRANTS: MUST ACCULTURATION BE A CONDITION OF AGENCY SERVICE?

Abstracted from an unpublished paper by Thomas W. Gray, Ph.D., MSW

PRACTICE CONTEXT AND CASE PRESENTATION

Ms. Li and her five children live in a Section 8 Public Housing unit, supported primarily through AFDC payments. Her oldest daughter, Pareth Ling, is enrolled in a GED course, but her attendance has been sporadic. She would like to complete high school, but feels strong obligations to her mother and the rest of the family. Her mother wants her at home to help with the children, handle various housekeeping responsibilities, and serve as interpreter as needed.

Ms. Li complains of headaches and difficulty sleeping. She dresses in traditional Cambodian garb. Her mother, father, and seven brothers and sisters were murdered, and a Cambodian therapist has stated that she may be suffering from Post-Traumatic Stress Disorder. She has been defined programmatically as displacing child rearing responsibilities to her teenagers, particularly to the client, 19-year-old Pareth. But in the Cambodian culture, this is quite normal, even to be expected.

Social services within the housing development are oriented toward economic independence and movement out of low-income housing. Ms. Li has expressed a desire to learn English and has been scheduled for ESL classes, but she does not attend. Agency staff have labeled her highly resistive: She says she will learn English when the children are grown. Her youngest child is 4 years old.

Pinderhughes (1989), in *Understanding Race, Ethnicity, and Power,* states that a counseling situation that ignores cultural issues is setting the client up for disempowerment and reoppression. Chan's (1992) work "contrasting beliefs, values, and practices," in *Developing Cross-Cultural Competence,* suggests ten potential impasses in worker–Cambodian client relationships that may be attributable to cultural differences between the Cambodian culture and the Eurocentric culture of the United States. These are included below, with Cambodian/Asian values listed first.

1. Family is understood as the primary unit versus the individual as the primary unit.
2. Family solidarity, responsibility, and harmony versus individual pursuit of happiness, fulfillment, and self-expression.
3. Continued dependence on family is fostered versus early independence is encouraged.
4. Hierarchical family roles and ascribed status are emphasized versus variable roles and achieved status.
5. Parent–child (parental) bond is stressed versus husband–wife (marital) bond is stressed.
6. Parent provides authority and expects unquestioning obedience and submission to

structure versus parent provides guidance, support, explanations, and encourages curiosity and critical/independent thinking.

7. Family makes decisions for the child versus child is given many choices.
8. Children are extension of parents versus children are individuals.
9. Parents ask: "What can you do to help me?" versus parents ask: "What can I do to help you?"
10. Older children are responsible for the siblings' actions versus each child is responsible for his or her own actions.

Many Eurocentric values are congruent with the values of the agency, such as individualistic focus, independence, and success/performance/achievement orientation. The ethical dilemma then becomes honoring culturally specific family structures and life orientations versus following agency program and policies. It can be stated as:

Client Self-determination v. Agency Policy and Values

RESEARCH AND RELATED LITERATURE
Honoring Culturally Specific Family Structures and Cambodian Life Orientations.
Draine and Hall (1986) state: "Cultural understanding in one's . . . culture occurs early and is typically established by age 5." We use these groundings to interpret our reality, to think, feel, and behave in a manner that provides safety and adaptiveness. Our culture becomes an integral part of our lives, and we become culturally programmed. As such, it remains outside of our conscious awareness.

When attempting to function within a second culture, we continue to interpret reality with our original, culturally specific cognitive structures, assuming that these interpretations are "right." These orientations may prove quite ineffective for cross-cultural work. Discomfort may manifest itself and be expressed in such emotional or physical ways as "frustration, anger, depression, withdrawal, lethargy, aggression, and/or illness" (Lynch & Hanson, 1992, p. 24). The client may distance him- or herself, as may the worker.

Axelson (1993, pp. 43–44) suggests cultural minorities may choose one or a combination of four positions in cross-cultural situations: (1) They may accept mainstream conditions to the extent of reducing primary group identity and suppressing various personal psychological needs "in order to gain success." (2) They may compromise with mainstream standards by blending and harmonizing distinctive cultural aspects with demands of the larger society. (3) They may revolt against the dominant cultural conditions, seeking to change the standards of "acceptable behavior." (4) They may withdraw "into the security of familiar cultural . . . patterns with which the person most clearly identifies and . . . can readily gain self-respect," providing for personal needs for security, status, and social relationships. Each position is espoused at a price: The first can frequently result in ridicule from the primary group. The second can be extremely stressful, demanding constant personal monitoring to bring congruency in many social roles. The third can be fraught with constant anger, hostility, resentment, and explicit "retaliatory hostility" from the dominant culture. The fourth can lead to a sense of

(*continued*)

CASE STUDY 3.3   CONTINUED

imprisonment and suffering, "life apathy," depression, grieving to a sense of loss of meaning in life and feelings of "nonbeing."

Chan (1992) suggests that cross-cultural competence can be built by workers through (1) self-awareness, (2) knowledge specific to each culture, and (3) skills that enable the worker to engage in successful interactions.

The NASW Code of Ethics requires workers to be culturally sensitive and addresses this issue in several sections. Section 1 states that:

> Social workers should understand culture and its function in human behavior and society, recognizing the strengths that exist in all cultures. (1.05a)
>
> Social workers should have a knowledge base of their clients' cultures and be able to demonstrate competence in the provision of services that are sensitive to clients' culture and to differences among people and cultural groups. (1.05b)
>
> Social workers should obtain education about and seek to understand the nature of social diversity and oppression with respect to race, ethnicity, national origin, color, sex, sexual orientation, age, marital status, political belief, religion, and mental or physical disability. (1.05c)

In reference to broader responsibilities:

> Social workers should engage in social and political action that seeks to ensure that all people have equal access to the resources, employment, services, and opportunities they require to meet their basic human needs and to develop fully. (6.04a)
>
> Social workers should act to expand choice and opportunity for all people, with special regard for vulnerable, disadvantaged, oppressed, and exploited people and groups. (6.04b)
>
> Social workers should promote conditions that encourage respect for the cultural and social diversity . . . promote policies and practices that demonstrate respect for difference. (6.04c)
>
> Social workers should act to prevent and eliminate domination . . . against any person or group. (6.04d)

Demographic changes are also demanding cultural competency. U.S. Census Bureau Statistics for 2000 show that the Hispanic population in the United States has doubled between 1980 and 2000 and that percentages of other races and ethnicities have also increased (www.censusscope.org/us/chart_race.html). Current statistics drawn from U.S. Census reports note that the U.S. population is now 69 percent White, 12 percent Black, 11 percent Latino, 4 percent Asian/Pacific Islander, 1 percent Native American and "other," and 2 percent multiracial (Herndon, 2001). The non-white percentage of the population is expected to continue to increase, both through immigration and a higher birth rate.

Traditional Asian and Cambodian orientations espouse philosophical positions of fatalism, tradition and living with the past, and contemplative circular thinking. Our dominant culture emphasizes "personal control over environment and one's fate, change and a future orientation, and analytic linear thinking." The traditional Cambodian culture emphasizes a collectivist social orientation and group welfare, collective responsibility and obligation, while the dominant culture emphasizes individual autonomy, independence, and self-reliance. Hierarchy, role rigidity, and "status defined by ascription," are generally emphasized within traditional Cambodian positions, while the dominant culture emphasizes equality, role flexibility, and status defined by achievement.

Honoring Program Imperatives and Obligations: An Expression of an Anglo-European Life Position. The *stated goals* of the agency program include

1. Empowering residents to take control of their lives through various self-sufficiency initiatives.
2. Providing a comprehensive and integrated program of social services.
3. Helping families become economically self-sufficient.

The housing project agency utilizes case management to provide services.

> Central to case management is the function of linking clients with essential resources and empowering clients to function as independently as possible in securing the resources they need. (Hepworth & Larsen, 1992)
>   Social work case management is a method of providing services whereby a professional social worker assesses the need of the client and the client's family when appropriate, and arranges, coordinates, monitors, evaluates, and advocates for a package of multiple services to meet the specific client's complex needs. (NASW, 1992)

The effectiveness of case management in providing services to people with multiple needs has been documented in a number of studies, which include: "Case Management in Health Care," by Loomis (1988), "A Social Work Practice Model of Case Management," by Moore (1990), and *The Practice of Case Management*, by Moxley (1989).
    Implicit and embedded in case management are the stated objectives and values of the social work profession, which include the dignity and worth of the individual and a commitment to social justice and integrity. The case management approach is congruent with Anglo-European values (Hanson, 1992b). Relevant to this dilemma are commitment to change, human equality, individualism, self-help, competition, future orientation, an action/goal/work orientation, directness, materialism, and personal control over the environment. As a tendency, teleological and utilitarian ethical positions would be more congruent with this life position.
    Section 3 of the NASW Code of Ethics supports the obligation of the worker to the practice setting:

> Social workers generally should adhere to commitments made to employers and employing organizations. (3.09a)
>   Social workers should work to improve employing agencies' policies and procedures. (3.09b)
>   Social workers should . . . ensure that employers are aware of the social workers' ethical obligation as set forth in the *NASW Code of Ethics*. (3.09c)

(*continued*)

CASE STUDY 3.3   CONTINUED

> Social workers should not allow an employing organization's policies, procedures, regulations, or administrative orders to interfere with their ethical practice of social work. (3.09d)

AUTHOR'S REFLECTIONS, REASONING PROCESS, AND RESOLUTION

The worker follows the worldview of the client as able, while recognizing that personal values might conflict with some Cambodian values. The worker values both "accomplishment" (Anglo-European) and "being" (Cambodian). Values include oneness of people, spiritual connection, sharing of power, compassion, perseverance, accomplishment, flexibility, and fairness/justice.

Loewenberg and Dolgoff (1992) state: "To thine own self be true." For purposes here, "To thine own self, be aware" might be more appropriate. From a postmodernist, social constructionist position, values and beliefs are understood as forever with us, shaping our perceptions and actions (Goldstein, 1990; Nelson, Megill, & McCloskey, 1987).

The worker and the client are in a relationship. The shape of that relationship, and the response of the client, are strongly influenced by the theoretical orientation(s) assumed by the worker. The ethically defined choices available are in some ways prefigured by the orientation chosen.

The Kantian theory of obligations, the utilitarian theory of consequences, and the liberal individualism theory of rights tend to come out of the positivistic science tradition. These theories move epistemologically from several assumptions, among them (1) a separation of subject from object, and by corollary, worker from client, and (2) judgments formulated from "firm universal principles" (Beauchamp & Childress, 1994). Critics of the "obligations/consequences/rights" orientations suggest they can only provide limited insight into what should be much broader conversations on moral decision making (Baier, 1985).

The ethics of care orientation emphasizes relationship, contextually given relationships, compassion, sympathy, discernment, sustenance, and care. Beauchamp and Childress (1994) suggest: "The care perspective is especially meaningful for roles such as parent, friend, physician, and nurse, [and social worker] in which contextual response, attentiveness to subtle clues, and the deepening of special relationships are likely to be more momentous morally than impartial treatment," typical of traditional theories. Moreover, "in any hierarchical situation, systems of any kind, the people in power define reality" (Pinderhughes, 1989). We can mitigate this imbalance by selecting an ethical theoretical base that works to minimize hierarchial influence.

Instead of being viewed as resistant, a culturally sensitive ethics of care approach might be to understand Ms. Li as possibly fearful of authority and involvement in a cultural community that is foreign to her. Pressure may drive her further into her house, possibly into depression, hurting individuals and family structural ties. Compassion from an ethics of care would suggest the worker tread easy and remain aware of imbalances in the worker/client relationship.

A communitarian theory might be chosen as a supplemental framework. This orientation has grown out of reactions to social and familial fragmentation, understood as due to the individualism espoused by advanced industrial societies (Beauchamp & Childress, 1994). It can serve as criteria for judging actions that do or do not reinforce and promote communal and family values, cooperative virtues, and goals and obligations built up from and within historically constituted groups. Family is understood as communal and includes parents and children involved in complementary roles and responsibilities. These roles, responsibilities, and obligations are understood as historically constituted.

The communitarian ethics approach closely approximates the Asian/Cambodian life orientation presented previously. This framework tilts the worker in the direction of the cultural side of the previously presented dilemma.

One must begin by redefining the client as the family, rather than Pareth. This is not altogether in opposition to the program imperative that states: "Helping families become economically self-sufficient"—though family in this context is understood in "American" family terms of performance and achievement. Focus needs to be given to family solidarity and responsibilities, as understood from the Cambodian orientation.

Ms. Li, the hierarchial head of the family, places her responsibility to her children above her desire to learn English. Pareth has also expressed a sense of responsibility to her mother and family ties and a willingness to delay GED studies. Continued dependence and integration within ascribed family roles is expected and fostered.

An appropriate goal perhaps would be to help facilitate better linkage to a Buddhist temple. Ms. Li describes herself as Buddhist, though only visiting the temple on New Year's Day. The Buddhist orientation is consistent with an ethics of care/relationship perspective.

The worker may also advocate that the agency move toward greater cultural competency, a value supported by the NASW Code of Ethics. Cross, Bazron, Dennis, and Isaacs (1989) might perceive the agency as being in "cultural blindness," espousing a set of convictions, values, behaviors, and/or policies seen as "unbiased." The consequence of this "universal" philosophy is assimilation of cultural values into the Eurocentric (dominant) melting pot.

A "culturally proficient" agency "improves services . . . actively seeks advice and consultation from a variety of ethnic communities and include such practices into the organization." Communication and mutual support between agency and Buddhist Temple would possibly both assist Ms. Li and establish a valuable link to enhance "cultural proficiency."

"A professional [case management] social worker assesses the need of the client and the client's family when appropriate, and arranges, coordinates, . . . and advocates for a package of multiple services to meet the specific client's complex needs" (NASW, 1992). These approaches would enhance "respect and appreciation for individual and groups differences; willingness to persist in efforts on behalf of clients despite frustrations, and commitment to social justice . . . for all members of society" (NASW, 1981).

QUESTIONS FOR THOUGHT AND DISCUSSION

1. Traditionally, the "melting pot" philosophy has encouraged immigrants to assimilate and acculturate, and to "blend" with the dominant Euro-American "culture." However, recently, attention and interest have focused on a view that suggests the value of maintaining "cultural pluralism." What are the social, economic, and historical factors that might have influenced this shift?

2. Do you think that immigrants from Asian countries have a more difficult time "adjusting" to their new country and its culture than those from European countries, such as Russia or the Eastern Bloc? Why?

3. One of the "hot" issues today involves bilingual education. Do you think that there is a value in a commonality of language, and that, therefore, English, the established language of the United States, should be the only official language and the only one in which business, social services, and education are conducted? If you believe that these should be available in each person's language of choice, how would you meet the need for the enormous diversity of languages that are spoken by individuals in this country? Would you give some languages "preferential status"? What would you base this on?

4. If you are working with clients who are culturally and/or ethnically different from you, what do you see as your personal responsibility in terms of gaining the needed skills for a culturally sensitive practice? How might you gain these skills?

5. It is difficult to see and understand our cultural biases: We are *inside* our culture, in a sense, and have integrated a particular perspective. As best you can, what do you see as some of the cultural biases that you hold? How might these impact on a client of another culture?

CASE STUDY 3.4

CONFIDENTIALITY IN A SPECIAL SCHOOL SETTING: WHAT IS THE STUDENTS' BEST INTEREST?

Abstracted from an unpublished paper by Patricia Dejesus, MSW

PRACTICE CONTEXT AND CASE PRESENTATION

A private day school for children and adolescents ages 8 to 21 with emotional and/or behavioral issues, learning disabilities, mental retardation, and autism provides students with a low teacher-to-student ratio, behavior specialists, family specialists, vocational specialists, speech and language therapists, occupational and physical therapists, social workers, and psychologists. The social workers and psychologists on staff provide individual and group counseling to those students who are in need of mental health services.

Most students receive services through a broad range of specialists, and the school's policy favors a high level of communication between team members, especially between family specialists, teachers, and counselors. Confidentiality is an issue when information revealed in therapy sessions is potentially useful for the student's team members. The right of confidentiality for the student versus the agency policy of a high level of communication and disclosure in the interest of helping the student becomes a difficult issue for the counselor.

The dilemma may be stated as:

Students' Right to Confidentiality v. Agency Policy of Open Communication among Professional Staff

RESEARCH AND RELATED LITERATURE

Social workers' ethical responsibilities to their clients are addressed in the NASW Code of Ethics. The NASW Code of Ethics (1996) states that social workers should not divulge any confidential information shared by a client without valid consent from the client or the person legally responsible for that person, as in the case of an underage child or adolescent. It also states that "social workers should protect the confidentiality of all information obtained in the course of professional service, except for compelling reasons . . . this does not apply when disclosure is necessary to prevent serious, foreseeable, and imminent harm to a client or other identifiable person . . ." (NASW Code of Ethics, 1996, p. 10). The NASW Code of Ethics further directs that clients should be informed about disclosure of confidential information and the possible consequences, any limits to confidentiality that are seen, and the fact that records should be maintained to ensure privacy. The NASW Code of Ethics also addresses the responsibilities of social workers to their practice setting. "Social workers *generally* [italics added] should adhere to commitments made to employers and employing organizations" (NASW Code of Ethics, 1996, p. 21). It also states, however, that social workers should make

(continued)

CASE STUDY 3.4   CONTINUED

known to their agency the ethical obligations presented in the NASW Code of Ethics (3.09(c) p. 21) and that an employing agency's policies or administrative orders should not interfere with the ethical practice of social work (NASW Code of Ethics, (3.09(d), p. 21) 1996).

In a 1992 position statement regarding the school social worker and confidentiality, NASW states:

> Assurance of confidentiality is important because it enables people to seek help without fear of such results as stigma, retaliation, disapproval, or damage to other relationships. Confidentiality encourages both full disclosure, which is essential for effective treatment, and the maintenance of trust, the means by which treatment is effected. (p. 38)

In most states, clients have a legal right to privileged communication. However, there are exceptions and extenuating circumstances that may affect this privilege, such as school policy requirements or obligations to third parties. The NASW Commission states that the school social worker has ethical obligations to parents, school personnel, and community in addition to the student. NASW guidelines include: Student and guardian must give informed consent to any disclosure; requests for information from outside agencies must be in writing and state the purpose of the request; students should be involved in the process when information is going to be discussed outside a session and be informed of the purpose of the disclosure; students should be informed of their rights regarding disclosure of information; team meeting members should maintain confidentiality of information shared, and students and guardians must agree to such sharing; all information shared should be related to the best interest of the student; because all states have laws regarding abuse and neglect reporting, students should be informed about these laws as protections for their safety; as well, students should understand that revealing plans of harm to self or others is not bound by confidentiality. The legal ruling in the case of *Tarasoff* v. *Regents of the University of California* (1976) set a precedent that therapists must warn intended victims. The rights of students to confidentiality when receiving drug or alcohol treatment and regarding pregnancy or sexually transmitted diseases varies from state to state (NASW Commission, 1992).

A school social worker stated that school settings often expect a high level of communication between professionals concerning the students, so confidentiality can become an issue. When information may need to be shared because it could be helpful to other professionals who work with the student, precautions should be taken to share only what is necessary. General statements may be used rather than specific details. Specific consent should be obtained when information is to be shared outside of the school. The social work profession holds confidentiality for clients as an ethical standard, and this social worker believed that this should take precedence over the school's policy when the two are in conflict (Bazis, 1997).

"Although social workers readily accept the obligation to protect client's rights to confidentiality and informed consent, this mandate is rarely evenly applied to children" (Berman-Rossi & Rossi, 1990, p. 195). Berman-Rossi and Rossi (1990) feel that since the social worker is providing services within the child's environment, there is more contact and therefore a higher risk for ethical dilemmas arising from the perceived need of others for information. "The social worker is called upon to help the child to make use of the school as well as to enable the school to become useful to the child" (Berman-Rossi & Rossi, 1990, p. 196). What are the implications regarding confidentiality when a school social worker shares information with teachers or others in the school in order to inform them of problems in the student's life that could make them more understanding of the child's behavior? Berman-Rossi and Rossi (1990) state:

> At formal team meetings, the normative inclination and expectation is that material assumed to be relevant to understanding the child will be shared. To do less, it is believed, denies the student the opportunity to benefit from an informed staff and an increasingly responsive environment. If the social worker separates himself or herself too stringently from the school environment, ultimately other staff will be alienated. Isolation behind the shield of confidentiality may isolate the child as well and render the worker's practice ineffective. (p. 201)

Berman-Rossi and Rossi (1990) also discuss parental rights issues in regard to confidentiality. The parents or legal guardians of children under 18 retain decisional and consent rights. The parents transfer that right to the school staff in many circumstances, based on the belief that a child under 18 does not have the cognitive or emotional capability to make decisions. Berman-Rossi and Rossi (1990) present research suggesting that although parental consent is justified at times, children are much more capable of making informed decisions on their own behalf than might be thought. They suggest that many adolescents, and some younger children, have cognitive and emotional levels mature enough to understand the issues of confidentiality and informed consent. They also found that children felt more positive and reacted with more self-confidence when they were afforded the rights of confidentiality. They feel that it should be assumed that children can participate in making decisions concerning what is best for them. Children should be given information concerning their rights at a level they can understand and should be informed that they have the right to say what information will be shared. Children must also be told that the worker cannot keep confidences about someone hurting them. Children can sign permission slips for sharing information along with the parent or guardian. Requests for information should be discussed with the child, can participate in deciding what information will be shared at meetings concerning him or her (Berman-Rossi & Rossi, 1990).

Sidney Kardon (1993) does not feel that withholding improves the student's functioning in the school and that sharing of information is beneficial to serving the student's best interest. He feels that a systems or ecological model can promote a more beneficial relationship for the student in the school setting. Kardon states that the student–teacher relationship is very important to a student's success in school and that the social worker should work to enhance this relationship. "Confidentiality is not the domain of the social worker within the school. It is the domain of the professional staff. If one believes the whole point of the social worker–student interaction, whether verbal, play, or consultative, is to enhance the student's relatedness to school, then the notion of confidentiality becomes less important" (Kardon, 1993, pp. 249–250).

(continued)

CASE STUDY 3.4 CONTINUED

Reviewing the NASW Commission position statement, Kopels feels that the ethical obligation is to the student alone, not to parents or school personnel, and that all decisions to reveal information must be based on the social worker's responsibility to the student. Confidentiality must only be broken for "compelling reasons" (Kopels, 1993, p. 251). The ethical obligation to keep confidentiality may make it more difficult at times for the social worker when performing his/her job in the school setting but it is necessary (Kopels, 1993).

AUTHOR'S REASONING, REFLECTION, AND RESOLUTION

Ethical decisions generally are affected not only by our own individual values, but also by the values of our clients and those of the society in which we live. Societal values are an important consideration because they provide the setting in which ethical decisions are made. Our society values hard work, productivity, achievement, and self-sufficiency. Youth, money, education, family, love, and health are also desirable. Rights such as life, justice, privacy, freedom, equality, and democracy are believed to be essential.

Confidentiality is a part of the right to privacy—to decide what information can be made public knowledge or shared with another individual or group. Freedom to express oneself and good mental health are important societal values that are affected by confidentiality issues.

An absolutist position would mandate confidentiality at all times, whereas relativists would suggest that circumstances such as settings and intended purposes of sharing information should be considered. Additionally, deontologists guided by the motive of the action (Loewenberg & Dolgoff, 1996) would suggest that if confidentiality was violated because it was viewed to be in the best interests of the child, it could be viewed as a good and appropriate. Consequentialists like John Stuart Mill and Sigmund Freud, who view the good in the results, were considered to be relativists (Loewenberg & Dolgoff, 1996). Gewirth states that the right to basic goods takes precedence over the right to other goods (as cited in Reamer, 1990). An example given by Reamer (1990) is that the value of a person's well-being takes precedence over an individual's right to confidentiality. This is upheld by the *Tarasoff* case (1976), which said that confidentiality must be broken when there is a threat to the well-being of someone.

The NASW Code of Ethics addresses both confidentiality and obligation to practice settings. Ethical standards, section 1.07, deals with privacy and confidentiality. The Code of Ethics states that

> . . . social workers should protect the confidentiality of all information obtained in the course of professional service, except for compelling reasons. The general expectation that social workers will keep information confidential does not apply when disclosure is necessary to prevent serious, foreseeable, and imminent harm to a client or other identifiable person or when laws or regulations require disclosure without a client's consent. In all instances, social workers should disclose the least amount of confidential information necessary to achieve the desired purpose . . . (1.07(c), p. 10).

The Code of Ethics also addresses the social worker's responsibility to the practice setting. Section 3.09 states that social workers should honor commitments made to the agency that employs them. However, it also states that social workers should not let an employing agency's policy or procedures "interfere with the ethical practice of social work" (p. 21). There could be an area of conflict between what the agency requires or requests and what the social worker feels is his or her obligation to the social work standard of confidentiality.

The school in which the dilemma occurred developed guidelines concerning the confidentiality of student educational records that became part of their Policy and Procedure Manual. The policy originally concerned educational records only and did not include records maintained by psychologists, social workers, or other professionals. Because it did not address the important issue of confidentiality of sensitive information, an addendum was made that stated that the privacy of the student and the student's family was of overriding importance. All information written or known about a family or student was considered privileged and confidential. Also, information about students or families was to be discussed only with those staff members directly concerned and then only for professional reasons.

The author's personal values related to this dilemma include respect for life; self-determination; truthfulness; promise keeping; and respect for children, their feelings, opinions, and rights, including privacy and information. The therapeutic alliance as a tool for positive growth and change is also a strong personal value. It is recognized that personal biases may have affected this values hierarchy: This worker also has a concern that children are often not given the same respect afforded others, which is harmful to their self-concept.

The literature review presented several choices of action for the school social worker. There was support for the right of confidentiality for the student, as well as for a school (agency) that promotes a high level of communication and disclosure regarding the student. One option is to keep all information confided by the student to the social worker confidential. The NASW Code of Ethics (1996) states that confidentiality of information when received while in professional service should be honored. This would honor the societal value of right to privacy. The value of trust within the student–social worker relationship would also be honored. Legally, this is supported in most states by a client's right to privileged communication. Berman-Rossi and Rossi (1990) support this choice by stating that children are mature enough to understand issues of confidentiality and react positively and with self-confidence when given this right. Kopels (1993) thinks that there is an ethical obligation to the student alone, and the agency's rights should not take precedence over the student's. But what if the social worker has been told by the student that he or she intends to harm him or herself or someone else? This author's personal value of the right to life, which is the first on my list of values, would be in conflict with this position of strict and absolute confidentiality.

A further option would keep all information received from the student confidential unless there is foreseeable or imminent harm to the student or to others. The student should be informed of these limitations to confidentiality from the beginning of therapy. This honors the societal values of health and right to life. All literature that supported

(continued)

CASE STUDY 3.4   CONTINUED

the student's confidentiality also supported that disclosure should be made in instances of imminent or foreseeable harm. This choice would follow the relativist ethical principle, which states that a value is affected by the particulars of the situation and therefore cannot be absolute. This would also be in line with personal values of right to life and keeping confidences, within limitations.

Another option is also to obtain the student's permission in each instance before sharing any information and to rely on the student's judgment as to what can or cannot be shared, providing the student with the reasons that sharing information might be in his or her best interest. This option limits parental consent and assumes that students will always be able to make reasoned decisions in their own interest, which may not be possible.

Asking parents or guardians of children to make these decisions is also an option. The NASW Commission on Education Position Statement (1992) says there is an ethical responsibility to more than just the child. Berman-Rossi and Rossi (1990) say that age does complicate the issue of confidentiality because children are believed to lack the cognitive or emotional capability to make decisions regarding what information should and can be shared with others. Because the setting here is a school for severely emotionally disturbed children, parents may indeed need to be responsible for decisions regarding their children. However, this option does not support the author's personal values of children's rights and self-determination.

A final option related to confidentiality is to obtain prior permission from both the student and parent. The NASW Commission on Education Position Statement (1992) supports keeping the confidentiality of the student unless permission is obtained from both the child and parents. This option supports both social work ethics and personal values.

In support of agency policy, NASW supports a social worker's responsibility and commitment to his or her practice setting. Sharing information affords others a better understanding of the child and his or her circumstances. As Berman-Rossi and Rossi (1990) state, sharing information enables the school to be more effective in working with the child. The consequentialist position might argue that if breaking a confidence is helpful to others working with the student, then the good (help) outweighs the bad (breaking confidence). Kardon (1993) states that in a school setting, confidential information is the property of the professional staff, not just the social workers, because the whole reason for a school social worker is to enhance the student's success at school. This would definitely favor the society values of education and achievement and effective treatment. However, the writer's personal value of keeping confidences and self-determination would be compromised in this situation.

A more limited stance might be to share only information that is needed or essential in fulfilling the child's educational goals, in a general way without breaking confidences. If confidential information needs to be shared for the sake of reaching educational goals, then permission would be obtained from the student and parent in order to protect the right to self-determination. This supports the value of informed consent but also supports breaking confidentiality if there is imminent harm foreseeable for the student or others. The NASW Code of Ethics (1996) says that a social worker should not let agency policy interfere with the ethical practice of social work, which protects the confidentiality of clients, but it also supports the social worker's obligation to his or her agency. Such a relativist position would support sharing confidential information only as necessary to other professionals in the school who are helping the student to reach his or her educational goals. This position would also support personal values.

The two values of confidentiality of the student and agency policy of disclosure may come into conflict at times. In Alan Gewirth's (1978) hierarchy of values, the individual's right to well-being, which is a basic right, should take precedence over his or her right to confidentiality. Confidentiality has to be broken if there is an intent to harm oneself. Gewirth's second guideline is that an individual's right to well-being should supersede another person's right to choose confidentiality. This is supported by the *Tarasoff* case (1976). Another guideline states that a social worker who freely consents to abide by a set of laws (agency policy) should adhere to that set of laws. This would make it important, then, for a social worker to know the agency's policy on confidentiality before accepting a position with that agency in order to see if its policy is compatible with the worker's position on confidentiality.

Having considered all of these options, the worker believes that the best resolution is to keep all confidential information private unless there is a possibility of imminent harm. Information that would be helpful to the student's educational goals may be shared if it can be done in a general way without breaking confidences. If there is a specific piece of information that would be helpful to others working with the child, consent for sharing the information would be obtained from student and parent, and the student him- or herself would be encouraged to share the information, thus empowering the student as well as providing helpful information to the staff.

QUESTIONS FOR THOUGHT AND DISCUSSION

1. Privileged communication as a legal right for social workers varies from state to state. It is very important for social workers to be cognizant of the protections and limitations to confidentiality in the state in which they plan to practice. Through consultation with NASW, the Internet, and an exploration of local codes and laws, determine the status of privileged communication for social workers in the state in which you plan to practice.

2. Personal values strongly influence the position of professionals regarding the rights of children to confidentiality. What factors would influence your decision? Do you believe the age of the child is an important issue? The rights of parents? Potential for risk to the child? To others?

3. Because of the structure of the social work profession, client confidentiality is compromised by the worker–supervisor relationship. Are there ever times when you believe the client's right to confidentiality should supersede the traditional worker-supervisor relationship?

4. School settings include professionals, paraprofessionals, and employees. Do you think information-sharing should be done at all levels if it is for the benefit of the child, or only on the professional level? What are the potential differences between sharing confidential information with other professionals, with paraprofessionals, and with staff?

5. If you share confidential information that you believe is in the best interest of a child with another professional working with the child, such as a teacher, what is your expectation for the confidentiality of the material you shared? May the teacher share the information with a teacher aide? With the school's bus driver? With a parent?

■ ■ ■ ■ ■ ▬▬▬▬▬▬▬▬▬▬▬▬▬▬▬▬▬▬▬▬▬▬▬▬▬▬▬▬

CASE STUDY 3.5
AN EMPLOYEE ASSISTANCE COUNSELOR'S DILEMMA

Abstracted from an unpublished paper by Mel Hall-Crawford, MSW

PRACTICE CONTEXT AND CASE PRESENTATION

Employee assistance programs (EAPs) are increasingly being utilized in both the private and public sector, with the general goal of addressing employee problems that impact on work performance and conduct, on their attendance, their reliability, and on other issues that affect their ability to perform their assigned tasks in an optimal manner. Programs are generally available to employees through self-referrals or through either formal or informal referrals by supervisors. They are, therefore, generally unlimited in terms of the types of problems that may be addressed.

Elena, a Japanese American woman, is a self-referred employee in a large corporation, who asks for assistance from the employee assistance program due to the great deal of difficulty she is experiencing in performing her job duties as a policy analyst. She recently separated from her husband and describes their relationship as filled with anger and mistrust. However, since he has left, she has become very frightened of being alone, and she feels very isolated, both at work and in her personal life. Her job is her sole source of support and, beyond that, her sole opportunity to interact with others.

Elena feels that she has been assigned an impossible task of creating a database, a project that she has been working on for over two years. She is frustrated by the lack of clarity from her supervisor regarding expectations and expresses concern that her job is in jeopardy. Elena says she stares at a blank computer screen in her office hour after hour, getting almost nothing done, and has actually curled up on the floor and cried on occasion.

Though Elena repeatedly refuses suggestions of involving her supervisor in these discussions, the worker feels strongly that this is advisable in order to determine (1) if things are as bad as Elena describes them and (2) if perhaps the supervisor could clarify what was expected of Elena so that her job performance could improve. However, the worker is also concerned that bringing this situation out into the open might further jeopardize Elena's job security in that such a meeting would spotlight Elena's performance and force the supervisor to examine the severity of the situation. After many discussions, Elena reluctantly consents to involve her supervisor.

During the meeting, her supervisor indicates that she wants to be supportive of Elena, but she also acknowledges that Elena's emotional state is indeed affecting her work performance. Elena breaks down in tears at this, but finally it is agreed that the supervisor will work with her to help her gain a better sense of how to proceed with her assignment and will also give her other intervening projects that would give Elena a sense of closure and accomplishment in her job. The worker agrees to help Elena deal with the larger issue of her depression and emotional problems by exploring other treatment options and by continuing counseling.

(continued)

CASE STUDY 3.5   CONTINUED

Following this meeting, Elena receives an informal performance appraisal rating her work at "satisfactory," a decline from prior ratings of "excellent," and a bad rating by general corporation standards. She believes that her job is in jeopardy and that the bad rating would make it difficult, if not impossible, for her to find another position.

The worker feels an obligation to protect Elena's best interest, but she is unsure whether she should continue to try to resolve Elena's work situation without further involving the supervisor or to urge that the supervisor be brought in as a consultant to the process in an effort to gain needed perspective and clarification. There is also a concern about whether the worker's urging Elena to consent to supervisory involvement infringes upon her self-determination. Because Elena's job appears to be in greater jeopardy since the involvement of her supervisor, the worker feels responsible.

However, the worker is also concerned about the larger ethical dilemma: What is her obligation to her client and to the employer of both herself and Elena? What if her obligation to her employer (to support and maintain optimum job performance for employees, which might in this case mean terminating Elena) and her obligation to her client (to keep her in a stable job situation, through which she is able to support herself) conflict?

The dilemma may be stated as:

Worker's Obligation to Employer v. Worker's Obligation to Client

RESEARCH AND RELATED LITERATURE

A definition of occupational social work must be the starting point for an exploration of this issue. Googins and Godfrey (1987) define occupational social work as being "a field of practice in which social workers attend to the human and social needs of the work community by designing and executing appropriate interventions to insure healthier individuals and environments" (p. 38).

EAPs help organizations by reinforcing their basic management principles and goals to employees (Googins & Godfrey, 1987). Assuming that one of an employer's basic principles and goals is employee job productivity, an EAP counselor has a responsibility to help an employee whose job performance is not meeting the employer's expectations.

There has been some discussion in the literature regarding the dilemma that employee assistance programs/counselors encounter when the interests of the employee and the employer may be in conflict. Loewenberg and Dolgoff (1992), in addressing "who is the client?", point out that "traditionally, a client was defined as the person(s) who engaged the practitioner and paid her a fee. Alternately, the client is the person (or the system) whose behavior is to be modified or changed by the professional's intervention" (p. 93). In this framework, however, an employee assistance counselor's "client" is the employing organization who is paying his or her salary as well as the employee who has come to the counselor for help. Or stated another way, the EAP counselor has an obligation to both the employee and the employer. Factoring in a social worker's ethical responsibility to the employer (Wells, 1986), the dilemma arises when a social worker or EAP counselor experiences difficulty in delivering effective service or affecting positive change in accordance with the employer's mission for the program.

Kurzman (1988) distills the issue in terms of the fundamental conflict between the profession's commitment to people's well-being and industry's dedication to profits. He poses the question "whose agent are we?" in light of circumstances when "organizational goals—in this situation productivity and profit maximization—are not entirely congruent with client needs" (p. 21).

Briar and Vinet (1985), while not explicitly advocating the employee's needs over those of the employer, point out that this approach or ordering of priorities "infinitely expands opportunities for the professional to address unmet needs of employees" (p. 351).

An interesting theme that has arisen in the literature reviewed is that when such a conflict arises between the best interest of the employee and the employer, a holistic or systems approach may be appropriate. Googins and Godfrey (1987) suggest that a systems approach to problem solving in the workplace is advantageous as problems exist within a specific context and addressing the problem may necessitate micro and macro solutions. "The EAP practitioner, joined by others in the workplace with similar humanistic functions, can help to promote new perspectives on corporate investment in employees and their families, consumers, and the wider community" (Briar & Vinet, 1985, p. 357). One caveat to this approach is that the employee must be comfortable with and must consent to the course of action that he or she feels is in his or her best interest. Overall, this perspective in the literature suggests that even when the employee's situation is at odds with the employer's expectations, the employee assistance counselor can be creative and endeavor to produce a positive outcome outside of the traditional relationships and ways of operating.

A review of the Code of Professional Conduct for Certified Employee Assistance Professionals (CEAP; Employee Assistance Certification Commission, 1994) touched on the ethical dilemma at hand in Section 1 of the Code of Conduct that deals with the workplace. Subsection c states *Human Resources Management:* The CEAP will seek to use all appropriate organizational resources in resolving job performance problems due to employee personal problems. The goal is to seek solutions for returning the employee to acceptable work performance." There is no guidance, though, as to what should be done, what the goal should be if the employee's work performance continues to be unacceptable, or what the obligation is to the employer.

In summing up the research and literature reviewed with regard to this ethical dilemma, it is clear that one of the primary goals of EAPs is to help employees with problems, personal or job-related, so that their work performance will improve. The literature acknowledges that there is a dynamic tension between individual human needs and the needs of the work organization but offers little guidance on how to deal with these needs when they come into conflict. This may be attributable to several factors: (1) Every situation is unique, and therefore it is difficult to speak broadly or in categorical terms; and (2) the field of occupational social work, while not new, is still evolving and has not received mainstream social work attention. Briar and Vinet (1987)

(*continued*)

CASE STUDY 3.5   CONTINUED

point out that "it is often argued that ethical discussions can deter the progress of human services in the workplace, especially if future service developers perceive value dilemmas as hazardous roadblocks" (p. 342).

AUTHOR'S REFLECTIONS, REASONING PROCESS, AND RESOLUTION

Values are concerned with what is good and desirable (Loewenberg & Dolgoff, 1992). In attempting to frame this issue in terms of general values derived from society, it is clear that the Protestant work ethic is an underlying principle. Our society places great value on hard work and having a job. "Work for economic gain is the way to success, a sign of personal morality, and a moral obligation" (Day, 1989, p. 7). Related to the Protestant work ethic is the societal value that productivity at work is good and desirable, and the converse is also true in that lack of productivity is viewed as a problem and is not well regarded.

Briar and Vinet (1985) take the position that employee assistance professionals derive their values from "ethical beliefs in the integrity and human potential of each individual, his or her right to self-expression . . . , and the centrality of human welfare above and beyond other potential overriding organizational goals, such as profitmaking, efficiency, and productivity" (p. 343). This vantage point would suggest that the client's best interest would take primacy over the employer's.

One value that emerged from researching the issue was that employing organizations recognize they have a responsibility to offer help to their employees who may be having personal or job-related problems, because ultimately such help will benefit the organization through improving the employees' performance. It also helps the organization by enhancing its image as being socially responsible. However, the outer limits of the employer's obligation to continue employing a worker whose performance, despite her seeming best efforts, is not easily amenable to improvement are uncertain.

Personal responsibility is another value on which our society places an emphasis. In this case, an individual or employee has a responsibility to take care of him- or herself, to seek help when necessary, and to deal with the consequences of his or her decisions. Elena wants help with her problems and has taken the initiative of seeking help from the employee assistance program.

Ethics deal with what is right or correct (Joseph, 1983; Loewenberg & Dolgoff, 1992). In this instance, there is a tremendous ethical responsibility for the client's best interest but there is also an ethical responsibility to the employer. The dilemma is best considered in terms of ethical relativism (Loewenberg & Dolgoff, 1992). What makes it so difficult is that one cannot always be sure if the anticipated consequence will occur. However, in this situation of conflict between the obligation to the employee versus the obligation to the employer, one has to prioritize to whom there is primary and secondary responsibility.

Another ethical principle relevant to this situation is the client's right to self-determination. If a client is adamant about not proceeding with the course of action recommended by the practitioner, unless there is a serious threat or harm to the client or another person, it seems that the practitioner is bound to honor the client's position.

However, again there can be gray areas in a situation in which a client agrees to a practitioner's recommendation, but both have trepidations about the course of action and are not sure about the outcome or repercussions.

Several of the core values in the NASW Code of Ethics (1996) relate to the situation that is the subject of this paper. These are: Value I—service and my desire to help an employee in need, drawing on my knowledge, values, and skills; Value II—respecting the dignity and worth of the employee; Value IV—understanding the importance of my relationship with the employee and our effort together to deal with her situation at work.

Section 1, Social Workers' Ethical Responsibilities to Clients, has several subsections that are relevant to the ethical dilemma that is being discussed here. Specifically, subsection 1.01, which deals with commitments to clients, seems pertinent in that this worker believes that the interest and welfare of the individual employee is primary. However, the worker also recognizes a responsibility to the larger organization. Subsection 1.02, which addresses self-determination, must be a consideration as the worker believes she may have infringed on client self-determination by bringing in the supervisor. Subsection 1.06a, relating to conflict of interest, makes the point that social workers should be alert to and avoid conflicts of interest.

Amplifying the possibility of a conflict of interest, Section 3 of the Code deals with ethical responsibilities in practice settings (NASW Code of Ethics, 1996). Subsection 3.09 speaks to the importance of social workers adhering to their commitments to their employers and of not allowing the policies and procedures of the agency to interfere with their ethical practice of social work.

Based on the above exploration and discussion in this ethical model, I believe appropriate ordering of the values/principles relating to this ethical dilemma are as follows: (1) In general, the employee's best interest is primary over the interest of the employer; (2) the worker needs to honor the client's right to self-determination; (3) the worker should act in the client's best interest and not encourage unnecessary risks that may conflict with the secondary client or, in this case, increase job jeopardy; (4) if a conflict of interest arises between the employee and the employing organization, the worker should try to balance the interests of both parties and find a mutually agreeable accommodation. However, in the absence of that, it still behooves the social worker to work on behalf of the individual as opposed to the organization, as the impact on the individual is greater, and his or her access to resources can be rather limited.

The worker is aware that her personal values impact strongly on ethical decision making. These include compassion and caring, respect, equity, balance, loyalty, honesty, and consistency. Though considering herself mostly a relativist with a touch of absolutist, the worker believes that things need to be taken in context and looked at in terms of the result and that it is important to be open-minded and flexible in judging what is right or wrong.

If the worker determines that her primary obligation is to Elena's best interest, she would choose to continue working with Elena in individual sessions without further supervisory consultations and/or seek outside resources for treatment for Elena, such as a day treatment program or a therapy group. This course of action would be supported by the belief in Elena's integrity and her right to human welfare. She needs the job, and her

(continued)

CASE STUDY 3.5   CONTINUED

functioning at work *might* improve, despite little evidence for this thus far. This choice would honor Elena's self-determination as well. However, the worker also wonders if it is in Elena's ultimate interest to lose her job, or be threatened with losing it, as this might help her to "pull herself together."

If the worker determines that her obligation to her employer is primary, she would make herself available to the supervisor for consultation. She would exercise caution in protecting the confidentiality of information Elena has shared in sessions, but would be open to assisting with direct interventions to improve Elena's work performance. The worker would of course let Elena know that she would be consulting with her supervisor and be available to Elena should crises occur.

On a different and higher level, addressing the obligation to the employer, the issue of an underfunctioning employee could be raised generically with the Human Resources Department and other appropriate personnel in management to explore what options or guidelines might be created. The underlying position here is that it is in the employer's best interest to retain employees rather than to let them go. It is more costly and disruptive to hire and train someone new unless it is clear that the incumbent employee is unable to meet his or her job responsibilities over the long run.

As a resolution, the worker has opted for the ethical stance that supports obligation to the client as primary. This position is a relativist one: If the client/employee were breaking clearcut rules or harming others in the workplace, the worker's obligation to the employer would probably override the obligation to the employee. The worker believes that Elena is not hurting anyone. She is not breaking any clearly stated work rules. She may be breaking some unspoken rules (by being unproductive in her job), but she needs her job to survive. She has far fewer resources than her employer. This worker feels that she is supported by the NASW Code of Ethics, which states that: "in general, clients' interests are primary."

The worker believes Elena's supervisor has her own responsibility in this situation. She is aware of Elena's poor job performance and depression and can take her own steps, independent of the worker's involvement, to deal with the situation. The lines of accountability and obligation appear to this worker to be quite different for herself, as an employee of the EAP, and for Elena's supervisor. Each must therefore follow the path that appears ethical and just from her vantage point and from her own values.

QUESTIONS FOR THOUGHT AND DISCUSSION

1. The worker here takes the position that she will regard her obligation to the client as primary because she is not breaking rules or harming others. Do you agree that no one is being harmed here by Elena's poor job performance? Who may be harmed?

2. The worker recognizes that she is a relativist and that she is making decisions based on the characteristics of each individual case. Yet she takes the position that she does because Elena is not "breaking rules" or "harming anyone." Is this also a relativist

position? How would you define "breaking rules" or "harm"? Would the *definition* hold absolutely for you?

3. What about "breaking rules" in other settings? Would this be more or less justified in settings such as a residential treatment center, an income distribution program, a school? If you believe the importance of adhering to rules varies by setting or by some measure of degree of severity of rule-breaking, how would you justify this relativist position?

4. Placement in an EAP may be creating issues of loyalty and responsibility not faced by workers in other settings. How does this setting differ from a social agency setting? From other host settings?

5. The worker raises the very interesting question of whether, and under what circumstances, an employer is also a "client." Do you believe that an employer can be a client?

■ ■ ■ ■ ■ ▬▬▬▬▬▬▬▬▬▬▬▬▬▬▬▬▬▬▬▬▬▬

CASE STUDY 3.6

GROUP THERAPY: CLIENT NEEDS AND FISCAL VIABILITY

Abstracted from an unpublished paper by Thomas C. Bertone, MSW, CSC

PRACTICE CONTEXT AND CASE PRESENTATION

Originally founded to provide free health, mental health, and social services to the gay and lesbian community, this intern's agency currently serves anyone infected or affected by HIV/AIDS. The number of clients in need of services has forced the agency to reconsider funding issues, and Medicaid reimbursement through the Ryan White Act and sliding scale fees from clients supplement the decreasing donations and grants in funding services. Ongoing funding through the Ryan White Act is dependent upon the numbers of HIV/AIDS clients being served.

The agency is restructuring at all levels in order to provide more efficient and cost-effective care compatible with managed care approaches, and there is a greater emphasis on groups as the treatment modality of choice, although clients clearly state preferences for individual therapy.

During the intake process, it is the worker's responsibility to develop a psychosocial history of each client and make a preliminary diagnosis, give a brief presentation at the department meeting, and assist in discussion that will result in a consensual disposition. The decision that is reached is strongly affected by the client's potential for funding the services. Referral outside the clinic to a worker who accepts a very few clients pro bono, a long wait for services, or referral to group treatment are the options of choice for clients who are not eligible for Ryan White funds and do not have the ability to pay for services.

Many clients have painful issues that are rooted in past experiences; others are ashamed of their HIV status and have kept this a secret. They have come to this agency for service because of its reputation in the community with the gay and lesbian and HIV/AIDS populations. They do not feel comfortable in a group situation. On the other hand, the agency will not survive financially if services are delivered without reimbursement. The need for services is great, and a greater number of people in need of service can be helped through use of the group modality. The worker is also caught in this dilemma: Should individual treatment be "pushed" at case presentations, to protect the needs of clients, or should the worker "push" group therapy with the client, even though this may not be in his or her best interest?

The dilemma that will be addressed is:

**Client and Worker's Concept of v. Fiscal Viability of the Agency
Best Interest of Client**

RESEARCH AND RELATED LITERATURE

Managed Care. Managed care has evolved in response to the rising cost of healthcare and is an attempt to provide services that are more cost-effective while maintaining a high quality of care. It was hoped that the competition among HMOs and other managed care organizations would help keep the costs of medical care down. However, "health care has so many special characteristics that efforts at competition have had the opposite effect from the one intended, as well as many other unintended consequences" (NASW, 1993).

Geller (1996) cites three definitions of managed care provided by Croze (1995):

> For detractors of managed care, managed care means "care managed by someone else." For those seriously interested in managed care, managed care means "[a]ny measure that from the purchaser's perspective favorably affects the price of services, the site at which services are delivered or received, and/or their utilization." Or, "[a]n arrangement or system in which there are financial, administrative, organizational, and monitoring constructs whose end is to minimize resource allocation and maximize efficiency and quality." (Geller, 1996, p. 225)

NASW (1993) says there cannot be one definition of managed care because it takes many forms. However, most programs follow the "medical model" of treatment. This model "focuses primarily on elimination or treatment of the symptom, versus a 'social health model,' which views the patient from a biopsychosocial perspective" (p. 169). NASW (1993) also notes that the rapid growth in the number of managed care plans makes it difficult to adequately assess their quality and ability to meet healthcare needs. It is further stated:

> Managed care is a neutral concept and should not be automatically evaluated as desirable or undesirable. However, forces in the present market can and often do distort health and mental health–providing organizations, leading to inequities that should be understood and challenged. . . . (NASW, 1993, p. 170)

Given these caveats, NASW has developed a resource guide to help social workers function in the managed care environment in an effective way (Jackson, 1995).

While most journal articles were critical of managed care, the positive exceptions are interesting: Trugerman (1996) notes that while many dismiss managed care out of hand, there is a lack of understanding of the various ways managed care can work. "It is actually possible to manage 'care' *and* reduce costs *and* increase access to behavioral health services" (p. 261). Dallek (1987, 1994) sees value in the potential for serving the needs of the poor. NASW's policy paper (NASW, 1993) recognizes the effectiveness of managed care programs for Medicaid-eligible individuals and families. In 1994, Bruce M. Fried, the Director of the Office of Managed Care in the Department of Health and Human Services, said ". . . managed care offers the greatest opportunity to address the problems of access, quality and cost. . . . Managed care has done a terrific job in demonstrating its effectiveness at controlling costs. . . ."

Negative critiques of managed care are easy to find. As an example, Munson (1996) fears that the move toward managed care is changing mental health services "from a humanitarian commitment to a private industry" (p. 243). He further states: "In the coming years, the social work profession will have to confront a market orientation to mental health services that challenges the basic social commitments of our profession" (p. 244).

(continued)

CASE STUDY 3.6   CONTINUED

Managed care has led to the development of predetermined protocols for treatment, including time limits and modes of treatment (cf., e.g., Geller, 1996; Mone, 1994; Munson, 1996). As Munson (1996) points out: "There is no documented research that any of these actions result in more efficient treatment, or greater productivity" (p. 246). Furthermore, two independent studies cited by Munson (1996) have shown the effectiveness of longer-term treatment, which is not supported by managed care. Munson (1996) cites eighteen principles that were contained in the 1990 NASW Code of Ethics that conflict with managed care guidelines and calls for developing models of clinical advocacy, echoing NASW's policy statement on managed care (NASW, 1993). Geller (1996) focuses his attention on the development of managed behavioral healthcare, with a specific focus on those individuals with severe mental illness. He sees that managed care "is really about managing time. . . . the patient appears to have left the foreground, to be replaced by resource management" (Geller, 1996, p. 223).

Concerns have also been raised about confidentiality, especially when a therapist must discuss details of a client's case with a "gatekeeper" at the managed care company, who may not be adequately trained in mental and behavioral health and may be unable to make informed individual judgments but may rely on formulas or predetermined guidelines in decision making. To address this problem, the NASW resource guide for managed care (Jackson & Beinecke, 1995) states: "Treatment will be more results focused; the primary goal will be to change behavior, not to facilitate personal growth or resolve long-standing intrapsychic conflicts or to address the root causes of dysfunction" (p. 56). NASW's policy statement on managed care (1993) also states that: "[m]ental health services without restrictions lead to savings in the long run because help with emotional and other mental problems reduces the use of other health care" (p. 170).

Group Treatment.   The positive aspects of group therapy have been discussed by various authors (e.g., Northern, 1988; Porter, 1993; Shulman, 1992). Northern (1988) notes mutual support, the quality of the relationships, the "universalization" of feelings and problems, the "instillation of hope," the "acquisition of knowledge and skills," and reality testing as positive factors (pp. 11–13). Shulman (1992) describes the group as a mutual aid setting where members can help each other address their individual problems, look at formerly taboo areas in a supportive environment, and use the group to rehearse new ways of relating to people.

Alperin (1994) critiques managed care for its focus on

> symptoms that provide an *identifiable* impairment in functioning. Almost completely disregarded are those symptoms that are intrapsychic and, therefore, not always directly observable in day-to-day functioning, such as sadness or poor self-esteem. Also ignored are the underlying intrapsychic conflicts creating these symptoms. (p. 140)

Porter (1993) believes that group therapy is most effective when interpersonal exploration occurs because within the group process "multiple transferences can be explored"; there can be a "corrective family experience"; there can be an opportunity to test new behaviors; obstacles to growth become apparent and can be dealt with; and "special forms of ego support" are provided (pp. 311–312). Porter (1993) also notes that severely borderline or narcissistic individuals, persons who are extremely paranoid or shy, persons who are psychotic, and individuals in crisis might not do well in a group setting.

Assuming a client is appropriate for group treatment, how effective is this type of intervention? Piper, Dabbane, Bienvenu, and Garant (1984) conducted a comparative study of short-term individual (STI), short-term group (STG), long-term individual (LTI), and long-term group (LTG) therapies to test out their hypothesis that "not all treatments can be expected to maintain their effectiveness in abbreviated forms" (p. 269). Patients placed in one of these four types of treatments had a followup assessment six months after termination. The authors concluded: "The best outcomes were associated with LTG therapy and STI therapy and the worst outcomes with STG therapy" (p. 275). They further concluded that the most cost-effective form of treatment was short-term individual therapy. However, Winegar, Bistline, and Sheridan (1992) studied the use of group psychotherapy in a managed care setting and showed greater staff productivity and increased staff morale, as well as client satisfaction.

AUTHOR'S REASONING, REFLECTION, AND RESOLUTION

General Values. Societal values most prominent in the literature review were health (including mental health), efficiency, cost-effectiveness, profit, quality of care, access to care, privacy/confidentiality, and professionalism. Health, both physical and mental, is the underlying value of this whole dilemma. Both sides support the health and well-being of the clients. Efficiency and cost-effectiveness appear to be the underlying principle in managed care programs; however, profit is also a value for them. Quality of care and access to care are values held by supporters of both sides of the current dilemma. Confidentiality appears to be more greatly valued by clients and workers than managed care companies, and important professional issues about who makes decisions for clients needing treatment abound.

Ethical Principles. This writer would use the ethical principles of Gewirth (cited in Reamer, 1990) and those proposed by utilitarianism (Reamer, 1990). From Gewirth, one can evaluate how well the core goods are being served and protected using his six guidelines. From the utilitarian perspective, one can consider whether the greatest good for the greatest number is being achieved. In this regard, the writer would lean toward act utilitarianism, where there is a greater emphasis on the individual than with rule utilitarianism.

Code of Ethics. NASW Code of Ethics (NASW, 1996) sections relevant to this dilemma include concern for the client's well-being (1.01); informed consent, especially regarding limits to service due to third-party payers, the need to be informed about alternatives, and the risks to confidentiality (1.03a, e; 1.07c, e, h, l); conflicts of interest (1.06a); dealing with termination of services (1.16b, e); administrative responsibilities for advocacy on behalf of clients (3.07a); social workers' commitment to employers (3.07a); social workers' responsibilities regarding improving policies and

(continued)

CASE STUDY 3.6   CONTINUED

services (3.07b); the integrity of the profession (5.01a); the evaluation of policies, programs, and practice (5.02a); and social and political action on behalf of those we serve (6.04a, b).

The main area of conflict in this list of ethical standards is between the concern for clients' well-being and the need to treat the clients within the parameters of the third-party payer (1.03a, 1.03e, 1.07, 1.16b) and agency policy (3.07a). These latter standards raise the issue of limitations to service and confidentiality, which often go against the well-being of clients directly and indirectly through their effect on adequate treatment.

Client Values. Grounded in the intake interviews, client values include quality of life, health, self-esteem, self-sufficiency, self-determination, personal dignity, friendship, family of origin, employment, and, in some cases, faith.

Agency and Department Values. The mission statement states that is the department's aim to provide comprehensive services from a "client-centered and client-strengths approach, offering the community an alternative to traditional mental health and addiction services." Self-determination, empowerment, and accessibility are valued, and the agency's primary goal is "to maintain, enhance, and assure the quality of services in each of the existing programmatic areas."

Proposed Hierarchy of Values. These values best reflect those of all interested parties to this dilemma: client well-being, self-determination, health, accessibility of care, professionalism, privacy/confidentiality, and efficiency.

Personal Values and Ethical Stance. The writer recognizes a personal bias against the way managed care is currently operating and tends to prefer psychoanalytic concepts and methods in working with my clients. These biases cause distress when group work is offered to clients who might best be served with individual therapy. Personal values, grounded in the Christian faith, include justice, self-determination, equality, respect (of self and others), honesty, responsibility, family, friendship, education, and simplicity.

Ethical Options
Worker's Perception of Client's Best Interest. It is recognized that the worker's personal biases and values may strongly affect perception of best interest, which generally tends toward individual therapy for most clients of the agency. Within this framework, one option is to do nothing—that is, to allow the status quo to remain, providing it is not causing any harm to the client. Following agency policy, finding a group for the client could provide some relief and also connect the client to sources of support. However, underlying issues may not be addressed.

A second option would be to push for individual therapy for clients, thereby maximizing well-being and respecting the client's stated wishes. This would place client well-being ahead of rules and regulations, as suggested by Gewirth. However, given insufficient personnel, clients may be forced to wait for long periods before beginning individual therapy.

Another possibility would be to refer the client to another agency or therapist, in spite of the client's self-determined choice to come to this agency. This option depends upon the availability of alternatives and would impact the clinic's fiscal viability.

A compromise option could involve the client in time-limited individual therapy prior to being placed in the group, thus meeting the client's need while respecting the clinic's fiscal concerns. In terms of act utilitarianism, this would be the exception to the principle of having most clients seen as part of group therapy, showing more consideration of individual needs while respecting the needs of the greater number (i.e., to maintain a fiscally viable clinic).

Fiscal Viability. Options here, this worker believes, can be inherently threatening to client well-being. Any threat to client well-being diminishes professional integrity and violates the principles set forth by Gewirth in terms of rules and regulations taking priority over basic goods (in this case, client well-being).

An act-utilitarian approach might be more conducive to options on this side of the dilemma: Maintaining a general policy of using group interventions need not eliminate the possibility of exceptions when cases warrant them. This respects client well-being, self-determination, and accessibility to care, but would involve the staff in difficult decision making.

One option for fiscal viability is the compromise described above: some individual therapy along with group therapy. This would not be the best solution for fiscal viability because of the time and resources that individual therapy can take away from group therapy. However, given the fact that individual therapy costs more than group therapy, it could generate more needed income.

A second option would be to maintain groups that focus on different problems, communication styles, and interests, so that individual needs might best be met. However, given the variety of needs with which people come into the clinic, how probable is it that any group would be suitable? Do we ignore some symptoms or underlying issues in order to "fit" a client into a particular group? What will this do to clients' well-being? What about the right to receive proper care? What about our sense of maintaining professional integrity?

A final option is long-range: developing ways of increasing funds from other sources. In a time of budget constraints and funding cutbacks, this could be a challenging, though ultimately rewarding, enterprise.

The Writer's Ethical Position. The combination of individual and group therapy best respects the values of client well-being, self-determination, access to care, and professionalism, while being sensitive to fiscal viability, and thus also would be in keeping with the principles of act utilitarianism. The worker's bias toward the client's mental well-being as a basic core good that takes precedence over the clinic's needs is evident, but consideration is also given to fiscal viability, without which client services cannot exist.

(continued)

CASE STUDY 3.6   CONTINUED

From a utilitarian perspective, the issue of distribution of resources to meet the needs of the greatest number cannot be ignored. Most clients come to the clinic because of its sensitivity to working with gay and lesbian issues and persons with HIV/AIDS. The clinic is seen as a place where this special population can receive affordable care. These special situations, along with the growing number of persons with HIV/AIDS coming to receive mental health services, make the consideration for the distribution of resources all the more urgent. To be able to provide the services demanded of it at the present time, the clinic seeks reimbursement from Medicaid and Ryan White funds. One of their requirements is that a certain number of clients be seen. Because of decreased staffing, groups are the only means to do this, although the use of interns is also beneficial in providing services at no cost to the agency.

While the overall fiscal viability of the agency is important if any type of service is to continue, individual needs must be considered and exceptions made. Making the exception to provide individual therapy in certain cases does not preclude a major allocation of resources to group treatment. Furthermore, time spent in individual therapy can prepare a client to move into group therapy at a later point. Then, clients' needs are being met, and the clinic is able to serve more clients using less staff and resources.

QUESTIONS FOR THOUGHT AND DISCUSSION

1. Many agencies maintain internship programs to meet the needs of their service populations within restricted budgets. Although there is attention and interest in students' learning, the agency's primary interest is in using the students to provide services for clients. Do you feel that this is fair to students, especially given the fact the students pay for field work credits?

2. Confidentiality and privacy issues can be addressed in group therapy. If you were leading a group, how might you address these issues with group members?

3. An act-utilitarian position, such as that espoused by the writer, demands that individual consideration be given to each case prior to making a decision, so that the decision can best meet the needs of all concerned. This method requires a much greater expenditure of time and, in this instance, would involve the time of all of the professionals at the departmental case disposition meetings. Do you believe this use of time, in an agency already understaffed and fiscally at risk, can be justified?

4. What alternative methods could be used for individualized decision making for clients at this agency? What are the advantages and disadvantages of each method?

5. If this agency had the possibility of providing individual therapy to 10 new clients a month and received 60 new cases per month, each preferring individual therapy, what might be a fair way to determine who receives those 10 places?

REFERENCES AND BIBLIOGRAPHY

Case Study 3.1

Allen, E. (1988). Reservations about advance directives. *Health and Social Work,* 72–74.

Beauchamp, T. L., & Childress, J. F. (1994). *Principles of biomedical ethics* (4th ed.). New York: Oxford University Press.

Bernstein, B. E. (1978, March). Malpractice: An ogre on the horizon. *Social Work,* 106–112.

Cohen-Mansfield, J., Kerin, P., Pawlson, G., Lipson, S., & Coleman, N. (1988). Advance directives preserve autonomy despite incapacity. *Health and Social Work,* 71–72.

Interviews with professionals at [Name withheld] Partial Hospitalization Program.

Kopels, S., & Kagle, J. D. (1993, March). Do social workers have a duty to warn? *Social Service Review, 73,* 101–126.

Lindenthal, J. J., & Thomas, C. S. (1984). Attitudes toward confidentiality. *Social Work,* 151–159.

McGough, L. S., & Carmichael, W. C. (1977). The right to treatment and the right to refuse treatment. *American Journal of Orthopsychiatry,* 307–320.

National Association of Social Workers. (1996). *NASW Code of Ethics.* Washington, DC: Author.

Partial Rehabilitation Manual (1994). Name withheld.

Perlman, H. H. (1965). Self-determination: Reality or illusion? *Social Service Review, 39,* 410–421.

Reamer, F. G. (1987). Informed consent in social work. *Social Work,* 425–429.

Reamer, F. G. (1990). *Ethical dilemmas in social service* (2nd ed.). New York: Columbia University Press.

Rothman, J. (1989). Client self-determination: Untangling the knot. *Social Service Review, 63*(4), 598–612.

Sehdev, H. S. (1976). Patients' rights or patients' neglect: The impact of the patients' rights movement on delivery systems. *American Journal of Orthopsychiatry,* 660–669.

Spirer, J. (1995). Personal communication. Washington, DC.

Case Study 3.2

Beauchamp, T. L., & Childress, J. F. (1994). *Principles of biomedical ethics.* New York: Oxford University.

Brod, B. J. (1987). Coordinating and distributing emergency clinical information by computer. *Social Work, 32*(6), 542–543.

Gewirth, A. (1978). *Reason and morality.* Chicago: University of Chicago Press.

Lanman, R. B. (1980). The federal confidentiality protections for alcohol and drug abuse patient records: A model for mental health and other medical records? *American Journal of Orthopsychiatry, 50*(4), 666–677.

Mutschler, E. (1990). Computerized information systems for social workers in health care. *Health and Social Work, 15*(3), 191–196.

National Association of Social Workers. (1996). *NASW Code of Ethics.* Washington, DC: Author.

Nurius, P. S., & Hudson, W. W. (1988). Computer-based practice: Future dream or current technology? *Social Work, 33*(4), 357–362.

Nye, S. G. (1980). Patient confidentiality and privacy: The federal initiative. *American Journal of Orthopsychiatry, 50*(4), 649–658.

Schrier, C. J. (1980). Guidelines for record-keeping under privacy and open access laws. *Social Work, 25*(6), 452–457.

Schuchman, H. (1980). Confidentiality: Practice issues in new legislation. *American Journal of Orthopsychiatry, 50*(4), 641–648.

Case Study 3.3

Axelson, J. (1993). *Counseling and development in a multicultural society*. Baltimore: Paul D. Brookes.

Baier, C. (1985). *Postures of the mind*. Minneapolis: University of Minnesota.

Beauchamp, T. L., & Childress, J. F. (1994). *Principles of biomedical ethics*. New York: Oxford University.

Borel, A. C. (1983). Mathematics: Art and science. *Mathematical Intelligence, 5*(4), 9–17.

Canda, E., & Phaobtong, T. (1992, January). Buddhism as a support system for Southeast Asian refugees. *Social Work, 37*(1).

Chan, S. (1992). Families with Asian roots. In E. Lynch & M. Hanson (Eds.), *Developing cross-cultural competence*. Baltimore: Paul D. Brookes.

Cross, T. L., Bazron, B. J., Dennis, K. W., & Isaacs, M. R. (1989). *Toward a culturally competent system of care*. Washington, DC: Georgetown University Child Development Center.

Draine, C., & Hall, B. (1986). *Culture shock: Indonesia*. Singapore: Times Books. In E. Lynch & M. Hanson (Eds.) (1992), *Developing cross-cultural competence*. Baltimore: Paul D. Brookes.

Goldstein, H. (1990, May). Strength or pathology: Ethical and rhetorical contrasts in approaches to practice. *The Journal of Contemporary Human Services*.

Hanson, M. (1992a). Ethnic, cultural, and language diversity in intervention settings. In E. Lynch & M. Hanson (Eds.), *Developing cross-cultural competence*. Baltimore: Paul D. Brookes.

Hanson, M. (1992b). Families with Anglo-European roots. In E. Lynch & M. Hanson (Eds.), *Developing cross-cultural competence*. Baltimore: Paul D. Brookes.

Hepworth, D., & Larsen, J. (1992). *Direct social work practice*. Pacific Grove, CA: Brooks/Cole.

Herndon, R. (2001, March 31). The nation's new mix. *Los Angeles Times*, p. 4.

Housing Commission. (1991a). The [Name Withheld] Commission: Working toward a balanced housing supply.

Housing Commission. (1991b). Proposal for economic empowerment demonstration program.

Housing Commission. (1994). The [Name Withheld] commission: A financial portrait.

Levy, C. (1973). The value base of social work. *Journal of Education for Social Work, 9*, 34–42.

Levy, C. (1979). *Values and ethics for social work practice*. Washington, DC: National Association of Social Workers.

Loewenberg, F. M., & Dolgoff, R. (1992). *Ethical decisions for social work practice.* Itasca, IL: F. E. Peacock.

Loomis, J. F. (1988). Case management in health care. *Health and Social Work, 13,* 219–225.

Lynch, E. (1992). Developing cross-cultural competence. In E. Lynch & M. Hanson (Eds.), *Developing cross-cultural competence.* Baltimore: Paul D. Brookes.

Lynch, E., & Hanson, M. (1992). *Developing cross-cultural competence.* Baltimore: Paul D. Brookes.

Moore, S. (1990). A social work practice model of case management. *Social Work, 35.*

Moxley, D. P. (1989). *The practice of case management.* Newbury Park, CA: Sage Publications.

National Association of Social Workers. (1981). NASW working statement on the purpose of social work. *Social Work, 26*(6).

National Association of Social Workers. (1992). *NASW Standards for Social Work Case Management.* Washington, DC: National Association of Social Workers.

National Association of Social Workers. (1996). *NASW Code of Ethics.* Washington, DC: Author.

Nelson, J. S., Megill, A., & McCloskey, D. (1987). *The rhetoric of the human sciences.* Madison: University of Wisconsin.

Pinderhughes, E. (1989). *Understanding race, ethnicity, and power.* New York: The Free Press.

U.S. Census Bureau. www.censusscope.org/us/chart_race.html

Case 3.4

Bazis, C. (1997). *Confidentiality in a school setting* (personal communication).

Berman-Rossi, T., & Rossi, P. (1990, April). Confidentiality and informed consent in social work. *Social Work in Education,* 195–207.

Frankena, W. (1973). *Ethics* (2nd ed.). Englewood Cliffs, NJ: Prentice-Hall.

Kardon, S. (1993). Confidentiality: A different perspective. *Social Work in Education, 15*(4), 247–250.

Kopels, S. (1993). Response to "Confidentiality: A different perspective." *Social Work in Education, 15*(4), 250–252.

Loewenberg, F. M., & Dolgoff, R. (1996). *Ethical decisions for social work practice.* Itasca, IL: F. E. Peacock.

National Association of Social Workers. (1996). *NASW Code of Ethics.* Washington, DC: Author.

NASW Commission on Education Position Statement. (1992). The school social worker and confidentiality. *School Social Work Journal, 17,* 38–45.

Phillips School for Contemporary Education. (1976). *Policy and procedures.* Annandale, VA: Author.

Reamer, F. G. (1990). *Ethical dilemmas in social service* (2nd ed.). New York: Columbia University Press.

Case Study 3.5

Briar, K. H., & Vinet, M. (1985). Ethical questions concerning an EAP: Who is the client? (Company or individual?). In S. H. Klarreich, J. L. Francek, & C. E. Moore (Eds.), *The human resources management handbook: Principles and practice of employee assistance programs.* New York: Praeger.

Day, P. (1989). *A new history of social welfare.* Englewood Cliffs, NJ: Prentice-Hall.

Employee Assistance Certification Commission. (Revised, 1994). *Code of Professional Conduct for Certified Employee Assistance Professionals (CEAP).* Arlington, VA: Employee Assistance Professionals Association.

Googins, B., & Godfrey, J. (1987). *Occupational social work.* Englewood Cliffs, NJ: Prentice-Hall.

Joseph, M. V. (1983). Ethical decision-making in clinical practice: A model for ethical problem solving. In C. B. Germain (Ed.), *Advances in clinical practice* (pp. 207–217). Silver Spring, MD: National Association of Social Workers.

Kurzman, P. A. (1988). The ethical base for social work in the workplace. In G. M. Gould & M. L. Smith (Eds.), *Social work in the workplace.* New York: Springer Publishing.

Loewenberg, F. M., & Dolgoff, R. (1992). *Ethical decisions for social work practice.* Itasca, IL: F. E. Peacock.

National Association of Social Workers. (1996). *NASW Code of Ethics.* Washington, DC: Author.

Wells, C. C. (1986). *Social work ethics day to day: Practice guidelines for professional practice.* New York: Longman.

Case Study 3.6

Alperin, R. M. (1994). Managed care versus psychoanalytic psychotherapy: Conflicting ideologies. *Clinical Social Work Journal, 22,* 137–148.

Croze, C. (1995). Medicaid waivers: The shape of things to come. *Proceedings of the Fifth Annual National Conference on State Mental Health Agency Services Research and Program Evaluation* (pp. 324–338). Alexandria, VA: NASMHPD.

Dollek, G. (1987). The quality of medical care for the poor in Los Angeles County's health and hospital system. Los Angeles: Distributed by Legal Aid Foundation of Los Angeles.

Dollek, G. (1994). State oversight of Medi-Col managed care plans: How well does California protect poor families? Los Angeles: Center for Health Care Rights.

Feel better? (1996, February 2). *Business Week, 3464,* 8.

Geller, J. L. (1996). Mental health services of the future: Managed care, unmanaged care, mismanaged care. *Smith College Studies in Social Work, 66,* 223–239.

Gray, C. (1997). Class notes from Social Work with Small Groups, Class 3. Washington, DC: The Catholic University of America.

Jackson, V. H., & Beinecke, R. H. (Eds.). (1995). *Managed care resource guide for social workers in agency settings.* Washington, DC: NASW Press.

Mone, L. C. (1994). Managed care cost effectiveness: Fantasy or reality? *International Journal of Group Psychotherapy, 44,* 437–448.

Munson, C. E. (1996). Autonomy and managed care in clinical social work practice. *Smith College Studies in Social Work, 66,* 241–260.

National Association of Social Workers (NASW). (1993). Managed care: Policy statement approved by the NASW Delegate Assembly, August 1993. In NASW (1994), *Social work speaks: NASW policy statements* (3rd ed., pp. 169–175). Washington, DC: Author.

National Association of Social Workers. (1996). *NASW Code of Ethics.* Washington, DC: Author.

Northern, H. (1988). *Social work with groups* (2nd ed.). New York: Columbia University Press.

Piper, W. E., Dabbane, E. G., Bienvenu, J. P., & Garant, J. (1984). A comparative study of four forms of psychotherapy. *Journal of Consulting and Clinical Psychology, 52,* 268–279.

Porter, K. (1993). Combined individual and group psychotherapy. In A. Alonso & H. Swiller (Eds.), *Group therapy in clinical practice* (pp. 309–341). Washington, DC: American Psychiatric Press.

Reamer, F. G. (1990). *Ethical dilemmas in social service* (2nd ed.). New York: Columbia University Press.

Shulman, L. (1992). *The skills of helping* (3rd ed.). Itasca, IL: F. E. Peacock.

Trugerman, A. (1996). All managed care is not equal. *Smith College Studies in Social Work, 66,* 261–272.

Winegar, N., Bistline, J. L., & Sheridan, S. (1992). Implementing a group therapy program in a managed-care setting: Combining cost effectiveness and quality care. *Families in Society, 73,* 56–58.

CHAPTER FOUR

NASW ETHICAL STANDARD FOUR

Social Workers' Ethical Responsibilities as Professionals

INTRODUCTION

Provisions of Code

The fourth section of the NASW Code of Ethics' Ethical Standards addresses expected standards of professional conduct and comportment. Close examination of the tenets of this part of the code reveals that, while it is phrased specifically for social workers, such standards may be considered to be the norm for professions in general. Standards of competence, discrimination, private conduct, dishonesty, fraud and deception, impairment, misrepresentation, solicitation, and acknowledging credit appear in many professional codes of ethics and/or ethical standards. Thus, this section may, in part, define what is meant by being a professional—specifically, a social work professional.

The first subsection, 4.01, directs the social worker to "accept responsibility or employment . . . on the basis of existing competence" (4.01a) and to "become and remain proficient in professional practice" (4.01b). Practice should be based only on recognized professional knowledge and ethics (4.01c).

The following three subsections address the obligation not to practice, condone, facilitate, or collaborate in any form of discrimination (4.02), dishonesty, fraud, or deception (4.04), and to conduct oneself in private in a manner that does not compromise one's professional responsibilities (4.03).

Impairment is a difficult and painful issue: an obligation of each worker, that may, if not met, place a responsibility on professional colleagues. Self-monitoring is preferred, but in the event that a social worker does not fulfill this professional duty, it is the obligation of colleagues to intervene. This "fallback" position in terms of the impairment of any professional is stated in subsection 2.09, Impairment of Colleagues.

The professional obligation of each social worker is not to allow "personal problems, psychosocial distress, legal problems, substance abuse, or mental health difficulties to interfere" with the performance of professional responsibilities (4.05a). Workers whose problems do interfere must seek professional help, adjust workload, terminate practice, or take other steps to "protect clients and others" (4.05b).

In terms of misrepresentation, the Code obligates social workers to make a distinction between "statements and actions" made as a private individual and those made as a member of the social work profession (4.06a). When speaking on behalf of professional social work organizations, workers are required to "represent the official and authorized positions" of such organizations (4.06b).

Returning to the issue of representation of professional credentials, the Code obligates social workers to represent themselves fairly and accurately and to correct any inaccuracies in others' representations of their qualifications (4.06c).

Professional comportment also prohibits social workers from soliciting clients who are potentially vulnerable to exploitation (4.07a) and from soliciting endorsements from persons who are similarly vulnerable (4.07b). Social workers should also take credit only for work actually performed (4.08a) and acknowledge the work and contribution of others (4.08b).

The Cases

The first case presented addresses a difficult issue: A social worker in the course of her professional practice realizes that she has handled two potentially suicidal clients very differently. Both clients asked that the social worker hold in confidence their verbalizations of their plans for suicide. In one case, the social worker chose to violate confidentiality and contact the police to have the client confined and treated. In the other, she chose to maintain confidentiality. The second client successfully effected her plans and committed suicide.

The social worker understood why she had handled the two cases differently: The differences were related to her evaluation of the potential life quality of each client, were she or he to continue to live. However, she questioned whether, as a professional, her reasons were sufficient and also whether she should have acted consistently in all instances of suicidal threats.

Clients with strong dependency needs that are unmet in their social environment often have difficulty terminating with a worker whom they have viewed as supportive, helpful, and interested. Despite referral to another worker, the clients may cling desperately to their original worker, begging not to be abandoned, asking to redefine the relationship on a social basis. However, professional ethics preclude such redefinitions. Dual relationships, in the interests of protecting the client from possible exploitation due to the inequality between client and worker in the relationship, are clearly proscribed by the Code of Ethics.

This dilemma confronts the worker in the second case presented. She has worked diligently with the client over a period of many months. She has initiated transfer and termination of her services. The client pleads for a continued relationship, citing her need for the worker. The worker must consider her obligation to meet the needs of the client, to the primacy of the client's interests, and to her professional obligation to the Code of Ethics. At first glance, the worker's overriding obligation is clearly to the Code of Ethics. However, dual relationships are proscribed only when there is the "*risk* of exploitation or *potential* harm" (1.06c, emphasis added). This leaves some room for interpretation by the worker.

A social worker who is a recovered alcoholic presents a difficult personal and professional dilemma in the third case. He regularly attends 12-step meetings at his field placement agency, which focuses on a small and closely knit population. He shares his experiences and mentors new 12-step attendees, many of whom are served by his agency. Some of these are clients assigned to him for professional service. In the context of the goals and methods used in the 12-step program, or indeed in any self-help support group context, what is an ethically professional relationship with clients?

What is the worker's personal obligation to himself, and how is this impacted by his new professional position as a social worker? Should he attend a different group, sacrificing his own personal best interests to those of his clients? As personal relationships and interaction are an important part of 12-step programs, should he continue these kinds of relationships now that he has a professional role? What is the potential impact of dual relationships on clients? This difficult issue can provide challenges to professionals in many social work contexts, as self-help groups are an important and commonly used resource for clients and professionals alike.

In the fourth case presented, a physician has asked the hospital social worker to plan for a patient. Because the patient is unable to communicate, the social worker initiates planning with his spouse. The physician has ordered referral for long-term care, while the spouse is adamant in her desire to take the patient home. This appears to be a potential conflict between client self-determination and (physician's) perception of client's best interests, which would be addressed in Section 1 of the Code, Obligations to Clients, Section 2, Obligations to Colleagues, and Section 3, Obligations to Practice Settings.

However, the author has viewed the conflict in different terms: Empirical knowledge suggests that the elderly are indeed at high risk of accidents and harm, but meaning-of-life issues are also important to well-being; ethical obligations support self-determination but also the worker's obligations to the client's well-being. The worker, in subsection 4.01c, is obligated to practice based on both empirical knowledge and social work ethics. Social work core values support a commitment to "well-being," which generally would seem to include physical, mental, and emotional well-being. How can the worker balance these seemingly conflicting obligations?

CASE STUDY 4.1

WHEN A CLIENT THREATENS SUICIDE: CLIENT AUTONOMY AND PROFESSIONAL OBLIGATION

Abstracted from an unpublished paper by Gigi Stowe, MSW

PRACTICE CONTEXT AND CASE PRESENTATION

An urban community service agency addresses special client issues, such as substance abuse, teenage pregnancy, children with difficulties in school, residential treatment for chronic mental illness, and court-mandated clients. Upon intake, clients are informed of their right to confidentiality and its limitations: the threat of harm to self and others. An agreement is signed in the record supporting the client's understanding of this agency policy.

The agency's policy with suicidal clients requires the utilization of the least restrictive measures possible. These range from verbal guarantees of safety, to a contract not to harm self, to hospitalization and confinement. It is the responsibility of the worker to assess each situation and take the appropriate action to guarantee a client's physical safety.

Two suicidal clients are presented to the caseworker within a common span of time. Client A is a 19-year-old African American male, with significant recent losses. In particular, the recent breakup of a long-term romantic relationship has been difficult, and he is now threatening suicide. His former girlfriend is with him during this interview. In previous interviews, the client has told the worker of his pride in his employment, his intention of going to college, and the extensive support system in his community.

The worker's assessment of Client A is that his verbalizations, as well as his gestures during the interview, are designed more to elicit his girlfriend's sympathy and attention than to be actual statements of intent. Nevertheless, as he has made the statement that he plans to commit suicide and refuses to retract it, the worker determines that her course of action must be to notify the police and to detain the client. She proceeds to do so, and Client A is immediately hospitalized and treated.

Client B is a 40-year-old white female, who was found, unconscious, lying in a park. Her story is one of extremely severe sexual, physical, emotional, and verbal abuse during the entire course of her life. Her father had, since early childhood, raped, beaten, and cut her, and inflicted invisible scars on her psyche. She is isolated from her family and has no social contacts. Due to her severe depression, she is unable to hold a job. She is unable to make friends due to frequent dissociations, panic attacks, and basic insecurity. She cannot return to school due to her inability to concentrate. She spends her days running, swimming, self-mutilating, and engaging in bulimia. She has a history of multiple suicide attempts, hospitalizations, and treatments and tells the worker she only wants to be allowed to die. While the worker would like to believe that, with time and therapy, she can be helped to find a reason for living, her history seems to render such hope nearly

(continued)

CASE STUDY 4.1 CONTINUED

impossible. The worker decides to continue to try to motivate her toward life, but takes no steps to detain her forcibly from committing suicide. Client B commits suicide.

These two side-by-side events, so different, yet so similar, are resolved with striking differences. In each case, the worker used reasoning and reflection, care and concern, and the best of her professional skills in addressing the problem. Yet her courses of action differed markedly, and the implications of these differences were, literally, vital. The differences that the worker perceives as significant could be justifiable, or not, depending on the ethical position taken.

Although the simplest course of action suggests that agency policy be followed in all instances, the worker is conflicted. While the client's personal situations were very different, their statements of ultimate intention were the same. Should the worker, to honor consistency, make the same decision in each case, no matter what the surrounding issues might be? Or should the worker consider each case individually and base her decisions on that evaluation? What role, if any, should the worker's perception of the quality of the client's life have in her assessments and decisions? What role, if any, should the client's own perception have?

In both cases, the issue of client autonomy is presented. The worker violates Client A's in the service of what she believes to be his excellent future potential for a good quality of life. She supports Client B's autonomy based on both the worker and client's assessment that good quality of life is not possible for this severely disturbed individual. Her autonomous wish appears "rational" to the worker. Client A's does not.

The dilemma is thus stated as:

(*Prevent Harm*)

Client Autonomy v. Professional Obligation to Prevent Discrimination

RESEARCH AND RELATED LITERATURE

Neither suicide nor assisted suicide is, at present, a crime under the statutes of any state in the Union. However, a majority of states do make it a crime to *assist* with a suicide (Chase, 1986). It seems to this author, however, that there must be some logical difficulty in punishing someone who assists with an act that is not itself illegal.

There is some lack of clarity in definitions of "autonomy," which range from "self-governance" to "freedom," and these variations can affect the interpretation of professional obligations. In a civilized society, restrictions must necessarily be placed on individual freedoms that trespass on the liberty of others. However, this would not appear to clearly be applicable to suicide, and even the law declines to impede the individual from harming him- or herself.

A number of sources have actually addressed the relationship between autonomy and suicide. For example, the *Encyclopedia of Social Work* states that "practitioners usually see individuals who are experiencing temporary impulses to kill themselves. These impulses occur in response to a loss, to interpersonal conflict, and to other distressing life events, or they may be secondary symptoms of depression or psychosis. Few people who have these impulses appear to be free or autonomous" (*Encyclopedia*, 1987, p. 744). Beauchamp and Childress appear to agree with this position by stating that "many persons who commit suicide are either mentally ill, clinically depressed or destabilized by a crisis and are therefore not acting autonomously" (Beauchamp & Childress, 1994, p. 386).

In another discussion of the subject, Beauchamp and Childress ask, "Do individuals have a moral right to decide about the acceptability of suicide and to act unimpeded on their convictions? If suicide is a protected moral right, then the state and other individuals such as health professionals have no legitimate grounds for intervention in autonomous suicide attempts" (Beauchamp & Childress, 1994, p. 386).

Further support for the decision not to intervene is provided by John Stuart Mill: "Intervention is justified to ascertain or establish the quality of autonomy in the person; further intervention is unjustified once it is determined that the person's actions are substantially autonomous" (Mill, 1977, p. 76).

Professional values, as addressed in the Code of Ethics, stress the social worker's primary responsibility to clients. However, in the case of a client who expresses an autonomous desire to kill him- or herself, it's unclear whether the obligation is to support the exercise of autonomy, or to prevent harm to the individual. Because both the obligation to self-determination and to the prevention of harm are given similar weight in the Code of Ethics (both are in the same subsection, 1.02), and "harm" is not clearly defined, absolutist and relativist positions would lead the worker to different courses of action.

It is obvious that this problem is not unique to the worker—it has been addressed by many in different times and circumstances. Attempts to work through the issues seem to lead to conclusions that are useful but do not address the specific problem. As my clients have mental problems, does this limit their autonomy? Where does it place my responsibility? How should "harm" be defined?

There is a professional obligation, clearly, to the primacy of client interests, as supported by Section 1 of the Code of Ethics. Prominent in this section is the client's right to self-determination; however, this may be limited in cases of imminent, foreseeable harm. If one expands the concept of "harm" from the physical to the mental, and includes quality-of-life issues as well, however, the perception of what constitutes "harm" may change markedly. In one case, it would seem, the worker focused on the physical harm that suicide would engender—the harm of death. In the other, the worker gave stronger weight to considerations of quality-of-life issues within the definition of "harm"—including mental harms, which, to the worker, seemed to override the physical ones.

The worker has a professional obligation, as noted in Section 4 of the Code of Ethics, to prevent discrimination: "Social workers should not practice, condone, facilitate, or collaborate with any form of discrimination on the basis of race, ethnicity, national origin, color, age, religion, sex, sexual orientation, marital status, political belief, or mental or physical disability" (4.02). Mental disability was an issue in both of these cases. However, the worker's perception of the mental disability of the first client was that of a transient disability, amenable to treatment. The client could be expected to return to a good quality of life with professional intervention.

Perception of the mental disability of the second client, however, led the worker to believe that this was extreme, unresolvable, and thus precluded any possibility of a

(continued)

CASE STUDY 4.1   CONTINUED

quality of life that would be acceptable to the client. Discrimination in the case of the middle-aged client can be based on her mental disability, which, in the worker's perception, would render impossible a reasonable quality of life and thus is included in the worker's definition of "harm."

AUTHOR'S REFLECTIONS, REASONING PROCESS, AND RESOLUTION
This dilemma is clearly embedded in society, and societal values must play a role in influencing the positions of each individual involved. "Society" values human life, yet it allows for the death penalty, abortion, and war, and societal values are often fraught with contradiction and conflict. It values life, liberty, and equal opportunity to pursue wealth, power, education, and happiness. Because there are so many contradictions in societal values, it is difficult to obtain clear direction from them, and the worker finds that she must rely strongly on her own values as well.

The lack of clarity about what constitutes "harm" in the Code of Ethics may be a reflection of the lack of clarity in the perception of "harm" in the wider society. Thus, it would seem, the worker's personal values became more central to her decision making. This course of action, however, led to actions that can be interpreted as discrimination. Discrimination in the case of the young man might be evidenced in the restriction placed on his self-determination by the worker's decision to confine him to prevent physical injury. Discrimination in the case of the middle-aged woman might be evidenced by the worker's evaluation of quality-of-life potential with severe mental illness.

While seeking to avoid discrimination and to arrive at a position of consistency in regard to suicide threats, the worker, on reflection, determines that the appropriate course of action is to evaluate each case on an individual basis, thus taking a relativist position. The concept of free will, and free choice, is a valuable one and applies to the worker as well as to the clients.

However, the ethics of the profession with which the worker has chosen to identify may limit the complete exercise of free will in deciding on actions in individual cases. While the author thinks that intuition is a valuable tool in making professionally sound decisions, there is still the necessity of supporting the intuition with rational arguments and processes in order to provide some structure. It would seem that, while it is important to retain the ability to tailor decisions and actions to the specific needs of each individual circumstance, it might be possible to develop a *procedure* that would be universally applicable and would provide a structure for thought. Procedural justice would uphold the strong social work commitment to social justice.

In conclusion, this writer believes that it is important to professional functioning, and to both professional and personal values, that each case, each situation, be evaluated and treated as unique. Careful use of intuition as a tool to guide the worker in assessments can assist in this process.

However, in order to provide some of the consistency that may be necessary for professional functioning and minimize any possible discrimination, the author believes that workers need to develop a structure and a procedure that will ensure adequate evaluation and reasoning and impartial assessments, while maximizing client autonomy and permitting individual treatment.

QUESTIONS FOR THOUGHT AND DISCUSSION

1. One consideration, possibly useful in evaluating client autonomy, is the theory of first and second order autonomy, as explained by Dr. Eric Cassell. A client makes an autonomous choice: in the case of Clients A and B, of coming to the agency for assistance. This "first order" autonomous choice may limit future autonomy in various ways: agency policy and worker values and position, for example, may impact client autonomy. However, within these limits, the client continues to maintain second order autonomy: He or she may choose to confide suicidal thoughts in the worker or not to confide them. If he or she chooses to confide in the worker, as both of these clients have done, future autonomy is further restricted by potential intervention, for which the authority has been given to the agency and worker by the client's original autonomous choice of seeking help. Using this line of reasoning, how might you address Client A? Client B?

2. To whom should an individual desiring to commit suicide have to justify his or her position?

3. If you feel that there are times when suicide is justifiable, such as intractable pain or terminal coma, would you include mental pain and suffering as well as physical pain and suffering as justifiable reasons for committing suicide?

4. In support of client autonomy, what is your position on assisting or supporting a suicidal client? In your professional capacity as advocate and enabler, should you also assist the client to commit suicide? What role do your own personal values play in this decision?

5. Do you see a difference between "suicide" and "euthanasia"? What is it?

CASE STUDY 4.2

"NOW THAT YOU'RE LEAVING, WHY CAN'T WE JUST BE FRIENDS?"

Abstracted from an unpublished paper by Joanna P. Martin, MSW

PRACTICE CONTEXT AND CASE PRESENTATION

A community-based agency provides case management services to disabled persons in order to reduce the risk of premature institutionalization, maximize client self-sufficiency, and/or reduce the risk of client self-neglect. The service is free of charge to county residents, and referrals can be made by any concerned individual including the client.

The client, Ms. K., was having difficulty in independent living as a result of her disability. She had limited financial resources and had encountered a series of lifelong losses and thus had no informal support system. She describes difficulty with "rude" caseworkers in the past, who had time limitations and overwhelming caseloads, "tossing (her) around" from one worker to another. She felt at a breaking point.

The client–worker relationship developed rapidly, with trust and cooperation in setting and successfully implementing goals. When, at the end of the internship, it became necessary for the worker to transfer her case, the client verbalized fear, stress, and a deep sense of abandonment. She asked to continue the relationship, saying, "Why can't we be friends?" and insisting that she "couldn't survive" without the worker.

The worker felt bound to the primacy of her client's needs and interests, but also to a professional obligation to the Code of Ethics, which clearly proscribed such relationships. Should her obligations to the Code of Ethics be considered before her obligation to the client?

The dilemma she faced can be stated as:

Primacy of Client Needs v. Obligation to Code of Ethics

RESEARCH AND RELATED LITERATURE

The Primacy of Client Need

Definition of Client Need. Some authors have argued that "the presenting problem," or the need presented at the onset, is merely a fraction of the client's overall needs (Biestek, 1957). This implies that although the objectives in the initial contract have been met, other needs can emerge in the interim, creating more work for the professional as well as for the client. Primacy of client need might suggest that the obligation of the worker may extend beyond the fulfillment of initial goals.

The Program/Agency, Its Policy and Focus. According to agency policy, although mental health and emotional needs are addressed in the client's care plan, it is not the social worker's overall responsibility to work on such needs: The social worker's responsibility is to conduct an assessment of long-term care needs and to develop an appropriate care plan for the client (Maryland Department of Human Resources, 1993).

Should there be a need for ongoing counseling or psychotherapy, the worker should refer the client to an appropriate resource and assist with access, if necessary (Maryland Department of Human Resources, 1993).

Theoretical Considerations. An ethics of care seems appropriate in considering Mrs. K.'s needs. "Caring" can be defined as having an emotional commitment to, or a willingness to act on behalf of, another person with whom one has a significant relationship. Proponents of this theory argue that the moral relationship one develops has to do with feeling for, and immersing oneself in, another human being. The moral response one must give when working with vulnerable, dependent, and ill persons, such as Ms. K., should be attached to the client's need(s). The worker should develop an insight into and understanding of the client's individual circumstance, needs, and, of course, feelings when arriving at an ethical decision (Beauchamp & Childress, 1994).

Obligations to the Code of Ethics
Professional Obligations. While the profession's core value of <u>service</u>, to uphold providing what the client self-determines, places an important obligation on the worker, so also does the core value of the dignity and worth of the person, which might be compromised if the worker accedes to the client's request and engages in a dual relationship. The core value of <u>integrity</u> also places on the worker awareness of the profession's ethical principles and standards and expects the worker to practice in a manner that is consistent with them. While this is no longer "practice" in the formal, direct sense, a relationship initiated in the professional context is held to standards of professional ethics both during and after the formal service to the client.

The obligation to refrain from dual relationships is clearly stated in subsection 1.06c of the Code of Ethics: "Social workers should not engage in dual or multiple relationships with clients or former clients in which there is a risk of exploitation or potential harm to the client. . . . (Dual or multiple relationships occur . . . simultaneously or consecutively.)" This is reinforced in subsection 4.01c, which states, "Social workers should base practice on . . . knowledge . . . relevant to social work and social work ethics."

Empirical knowledge suggests the existence of the potential for harm and exploitation of clients in dual relationships. The Code of Ethics proscribes such relationships under those conditions.

Agency Policy. Agency policy provides little guidance regarding whether one should or should not engage in dual, nonsexual relationships with clients. However, a supervisor at the agency stated that these types of relationships are considered unprofessional because they are, in the long run, (1) damaging, or potentially harmful, to the professional and (2) damaging to the client, and it's strongly recommended that boundaries be drawn between workers as professionals and individuals as clients.

In a national study of social workers, psychologists, and psychiatrists, only a small percentage of those surveyed felt that nonsexual relationships outside of professional boundaries with clients are never ethical (Borys & Pope, 1989). Unfortunately, little research has been done pertaining to the ethics of nonsexual relationships among

(*continued*)

CASE STUDY 4.2   CONTINUED

social workers and clients (Kagle & Giebelhausen, 1994). The literature suggests that when it comes to nonsexual relationships with clients, workers are guided primarily by their own values and judgments of what professionals should and should not do.

Theoretical Considerations. A consequentialist would look at the consequences of actions (Reamer, 1990) and could argue that Ms. K. might eventually become exploited if the worker and client were to form a "friendly, nonsexual" relationship (Kagle & Giebelhausen, 1994); this can be due to the distinctively different roles a professional and a "friend" play. Deontologists, such as Kant, might also object, for the exploitation potential would suggest that clients could be treated as a means, rather than with the respect and dignity to which all human beings were entitled. Additionally, a professional relationship is a fiduciary one, while a friendship is not (Kagle & Giebelhausen, 1994; Kutchins, 1991). Thus, stepping outside the boundaries of the professional relationship can ultimately have negative consequences for the client.

AUTHOR'S REFLECTIONS, REASONING PROCESS, AND RESOLUTION
Two ethical principles against which to judge possible solutions are nonmaleficence and beneficence, the provision of benefits or "all forms of action done for the benefit of others" (Beauchamp & Childress, 1994, p. 260). Both relate primarily to the worker's obligation to the client's well-being; for example, many authors argue that it is potentially harmful for the client when the worker and client engage in dual relationships (Kagle & Giebelhausen, 1994). Engaging in such acts could inflict harm. It may be difficult for even the most well-intentioned worker to consider all of the possibilities for harm to the client that could result from changes in the relationship. Would the shift from professional to friend benefit Ms. K.? Would it help or hinder her? One must also weigh the possible goods of such an act against the possible harms when determining its beneficent qualities.

While the Code of ethics supports client self-determination and leaves to the social worker's discretion whether there is "risk" of potential exploitation and harm, adherence to the Code generally proscribes such dual relationships.

Ms. K. wants the social worker to treat her as an individual with individual needs, not as a typical "case." Though she verbalizes the desire to shift to a friendly relationship, an unequal balance would continue since Ms. K. views this as a way of meeting her own needs primarily, rather than mutual needs, which characterize a friendly relationship.

Using Gewirth's system of hierarchy, and applying it to social work, the worker should consider that

1. The client's right to well-being *takes precedence over* the client's right to freedom, independence, and individuality.
2. The client's right to freedom and independence *takes precedence over* the client's right to equality.
3. The client's right to equality *takes precedence over the* worker's right to self-determine. (Hepworth & Larsen, 1993; Reamer, 1990)

The worker personally values well-being, safety, physical and mental health, freedom and justice, individuality, self-determination, education, and work and sees these as important goals for her clients as well, recognizing that she and a client may define each of these differently.

A professional concern for ensuring that Mrs. K. optimizes her opportunities to attain these goals leads the worker to determine that they would best be served by remaining within the boundaries of the professional relationship. This recognizes client need, but seeks to meet it within the agency's professional services. Recognizing the potential negative effects of transfer and termination, the worker attempts to minimize these by structuring termination to include sharing the reasons for her decision with the client, providing ample opportunity for the client to work through her feelings of abandonment and loss with the worker, discussing the client's needs in person with the new worker, visiting the client with the new worker, and supporting the client's transition.

Recognizing that a social support system in the community is important to this client's well-being, the worker can suggest and encourage the exploration of community supports as a possible goal/focus for future social work intervention. In so doing, she facilitates meeting the expressed needs of her client through appropriate use of professional intervention.

QUESTIONS FOR THOUGHT AND DISCUSSION

1. Are there ever instances where a relationship with the client outside of professional boundaries may be justified? What might be a situation where there is no "risk of exploitation or potential harm" to the client? Do you think that it makes a difference if such a relationship is concurrent with the professional relationship or follows it?

2. In many communities, especially smaller ones, the worker may find her- or himself with a referral for service from a client who is known to the worker. In such circumstances, the worker may need to refer the client to another worker. How would you define the circumstances where such referrals are necessary? What about relatives (close?) (distant?), friends (close?) (distant?), members of your church, club, community group? Your children's friends? Parents of your children's friends? Relatives of co-workers? Friends of a family member, or of a close friend? And, of course, how would you define "close" or "distant"?

3. In some circumstances, it may not be possible to refer such clients elsewhere, due to distance, lack of available services or workers, and so on. If there is a clear need for service, is it preferable that this be unmet, or that you accept the client? If you do so, how might you design and structure your relationship to minimize the potential negative effects?

4. Though you may not be working with the person, you may find that someone you know well is a client of your agency. What are some of the ethical issues that you need to consider? How might you address them?

5. It is possible that you might begin to work with a client, then discover that there is involvement with someone that you know well, are related to, and so on. How might you address such a situation?

■ ■ ■ ■ ■ ▬▬▬▬▬▬▬▬▬▬▬▬▬▬▬▬▬▬▬▬▬▬▬▬▬▬▬▬▬▬▬▬▬▬▬▬

CASE STUDY 4.3

THE PROFESSIONAL IN PEER SUPPORT GROUPS: WHERE DO WE FIT IN?

Abstracted from an unpublished paper by Mickey J. W. Smith, MSW, CAC

PRACTICE CONTEXT AND CASE PRESENTATION

A large, nonprofit, community-based organization provides a wide variety of health-related services to the gay and lesbian and HIV-infected population. Community members, professionals, consumers, and volunteers use a variety of the services provided by the agency. This is the only agency in the area that provides substance abuse and mental health services to the gay and lesbian community.

Traditionally, the substance abuse social workers have themselves been prior substance abusers currently in recovery. They attend 12-step meetings of Alcoholics Anonymous (AA) or Narcotics Anonymous (NA) and may be in the same meetings as their clients, who have signed a treatment contract to attend at least five 12-step meetings a week.

Because of the small size of the gay and lesbian recovery community, clients and social workers attending the same groups may become involved in outside interactions or relationships. There is a potential for the formation of dual relationships, especially once a client is discharged from the program. This potential is heightened due to the size of the groups and the kinds of relationships that support recovery. However, the worker also has a personal obligation to self to attend meetings and participate in activities that maintain personal recovery in the most supportive environment.

It is essential for social workers involved in this program to consider the following ethical dilemma:

Obligation to Self v. Professional Obligation to Client

RESEARCH AND RELATED LITERATURE

According to the Code of Ethics of the National Association of Social Workers (NASW), a dual relationship occurs "when social workers relate to clients in more than one relationship whether professional, social, or business" (1996, pp. 9–10). The dual relationship can develop whether the nonprofessional relationship starts before, during, or after the social work relationship (Kagle & Giebelhausen, 1994). To date, the majority of the literature that discusses dual relationships focuses on sexual relations between practitioner and client, and very little is written about nonsexual dual relationships. In fact, Kagle and Giebelhausen (1994) indicate that only two professional associations recognize that nonsexual relationships pose risks to clients and call upon practitioners not to engage in such relationships with current or former clients. The NASW Code of Ethics states that social workers should not engage in dual relationships with clients or former clients if there is a "risk of exploitation or potential harm to the client. In instances when dual or multiple relationships are unavoidable, social workers should take steps to protect clients" from such exploitation or harm. The local Certification Board for Professional Alcohol and Drug Counselors (DCCB/PADC) also includes wording that promotes avoidance of dual relationships with clients (DCCB/PADC, 1995).

Most of what has been written about nonsexual dual relationships focuses on the negative components or problems within these relationships. When a professional engages in a nonprofessional relationship with a client, boundaries become blurred and distort the nature of the therapeutic relationship (Pope & Vasquez, 1991). Since the bond between the professional and client extends beyond termination, it has been theorized that such dual relationships are not ethical with former clients as well as current ones (Kagle & Giebelhausen, 1994). Additionally, it has been reported in two articles that ostensibly nonsexual dual relationships can also lead to sexual intimacy between practitioners and clients (Coleman & Schaefer, 1986; Pope & Bouhoutsos, 1986)

The practitioner's judgment may also become impaired, and boundary issues can occur. The need of each party to be regarded positively may affect the relationship between client and worker (Corey, Corey, & Callanan, 1993). Although the perception is that both parties are equal in power in a nonprofessional relationship, in fact the professional still maintains the power, albeit often unacknowledged, without the obligation of professional conduct (Kagle & Giebelhausen, 1994). It is theorized in these instances that the attention shifts from the client to the practitioner, creating the appearance of shared power (Brown, 1985). Studies have also shown that actual professional behavior is often more ethical than professionals might assume, as supported by Borys and Pope (1989), who study compared the two kinds of relationships across three professions (social work, psychology, and psychiatry). Of particular interest is the question of the professional's becoming friends with a client after termination: 14.8 percent of the respondents reported that they believed that such an action is never ethical, while 69 percent of the respondents reported never engaging in such behavior.

Social workers also express discomfort or dissatisfaction with the barriers that exist between them and their clients (Loewenberg & Dolgoff, 1996). Often the therapeutic setting constrains the relationship in ways that may not be the most beneficial for the client. An example presented by Loewenberg and Dolgoff (1996) is the problem of anomie where the client is not connected to other people or resources. In a therapeutic environment only the symptoms are treated, without any work taking place on the core support network problem. In order to "fix" this problem, the client must establish more meaningful relationships, and some argue that the social worker provides the model for this form of relationship. One way the professional can act as a model for such a client would be to establish a relationship with the client outside the office or therapeutic environment. The client may benefit from interacting in the "real world" with an individual, the professional, who can model a positive social relationship. In addition, some believe that counselors and clients can handle social relationships while maintaining a therapeutic relationships as long as priorities remain clear (Corey, Corey, & Callanan, 1993).

Herlihy and Corey (1992) suggest that dual relationships are inherent in the work of all helping professionals, regardless of client population or work setting. Peer counselors are examples of positive, beneficial dual relationships. In one study, previous

(continued)

clients (alumni) were used as peer counselors or co-leaders in the treatment of clients convicted of driving under the influence (DUI) (Dan, 1992). Clients interacted with nonprofessional group leaders outside the treatment milieu, thus experiencing a positive peer culture similar to 12-step programs where individuals interact and learn both inside the support group environment and in social settings. Such peer-led models provide role models for change and an informal process of relationship building (Dan, 1992; Hopson & Beaird-Spiller, 1995).

A few authors have indicated that the nature of the community in which a social worker lives and practices may lead the social worker to have additional roles with a client (Corey, Corey, & Callanan, 1993; Loewenberg & Dolgoff, 1996). Generally, these discussions have focused on rural areas or small cities that are quite isolated from larger urban centers, not on specific communities within urban settings or larger cities close to urban centers. However, communities within large urban areas can, and do, share conditions similar to rural or isolated locations. Often, gays and lesbians are mistrustful of traditional health and human service agencies due to past lack of sensitivity to their needs (Mongeon & Ziebold, 1982). This has influenced their perception of which AA or NA meetings are safe to attend or potentially most beneficial to them as individuals.

**AUTHOR'S REFLECTIONS, REASONING PROCESS,
AND RESOLUTION**

The societal value of individual freedom to make decisions in one's personal interest must be weighed against the value of the good of the many, or the majority. Both client and worker must consider a number of factors that impact their decision about dual relationships. The worker must also consider whether the potential harms of attending meetings with clients outweigh the potential benefits to both clients and worker.

Personal autonomy, or a client's right to self-determination, is one of the first ethical standards described in the NASW Code of Ethics. Section 1.02 (NASW, 1996) explicitly states that, "Social workers respect and promote the right of clients to self-determination" (p. 7). This first section of the Code of Ethics, which focuses on the social worker's ethical responsibilities to clients, coincides with the societal value of personal freedom to make choices. When applying this principle, the professional moves away from a paternalistic relationship to the client (Smith, 1995) and toward client autonomy and empowerment. Section 6.04(b) states that "[s]ocial workers should act to expand choice and opportunity for all people" (p. 27). Of special relevance is standard 4.03, which focuses on the professional's private conduct. Unlike the support given to client choices, it indicates that the private conduct of the social worker should not be permitted to interfere with professional responsibilities (NASW, 1996). However, many clients believe that maintaining a connection to the treatment professional is important or valuable, and professionals generally agree that strong support networks for clients after termination of treatment are important to ongoing success.

There are a number of values and ethical principles relevant to this ethical dilemma. Judeo-Christian values support the intrinsic worth of each person, and the importance of giving help if needed (Day, 1989). If the overall welfare of the client is the worker's foremost priority, respect for the client's decisions appears to be vital. If the client wishes to initiate a dual relationship, the worker can respect that decision within client self-determination. Providing help to those individuals who seek it, grounded in altruism, was one of the major elements in this writer's choice to enter the social work profession. This includes placing the needs of clients above personal needs or other professional responsibilities. Maintaining a relationship where the worker is a surrogate parent or a surrogate friend may be very beneficial to clients. However, it is recognized that these kinds of relationships may ultimately affect the professional relationship in a negative manner by blurring professional boundaries. It is also recognized that the worker receives a secondary gain from the relationships: the satisfaction of continuing to help a client progress and feeling that the progress is in some measure due to the worker's efforts.

Should the substance abuse staff member who is also in recovery and attending 12-step meetings be in the same meetings as current or past clients? Does the professional limit his or her involvement in these support groups, which are often viewed by the professional as being as important to his or her own recovery as they are to the client's treatment and recovery? Or does the social worker continue attending the same meetings while maintaining no interactions with clients in these settings? Can the professional maintain nonprofessional relationships with clients as long as the professional boundaries are respected in the treatment environment? To focus on a specific course of action, it is important to consider these options: If a client, current or former, is at a meeting the worker attends, should the worker leave, stay and not speak in the meeting, or stay and share in the group? It is assumed that these three choices—not attending, not participating, and participating fully—will impact the actions of clients in initiating, or not initiating, an interest in a continuing dual relationship with the social worker. These choices will also strongly impact the social worker's own efforts to remain in successful recovery.

If the professional adheres to the concept that dual relationships with clients must be avoided in such an instance, he or she can act in two ways. First, the worker may decide to attend 12-step meetings that clients are unlikely to attend, primarily those outside of the agency and the gay-lesbian community. In limiting shared meeting attendance, the professional maximizes the ethical principle that the social worker's private conduct should not interfere with his or her professional responsibilities. It would also preclude clients' learning about a worker's perceived failures or setbacks, which could affect their regard for the social worker's professional abilities. However, it also limits the worker's access to meetings in an atmosphere that he believes would be personally most beneficial.

The social worker may also choose to remain at the meeting, but not participate. The rationale for not participating is similar to that above, with some differences: Boundaries would be maintained, but the worker could still set a positive example by attendance at meetings, modeling behaviors that are required by clients in treatment and positively impacting the client's success with recovery. Clients will also see that attending meetings is important and valuable, regardless of length of abstinence or professional training. However, attending and not participating is much less beneficial to

(continued)

CASE STUDY 4.3   CONTINUED

the worker, who can only be personally involved in a passive manner and thus cannot receive the needed personal benefits of active involvement.

The third choice, attending and participating fully, maximizes the worker's own potential for remaining in recovery and fully partaking of the 12-step program. There may be times that revealing personal information may be uncomfortable for the worker with clients present, so that some limitations in participation may occasionally occur. The worker would model full participation and commitment for clients, and demonstrate the positive results of engagement in the 12-step program. If dual relationships develop, the worker could self-monitor and limit involvement, focusing only on relationships that are ultimately beneficial to clients from both the clients' and the worker's perspectives. The worker could be open with clients in presenting potential problems that must limit the extent and quality of dual relationships.

After considering each of these alternatives, this worker has chosen to fully participate in the 12-step program and to maintain supportive relationships with clients outside of the boundaries of the professional relationship. Two rationales justify the decision to maintain such contact with former clients: First, as an individual in recovery, the worker has developed a clear understanding that addiction is treated most effectively in groups and with the help of other recovering addicts. This is achieved both through formal meetings and through interacting in real-world settings with other clean and sober individuals; one gains personal strength in recovery through assisting other people. The primary commitment when working with addicts and alcoholics is the recovery process, both personal and professional. In addition, this worker is indebted to the 12-step programs for the recovery which has resulted in his ability to enter an MSW program. This decision is also grounded in the cardinal professional the value of service to others, based on the larger Judeo-Christian value of helping those in need.

However, this process of self-examination has led the worker to understand that social interactions with former clients may not be the most professionally appropriate actions to pursue because (1) such interactions provide a level of gratification beyond that coming from professional duties while still attending AA or NA; (2) such relationships may impede the process through which the client terminates from the treatment program while still attending AA or NA; and (3) such interactions can be, and are, witnessed by other people in the community and may be perceived to be something that they are not.

Dual relationships can provide a false sense that treatment is still being provided and undermine the efforts of staff to develop and implement a discharge plan for a client. Enabling clients to remain in a dependent relationship limits their ability to move on in their lives. There is also a recognized personal gratification in knowing that the work done with clients is still wanted or needed as well as a sense of power and control that inhibits clients from developing their own support network. Since the gay and lesbian recovery community is so close-knit, there is cause for concern regarding the perceptions within that community.

While the worker believes the advantages to the client outweigh these disadvantages, there is a sincere recognition that these must be carefully considered in each case and a thoughtful, conscious decision made that ultimately places the good of the client in the primary position, as required by the Code of Ethics and the worker's personal value system.

QUESTIONS FOR THOUGHT AND DISCUSSION

1. The author has two personal gain considerations: maximizing his own recovery, and the gratification he receives from his work with clients and from feeling needed. Should these be considered equally in making the decision about dual relationships?

2. All social work professionals gain a sense of personal satisfaction in helping others. Sometimes, the need for personal satisfaction can impede professional judgment about the best interests of clients. Yet, in many ways this is a common human need. Should social workers always subsume their need for personal satisfaction to client need? How does one do that?

3. How can social workers become aware of their own needs for satisfaction, power, control, and client appreciation? How can you raise your own personal awareness of these issues?

4. Traditionally, certain helping contexts have relied heavily on peer involvement. This creates a supportive atmosphere that benefits both the helper and the helpee. However, when the helper becomes a professional social worker, additional concerns must be addressed. How do you feel professional education, or professional status, should impact upon the peer structure of self-help groups?

5. What is the role of a trained professional in a self-help group?

■ ■ ■ ■ ■ ▬▬▬▬▬▬▬▬▬▬▬▬▬▬▬▬▬▬▬▬▬▬▬▬▬

CASE STUDY 4.4

FIDELITY TO A CLIENT UNABLE TO COMMUNICATE

Abstracted from an unpublished paper by Marian D. Kaufman, MSW

PRACTICE CONTEXT AND CASE PRESENTATION

Mr. and Mrs. Smith have been married for sixty years. They are in their mid-eighties. In the past five years, Mr. Smith has suffered a series of strokes, leaving him unable to ambulate or to speak clearly. Two months ago, another stroke left him semicomatose. He was placed in a nursing home but, after three weeks, was admitted to the hospital with pneumonia and bed sores. Mrs. Smith feels that these are the result of poor care in the nursing home. Mrs. Smith is legally blind and walks with the aid of a cane. She is mentally acute, handles all the finances, and makes all the decisions for Mr. Smith. She has decided to take Mr. Smith home.

Social work intervention was requested by the physician, who feels that Mr. Smith's quality of care will be severely compromised. He is also concerned that Mrs. Smith may become ill or seriously injure herself trying to care for Mr. Smith. He would like Mr. Smith returned to the long-term care facility to ensure his safety, his quality of care, and Mrs. Smith's well-being. He feels that Mrs. Smith has made a poor decision.

Mrs. Smith is adamant about her decision. She tells the social worker that if Mr. Smith returns to the convalescent center, it will break his heart, and he will die. He has told her repeatedly that he does not ever wish be in a long-term care facility, and she considers that she is obligated by his statement. She also feels that the quality of care at the facility is poor, and that she could not further subject him to this. She states that two neighbors, who have been very devoted, will assist her caring for Mr. Smith. She feels that remaining together is vital to the well-being of both Mr. Smith and herself.

It is clear to the worker that Mrs. Smith has the right to make decisions on her husband's behalf. She is mentally competent and has been responsible for him since his stroke. Thus, "patient rights" devolve to her, as his representative. She is exercising these "rights" as surrogate decision maker by expressing her intention to take her husband home with her. However, the worker's primary obligation, to Mr. Smith as her client, suggests that she assess his needs separately from Mrs. Smith's understanding of them.

The social worker is caught in an ethical dilemma that places her obligation to support client self-determination, through the surrogate decision maker, against her obligation to safeguard the client's health and safety, which may be seriously compromised should Mr. Smith return home with Mrs. Smith.

The worker must consider two competing claims:

Self-Determination v. Health and Safety

These must be placed in the context of the worker's professional obligations, the recognized knowledge base, and the Code of Ethics.

RESEARCH AND RELATED LITERATURE

Much has been written on the issue of long-term care versus independent living for the elderly. Thompson et al. (1993) assess the amount of social support the caregiver needs as she or he assists an elderly family member. Social workers have an important role in educating and counseling families before such decisions are made, as well as in continuing to assist families at home as new needs arise. Often, the social worker is the only professional that is involved with the family from the beginning to the end of treatment (Nicholson & Matross, 1989).

The subject of safety has a central place in the literature. In 1985, there were 6.2 to 6.5 million older persons with one or more dependencies in activities of daily living. By the year 2020, this population will increase to 14.4 million, 4.2 million of whom will need nursing home care (Council on Scientific Affairs, AMA, 1993). During the next twenty to fifty years, the problem of how to care for frail elderly will become a major social issue.

Ranson (1990) notes that in 1984 the World Health Organization stated accident injuries ranked fifth among the leading causes of death, and, in the elderly, the rate is often higher for accidents than for infectious diseases. It has been proven that the effects of accidents in the home greatly increase the likelihood of invalidity, extended periods of medical care, and even death. Over half of all at-home accidents occur to persons over 75 years of age and have proven to have serious consequences (Ranson, 1990).

The use of home safety measures has not proven to be particularly successful in reducing the number of in-home accidents. Families often wait until after an accident to install them. Among households where smoke alarms, medic alert bracelets, and "panic buttons" exist, noncompliance is a problem (Devor et al., 1994).

At present, nursing facilities are only caring for 5 percent of the frail elderly population. Family caregivers are responsible for the vast majority of home healthcare (Council on Scientific Affairs, AMA, 1993). The demographic trend over the last generation has been for families to become geographically separated, usually due to career demands. The responsibility for at-home care often falls on elderly relatives, many of whom have health issues of their own.

Recently, much attention has been given to the rights of the elderly in terms of autonomy and self-determination. Nicholson and Matross (1989) note that the foundational values of freedom and independence are supported by the President's Commission for the Study of Ethics, Problems in Medicine, and Behavioral Research (1983), which defends a competent person's right to make decisions regarding medical procedures and overall treatment.

In cases where a client lacks decisional capacity, one of two standards of judgment is generally used. The first, substituted judgment, asked that the surrogate decision maker make the choice that the client would have made, has she or he been able (Wicclair, 1993, p. 53). Substituted judgments require that the decision maker know the client sufficiently well to be able to determine with some degree of certainty the action she or he would have chosen and be able to lay aside any personal interest in a specific course of action. Generally, family members or close friends fill this function (Wicclair, 1993, pp. 54–55). The second standard of judgment, best interest, considers harms and benefits and asks that the decision selected maximize benefits and minimize harms,

(continued)

CASE STUDY 4.4   CONTINUED

from the point of view of the decision maker. The person filling this function is presumed to be a reasonable person acting within what she or he believe to be the best interests of the client (Wicclair, 1993, pp. 58–59). Typically, then, social workers' decisions tend to be made from a best interest judgment perspective. The two decision-making processes can easily lead to potentially different courses of action.

Recent research emphasizes the relationship between a sense of control over one's life and positive outcomes in aging (Kapp, 1989). Though professionals in the field have a tendency to say, "If this patient is refusing the recommended discharge plan, it proves that the patient is incompetent," patients have the right to refuse care plans and also to make risky decisions (Dubler, 1988). Bart Collopy (1988) examines six case studies and describes the loss of freedom and dignity people experience in nursing homes.

The mission of the profession, as stated in the Preamble of the Code of Ethics, includes a commitment to (1) service, which the worker is attempting to provide; (2) social justice, which might support both the right to safety and the right to self-determination; (3) the dignity and worth of the person, also supportable through both sides of the ethical dilemma; (4) the importance of human relationships, which seems to obligate the worker to support of the marital bond; and (5) integrity and competence, both of which suggest that the worker has an obligation to act in a manner consistent with both the value and knowledge base of the profession.

The worker's obligation to the client is specified in Section 1 of the Ethical Standards of the profession. This stipulates that the worker hold as a primary responsibility the "well-being of clients" (1.01) and supports self-determination, except where there is a "serious, forseeable, and imminent risk to themselves or others" (1.02). Both of these obligations may be interpreted in a manner that could support either side of the dilemma—well-being will be affected by the worker's definition. Does it include physical well-being only, or also mental and emotional well-being? "Serious, forseeable, imminent risk" is also open to interpretation. Is it possible to clearly predict the kind of "risk" that says that harm *could* occur if the client returns home? While such harm can be "forseeable," many factors can impact on the degree of risk.

The worker also has the obligation to interdisciplinary collaboration defined in Section 2.03. The physician, as head of the multidisciplinary team working with the client, has taken a position in support of client safety and has asked that the social worker implement this. Collaboration would lead the worker to support his determination, although she may disagree. In the event of such disagreement, the Code states that the worker "[s]hould attempt to resolve the disagreement through appropriate channels. If the disagreement cannot be resolved, social workers should pursue other avenues to address their concerns consistent with client well-being" (2.03b).

Section 3.08, which addresses commitments to employers in the practice setting, is also applicable to the dilemma, since the structure of the practice setting establishes clear guidelines that seem to place determination of action on behalf of patients in the hands of physicians. Social workers who operate in a host setting, such as a hospital, accept this structure as part of their commitment to the agency.

Included in this section is the obligation to adhere to commitments to employers and also to ensure that employers are aware of the social workers' ethical obligations to the NASW Code and its practice implications. It also states:

> Social workers should not allow an employing organization's policies, procedures, regulations, or administrative orders to interfere with their ethical practice of social work. Social workers should take reasonable steps to ensure that their employing organizations' practices are consistent with the *NASW Code of Ethics.* (3.09d)

Further, subsection 4.01c asks that social workers "base [their] practice on recognized knowledge, including empirically based knowledge, relevant to social work and social work ethics."

AUTHOR'S REFLECTIONS, REASONING PROCESS, AND RESOLUTION

Our society values the dignity and worth of the individual, thus respecting each person's right to make decisions on his or her own behalf. Our society also values the maintenance of the family as a unit whenever possible. However, another strong American value is safety. We tend to think that everyone has a "right" to safety. When the two rights, freedom and safety, conflict, difficult problems can ensue.

It is difficult to assess Mr. Smith's values due to his inability to communicate. However, Mrs. Smith has stated that she believes it would "break his heart and probably kill him" to become institutionalized. She has promised him that this will never happen to him. She feels a duty to fidelity and to the honoring of her promises.

The social worker strongly supports the value of family integrity and feels that the efforts of an elderly couple to remain together should be supported wherever possible. Freedom is also an important value, and the worker might tend to be biased against persons or institutions that might tend to remove freedom from any person.

An ethically absolutist position could support either side of the dilemma. It is possible to reason that safety and health must come before other considerations, as a primary condition of life and quality of life. It is also possible to argue, with Kant, that a person's right to self-determination is unconditional (Loewenberg & Dolgoff, 1992). This is in accord with the strong support for self-determination in the Code of Ethics. W. D. Ross, a deontologist, would support Mrs. Smith's position based on the moral duty to fidelity (Frankena, 1973). Her obligation is to honor her promise. Normative relativism might argue that what is good for one individual might not be good for another. Therefore, each situation must be considered individually.

The Code of Ethics advocates the social worker's primary responsibility to the well-being of the client. While "well-being" is not defined, social work's core values would seem to include mental and emotional, as well as physical, well-being within this obligation. While empirical data support the incidence of harm and accidents in the elderly populations, especially the at-risk population, literature also supports the position that self-determination, and a sense of control over one's life, has a strong impact on the desired possibility of positive outcomes for the elderly. Thus, the commitment to use empirically based knowledge supports both sides of the dilemma.

(continued)

CASE STUDY 4.4   CONTINUED

A consideration of social work ethics, however, tends to support a position that would enhance self-determination as a foundational part of "well-being." A commitment to respect the primacy of a client's interests through self-determination, and to respect the client's own definition of "well-being," would support an ethical obligation to base practice on this as well.

In attempting to resolve this dilemma, the worker chooses to examine both of the original options. Additionally, a third option is considered: placement in an assisted living complex. This would allow the couple to remain together and retain some of the "comforts of home." While some self-determination might be sacrificed with this option, the increased margin of physical safety would seem to justify this position, combining both sides of the dilemma in a compromise that maximizes the benefits of both positions.

The third alternative would necessitate the sale of the Smith's home, an action to which Mrs. Smith might object. However, because this position maximizes both safety and self-determination, the worker feels comfortable suggesting and advocating for the third option. Should Mrs. Smith refuse, other potential options might include providing caregivers in the Smith home.

QUESTIONS FOR THOUGHT AND DISCUSSION

1. If Mrs. Smith decides to take Mr. Smith home, and the physician refuses to authorize the discharge, what role should the social worker assume? Is her primary obligation to the client's self-determination, to her employing agency, to the client's safety, or to the physician as head of the multidisciplinary team? What are the ethical implications for the worker if she is forced to make one of these choices?

2. Do you think that Mrs. Smith's autonomy rights, coupled with her personal values, could alone be sufficient justification for the support of planning discharge to home?

3. If the social worker chooses to advocate for Mr. and Mrs. Smith, and to support their discharge to their home, do you think that she is morally responsible if injury or harm is sustained by either of them?

4. In a multidisciplinary setting, such as this one, the social worker often does not have the ultimate authority to make decisions. If there is a disagreement between the position of the social worker and the head of the multidisciplinary team, what do you feel should be the role of the social worker? How would you implement "pursuing other avenues to address [their] concerns" (NASW, 2.03b)?

5. If Mrs. Smith is offered the "third alternative," refuses to consider it, and insists on taking Mr. Smith home, what then is the worker's responsibility? Do you think it is different in this circumstance than in question 2?

REFERENCES AND BIBLIOGRAPHY

Case Study 4.1

Beauchamp, T. L., & Childress, J. F. (1994). *Principles of biomedical ethics*. New York: Oxford University Press.

Brock, D. (1989). *Medical ethics: Death and dying*. Boston: Jones and Bartlett Pub.

Chase, R. N. (1986). Criminal liability for assisting suicide. *Columbia Law Review, 86,* 348–362.

Encyclopedia of Social Work. (1987). 18th ed., Vol. 2. Silver Spring: NASW.

Hamel, R. P. (Ed.). (1991). *Choosing death: Active euthanasia, religion, and the public debate*. Philadelphia: Trinity Press International.

Mill, J. S. (1977). *On liberty: Collected works of John Stuart Mill* (Vol. 18). Toronto: University of Toronto Press.

National Association of Social Workers. (1996). *NASW Code of Ethics*. Washington, DC: Author.

Ostrom, C. M. (1993, August 29). Law about helping suicide not explicit. *The Seattle Times,* p. A14.

Case Study 4.2

Beauchamp, T. L., & Childress, J. F. (1994). *Principles of biomedical ethics*. New York: Oxford University Press.

Biestek, F. (1957). *The casework relationship*. Chicago: Loyola University Press.

Borys, D., & Pope, K. (1989). Dual relationships between therapist and client: A national study of psychologists, psychiatrists, and social workers. *Professional Psychology: Research and Practice, 20*(5), 283–293.

Hepworth, D. H., & Larsen, J. A. (1993). *Direct social work practice: Theory and skills* (4th ed.). Pacific Grove, CA: Brooks/Cole.

Kagle, J. D., & Giebelhausen, P. N. (1994). Dual relationships and professional boundaries. *Social Work, 39*(2), 213–220.

Kutchins, H. (1991). The fiduciary relationship: The legal basis for social workers' responsibilities to clients. *Social Work, 36*(2), 106–113.

Maryland Department of Human Resources, Social Services Administration, Social Services to Adults, Code of Maryland Regulations (1993).

National Association of Social Workers. (1996). *NASW Code of Ethics*. Washington, DC: Author.

Reamer, F. G. (1987). Values and ethics. In A. Minahan et al. (Eds.), *Encyclopedia of social work* (18th ed., Vol. 2, pp. 801–809). Silver Spring, MD: NASW.

Reamer, F. G. (1990). *Ethical dilemmas in social service* (2nd ed.). New York: Columbia University Press.

Case Study 4.3

Beauchamp, T. L., & Childress, J. F. (1994). *Principles of biomedical ethics* (4th ed.). New York: Oxford University Press.

Borys, D. S., & Pope, K. S. (1989). Dual relationships between therapist and client: A national study of psychologists, psychiatrists, and social workers. *Professional Psychology: Research and Practice, 20*(5), 283–293.

Brown, L. (1985). Power, responsibility, boundaries: Ethical concerns for the lesbian feminist therapist. *Lesbian Ethics, 1*(3), 30–45.

Coleman, F., & Schaefer, S. (1986). Boundaries of sex and intimacy between client and counselor. *Journal of Counseling and Development, 64,* 341–344.

Corey, G., Corey, M. S., & Callanan, P. (1993). *Issues and ethics in the helping professions* (4th ed.). Pacific Grove, CA: Brooks/Cole.

Dan, D. (1992). The use of "alumni" in treatment of driving under the influence (DUI). *Alcoholism Treatment Quarterly, 9*(1), 77–83.

Day, P. J. (1989). *A new history of social welfare.* Englewood Cliffs, NJ: Prentice-Hall.

District of Columbia Certification Board for Professional Alcohol and Drug Counselors (DCCB/PADC). (1995). *Ethical standards for counselors.* Washington, DC: Author.

Herlihy, B., & Corey, G. (1992). *Dual relationships in counseling.* Alexandria, VA: American Association for Counseling and Development.

Hopson, R. E., & Beaird-Spiller, B. (1995). Why AA works: A psychological analysis of the addictive experience and the efficacy of alcoholics anonymous. *Alcoholism Treatment Quarterly, 12*(3), 1–17.

Kagle, J. D., & Giebelhausen, P. N. (1994). Dual relationships and professional boundaries. *Social Work, 39*(2), 213–220.

Loewenberg, F. M., & Dolgoff, R. (1996). *Ethical decisions for social work practice* (5th ed.). Itasca, IL: F. E. Peacock.

Mongeon, J. E., & Ziebold, T. O. (1982). Preventing alcohol abuse in the gay community: Toward a theory and model. *Journal of Homosexuality, 7*(4), 89–99.

National Association of Social Workers. (1996). *NASW Code of Ethics.* Washington, DC: Author.

Pope, K. S., & Bouhoutsos, J. (1986). *Sexual intimacy between therapists and patients.* New York: Praeger.

Pope, K. S., & Vasquez, M. T. (1991). *Ethics in psychotherapy and counseling.* San Francisco: Jossey-Bass.

Smith, M. W. (1995). Ethics in focus groups: A few concerns. *Qualitative Health Research, 5*(4), 478–496.

Whitman-Walker Clinic, Inc. (n.d.). *Volunteer resource manual.* Washington, DC: Author.

Case Study 4.4

Abramson, J. S. (1990). Enhancing patient participation: Clinical strategies in the discharge planning process. *Social Work in Health Care, 14*(4), 53–69.

Aneshensel, C. S., Pearlin, L. I., & Schuler, R. H. (1993). Stress, role captivity, and the cessation of caregiving. *Journal of Health and Social Behavior, 34*(1), 54–70.

Collopy, B. J. (1988). Autonomy in long-term care: Some crucial distinctions. *The Gerontologist, 28*(Supp. 1), 10–17.

Council on Scientific Affairs, American Medical Association. (1993). Physicians and family caregivers. *Journal of the American Medical Association, 26*(10), 1282–1284.

Devor, M., Wang, A., Renvall, M., Feigal, D., & Ransdell, J. (1994). Compliance with social and safety recommendations in an outpatient comprehensive geriatric assessment program. *Journal of Gerontology, 49*(4), M168–M172.

Dubler, N. N. (1988). Improving the discharge planning process: Distinguishing between coercion and choice. *The Gerontologist, 28,* 76–81.

Frankena, W. (1973). *Ethics* (pp. 26, 109). Englewood Cliffs, NJ: Prentice-Hall.

Hardwig, J. (1990). What about the family? *Hastings Center Report, 2*(2), 5–10.

Kapp, M. B. (1988). Forcing services on at-risk adults: When doing good is not so good. *Social Work in Health Care, 13*(4), 1–13.

Kapp, M. B. (1989). Medical empowerment of the elderly. *Hastings Center Report, 19*(4), 5–7.

Loewenberg, F. M., & Dolgoff, R. (1992). *Ethical decisions for social work practice* (pp. 42–44, 96). Itasca, IL: F. E. Peacock.

McCullough, L. B. (1985). Long-term care for the elderly: An ethical analysis. *Social Thought, 11*(2), 40–52.

National Association of Social Workers. (1996). *NASW Code of Ethics.* Washington, DC: Author.

Nelson, J. L. (1992). Taking families seriously. *Hastings Center Report, 22*(4), 6–12.

Nicholson, B. L., & Matross, G. N. (1989). Facing reduced decision-making capacity in health care: Methods for maintaining client self-determination. *Social Work, 34*(3), 234–238.

Ranson, R. (1990). Home safety: The challenge to public health. *Journal of Sociology and Social Welfare, 17*(1), 93–113.

Thompson, E. H., Futterman, A. M., Gallagher-Thompson, D., Rose, J. M., & Lovett, S. B. (1993). Social support and caregiving burden in family caregivers of frail elders. *Journal of Gerontology, 48*(5), S245–S254.

Wicclair, M. R. (1993). *Ethics and the elderly.* New York: Oxford University Press.

CHAPTER FIVE

NASW ETHICAL STANDARD FIVE

Social Workers' Ethical Responsibilities to the Social Work Profession

INTRODUCTION

Provisions of Code

In making a commitment to the field of social work, workers also take on a commitment to the profession of which they are a part. Social workers, both individually and collectively, represent the profession, and the commitment to professional values and behavior and to a solid base of knowledge is vital. The two subsections in this section address the profession's integrity, evaluation, and research.

Subsection 5.01 addresses the integrity of the profession as a whole. It advocates the maintenance and promotion of high standards of practice on the part of all members (5.01a). Social workers are also obligated to support the values, ethics, knowledge base, and mission of the profession through research, discussion, and responsible criticism (5.01b).

Time and expertise should be contributed to support and enhance the profession, such as teaching, research, consultation, legislative testimony, community presentations, and membership in professional organizations (5.01c). The next subsection encourages the contribution to the knowledge base of the profession specifically, and the sharing of knowledge with colleagues via literature, presentations, and conference participation (5.01d).

Subsection 5.01d addresses what may be, at times, a touchy situation—the obligation to prevent the unauthorized and unqualified practice of social work. Workers have advocated, and succeeded in having passed, licensure laws in every state, with specific qualifications, criteria, and levels of licensure. Social work agencies have, on the whole, respected such licensure. However, workers in host settings may find themselves confronted with unqualified and unauthorized (and unlicensed) "social workers" whose credentials do not include formal social work education. This may create problems for the worker on both a personal and institutional level as he or she seeks to rectify this misuse of professional titles. However, there is a strong obligation to work toward the maintenance of high professional quality of service, which involves reserving the title "social worker" for members of the profession alone.

Subsection 5.02 addresses evaluation and research, asking that workers monitor and evaluate policies, programs, and practice interventions (5.02a), facilitate evaluation and research (5.02b), and critically use the results of such evaluation and research in practice, keeping current with new developments in the field (5.02c).

In terms of research in social work, workers must consider consequences of such research and follow guidelines that protect participants (5.02d). These might include voluntary, written, full-informed consent for all participants (5.02e) or proxies if necessary (5.02f), informing participants of their rights to withdraw or refuse (5.02h), providing access to supportive services (5.02i), the protection from harm (5.02j), assurance of anonymity and confidentiality (5.02l), protection of identifying information unless proper consent has been obtained (5.02m), and the avoidance of dual or multiple relationships or conflicts of interest (5.02o).

Social workers should not design or conduct research or evaluation that does not utilize informed consent procedures (5.02g), should discuss collected information only with professionals or with persons professionally concerned (5.02k), should report findings accurately, and should educate themselves and others about proper research practices (5.02p).

The Cases

The first case presented in this section places the worker's professional integrity, her responsibility to the value base of the profession, and her obligation to utilize her knowledge and skill against the rights of clients to self-determine. In an adoption agency, the worker is presented with parents who desire immediate placement for their 3-month-old baby girl. They are clearly in crisis, are anxious, and under a great deal of stress. They are unaware of, and uninterested in, any resources or information available to assist them in caring for their child or in making any decisions for her welfare. They adamantly refuse any agency service other than immediate placement.

The worker is concerned that they are making a momentous decision without reflective thought and adequate information, both of which services she is professionally able and obligated to provide. Can she require that the parents accept counseling as a condition of placing their child for adoption when they clearly do not want this service? How can she meet her obligation to them, as well as to the profession?

In the second case, the worker in a rape crisis center is faced with difficult immediate decisions. Clients in crisis call for help and ask the worker to decide for them whether their rape should be reported to the police. The worker has no in-person contact with them, and her relationship is based only on the present telephone call. She has little information regarding the individual client's values, vulnerabilities, strengths, and weaknesses.

The professional values of justice, honesty, integrity, concern for the welfare of society and others suggest that the worker has an obligation to encourage the client to report the rape. The worker's agency, whose mission is to address issues of violence against women, encourages reporting.

However, statistics and studies about reporting rape force the worker to consider other issues as well. Very few reported cases reach the courts, and, of these, only a small fraction result in conviction. The process of reporting and prosecution is humiliating, embarrassing, and often painful for the victim. Is it justified to add to the victim's stress and vulnerability by encouraging reporting, when the chances of success in prosecution are so small? Is the worker not obligated, instead, to the protection of her vulnerable client and, therefore, to suggesting that the client not report?

In the third case, a young, pregnant, substance-abusing mother, sent to a substance-abuse treatment program by the court, is noncompliant. She also refuses prenatal care, for fear that the physician will condemn her substance abuse.

The worker's dilemma is painful: Should she support her client's right not to seek prenatal care? Should she protect the safety of the unborn fetus, who might be considered part of a "vulnerable population"? This mother is not seeking an abortion; she plans to have the child. However, she is placing the child at risk both through her substance abuse and through her refusal of prenatal care. The interests of society would seem to support the birth of healthy babies. The court system is not aware of this client's problem. Should the worker turn to the court for help?

The fourth case presents a conflict for the worker trying to support the values, ethics, and knowledge base of the profession. A medical social worker has a patient with terminal cancer, and patient and family want to continue treatment at the hospital. The physician feels that treatment is futile, and that the patient should be referred to hospice care, so that hospital resources could be utilized more appropriately. The patient and family associate hospice with death and refuse to consider this option.

The worker's primary obligation to her client, and that client's right to self-determination, would lead her to assist her client to remain in the hospital and to receive the care that she is requesting. However, she is working in a host setting: She also has an obligation to respect the expertise of other professionals and to follow written orders that are supported by hospital policy. She has a broader obligation to the optimal utilization of resources.

Although there is a case in this collection that addresses research issues, which are a primary focus in this section of the Code of Ethics, the particular dilemma, and the manner in which it is phrased, seems to place it, rather, in Section 6. Section 5 will be utilized primarily in the exploration of professional obligations. However, the interested reader is referred to "Case Study 6.5: Genetic Research: For the Good of This Subject or for (Future) Society?" (pp. 222–230).

CASE STUDY 5.1

"MY CLIENTS ARE IN A HURRY!": PROFESSIONAL INTEGRITY VERSUS CLIENT SELF-DETERMINATION

Abstracted from an unpublished paper by Shereen Rubenstein, MSW

PRACTICE CONTEXT AND CASE PRESENTATION

A private, nonprofit agency serves children in need of adoption services and their biological and adoptive parents. Located in a large urban center, the agency serves "hard-to-place" as well as "normal" children and has developed an excellent reputation for careful and thoughtful placement planning.

Mr. and Mrs. Smith desire to plan for adoption for their 3-month-old baby girl, Rachel. She has been diagnosed with cerebral palsy, possible blindness, and possible mild mental disability. The Smiths also have a 2-year-old son, whom they describe as "perfect."

The Smiths request immediate placement. They state that they have been considering adoption since the "nightmare" began at Rachel's birth, and they feel they can no longer continue to care for her. They express concern about their future responsibilities in raising a disabled child—"changing her diaper at 10 years of age and still at 21," "routinely massaging her gums," "gliding a tube down her throat for feeding while having (their) morning coffee," and so on. They have waited these three months to ascertain that there was no error in diagnosis, but now they have been assured that Rachel's condition is permanent, and they wish to proceed immediately. They have adequate financial resources to provide for Rachel, but they do not wish to be responsible for the cost of raising a disabled child. They expressly state that they do not wish to become involved in receiving any counseling from the agency: Placement services were all that was required.

In assessing the Smith's request, the worker feels that the Smiths are currently deep in crisis, mourning the loss of their "perfect" family, and unable to cope with the thought of a disabled child. They express a sense of failure and guilt, as well as confusion. Also, in attempting to assess whether the Smiths have explored other avenues, she determines that they are unaware of the resources and support services available to assist parents of disabled children.

It seems unwise to the worker for the Smiths to make a hasty decision without knowledge and reflection and without any counseling. Thus, the worker determines that it is not in their best interests to proceed without utilizing the professional skills available to them to ensure the best decision for their future. Placing Rachel without these services would violate the worker's professional integrity, her obligation to serve her clients with skill and competence, and the standards of the profession: "The professional social worker has the knowledge and skill necessary to assure a positive outcome and is, therefore, responsible for making the decision that will secure the optimum

(continued)

CASE STUDY 5.1   CONTINUED

benefit for the client" (Loewenberg & Dolgoff, 1992). Yet the clients are requesting placement immediately. The worker finds herself facing the dilemma of:

Client Self-Determination v. Professional Integrity

RESEARCH AND RELATED LITERATURE

A study conducted in the intensive care unit with parents of neonatal/ill infants found common manifestations of extreme emotional stress (Dillard, Auerbach, & Showalter, 1980). In addition to displaying signs of depression, loss of appetite, and high anxiety, many were struggling with a great amount of guilt. Forty percent felt that they were responsible for their baby's illness. Yet, of the more than 250,000 children born each year with a mental or physical handicap, the vast majority of parents do choose to parent them (Springen & Kantrowitz, 1990).

Feelings of guilt, failure, and helplessness are common among parents who have made an adoption plan for their disabled infants. They may feel they are incapable of creating, or raising, a healthy baby. Financial stress and feeling emotionally "wiped out" are two common emotions, but parents also fear making an error by "giving away" a child who is not really disabled. Adoption experts seek to help these parents view their decision as one made out of love. They can be told that being honest and loving the child enough to know that others can give their baby what they fear they cannot is a good decision, and this thought can aid the grief process. A period of grief often occurs post placement. Practitioners feel that the adoptive home is the better home for the child, because adoptive parents do truly desire the child (Springen & Kantrowitz, 1990).

A strong support network may be critical in making such decisions. In the 1970s, Cassel, Cobb, and Kaplan conducted separate studies that all indicated a strong social support network can greatly help someone who is experiencing a crisis (Mor-Barak, 1988). The Smiths' network, except for Mrs. Smith's father, all support the adoption plan for Rachel.

The Smiths support their arguments with deontological reasoning. They feel that adoption for Rachel is in the baby's best interest: that another family would better be able to love her, support her, and care for her. A deontologist such as Kant would find this reasoning morally and ethically acceptable, for "to have moral worth, a person's motive for acting must come from a recognition that he or she intends what is morally required" (Beauchamp & Childress, 1994).

Rights-based theory, such as liberal individualism, also supports the Smiths' decision, because "to have a right is to be in the position to determine, by one's choices, what others are to do or need to do"(Beauchamp & Childress, 1994). The Smiths' right to choose also gives them the right to expect that the adoption agency will implement their choice.

However, the worker's ethical code suggests other obligations and responsibilities. The social worker has an ethical responsibility to support the integrity of the profession, as stated in Section 5 of the Code, which obligates workers to maintain a high standard of practice (5.01a) and to "uphold and advance the values, ethics, knowledge, and mission of the profession" (5.01b). These support the worker's application of knowledge, skill, and competence to the client's problem. This would seem to preclude her acceptance of the Smith's requests without provision of services to ensure that they are making the best possible decision for their family.

The worker recognizes that the Smiths are in crisis, based on their behavior and levels of stress and anxiety. A loss of something or someone close is oftentimes a precipitating event that causes a crisis for a person (Gilliland & James, 1993). The loss of the normal, healthy child that the Smiths expected represented such a precipitating event for them. Other common manifestations of persons in crisis include feelings of guilt, depression, lowered self-esteem, anxiety, lack of appetite, and difficulty sleeping. The ability to rationalize, think logically, and make decisions may be impaired (Dixon, 1979). In speaking with the Smiths, the worker has become aware that most of these characteristics apply to them.

The Smiths also appear to lack information regarding resources to assist them with Rachel, and providing such information to them could be considered an extension of subsections 6.04a and b, which state that workers should act to ensure that all persons have access to the resources they need, as well as to expand the choices for all individuals. Early intervention services for the Smiths might include family training, counseling, home visits, case management, assessments, and respite care (Bishop, Rounds, & Weil, 1993).

A deontological approach to the dilemma suggests that it is important to properly assess a case and to offer the best possible services. Kant's argument that "morality is grounded in pure reason, not in tradition, intuition, conscience, emotion, or attitude such as sympathy" (Beauchamp & Childress, 1994) directs the worker to thoughtfully consider the issues involved prior to acting upon the Smiths' request.

AUTHOR'S REFLECTIONS, REASONING PROCESS, AND RESOLUTION

The Smiths appear to be receiving contradictory messages from society. On the one hand, society asks that parents shield and protect their children from danger and harm. On the other, it sends clear messages that healthy, cute little babies are desirable. On the one hand, parents who adopt disabled children are praised; on the other, discrimination against people with disabilities is rampant. The Smiths, and the worker herself, are caught in these contradictions.

In order to safeguard Rachel's interest, and enable the Smiths to make a reflective decision unencumbered with her care, the worker determines that Rachel may be placed in a foster home temporarily. While this would mean an adjustment for the baby, the worker feels that the removal of Rachel from their care would allow the Smiths the time and the distance they need to consider all of the possibilities open to them. As a condition of accepting Rachel into care, the worker would ask the Smiths to come in for counseling and provide them with the information they need to make an informed decision. This would maximize their self-determination, relieve the pressure for immediate adoption placement, and enable the worker to provide the needed services to the family.

If, after counseling and the provision of information, the Smiths continue to desire adoption for Rachel, the worker would accept her for placement.

(continued)

CASE STUDY 5.1   CONTINUED

Postscript. Before presenting the above plan to the family at their next appointment, the worker received a call from the Smiths. Unable to keep Rachel a moment longer, they have placed her for immediate adoption with another agency, who was willing to accept her without providing services to the family.

QUESTIONS FOR THOUGHT AND DISCUSSION

1. Unfortunately, the worker knows that placing Rachel in an adoptive home may not be as simple as the Smiths want to believe. Rachel may, indeed, remain in foster care for an extended period of time before a home is found for her. Should this fact influence her planning for the family?

2. The agency can provide a service that the Smiths desire: adoption. Is it ethical for the agency to require that, in order to obtain the desired service, clients be forced to accept services they explicitly do not want, which do not preclude providing the requested services?

3. If the determination of the "primary client" is not a part of agency policy, whose interests should this worker hold as primary? The Smiths, since they initiated contact with the agency? Rachel's, as she is unable to advocate for herself and is in need of the agency's service? Or the family as a whole, including the Smith's 2-year-old son? How might this lead to different courses of action for the worker?

4. The worker has determined that Rachel's best interest is her primary obligation. What, then, could be viewed as her ethical responsibility to the child from the moment that the Smiths request placement for her?

5. The Smiths are not responsible for Rachel's medical problems. They are, however, well able to provide for Rachel financially. Along with surrendering her for adoption, they are asking "society" to assume the financial burden of her care. Do you think they are justified in expecting society to pick up the tab?

■ ■ ■ ■ ■

CASE STUDY 5.2

RAPE: WHEN PROFESSIONAL VALUES PLACE VULNERABLE CLIENTS AT RISK

Abstracted from an unpublished paper by Eileen A. Dombo, MSW

PRACTICE CONTEXT AND CASE PRESENTATION

An urban rape crisis center is a private, community-based organization dedicated to ending all forms of violence against women through counseling and advocacy services to sexual assault survivors, through community education, coalition work with other local and national community organizations, legislative monitoring, and advocacy on relevant issues. The center maintains a 24-hour hotline staffed by social workers. Advocacy services include assistance in reporting to the police and/or pursuance of legal action and a companion program where workers accompany clients to hospitals, police encounters, and court appointments.

Hotline callers, like other survivors of sexual assault, often feel a loss of power or an ability to be assertive. Some clients decide that it would be empowering to report the rape to the police and/or take some legal action against the perpetrator. Others do not wish to pursue this course of action. Still others are uncertain of what course of action to pursue and ask the hotline worker's advice.

As a social work professional, the worker is strongly committed to the ethical principle of social justice, which is a core value and a mission of the profession, as stated in the Preamble of the NASW Code of Ethics. Thus, it would appear the worker's obligation is to encourage the caller to report the incident. This would raise public awareness and support accurate statistics. The perpetrator could be caught, face charges, and go to jail, thus protecting other women.

However, experience in the companion program has also enabled the worker to have an understanding of the difficulties victims encounter in the process of reporting. This process can be traumatic for many rape survivors who are not prepared for the insensitive and harsh treatment many receive from the police, hospitals, and legal system. Providing full and honest information about the process can dissuade a victim from reporting. Hotline workers who face this question during a single telephone contact know very little about the caller and are often uncertain of whether strong encouragement to report is in the best interest of the victim.

The dilemma can be stated as:

Professional Commitment to Justice v. Obligation to Client's Best Interest

RESEARCH AND RELATED LITERATURE

Estrich (1987) states that rape is the most underreported crime in our society. She states that underreporting affects how society perceives the crime; people assume that rape does not happen that often because of the low statistics. Estrich's findings support the

(continued)

CASE STUDY 5.2   CONTINUED

decision to urge the caller to report because it will raise awareness and statistics. The more survivors report, the more attention the issue of rape will get from the police, the courts, and society.

Koss (1985) found that only 10 to 50 percent of rapes are reported to the police. In an effort to increase reporting, Adams and Abarbanel (1988), workers at a rape treatment center in California, wrote a manual for colleges and universities to help them handle the issue of sexual assault. In the manual, they encourage administrators to adopt policies that encourage victim reporting of sexual assaults. They assert that reporting will help prevent assaults from happening to others and facilitate the provision of services to survivors. Clearly, the information presented by Estrich, Koss, and Adams and Abarbanel show the need for survivors to report rape because it will increase the awareness of the crime. The police department's Sex Offenses Branch stated that they would encourage all victims of rape to report immediately because this allows more evidence to be collected and increases the chances of successful prosecution.

However, 98 percent of the survivors who do press charges will never see their attacker caught, tried, and imprisoned; over one-half of the cases brought to prosecution will be dismissed; and one-half of convicted rapists serve less than one year in prison (Senate Judiciary Committee, 1993).

When a survivor decides to report, the police are contacted, and the survivor is taken to the hospital and given an examination, which includes an evidence collection procedure that is very detailed and sometimes painful. Interaction with the police and hospital staff can be traumatic: She must often wait for the police to respond to her call, then wait again in the hospital emergency room because her situation is not deemed to be a priority unless she is critically injured. Often, officers and hospital staff are not trained to deal with survivors of sexual assault, and frequently their own personal biases about rape and rape victims are revealed through their contact with the survivor.

After hospital procedures are completed, the survivor must fill out a report and may be taken back to the scene of the crime. A police investigation will follow and, depending on the amount of evidence the police are able to collect, there will either be an arrest or the case will be referred to the United States or the respective State's Attorney's Office for further investigation. If it is then determined that there is enough evidence to pursue, the survivor may have to appear in court and testify. In court, she is often made to answer questions that suggest she is to blame for the rape. This is also quite traumatic (Rape Crisis Center, 1995).

Estrich (1987) notes that many reported rape cases do not go much further than the police report due to lack of evidence. She states that, in many cases, authorities do not see the case as fitting the definition of rape and that they are "not treated as criminal by the criminal justice system" (Estrich, 1987, p.8). Bachman (1993) found that women did not report their rape because they felt it was too personal or they feared they would not be believed. Koss (1985) found that some victims are in such denial about the rape that they cannot bring themselves to report or feel they will not be believed. Professionals at the center agree in perceiving that reporting is often traumatic for the survivor and that the perpetrator is rarely brought to justice.

AUTHOR'S REFLECTIONS, REASONING PROCESS, AND RESOLUTION
Until someone is found guilty by a court of law, they are only the "alleged rapist." The burden of proof is on the victim. Since she must prove that the man accused of raping her actually did so, in effect, she is the one to be put on trial. Our society also values independence and individual privacy. "Proving" rape generally involves a loss of privacy: One's sexual history, and the experience itself, must be revealed in court, often an extremely traumatic experience for the victim.

The Code of Ethics provides guidance in resolving this dilemma. Section 1.01 addresses commitment to clients' well-being as a *primary* responsibility. The very next sentence in that section, however, suggests that the worker's responsibility to society may, at times, supersede this commitment. Section 1.03a explicates the obligation to informed consent. Section 1.06a addresses conflicts of interest. Is an obligation on the part of the worker to both social justice *and* best interest of client such a conflict? If so, should the worker inform the client of this conflict? Section 5.01b states the professional obligation to advance the mission, values, and ethics of the profession. This would seem to support the social justice side at least as strongly as the client's best interests side of the dilemma. Section 4.04 asks workers to be truthful with clients. Being truthful supports giving complete information about the problems and difficulties that the survivor may experience if she elects to report. It is often difficult to assess client values based on a crisis telephone call, and the worker may not be able to utilize such a call as a resource in decision making.

The worker values autonomy and independence and believes that empowerment can be a positive tool. Justice is power: Thus, reporting can be very empowering. However, the worker's experience has demonstrated to her that the criminal justice system is not sensitive to the needs of rape victims and that the likelihood of actually bringing the rapist to justice is slim. Thus, concern for the protection of the client from the sometimes harsh and insensitive process, combined with the small likelihood of success, leads the worker to believe that the risks associated with reporting may not be worthwhile if the client is herself reluctant to initiate the process.

Ultimately, however, this worker believes that it is her obligation to provide full and complete information to clients who ask about reporting and, indeed, to all clients. Such information supports and enhances empowerment for all clients, for it enables each to make the decision about reporting in accordance with her own values and understanding of herself. Where a client asks the worker's advice, provision of information can be supplemented with an exploration of client values and beliefs, thus ensuring that the decision made is truly that of the client's.

While social justice would support reporting rapes, it is not legally mandated that the social worker herself engage in such reporting. Social justice, in the sense of reporting crimes, can only be demanded by the survivor. Providing full information enables the survivor to be treated with consideration, respect, and justice.

QUESTIONS FOR THOUGHT AND DISCUSSION

1. In addition to providing information about reporting and the social justice issues involved to survivors of rape, does a social worker have any other social justice obligations here?

2. If you were in the position of the worker who wrote this paper, what would *you* do? How would you justify your actions? In your work, do you feel that it is more important to consider the individual or to support the best interests of society as a whole?

3. If you were providing information about issues related to filing suit and prosecution of perpetrators, would you provide this based on public literature, your own experiences with clients, your agency's experiences as a whole, or all of these? What do you think is "sufficient information"—enough to justify your having "informed" your client? Do you think it is ever possible to give clients *too much* information?

4. Rape crisis workers, like all crisis intervention workers, suffer from a high degree of burnout. How would you determine if this was affecting your response to the client who was asking advice about reporting? What symptoms would you look for in yourself and what would you do about them, if anything?

5. In this country, we believe a person accused of a crime to be innocent until proven guilty. Yet, in the case of rape, this often may mean that the victim is herself placed on trial, her privacy and freedom violated in order to "prove" guilt. What societal values support the "innocent until proven guilty" stance? What changes, if any, would you make in the current system to protect and assist the victim? How could these changes be justified in terms of societal values?

CASE STUDY 5.3

WHEN CLIENT SELF-DETERMINATION PLACES
AN UNBORN CHILD AT RISK

Abstracted from an unpublished paper by Patricia Y. Braun, MSW

PRACTICE CONTEXT AND CASE PRESENTATION

Mary is a young, pregnant client in a substance-abuse treatment center. Although she has been completely noncompliant with her program and has received warning letters, she cannot be terminated because of a county health regulation that stipulates pregnant women are health hazards and cannot be released into the general population. Mary was sentenced to six months incarceration for theft, but the sentence was suspended with the requirement that she comply with a substance-abuse treatment program. Mary refuses to get prenatal care until she is six months pregnant. She states that she is afraid the doctor will make her feel guilty for endangering her baby with her substance abuse.

The worker faces a painful dilemma:

Client Self-Determination v. Professional Obligation to Vulnerable Populations

(in the case the unborn child)

RESEARCH AND RELATED LITERATURE

Self-determination is a "condition in which personal behavior emanates from a person's own wishes, choices, and decisions. . . . It implies freedom from coercion and interference" (Abramson, 1985, p. 387). Individuals are entitled to make mistakes as well as to act wisely.

Prohibiting a pregnant woman from using drugs may infringe on the constitutional guarantee of liberty, privacy, and bodily integrity and the right of equal protection as well as the right to refuse health care. The Supreme Court decision of *Roe* v. *Wade* (1973) upholds a woman's right to personal privacy (Rosenberger & Goldstein, 1991). In the case of *Planned Parenthood of Southeastern Pennsylvania* v. *Casey* (1992), the Supreme Court held that "when the framers of the Constitution accorded basic human rights to 'persons' they did not intend to include fetuses. . . . and that the State can only intervene to protect fetuses and persons that fetuses become, so long as those actions do not infringe on the constitutional rights of the mother" (Andrews & Patterson, 1995, p. 59).

Most child abuse and neglect statutes exclude fetuses from their protection. Tracey (1994) maintains that even though the majority of states acknowledge that a large number of child maltreatment cases involve substance abuse once a child is born, the impact on parenting skills and specific consequences for the child cannot be documented effectively. Substance abuse per se is not evidence of child maltreatment. In Murphy and colleagues' (1991) study of research to date, they note that a number of studies fail to find a strong association between substance abuse and child mistreatment,

(continued)

CASE STUDY 5.3   CONTINUED

only that it plays a role in increased risk. In spite of their drug exposure, some children achieve age-appropriate social, emotional, and cognitive development (Davidson, 1991).

It can be argued that suggesting any criminal liability would discourage maternal/fetal bonding and work to undermine self-determination (Rosenberger & Goldstein, 1991). Mundahl and colleagues (1991) cite McGinley (1986) as saying "guilt, poor self-image, and lack of self-confidence in parenting often accompany a mother's substance abuse, adding to the risk of attachment difficulties" (p. 135). The bonding process is already fragile. Brazelton (1986) has said that if separated at birth, the mother could interpret the denial of contact as the lack of ability to care for her infant, which would erode attachment (Mundahl, VanDerWheele, Berger, & Fitzsimmons, 1991). Additionally, the removal of a newborn from the parents affects the parental right to care and custody of one's own child (Andrews & Patterson, 1995). The Adoption Assistance and Child Welfare Act of 1980—Public Law 96-272—states its goal as keeping the parents and child together whenever possible (Tracey, 1994).

If it is argued that Mary, due to her addiction, is not in the position to make reasonable choices, it is debatable whether it is just to punish someone for actions beyond their control (Duryea, Fontana, & Alfaro, 1978). The inability to be abstinent is the nature of addiction. Any potential abuse or neglect of a child is often related to personal problems and societal conditions beyond the control of parents, who often have inadequate resources to address their difficulties. But the self is never a fixed entity. Self-determination is an ongoing process where learning and growth contribute to better decision making. For this to happen, autonomy must take precedent.

The 1966 Supreme Court Gault decision recognized children as legal persons, saying "neither the Fourteenth Amendment nor the Bill of Rights is for adults alone" (Plum, 1991, p. 33). Plum maintains that "parental rights" should be relabeled "parental duty," and when a parent violates or fails to carry out their duty, the state must intervene.

In *Endresz* v. *Friedberg* (1969) the Supreme Court stated that every human being has the legal right "to begin life unimpaired by physical or mental defects resulting from the negligence of another" (Rosenberger & Goldstein, 1991, p. 340). In terms of whether the mother's privacy should be protected, Bailey, Hser, Hsieh, and Auglin (1994) write that the use of illicit drugs is not only not a fundamental right, but a crime. Johnson (1986) argues that the child's right to liberty from bodily restraints should be protected because its health depends largely on its mother's actions during pregnancy. Even *Roe* v. *Wade* stated that "the state does have an important and legitimate interest in preserving and protecting the potentiality of human life" (Rosenberger & Goldstein, 1991, p. 342). A mother has the same moral and legal obligations to care for her unborn child as she does after its birth.

The unborn have a right to develop in a healthy environment. Mundahl et al. cites many studies that show clear evidence that prenatal drug use is harmful to a fetus. Use may cause miscarriage or stillbirth. Rosenberger and Goldstein cite a 1990 study that found that, 50 percent of those born with cocaine exposure suffer strokes in the womb or during infancy (Rosenberger & Goldstein, 1991, p. 340). Infants may be premature;

have lower birth weights, motor difficulties, neurobehavioral problems, and difficult temperaments; and may fail to develop strong attachments to caregivers (Davidson, 1991). Toddlers have lower developmental scores, less representational play, and a tendency toward insecure attachment relationships. Older children may be hyperactive and have learning disabilities, attention deficits, and problems with short-term memory (Rodning, 1987).

Maternal drug use increases the likelihood of obstetrical and neonatal complications, resulting in mother/infant separation at birth. Disturbing the attachment process may result in personality problems, mood disorders, learning difficulties, and a higher risk of child abuse and neglect. Insecure or anxious attachment relationships have a lifelong impact on self-esteem and the ability to form relationships. A relapsed mother cannot provide the consistent warmth, availability, and affection that gives the child a sense of security.

The federal Child Maltreatment and Prevention Act of 1974 defines maltreatment as "where, through purposive acts or marked inattention to the child's basic needs, behavior of a parent/substitute or other adult caretaker caused foreseeable and avoidable injury or impairment to a child or materially contributed to unreasonable prolongation or worsening of an existing injury or impairment" (Ards & Harrell, 1989, p. 338). Drug use is evidence of parental inability to care for a child. "New York, California, Illinois, Florida, Minnesota, Utah, Indiana, Oklahoma, and Massachusetts have amended their child abuse statutes to require reports of suspected abuse or neglect to be made in cases of prenatal chemical exposure" (Gustavsson & Rycraft, 1993, p. 142). In New York, the Family Court Act has decided that if a person uses a drug that can result in unconsciousness, intoxication, hallucination, disorientation, or the impairment of judgment or execution of rationality, it "shall be prima facie evidence that a child who is the legal responsibility of such person is a neglected child" (Rosenberger & Goldstein, 1991, p. 343). In Illinois a mother was charged with manslaughter because of drug use during pregnancy, which resulted in the death of the infant (Mundahl et al., 1991).

Values found in the literature related to this issue include the right to self-determination, life, equal protection, privacy, health, bodily integrity, duty to care for one's children, and the importance of a close mother–child bond. In most cases, self-determination was an absolute value with the assumption being that every person has the ability to make free and rational choices and the ability to put those choices into effect. Barriers to reasoned decision making and the inability to act on those values was not recognized. The long-term consequences of making a poor choice and the extent and intensity of these consequences were not enough to override self-determination as a priority. The comparison of self-determination and the health of an unborn child is difficult. One can gather empirical evidence as to the consequences to the child, but it is difficult to quantitatively measure the effect of a temporary loss of freedom in a person's overall life.

The literature focuses on values as applicable to the individual—on protecting an individual against the state—and does not reflect the communal nature of our society. If the state took over the child rearing and fiscal responsibility for the child, no thought was given to the costs borne by that society or the welfare of the larger group.

(continued)

CASE STUDY 5.3   CONTINUED

The background of the authors affected their value positions. Lawyers were concerned with rights and protection thereof. Those advocating for children's rights (and all included fetuses as children) emphasized punitive measures for the mother rather than rehabilitation. Doctors focused on medical complications and the need for a healthy start in life for the fetus. What was medically preferable for the mother was not addressed. Social workers were concerned about attachment issues and family preservation. They saw the client system as much broader than the individual and focused on valuing the mother's motive and process of recovery rather than having a fixed rule of total abstinence as the desired outcome. They could be said to be ethical relativists, as they seemed to be more prepared to choose an option because it would lead to a desired result.

Gewirth would say that the greatest good is the balance between all affected parties. Principles to judge possible solutions include: (1) Every human being has the right to freedom and well-being; (2) one's basic rights can be said to be violated if one is deprived of life and health; (3) the individual's right to well-being takes precedence over another's freedom; (4) the individual's right to freedom takes precedence over his or her own well-being; (5) an individual's right to well-being may override laws and regulations; and (6) an individual has an obligation to prevent basic harm and promote the public good (Reamer, 1990). Loewenberg and Dolgoff (1992) would add the notion of the least harm or most easily reversible harm. Beauchamp and Childress (1994, p. 206) would consider whether there was the intention of inflicting harm. They would also say that there is a difference between a violation of a right, which is an unjustified action against a right, and an infringement of a right, which would be a justified action.

Two principles in the 1996 Revised Social Work Code of Ethics apply to this situation. In Ethical Responsibility to Clients, section 1.02 states that social workers will respect and promote the rights of clients to self-determination and assist clients in their efforts to identify and clarify their goals. Social workers may limit client's rights when actions are of an imminent risk to themselves or others. In this case the client has the right to choose to use drugs, but this right puts an unborn child's health at risk, which may jeopardize his or her opportunity to exercise the right of self-determination in the future. A second principle would be found in Social Work Ethical Responsibilities to the Broader Society. Section 6.01, on general welfare, states that social workers should promote the general welfare of society, from local to global levels, and the development of people and their communities. Social workers should advocate for living conditions conducive to the fulfillment of basic human needs and promote social, economic, political, and cultural institutions that are compatible with the realization of social justice.

These conflicting directions are particularly difficult for the worker in trying to meet her responsibility to the profession as a whole. Subsection 5.01a asks that social workers "work toward the maintenance and promotion of high standards of practice." Which course of action would best support these? Subsection 5.01b obligates workers to "uphold and advance the values, ethics, knowledge, and mission of the profession" and to "improve the integrity" of social work. How is that obligation best met in this case?

AUTHOR'S REFLECTIONS, REASONING PROCESS, AND RESOLUTION
It is to the benefit of society that its members be drug-free so that they can exercise their privileges and responsibilities as part of society. Living a life of addiction or in an environment of substance abuse does not promote the growth and well-being of people. To ameliorate this context of living is a worthy social work goal. Advocating for unborn children's rights would contribute to social justice. A tentative values hierarchy in which to work would be (1) respect for autonomy, (2) protection of life and well-being, (3) equality, (4) least or most easily reversible harm, and (5) privacy.

The worker's personal values include (1) self-determination, (2) respect, (3) self-actualization, (4) acceptance of difference, (5) equality, (6) empathy, (7) knowledge, (8) validation of others, (9) interpersonal relationships, and (10) transcendence.

Mary has exercised her right to self-determination by choosing a drug treatment program over a jail sentence, and within the program she chooses to continue to use drugs and attend sporadically. Mary's focus on herself is grounded in her constitutional rights. As a fetus is not fully recognized by law, issues of equality, denial of another's rights, or harm are not intervening considerations.

The worker has considered several options: (1) having Mary develop her own program of treatment at a level she felt she could commit to; (2) working with Mary's doctor to make prenatal visits less threatening, reducing her guilt and leading to more consistent care (the focus could shift from the fetus's health to Mary's health); (3) setting up a team consisting of Mary's probation officer, housing social worker, and substance abuse social worker, who would help her develop a recovery plan; (4) doing no more than is currently being done; (5) mandating that Mary enter an inpatient long-term treatment facility; (6) incarcerating Mary for noncompliance with substance-abuse program; (7) reporting Mary to Child Protective Services for neglect and having her parental rights terminated on the birth of the infant.

Mandating long-term inpatient treatment is this worker's option of choice. Mary is already part of the court system and is considered a public health risk. In recent weeks the local court system seems to be moving away from punitive measures to treatment. Mary has the disease of addiction, which is progressive and causes her to have little control over her behavior. Previous outpatient treatment attempts have failed to provide the stable environment for her recovery. Mary is in a chronic condition, with the disease life-threatening to both herself and the fetus if it is untreated. Dolgoff would concur that the protection of life, mother and fetus, must take priority over any issues of privacy, autonomy, or bodily integrity. Medical care is necessary because Mary cannot change through personal initiative. A successful outcome is more assured with an increased level of intervention.

Deontological theory would say that all individuals have the basic right to life and health and we are obligated to ensure this opportunity. The disease of addiction has handicapped Mary's free will, preventing her from making voluntary informed decisions. She cannot function autonomously in her present condition, and these basic rights are being violated. Thus, a temporary interference is justifiable until the condition of choice can be reestablished. It is not only the right thing to do for both individuals involved but also meets the standards of teleological theory's greatest good. Not only would this option provide Mary with the greatest chance of a stable recovery program,

(continued)

CASE STUDY 5.3   CONTINUED

it would protect the basic rights of life, health, and well-being of the fetus. Without treatment, both are at risk.

The ethics of care theory also applies, for the social worker is providing intellectual care in that she is knowledgeable about what Mary wants. Mary wants to be part of a treatment program whose goal is long-term recovery, instead of going to jail where the goal is forced temporary abstinence. She agrees with society's belief that abstinence is a good. Mary signed statements indicating she understood the rules and goals of the program and she developed and signed her individual treatment plan with her social worker. She was not angry or belligerent. She worried over the health of her fetus and did not want to harm it, but the disease has interfered in making positive healthcare decisions in its regard. Mary has communicated that she wants a home, a job, and to be reunited with her other children, all of which she would need a drug-free lifestyle to maintain. There was no client/worker value gap in this case. Mary has been autonomous but has been incompetent to carry out what she desires. Over time her deliberative capacity has diminished.

In this option, the values of self-determination for both mother and fetus are maximized, as well as life, equality, and least (or most easily reversible) harm. The worker's personal values of self-determination, respect, self-actualization, equality, empathy, knowledge, and relationships support this path. The Code of Ethics states that intervention is justified if it would help the client work toward her identified goal and would help limit those actions that are harmful to her. This option would also facilitate a drug-free lifestyle that is more conducive to getting her human needs met, as well as contributing to the good of the community.

QUESTIONS FOR THOUGHT AND DISCUSSION

1. The legal status of fetuses in this country is, at times, unclear, often leaving the social worker with little guidance. This tends to foster decision making based on personal values when the well-being of a fetus is at risk. Do you feel that you are professionally justified in intervening to protect the well-being of a fetus? Why or why not? Are the interests of society in the health of newborn infants a consideration for you? Are your religious or political beliefs?

2. Gewirth prioritizes individual rights by saying that a person's right to freedom takes precedence over his or her right to well-being—in other words, a competent individual may not be prevented from actions freely undertaken that harm him or her. (The order is reversed, however, if others may be harmed.) Do you agree? Under what circumstances, if any, do you feel that there is justification for limiting individual freedoms?

3. Do you believe that substance abuse *per se* is evidence of mental incompetence, which would then be used to justify the suspension of self-determination and freedom in favor of the imposition of "best interest" from another person, society, or yourself as its agent?

4. Fetuses can be harmed by means other than substance abuse, such as poor nutrition, inadequate medical care, reckless driving, smoking, refusal of routine prenatal vitamins, fatigue, excessive exercise, overwork, and so on. Do you believe that pregnant women should be monitored for the prevention of *all* possible harms to the unborn?

5. If a competent person chooses a lifestyle that places him or her at risk of illness or injury, and such illness or injury occurs, do you believe that the burden of cost and care should be placed on society? A specific example may help—an alcoholic has received a liver transplant and continues to abuse alcohol. Should he receive another? Consider that organs are often at a premium, and people can die waiting for them. Consider the cost of the care and surgery to all members of society.

■ ■ ■ ■ ■ ■

CASE STUDY 5.4

"DISCHARGE HER TO A HOSPICE *NOW!*"—A CONFLICT OF PROFESSIONAL LOYALTIES

Abstracted from an unpublished paper by Josephine K. Bulkley, J.D., MSW

PRACTICE CONTEXT AND CASE PRESENTATION

On an oncology service at a major university hospital, the worker has been assigned a terminal cancer patient—a mother of three young children, with a devoted and supportive husband and family. The physician has determined that further efforts are futile, thus making the patient's continued hospital stay an improper utilization of resources. He orders the social worker to refer the patient for hospice care.

Both patient and family associate hospice care with death. They do not accept the patient's poor prognosis and request continued care and treatment. The worker has attempted to present the hospice concept to the patient and family, and it has been adamantly refused. Rather, they are requesting continued hospital treatment and services.

Many patients receiving cancer treatment at this hospital are admitted to the oncology unit a number of times. Although some patients want hospice services, many do not and wish to receive all medical treatment, even palliative treatment not aimed at a cure, at the hospital. Some return to the hospital's outpatient clinic routinely for appointments with their primary attending physician, and they are admitted if a complication arises. Some patients choose to die in the hospital.

The central ethical dilemma involves a conflict between the social worker's ethical responsibility to abide by the policies, regulations, and recommendations of the employing organization (the hospital and medical staff) and her responsibility to advocate or protect the interest of the patient and family. The above case may be considered an example of conflicts in the duty of fidelity, "divided loyalties" (Reamer, 1990, p. 87; Beauchamp & Childress, 1994), or loyalties to multiple parties (Proctor, Morrow-Howell, & Lott, 1993). The practice situation noted above is described by Kugelman (1992) as follows:

> If a health care organization must depend for its existence on the rapid discharge of patients, and if for certain patients, such a rapid discharge does not serve their best interests, the social worker must make decisions regularly where no clear path toward the right action exists.

Loewenberg and Dolgoff (1992, p. 143) also state: "Organizational maintenance and survival demands may lead to rules which contradict the primary obligation of social workers to give priority to their client's interests."

The dilemma may be stated as:

Obligation to Client Advocacy v. Obligation to Employing Organization

RESEARCH AND RELATED LITERATURE

Obligation to Client Advocacy. In hospitals, the primary focus of most social work- ers' intervention is discharge planning and arranging adequate and appropriate care for patients after hospitalization (Proctor et al., 1993). A social worker who believes a par- ticular discharge plan is best for the client when the client wants something different is faced with a conflict between what he or she believes is in the client's best interest and fostering self-determination on the client's part. A study of ethical dilemmas experi- enced by sixteen hospital social workers revealed that the most common conflict in- volved the social worker's pursuit of the client's best interests and fostering the client's self-determination (Proctor et al., 1993). The study also found that this ethical conflict frequently arose where there was disagreement concerning discharge destination.

A fundamental ethical principle of social work practice (1.01(a), p. 7) is the so- cial worker's primary responsibility to the client (NASW, 1996). There is little doubt that a social worker should consider his or her client's interests as paramount. The obligation of fidelity is described by Beauchamp and Childress (1994, p. 430) as "Norms that specify . . . moral principles, . . . especially respect for autonomy, justice and utility. These principles justify the obligation to act in good faith to keep vows and promises, fulfill agreements, and maintain relationships and fiduciary responsibilities. In a hospital setting, social workers may have conflicts with medical staff because "a psychosocial understanding of client needs often leads social workers to disagree with physicians about treatment and discharge" (Proctor et al., 1993).

A client's right to self-determination is considered a fundamental precept of so- cial work and is a basic obligation of the worker. This obligation is accorded the utmost esteem by the profession (Rothman, 1989; Hepworth & Larsen, 1993). Biestek (1957) states:

> Today one of the firmest convictions of the profession of social work is that the person has an innate ability for self-determination and that a conscious, willful violation of the client's freedom by a caseworker is an unprofessional act which transgresses the client's natural right and impairs casework treatment or makes it impossible.

According to Abramson (1985, p. 387), self-determination "refers to that condi- tion in which personal behavior emanates from a person's own wishes, choices and de- cisions." The extent to which self-determination has priority over other values and principles "is a historical and continuing struggle" (Proctor et al., 1993). Moreover, Proctor et al. (1993, p. 171) note that self-determination "has been recognized as a pri- mary aspect of ethical issues arising in health care settings; patient bills of rights in many hospitals explicate the importance of self-determination."

The duty to promote a client's self-determination arises out of a basic moral prin- ciple regarding respect for autonomy. Autonomy may be defined as "a form of personal liberty of action where the individual determines his or her own course of action, in ac- cordance with a plan chosen by himself or herself" (Abramson, 1985). Beauchamp and Childress (1994) state autonomy "has acquired meanings as diverse as self-governance, liberty rights, privacy, individual choice, freedom of the will, causing one's own be- havior, and being one's own person." Drawing from the work of Alan Gewirth, Reamer

(continued)

CASE STUDY 5.4   CONTINUED

(1990) states that a basic ethical guideline in resolving a conflict between values or principles is that "An individual's right to freedom takes precedence over his or her own right to basic well-being." Thus, a social worker should respect an individual's right to choose to engage in self-destructive behavior, with two caveats. The client's decision must be voluntary and informed, and the consequences must not threaten the well-being of others (Reamer, 1990). According to Reamer (1990), as drawn from Gewirth, another person's well-being takes precedence over a person's right to freedom. Abramson (1981) notes:

> What of the patient's positive right to health care of which the medical aspect is only one component? What of the negative or autonomous right to be free of interference in the exercise of those rights? These rights are potentially violated every time a patient is discharged when medically ready, but is without emotional or social preparation, complete understanding of the reasoning behind the discharge, or informed consent to an aftercare situation that does not provide reasonable continuity of care.

Obligation to Employing Organization. Reamer (1990) states that "social workers are ordinarily obligated to abide by the rules and regulations of their employers." Levy (1976) further describes this obligation:

> The social worker owes specific ethical responsibilities to his employing agency. Foremost among these is the responsibility to act for, and represent the agency loyally and well—not without some thought to, and responsibility for, inequities and injustices that the agency may inflict on others, but unequivocally nonetheless—unless or until he severs his relationship with the agency.

This is not a matter of blind and rigid loyalty without regard for consequences, but a contracted obligation in the sense that if the social worker works for an agency, he or she works for and not against it. Second, the social worker does what the agency employs him or her to do in fulfilling the agency's declared purpose and service function, not something else.

A social worker who is employed by a hospital therefore has an ethical obligation to support the recommendations of the medical staff concerning patients. Under the current financial healthcare crisis, the hospital and medical staff have an economic interest in "efficient use of acute care beds for financial solvency" (Proctor et al., 1993), thereby encouraging rapid discharge of patients and avoidance of multiple or repeated hospitalizations.

A hospital's need to consider the most efficient use of scarce resources to ensure its survival (Kugelman, 1992, p. 65) is a legitimate interest on the part of doctors and hospitals, one justified by the principle in biomedical ethics called distributive justice (Beauchamp & Childress, 1994). Under utilitarian theory, which considers the greatest good for the greatest number to be its guiding principle, only the end or consequences are important, not the means. Stopping aggressive treatment with one patient is appropriate if more patients who have a greater chance of survival benefit.

Reamer (1990) raises the question of when a doctor should shift treating a dying patient aggressively to using less expensive efforts of making the patient comfortable and free of pain (suggested by a hospice approach) and divert such funds for the care of patients who have a greater chance of survival. A related concept is that of "medical utility," or allocation of scarce medical resources: ". . . it is morally imperative," according to Beauchamp and Childress, "to consider medical utility. . . . Differences in patients' needs and in their prospects for successful treatment are both relevant considerations" (1994, p. 382).

Moreover, Rothman (1989) discusses the issue of "external restrictions on choice," which he asserts competes with the primacy and efficacy of the principle of self-determination:

> The structure and nature of the service are often constrained by legal eligibility requirements—what clients may receive what services, the boundaries of practitioner activities, and requirements placed on clients by their situation or program. . . . Other contextual factors may cramp clients' wishes, such as their economic status . . . and family circumstances. . . . Analyses point out that ignoring reality encourages fantasy and may be self-defeating in the long run. . . . All practitioners are aware of agency boundaries as expressed in rules, standards and eligibility requirements, and types of services provided. Both clients and practitioners are subject to expectations and rules related to these structural conditions, with constraining consequences for the client's self-determination.

Rothman (1989) discusses the need to limit self-determination because of "competing professional considerations," especially relevant for hospital social workers. He states:

> Professional actions may be complicated and shaped by the ancillary position of human-service workers in institutions where they are in the minority and marginal to the predominant mission. Courts, hospitals, industrial settings, and penal institutions, for example, are ordinarily controlled by others who have goals variably compatible with those of human services. Consequently, the worker who "goes at the client's pace," and attempts to extend to the client the opportunity for self-determination, may be termed detrimentally "permissive" or "soft" by the other staff. The practitioner's difference in approach to clients/patients may make both sides feel that the worker is "out of step with the team."

Social workers in hospitals often make choices that support the hospital's or doctor's recommendations. Several studies illustrate this point. Kugelman (1992) conducted a qualitative study regarding twenty hospital social workers' responses to a fictional ethical dilemma involving obligation to a medical center versus an obligation to promote the patient's right to self-determination in refusing surgery for metastatic cancer. Half the participants were unable to maintain support for their client's wishes at the expense of the doctor's recommendations. Several workers noted issues concerning the doctor's or hospital's "power" in deciding to limit the extent of their advocacy role. Workers described fear of losing their jobs and feeling that it is the doctor's

(*continued*)

CASE STUDY 5.4   CONTINUED

decision, lack of respect for clients' rights, futility of supporting the patient, and need to persuade the client of the doctor's decision (Kugelman, 1992).

Walden, Wolock, and Demone (1990) also found that when presented with a vignette involving an elderly patient whose family wanted continued hospital care while the hospital was pressuring for discharge, most social workers did not choose the client-oriented response of advocating for the family. Interestingly, however, the study found that MSW students in hospital settings were more likely to advocate for the patient and less likely to demonstrate loyalty to the hospital or doctors.

The tendency of social workers in a hospital to support the hospital may be a reflection of their status in this host setting. There are significant pressures placed on social workers to rubber stamp or effectuate the recommendations of medical staff and a strong feeling of powerlessness to advocate a different position or one supporting the patient. One respondent in the Kugelman (1992) study stated: "I think what happens in the system is that people tend to say, this shouldn't be but I know it would be an exercise in futility." Another worker stated: "I tend to think that in hospitals when you [the social worker] start increasing, upping the ante, you usually lose" (p. 72).

AUTHOR'S REFLECTIONS, REASONING PROCESS, AND RESOLUTION

Ethical Theories.   Teleological or utilitarian theories justify the social worker's obligation to the hospital, professional colleagues, and society based on the need for rapid discharge, prevention of multiple hospitalizations, and the maximization of limited medical resources (Beauchamp & Childress, 1994; Reamer, 1990). These theories hold that certain actions are considered good because of their consequences in terms of promoting the "maximum good for everyone" and are less concerned about the individual (Loewenberg & Dolgoff, 1992). Moreover, utilitarian theories also justify persuading the client to accept hospice, as hospice would be likely to produce the best consequences or results for the patient and family. Thus, utilization of hospice care would benefit the patient and the patient's family, as well as the hospital, hospital staff, and other patients. According to Reamer (1990), most ethical decisions by social workers are based on utilitarian or teleological principles.

Deontological theories state that certain actions are intrinsically right. These would justify respect for patient autonomy and freedom, promoting self-determination, and accepting the client and her uniqueness and individuality. In addition, an "ethics of care" theory (Beauchamp & Childress, 1994) also justifies respect for the client's autonomy, and it values empathy, sympathy, and knowledge of the particular client's needs. According to Beauchamp and Childress (1994), ethics of care theory places

> emphasis on traits valued in intimate personal relationships, such as sympathy, compassion, fidelity, discernment, and love. Caring in these accounts refers to care for, emotional commitment to, and willingness to act on behalf of persons with whom one has a significant relationship. Noticeably downplayed are Kantian universal rules, impartial utilitarian principles, and individual rights. (p. 85)

The NASW Code of Ethics. In the Ethical Standards section of the Code of Ethics, more specific guidelines are provided for all social workers. Section 5 states that workers should maintain and promote high standards of practice and that they should uphold the "values, ethics, knowledge, and mission of the profession" (5.01a–b).

Relevant guidance is provided in several other sections as well. Section 1.01, the first ethical standard written into the Code, attests to the social worker's primary commitment to clients, and 1.02 develops this as an obligation to respect and support client self-determination. Section 2.03 asks that workers contribute to multidisciplinary discussion and try to resolve differences with other disciplines. Section 3 of the Code addresses responsibilities to practice settings, and 3.09 specifies commitment to employers, obligating workers to adhere to such commitments as well as to making employers aware of the worker's commitments to the NASW Code of Ethics. Subsection 3.09d states specifically, however:

> Social workers should not allow an employing organization's policies, procedures, regulations, or administrative orders to interfere with their ethical practice of social work. Social workers should take reasonable steps to ensure that their employing organizations' practices are consistent with the *NASW Code of Ethics.*

Thus the Code would seem to support and justify the worker's obligation to advocate and serve the best interests of the client and to support client self-determination, as primary.

Client and Worker Values. Client and worker values also impact on decision making and must be considered when attempting to reach a resolution. The client and family seem to share a strong commitment to their values, which include (1) caring, (2) privacy, (3) self-determination, (4) well-being, and (5) loyalty to each family member.

The worker's personal values include (1) loyalty and fidelity, (2) caring, (3) freedom, self-determination, and respect for autonomy, (4) justice, and (5) fairness.

Rationale for a Compromise Position. There are several options for action that would support one or the other side of the dilemma. However, the worker chooses to attempt to reach a compromise between the doctor's position and the client's desires. According to the associate director of the social work department, "ethical consults" are available when ethical dilemmas or conflicts arise needing immediate attention. Ethical consults may be convened within 24 hours and directly address issues facing the hospital and patients. The consult involves a team that includes a doctor, nurse, clergy member, lawyer, social worker, and usually the patient and family.

This worker clearly supports the client's right to self-determination and believes that she has an ethical obligation to advocacy on behalf of her client. Both her personal values, and those of her client and family, would support her advocacy for the right of her client to continue to receive care in the hospital. Additionally, the NASW Code of Ethics would appear to support the primacy of client interest in this conflict between client desires and hospital policies.

(continued)

CASE STUDY 5.4   CONTINUED

Nevertheless, because of the many factors noted above (i.e., the social worker's peripheral role in the hospital, the worker's duty to the hospital, and the very real issues of resource allocation), the option of seeking an ethical consult to attempt a compromise through a meeting of all the parties appears to be the optimal position in this situation. Taking a stand in complete opposition to an attending physician would likely result in numerous negative consequences, as well as prove to be futile, as described earlier in Kugelman's study.

QUESTIONS FOR THOUGHT AND DISCUSSION

1. Host settings, such as hospitals, schools, health clinics, places of employment, housing agencies, income transfer agencies (such as AFDC), hospices, justice systems, and so on, create a range of ethical issues for social workers. What do you feel to be the major ethical dilemmas social workers in such settings may need to address?

2. An important issue for workers in any host setting is a lack of power to influence the course of events relative to that of the host discipline. Yet the social work perspective adds an important piece to the overall work of the setting. What do you see as the unique contribution of social work in all host settings?

3. In host settings, workers are often more aware of the advocacy role that is an important part of the value base of the profession. Advocacy is often discussed as "case advocacy" and "class advocacy." Do you view your commitment as equally strong to both? Why or why not?

4. Employment as a social worker is a contractual obligation that asks workers to support the mission, policies, and procedures of the employing agency. How would you familiarize yourself with these? Would you do this before or after agreeing to employment?

5. Even in the most ideal of circumstances, a worker may find herself disagreeing with a particular policy for negatively affecting her client. In certain instances, she can choose to disregard it without drawing the attention of supervisor or colleagues. What are the negative effects of such an action for the worker herself, the client, the agency? Are there conditions or situations in which you would disregard agency policy? What are they?

REFERENCES AND BIBLIOGRAPHY

Case Study 5.1

Beauchamp, T., & Childress, J. (1994). *Principles of biomedical ethics.* New York: Oxford University Press.

Bishop, K., Rounds, K., & Weil, M. (1993). P. L. 99-457: Preparation for social work practice with infants and toddlers with disabilities and their families. *Journal of Social Work Education, 29*(1), 36–45.

Dillard, R., Auerbach, K., & Showalter, A. (1980). A parents' program in the intensive care nursery: Its relationship to maternal attitudes and expectations. *Social Work in Health Care, 5*(3), 245–251.

Dixon, S. (1979). *Working with people in crisis: Theory and practice.* St. Louis, MO: C. V. Mosby.

Gilliland, B., & James, R. (1993). *Crisis intervention strategies.* Pacific Grove, CA: Brooks/Cole.

Loewenberg, F., & Dolgoff, R. (1992). *Ethical decisions for social work practice.* Itasca, IL: F. E. Peacock.

Mor-Barak, M. (1988). Support systems intervention in crisis situations: Theory, strategies, and a case illustration. *International Social Work, 31,* 285–304.

National Association of Social Workers. (1996). *NASW Code of Ethics.* Washington, DC: Author.

Springen, K., & Kantrowitz, B. (1990, October 22). The long goodbye: When parents give a disabled child up for adoption, the pain often lingers. *Newsweek, 16,* 77–80.

Case Study 5.2

Adams, A., & Abarbanel, G. (1988). *Sexual assault on campus: What colleges can do.* Santa Monica, CA: Santa Monica Hospital Medical Center.

Bachman, R. (1993). Predicting the reporting of rape victimizations: Have rape reforms made a difference? *Criminal Justice and Behavior, 20*(3), 254–270.

Estrich, S. (1987). *Real rape: How the legal system victimizes women who say no.* Cambridge, MA: Harvard University Press.

Koss, M. P. (1985). The hidden rape victim: Personality, attitudinal and situational characteristics. *Psychology of Women Quarterly, 9,* 193–212.

National Association of Social Workers. (1996). *NASW Code of Ethics.* Washington, DC: Author.

Rape Crisis Center. (1995). *Rape crisis center training manual.* Author.

Senate Judiciary Committee. (1993). *The response to rape: Detours on the road to equal justice.* Washington, DC: Author.

Case Study 5.3

Abramson, M. (1985). The autonomy-paternalism dilemma in social work practice. *Social Casework,* 387–393.

Andrews, A. B., & Patterson, E. G. (1995). Searching for solutions to alcohol and other drug abuse during pregnancy: Ethics, values, and constitutional principles. *Social Work, 40,* 55–64.

Ards, S., & Harrell, A. (1989). Reporting of child maltreatment: A secondary analysis of the national incidence surveys. *Child Abuse and Neglect, 17,* 337–344.

Bailey, R. C., Hser, Y-I., Hsieh, S-C., Auglin, M. D. (1984, Winter/Spring). Influences affecting maintenance and cessation of narcotics addiction. *Journal of Drug Issue, 24* (1/22), 249–272.

Beauchamp, T. L., & Childress, J. F. (1994). *Principles of biomedical ethics.* New York: Oxford University Press.

Berger, C. S., Sorensen, L., Gendler, B., & Fitzsimmons, J. (1990). Cocaine and pregnancy: A challenge for health care providers. *Health and Social Work, 15,* 310–316.

Besharov, D. J. (1989). The children of crack: Will we protect them? *Public Welfare,* 8–11.

Brazelton, T. B. (1986). Issues for working parents. *American Journal of Orthopsychiatry, 56*(1), 14–25.

Davidson, C. E. (1991). Attachment issues and the cocaine exposed dyad. *Child and Adolescent Social Work, 8,* 269–284.

Duryea, P., Fontana, V. J., Alfaro, J. D. (1978). Child maltreatment: A new approach in educational programs. *Children Today, 7,* 13–16.

Gustavsson, N. S., & Rycraft, J. R. (1993). The multiple service needs of drug dependent mothers. *Child and Adolescent Social Work, 10,* 141–151.

Loewenberg, F. M., & Dolgoff, R. (1992). *Ethical decisions for social work practice,* Itasca, IL: F. E. Peacock.

Mundahl, L. D., VanDerWheele, T., Berger, C., & Fitzsimmons, J. (1991). Maternal-infant separation at birth among substance using pregnant women: Implications for attachment. *Social Work in Health Care, 16,* 133–143.

Murphy, J. M., Jellenek, M., Quinn, D., Smith, G., Poitrast, G., & Goshko, M. (1991). Substance abuse and serious child mistreatment: Prevalence, risk, and outcome in a court sample. *Child Abuse and Neglect, 15,* 197–211.

National Association of Social Workers. (1996). *NASW Code of Ethics.* Washington, DC: Author.

Plum, H. J. (1991). Legal response to child abuse and neglect: Assessment, treatment and prevention. *Child Abuse and Neglect, 15,* 31–37.

Reamer, F. G. (1990). *Ethical dilemmas in social service.* New York: Columbia University Press.

Rodning, C. J. (1987). The relationship between empathy and attachment. Unpublished Ph.D. dissertation, UCLA.

Rosenberger, E. H., & Goldstein, E. D. (1991). The legal consequences for children born of chemically dependent mothers. *Child and Adolescent Social Work, 8,* 339–346.

Tracey, E. M. (1994). Maternal substance abuse: Protecting the child, preserving the family. *Social Work, 39,* 534–540.

Case Study 5.4

Abramson, M. A. (1981). Ethical dilemmas for social workers in discharge planning. *Social Work in Health Care, 6*(4), 33–41.

Abramson, M. A. (1985, September). The autonomy-paternalism dilemma in social work practice. *Social Casework,* 387–393.

Beauchamp, T. L., & Childress, J. F. (1994). *Principles of biomedical ethics.* New York: Oxford University Press.

Biestek, F. (1957). *The casework relationship.* Chicago: Loyola University Press.

Hepworth, D. H., & Larsen, J. A. (1993). *Direct social work practice: Theory and skills.* Pacific Grove, CA: Brooks/Cole.

Kugelman, W. (1992). Social work ethics in the practice arena: A qualitative study. *Social Work in Health Care, 17*(4), 59–77.

Levy, C. S. (1976). *Social work ethics.* New York: Human Sciences Press.

Loewenberg, F. M., & Dolgoff, R. (1992). *Ethical decisions for social work practice.* Itasca, IL: F. E. Peacock.

National Association of Social Workers. (1996). *NASW Code of Ethics.* Washington, DC: Author.

Proctor, E. K., Morrow-Howell, N., & Lott, C. L. (1993). Classification and correlates of ethical dilemmas in hospital social work. *Social Work, 38*(2), 166–177.

Reamer, F. G. (1990). *Ethical dilemmas in social service.* New York: Columbia University Press.

Rothman, J. (1989). Client self-determination: Untangling the knot. *Social Service Review, 63*(4), 598–612.

Walden, T., Wolock, I., & Demone, H. W. (1990). Ethical decision-making in human services: A comparative study. *Families in Society: The Journal of Contemporary Human Services, 71*(2), 67–75.

CHAPTER SIX

NASW ETHICAL STANDARD SIX

Social Workers' Ethical Responsibilities to the Broader Society

INTRODUCTION

Provisions of Code

All professions have a special relationship to the society in which they are embedded. There is a contract, implicit in some areas, explicit in others, that exists between the profession and the society. Licensure, laws affecting professional conduct and privilege, malpractice laws, and other "official" mechanisms may be used to delineate and define the role of the profession in society.

In common with members of other professions, social workers have an ethical responsibility to the promotion of the "general welfare" of society. Because of the specific roles and functions that the social work profession assumes, and is granted, within the society, this obligation to the "general welfare" carries ethical responsibilities that affect the diurnal functioning of each professional. Social workers often act as the "agents" of society, performing such functions as administering its social programs; caring for those who are weak, young, old, or otherwise unable to care for themselves; working to improve the individual and collective position of the disadvantaged members of society; helping to ensure social justice for all; and preserving for all of society the safety and the basic freedoms that are inherent in its structure.

The Preamble of the Code of Ethics outlines social work's commitment to social justice and advocacy as follows:

> Social workers promote social justice and social change with and on behalf of clients . . . are sensitive to cultural and ethnic diversity and strive to end discrimination, poverty, and other forms of social injustice. These activities may be in the form of . . . advocacy, social and political action, policy development and implementation.

Social justice is a core value of the profession. This translates into the ethical principle "Social workers challenge social injustice":

Social workers pursue social change, particularly with and on behalf of vulnerable and oppressed individuals and groups of people. . . . [C]hange efforts are focused on issues of poverty, unemployment, discrimination, and other forms of social injustice . . . to promote sensitivity to and knowledge about oppression and cultural and ethnic diversity. ("Ethical Principles," Code of Ethics)

Section 6 of the Ethical Standards of the Code of Ethics provides more specific guidance for social workers in fulfilling these obligations.

Subsection 6.01 asks social workers to promote the "general welfare of society," from local to global, and to advocate for conditions that allow the fulfillment of basic human needs for all. Social justice may be promoted through "social, economic, political, and cultural values and institutions."

The commitment to respect for diversity, both social and cultural, is extended from the United States to a global level. Social workers "should promote policies and practices that demonstrate respect for difference," expand cultural knowledge, advocate for culturally competent programs and institutions, and safeguard the rights and equity of all (6.04c).

Social workers also have a commitment to help educate the public about these issues, to encourage participation (6.02), to provide services in public emergencies (6.03), and to act to prevent exploitation and discrimination (6.04d).

The Cases

The majority of ethical dilemmas encountered by professionals in relation to society concern the dual obligation to clients and to the broader society. Others relate to issues such as meeting the needs of present members of society versus ensuring the welfare of future members and conflicting obligations to society and employing agency. Often, ethical issues that involve the "general welfare" imply an understanding of the general values of a society—a necessary precondition for the promotion of its welfare. The task of defining these values, in itself, can be difficult in this diverse, multicultural country. Society defines and regulates itself through the enactment of laws and policies that support its foundational values. As agents of society, as well as members, social workers are responsible for administering and upholding the laws that the society has made. This responsibility assumes greater dimensions when a worker has responsibility for the members of society who cannot advocate for themselves: children, the elderly, the mentally disabled or incompetent, and others.

These obligations also contain the possibility of ethical dilemmas, especially when the laws are in conflict with workers' own values, their perception of their clients' best interests, or the values of the profession as a whole. The case examples included in this chapter illustrate some of these areas of ethical conflict for professionals.

The first case presents a classical confidentiality/duty-to-warn dilemma, often faced by workers whose populations include HIV-positive clients. The worker's problem is additionally complex because the agency's policy seems to support maintaining confidentiality, and the laws pertaining to duty to warn in the case of HIV infection are less clear than in verbalized threats of injury by violence. In considering this case, and the worker's resolution, it is interesting to see how vital a role her own values play in her decision.

The worker in the second case is confronted with an adolescent who informs her that he is planning to resume dealing marijuana. He has been in treatment for eight months and has made significant progress in school performance, behavior at home, and sociability. She must consider whether her primary obligation is to report his plan to the authorities, when there is no legal obligation for her to do so, or to maintain confidentiality and continue to attempt to work with him, addressing this problem in treatment.

The third case presents a situation that carries the potential for serious harm when a client on parole infers to the social worker that she is carrying a concealed weapon in order to protect herself from potential physical danger from an ex-spouse and other men. The client lives in a high-crime neighborhood, and the threats made against her are believable. She has made excellent progress in group therapy and is almost ready for graduation from the program. How should the worker address this problem? If it is reported to the parole officer, the client risks reincarceration and a loss of all the gains she has worked so hard to achieve. Additionally, the worker has conducted an informal survey of her group, asking how many members had access to guns. A majority responded in the affirmative. Should all of them be reported? However, if suspicion of possession of concealed weapons is not reported, the relationship between the agency and law enforcement is jeopardized and the worker models deception and co-optation to the client and group members. Innocent people, as well as the client and others directly involved, may be injured. There is no written agency policy to support either decision, and time is of the essence.

A particularly dilemma-laden conflict is presented in the fourth case in this chapter, society's obligation to protect the well-being and rights of its chronically mentally disabled homeless members. Must these two concepts, rights and well-being, remain always in conflict? Who decides how "well-being" is to be defined, the client or the policy maker? The author, working in an advocacy program, must try to determine the best interests of this special population in order to support the policies that best serve their interests.

The fifth case presents an unusual setting for a social work dilemma: the institutional review board of an organization funded with public monies, engaged in genetic research. The social worker is a member of the board, which is considering the issue of providing information on study results and genetic counseling to subjects. While there are strong arguments in support of the rights of subjects to the benefits of research, provision of these benefits is costly and will endanger the entire study. Thus, the worker must consider the rights of the individuals involved versus the potential good that can accrue to all members of (a future) society from the findings of the research, then make a recommendation to the board.

The last case in this section addresses a broad moral issue related to immigration policy. Immigration policies in the United States have varied markedly over the years, but have never specifically addressed certain ethical obligations that the United States might have a very "special" population. Immigration has been limited for many years, through the use of a variety of standards and criteria. The worker believes that it might be ethical for preferential status to be granted to immigrants who have sought refuge because of events in their country that have been supported and/or exacerbated by the military presence of the United States. Do we, the social worker asks, have a greater obligation to support these applicants for immigration status? Should we, as a profession, advocate for preferential treatment? Does the presence of the United States military on the soil of another country obligate it to special consideration for its refugee population? Does it create a special relationship that differs from that of other potential immigrants?

■ ■ ■ ■ ■ ▬▬▬▬▬▬▬▬▬▬▬▬▬▬▬▬▬▬▬▬▬▬▬▬▬▬▬▬

CASE STUDY 6.1

HIV: THE CONFIDENTIALITY/DUTY-TO-WARN DILEMMA

Abstracted from an unpublished paper by Robin E. Rolley, J.D., MSW

PRACTICE CONTEXT AND CASE PRESENTATION

The policy at a suburban community services agency states that agency social workers have a duty to uphold the right of HIV-positive clients to confidentiality. It further states that if a worker is aware that an HIV-positive client is endangering the safety of others, and refuses to refrain from high-risk practices, he or she must seek advice from his or her immediate supervisor. A number of persons in the administrative hierarchy must be consulted, in turn, before any action is undertaken. This policy has been interpreted by social workers as favoring the right to confidentiality over the duty to warn sexual partners in cases of high-risk sexual practices where the client refuses to warn partners.

The dilemma faced by social workers at this agency may be addressed at more than one level. On a societal level, the professional has a duty both to maintain confidences and to promote the general welfare of society by preventing harm to its members (the duty to warn). On an individual client level, there is a duty to respect the client's right to privacy and confidentiality, as well as to self-determination. On the level of employing agency, the worker has the obligation to follow agency policy (maintain confidentiality), but also has a responsibility to personal values, which, in this author's case, place the public good over individual rights. Employment may thus violate personal values, creating a difficult personal ethical dilemma.

In deciding which dilemma to focus on, the worker recognizes that she is already making an ethical decision. Because of her strong personal commitment to the "general welfare," she has chosen to address her obligation to respect the client's right to confidentiality versus her "general welfare" commitment. Research and literature, therefore, will be presented to assist the reader in addressing this first issue, which has been stated as:

Confidentiality v. Duty to Warn

RESEARCH AND RELATED LITERATURE

Articles on this subject regarding the obligations of therapists and medical doctors support both sides of the dilemma, but do not offer a definitive resolution. Yu and O'Neal (1992) report, "no case involving confidentiality and an AIDS client has been litigated so the legal precedent of settling the dispute regarding breaching confidentiality has yet to be determined" (p. 425). Arguments for both sides tend to either apply or distinguish this issue from the landmark case of *Tarasoff* v. *The Regents of the University of California* (1976).

Those who find the *Tarasoff* decision applicable focus on four aspects of the court's holding: the existence of a special relationship, the assessment of dangerousness, an

(continued)

CASE STUDY 6.1   CONTINUED

identifiable victim, and appropriate action by the therapist (Lamb, Clark, Drumheller, Frizzell, & Surrey, 1989). The decision determined that therapists have a "special relationship" with clients that causes them to assume some responsibility to the safety of the patient and also of third parties (Lamb et al., 1989). In an HIV-related situation, the assessment of danger involves three general factors: medical diagnosis, extent of involvement in high-risk behaviors, and use of "safer sex" techniques (Lamb et al., 1989). Therapists, according to *Tarasoff,* are not obligated to investigate to determine the identity of an intended victim, but might, in some instances, be able to arrive at this with thought (Lamb et al., 1989). The fourth criterion, "appropriate action," mandates reasonable care, and actions might involve detaining, warning, and/or protecting. The most frequently used intervention is hospitalization. Breaching of confidentiality is ranked fourth (Lamb et al., 1989).

Criteria for invoking "duty to warn" based on *Tarasoff* generally requires that (1) the therapist have knowledge of HIV infection; (2) unsafe behavior occurs on a regular basis; (3) behavior continues even after counseling; and (4) HIV transmission will be the likely result (Harding, Gray, & Neal, 1993, p. 300).

In sum, those in favor of duty to warn cite the *Tarasoff* precedent and public health laws (attempt to prevent spread of infectious diseases), the therapist's potential liability, and the need to limit confidentiality to protect others from harm.

In favor of maintaining confidentiality, one might distinguish between a "direct verbal threat," as in *Tarasoff,* and the passive threat posed by HIV-positive clients, where the intention to infect is not usually verbalized (Harding, Gray, & Neal, 1993, p. 301). Another possible distinction would establish that the sexual partners of an HIV-positive client have the choice not to engage in high-risk sexual activities or needle sharing.

Kain (1988) suggests that breaching confidentiality with HIV-positive clients will increase the discrimination against them in obtaining or maintaining housing, insurance, and employment. He also maintains that therapists might breach confidentiality based on their own moral, religious, or political biases.

Another argument in support of maintaining confidentiality suggests that, through the therapeutic relationship, social workers can educate clients on safer practices, encourage them to voluntarily inform their partners and maintain their roles as client advocates. Social workers may also face liability in breaching confidentiality as case law in certain states rejects the application of *Tarasoff.* Social workers may be found guilty of breach of confidentiality (Morrison, 1989, p. 169).

No matter which position is taken, all the literature strongly upholds the social worker's responsibility to know the laws of his or her state, as well as the policies of his or her employer. In this worker's agency, policies uphold confidentiality. There are no laws in the state applying the *Tarasoff* decision, although statutes require that mental health service workers have a duty to take precautions to protect third parties only when a client has verbally, or in writing or sign language, communicated serious bodily injury to a readily identifiable third party.

Workers in agency settings are also obligated to consult with agency policy and values. The agency in which this dilemma occurs would seem to value privacy and self-determination over the societal good. The state statutes seem to support a duty to warn, though several means are suggested for the fulfillment of that duty.

The Code of Ethics places the worker's commitment to the client as primary and supports self-determination. However, it states that a worker may limit a client's self-determination when "clients' actions or potential actions pose a serious, foreseeable, and imminent risk to themselves or others" (1.02).

The rights of clients to privacy and confidentiality are addressed and state that social workers must keep in confidence all information shared by clients except for "compelling professional reasons" (1.07c). Such reasons include the "serious, forseeable, imminent risk" alluded to above.

Limitations to privacy and confidentiality are addressed more fully in subsection 1.03a, on informed consent:

> Social workers should use clear and understandable language to inform clients of the purpose of the services, risks related to the services, limits to services because of the requirements of a third-party payer, relevant costs, reasonable alternatives, clients' right to refuse or withdraw consent, and the time frame covered by the consent.

While the intent may have been to include, as a "risk," the obligation of the social worker to warn others "at risk" from a client's behavior, this is not specifically included here.

On the other hand, Section 6 of the Code seems to support the worker's obligation to warn. It is clearly stated in subsection 6.01 that social workers have an obligation to the "general welfare" of society. This could be applied to individual members within the society, such as partners of the client, as well as society as a whole, in terms of the prevention of the spread of HIV infection.

The worker also has an obligation to "expand choice" for all persons, "with special regard for vulnerable, disadvantaged, oppressed, and exploited people and groups" (6.04a). Informing individuals who could potentially contract HIV would seem to be expanding choices for them. They can also be considered to be a particularly vulnerable and possibly exploited population, thus one to whom the social worker has a special responsibility (6.04b).

AUTHOR'S REFLECTIONS, REASONING PROCESS, AND RESOLUTION

Societal values favor individual rights, such as freedom, self-determination, and privacy, and the good of society, such as concern for the well-being of others, public safety, and justice. Those values favoring individual rights tend to support the maintenance of confidentiality, while those favoring the good of society support the duty to warn third parties. Our society also tends to accept the concept that "majority rules."

Two relevant ethical principles applicable to this debate are the utilitarian principle of the greatest good for the greatest number and the Kantian principle that people "should always be treated as ends in themselves, that is, as rational, autonomous (self-determining) agents" (Cohen, 1990, p. 283). Both can be interpreted to support either side of the debate.

(continued)

CASE STUDY 6.1 CONTINUED

Promoting the greatest good for the greatest number supports confidentiality in that it might lead a greater number of HIV-positive clients to seek treatment, thus reducing the risk to the society at large (Cohen, 1990). On the other hand, the greatest good for the greatest number could also mean the recognition of the utility of the duty to warn third parties, to protect them from pain and death.

One interpretation of the Kantian principle is that "consistent application of respect for persons as autonomous agents demands . . . confidentiality be respected." On the other hand, clients who fail to inform their partners of their HIV status are treating the partner as a means, not as an end (Cohen, 1990, p. 283).

In evaluating all the above, a tentative values hierarchy might place general well-being, public safety, and justice above privacy, self-determination, and individual rights. This hierarchy agrees with the worker's personal values as well, as the author perceives her greater responsibility as being toward the general welfare of society and, therefore, toward a duty to warn or protect third parties. However, she would first attempt to resolve the dilemma within the therapeutic relationship by encouraging the client to share information about HIV-positive status with at-risk others and/or to use safer practices. Should this approach not resolve the issue, she would act to protect and warn persons at risk.

This position is based on the worker's personal values, as well as the legal precedents and ethical principles considered. It is supported by the broader utilitarian position that the greater good is achieved through direct intervention to prevent harm to members of the society. While this decision is contrary to the policy of the agency, the worker feels it is strongly supported both legally and ethically. The ethical dilemma that presents itself by this resolution, the nonadherence to agency policy, would also need to be addressed by the worker, for it would create a serious breach of trust by the worker to the practice setting, a violation of Section 3 of the Code of Ethics. Resolving one dilemma in the way that the worker feels is best, therefore, creates another that will also involve choices of action by the worker.

QUESTIONS FOR THOUGHT AND DISCUSSION

1. This author chooses to address the issue of confidentiality versus duty to warn in cases of HIV-positive clients, at least to some extent, because she is aware of a strong value difference between herself and the agency in this regard. What are some of the ethical ramifications of employment in an agency with whose policies you disagree?
2. Are there any policies that would preclude your employment in a social agency or other setting that employs social workers? How would you investigate a prospective employer's policies on the issues you feel strongly about?
3. The issue of primary responsibility—to an individual client or to the well-being of the society at large—is not limited to the spread of infections diseases, such as AIDS. This issue frequently confronts social workers. What do you see as your primary obligation?

4. Social workers in the course of treatment may become aware that a client is inappropriately using society's resources. There is no "imminent danger," no "intended victim"—just a breach of society's trust on the part of the client. Would you feel an obligation to take action under such a circumstance? What action would you take?

5. Are there other sources or foundations for the values of society than simple "majority rules"? What are these other sources? How should they interact with the concept of "majority rule"?

■ ■ ■ ■ ■ ▬▬▬▬▬▬▬▬▬▬▬▬▬▬▬▬▬▬▬▬▬▬▬▬▬▬▬

CASE STUDY 6.2

DEALING DRUGS: CAN CONFIDENTIALITY EVER BE JUSTIFIED?

Abstracted from an unpublished paper by Julie B. Goodale, MSW

PRACTICE CONTEXT AND CASE PRESENTATION

An adolescent in a suburban high school with a personal history of violence had been heavily involved with dealing marijuana. Through court intervention, he was transferred to a different high school and asked to meet with a youth services social worker.

The social worker has been seeing the client for approximately eight months on a weekly basis. During this time, a relationship of trust has developed that has enabled the client to discuss his problems and ask for help from the worker. The client has remained in school, passed his courses, and functioned outside of school without recourse to any violence. He regularly keeps appointments. The worker is encouraged by his progress and feels that his continued trust and the therapeutic relationship could be pivotal for the client's future.

Although the young man at first refrained from selling drugs, he has recently been contacted by his former supplier, who convinced him that he should go "back into the business." He has confided to the social worker that he plans to resume selling drugs in the immediate future. The worker has been unable to dissuade him from his intention to resume selling marijuana. He does not consider this a "serious drug" and says, "If I don't do it, someone else will. I might as well be the one getting the money!" The worker is concerned that harm to society will result from the client's resumption of drug dealing.

On the other hand, the client has made solid gains during the time she has worked with him. He trusts her and has been able to work well with her, sharing information, accepting support, and sustaining the gains. If the worker reports his intention to authorities, she places at risk her continued work with this client, his trust of her, and the maintenance of his gains. While she is distressed with his intention to deal drugs, she wonders if it would be more helpful, both to him as an individual and to society as a whole, if she continues to work with him and attempts to address his drug dealing in the course of her contacts with him.

The dilemma maybe stated as:

Confidentiality v. Obligation to Society

RESEARCH AND RELATED LITERATURE

Confidentiality is the right of the client and is clearly stated in the Code of Ethics, Section 1, which states:

> Social workers should respect clients' right to privacy. . . . Once private information is shared, standards of confidentiality apply [1.07a]. Social workers should protect the confidentiality of all information obtained in the course of professional service, except

for compelling professional reasons. The general expectation. . . . does not apply when disclosure is necessary to prevent serious, foreseeable, and imminent harm to a client or other identifiable person or when laws or regulations require disclosure without a client's consent [1.07c].

The underlying belief is that mutual trust is essential to the maintenance of a therapeutic relationship between a client and a worker (Seelig, 1990). This relationship enables changes in the client's attitude, behavior, and functioning.

The Code of Ethics also obligates social workers to the primacy of client interests and to trustworthiness. These suggest that, professionally, the worker should act so as to retain the client in treatment and should continue to provide services to him.

However, Section 6 of the Code also obligates the worker to support the best interests of society and the general welfare. In Section 6.01, social workers are obligated to "promote the general welfare of society."

Among social workers, it is commonly accepted that it is unethical to disclose information shared in confidence. Such information should not be shared with third parties (Reamer, 1990). Also, according to Moore (1994), "Implied in the issue of confidentiality is the notion of the individual's right to privacy" (p. 165).

There are a few exceptions to the obligation of workers to preserve confidentiality. These are: (1) if the client is in danger of harming self or other; (2) if the client and social worker mutually agree to tell a third party; (3) if the social worker is subpoenaed to testify in court.

It is unclear whether selling marijuana constitutes harm as intended in the first exception to the obligation to confidentiality. A person is under no legal obligation to inform the authorities of illegal activities. Failing to be a good samaritan is not a crime (Forer, 1986).

The policy of the agency does not clearly and unequivocally mandate reporting of drug dealing. Rather, situations are addressed as they occur on a case-by-case basis, and a course of action is determined that seems appropriate to the individual client. Colleagues at the agency, when consulted, stated that they did not feel that dealing marijuana constituted harm as intended in the exceptions to the obligation to confidentiality.

Although there may be no legal responsibility, there are other reasons for people to act on behalf of others. According to Senator Orrin Hatch (1992), "Individual responsibility . . . is *the* first principle of limited government" (p. 959). The United States was founded on a principle of individual freedom without interference from large governing bodies. However, a limited government can only be feasible if the people in that society are able to govern themselves, both socially and individually (Hatch, 1992). Individual responsibility is a necessary precondition for a civilized legal order (Calabresi & Lawson, 1992).

The courts and the entire justice system depends on citizens' actions (Forer, 1986). Calabresi and Lawson (1992) state that "without a sense of personal honor—and, more importantly, a sense of shame—any form of social organization is doomed" (p. 957). There have been documented cases where the public interest supersedes the client's right to privacy (Moore, 1994), the most notable being *Tarasoff* v. *The Board of Regents of the University of California,* the landmark precedent in duty-to-warn cases.

(continued)

CASE STUDY 6.2 CONTINUED

In the current dilemma, one can presume that society at large is the "intended victim." The client may sell drugs to someone who overdoses or drives while under the influence and kills or injures an innocent bystander. Dealing drugs possesses potential for harm to others, both users and the general public.

In attempting to protect members of society from the harms of drugs, federal laws make drug use and dealing a crime. While the worker is not mandated to report illegal actions, as noted above, there are ethical issues involved as well in protecting knowledge of criminal activity.

AUTHOR'S REFLECTIONS, REASONING PROCESS, AND RESOLUTION

One ethical theory that is applicable to this dilemma appears to be utilitarianism. Utilitarianism derives from a consequentialist, or teleological, perspective in that the major thrust and concern are the consequences of a course of action. Utilitarians seek "the greatest good for the largest number of people" (Loewenberg & Dolgoff, 1992, p. 42). In determining a course of action, utilitarians consider the needs of everyone affected, and the ultimate course chosen should be the one that produces the "maximal balance of positive value over disvalue" (Beauchamp & Childress, 1994, p. 47).

Act utilitarianism asks, "What good and bad consequences will result from *this* action in *this* circumstance?" (Beauchamp & Childress, 1994, p. 50). In considering the dilemma in question, one might note that a bad consequence, clearly, is that the client's trust will be broken and the client, who is in need of treatment, will likely leave therapy. A good consequence might be that one less person is dealing drugs, reducing the exposure for the potential harm to drug use. However, it is unclear in this particular situation whether another person would be recruited to take the client's place, as he contends, thus negating any potential positive effect.

If one considers simply the greatest good for the largest number of people, the interests of society in preventing additional exposure and access of its members to drugs clearly provides the utilitarian answer. Our society clearly values autonomy and personal freedom. Applying these to this situation would seem to support the right of the client to make money in any way that he chooses. If he chooses to violate the law, he has the freedom to do so, unless caught. Members of society may also exercise personal freedom and autonomy in choosing whether to risk the potential harms of using marijuana. Another societal value, safety, conflicts with freedom and autonomy in this instance, however. Drugs endanger users as well as others, and this knowledge creates the laws that currently exist against using and selling drugs.

The client values money, power, and status. According to him, he was the "best" marijuana dealer in the area. He is not concerned about responsibility to others or to society as a whole, nor does the illegality of his actions trouble him.

The worker values honesty, truth, justice, education, and job training. These values have led the worker to cooperate with authorities in the past in ensuring justice and protecting society. She does not agree with the position of taking an "easy out"—selling drugs, rather than staying in school and learning a skill.

On the other hand, the worker values trustworthiness very highly. She is concerned with trying to maintain her relationship with this client, and she feels that breaching confidentiality and reporting his drug dealing would cause the client to terminate much-needed treatment. Also, she feels that breaching confidentiality would reflect negatively on her own professional self-concept.

Five potential options for action are suggested in examining this dilemma. First, the worker can choose to maintain complete confidentiality, telling no one of what the client has confided in her. Second, the worker may inform her supervisor, with the request that confidentiality be maintained by the supervisor as well. Third, the worker may elect to inform the police or drug enforcement agency. Fourth, she may choose to inform the school authorities and cede to them the responsibility for future action. Fifth, she may inform the client's parents and attempt to enlist their assistance in discouraging the client from pursuing his stated intentions.

The social worker feels confidentiality is the right of the client. The client assumed that the information shared would not be divulged, and the Code of Ethics does not seem to provide clear and specific guidance in this area. The worker's respect for autonomy and personal freedom lead her to the conclusion that the client has the right to determine his own course of action, just as the potential users of his services have the right to determine theirs. Her strong commitment to trustworthiness causes her to feel that the best service that she can render to the client—and, by extension, to society as a whole—is to keep the client in treatment and to try to assist him to reflect on, and perhaps to reconsider, his decision.

The worker would share information about her client with her supervisor, asking that the supervisor maintain the client's confidentiality. As the policy of the youth service agency does not require the reporting of drug use or dealing, this position would not be a violation of commitments made but, rather, a support for future growth and change for this client.

QUESTIONS FOR THOUGHT AND DISCUSSION

1. A possible position with regard to reporting responsibilities states that, due to the nature of the client/worker relationship, there is an obligation on the part of the worker to prevent harm that may be perpetrated by the client, which differs from the obligation of members of the general public. The relationship between client and worker differs from that between the client and any other member of society. This difference creates additional obligations on the part of the worker. Do you feel that this is a valid position? How would you describe this difference in relationship and responsibilities?

2. Another way to look at the dilemma presented here keeps the focus on the welfare of the general public on both sides of the equation. Reporting the client's actions might serve the immediate interests of society by removing him from the street. Maintaining the client in treatment serves the long-range interests of society by potentially changing his approach to the issue of drugs and removing the possibility of harm through therapy. Which approach do you feel most clearly meets the obligations to the good of the general public that the profession holds?

3. The client is selling marijuana, a drug that is considered among the least harmful of controlled substances. Should the particular drug the client is dealing affect your decision to maintain or breach confidentiality? Is all drug use equally bad, equally harmful?

4. The client's rationale for deciding to resume selling marijuana is, "If I don't, someone else will." There is justification for this position. Should this have any effect on your decision in this dilemma?

5. The worker plans to share the information about the client's dealing with her supervisor, in order to receive guidance in working with him. Though the policy of the agency seems loose and nonspecific in this regard, the supervisor's personal values may dictate a different course of action from that on which the worker has decided. Can, and/or should, a worker bind a supervisor to a decision that she has made independently? What options might the supervisor feel to be necessary to her own fulfillment of her obligations and responsibilities?

CASE STUDY 6.3

LIMITING SELF-PROTECTION FOR VULNERABLE CLIENTS: AN ACCEPTABLE RISK FOR THE PROTECTION OF SOCIETY?

Abstracted from an unpublished paper by Stephen Hardstack, MSW

PRACTICE CONTEXT AND CASE PRESENTATION

Jocelyn is a 44-year-old woman who has been mandated by the U.S. Parole Office to complete a six-month program of group psychotherapy and drug education at a private urban substance abuse clinic. She was convicted for her role as a cross-country cocaine courier and subsequently served a sentence in a federal prison. At the time of her arrest, she tested positive for cocaine use, but since then has not tested positive during twice-weekly drug screens required by the program. She is divorced and has three children—ages 17, 13, and 8—who are currently being cared for by her ex-husband's mother and grandmother. She would like to regain custody of the children, is looking for a job, appears both street-smart and intellectually intelligent, and is forthright and often incisive when she participates in group therapy. She is several weeks from graduating from the program.

Jocelyn and her husband James divorced while she was in prison, and she states that he facilitated her involvement with drugs. At present, she is living with her sister Karen, three blocks down the same street that James lives on, in a high-crime area. James previously has come onto Karen's property, verbally abusing and physically threatening Jocelyn, so a restraining order was obtained. However, when he sees her on the street, he sometimes stares her down or yells at her; mutual acquaintances have also reported that he has made threats against her.

During therapy, Jocelyn has discussed the dangers of an unescorted woman's mandated attendance at Narcotics Anonymous (NA) meetings. She says that when she walks to meetings, she is accosted by solicitations to buy drugs or have sex, with accompanying unwelcome physical contact from the solicitors. Patting her purse, Jocelyn related that she carries "all the protection she needs" to deal with these various threats, seemingly implying that she was carrying an illegal concealed weapon. As followup in a subsequent session, the worker asked how many clients had access to a gun, and Jocelyn was one of the majority who raised a hand. Jocelyn has also shared her ex-husband's current behavior and threats and has stated that she will not allow herself to be assaulted by James or any other man ever again.

The worker is concerned about the degree of endangerment a concealed firearm represents to the agency and its clients, to society at large, and potentially to Jocelyn and James. This concern would support acting to restrict Jocelyn's access to a handgun. On the other hand, the sense of self-protection she derives from carrying a concealed weapon may assist her in coping with the perceived threats posed by her ex-husband and by the dealers and hustlers who hang around NA meetings hoping to prey on struggling, vulnerable attendees.

(continued)

CASE STUDY 6.3   CONTINUED

The dilemma to be addressed, then, may be stated as:

Client Safety v. Safety of Society

RESEARCH AND RELATED LITERATURE
The agency has no written policy regarding the carrying of firearms on the premises. However, it is subject to local law, which severely restricts possession or use of handguns despite the Second Amendment of the Constitution, which states: "A well regulated Militia, being necessary to the security of a free state, the right of the people to keep and bear Arms, shall not be infringed."

While the agency has no written policy, there is one precedent: A client directly told the agency supervisor he was carrying a concealed weapon. The supervisor asked to see it, ejected six live cartridges, and returned the weapon with the admonition to the client never to repeat this incident. In return, the supervisor agreed not to report the incident to the client's parole officer.

The literature shows that social workers have legitimate job safety concerns. Star (1984) found that "some clients are potentially violent and pose a serious threat to the physical safety of social workers employed in outpatient settings." Confirming this observation, a study by Mace (1989) of 799 social workers found that one-quarter of the participants reported being assaulted by a client. Verbal abuse and physical assaults by clients and by paraprofessionals were also reported in a study of 121 social work students and 96 field instructors (Tully, Kropf, & Price, 1993). Thus, a client possessing a weapon in an agency setting clearly might also be considered a dangerous threat.

However, the surrounding environment lends validity to the need for self-protection. Some local residents feel that the seemingly arbitrary nature of jurisdictional gun laws precludes taking the more restrictive law in their jurisdiction seriously. For example, the trial of TV commentator and newspaper columnist Carl Rowan on charges of violating District of Columbia gun control law ended in a hung jury (Lewis, 1988). On the other hand, it can be argued that society needs to be protected from people with guns, especially if the gun is not legally possessed, since that type of gun may also be intended to fulfill an unlawful use that will cause harm to others and because violent crime is now characterized as an epidemic in the United States (Chafee, 1992).

AUTHOR'S REFLECTIONS, REASONING PROCESS, AND RESOLUTION
The Hobbesian fear of a violent death may or may not be a motivation by which people contract to form and maintain a civil society. In some parts of our society, a wrong look, driving into the wrong neighborhood, or even being too close to a window when an incident involving a gun occurs may result in tragic consequences to an unwitting victim. Violence occurs easily because, in the view of so many, life is cheap. For some people, respect is all-important, and loss of face is to be avoided at any cost. Primary among ethical principles, the right to one's life is fundamental—hence, society values safety.

Jocelyn has evidently made a decision that her own personal safety—indeed her own life—may be dependent on her ability to defend herself with a firearm. Members of her treatment group share with her the need for empowerment that a firearm provides. In conversation with the agency director regarding the validity of the informal treatment group poll result—where a majority of clients claimed to have access to a gun—the director stated that his ten years of experience led him to believe that the result certainly had face validity.

The Ethical Standards section of the NASW Code of Ethics specifies the worker's obligations to the client. Commitment to clients (1.01) states that the client's interests are generally "primary," but may on occasion be mitigated by responsibility to society. This question is, of course, fundamental to the ethical dilemma. It is not known whether the client merely derives a sense of security from carrying a gun or would actually fire it if she felt threatened. If fired, harm may result to an innocent or intended victim, precluding any other less harmful alternative such as flight, mediation, or law enforcement assistance. Self-determination (1.02) may imply that even for involuntary clients, those who are committed to recovery (and risk danger attending mandated NA meetings) should be supported. This right may be limited only when a "client's actions pose a serious, foreseeable, and imminent risk." It is not possible to state positively that all three of these conditions are met in this incident. If they were, then "duty to warn" the intended victim would have to be considered.

The client's vulnerability within the context of mandated treatment and within her present living environment should also be considered, because there is a potential for incarceration if handgun possession is reported. Should decisional authority rest with the worker alone, or in conjunction with the client or supervisor (Consultation, 2.05)? Is this a clear-cut legal matter for the parole office or even law enforcement to handle? The Code of Ethics clearly defines the responsibility of individual social workers to the broader society, the background within which the dangers associated with this dilemma must be considered. Who has the ultimate responsibility?

The last section in the Code of Ethics deals with the worker's responsibilities to society. The paragraph entitled Public Emergencies (6.03) may be loosely connected to this case, but, in the best judgment of the worker, Jocelyn is not likely to create such a situation, armed or unarmed. There does seem to be a clear need for "macro level" intervention to improve social welfare (6.01) and especially for addressing the issues of vulnerable, disadvantaged, oppressed, and exploited people (6.04) such as Jocelyn and her neighbors. Changing the environment so that there is no further need for firearms for individual protection is a clear social work obligation. Unfortunately, that will not resolve the present problem.

The social worker believes her client values her family and reunification with her children. Her self-determined commitment to ongoing sobriety, her adherence to clinic and parole rules, and her own statements support her motivation to make changes in her life. A tentative external hierarchy that might be proposed would be (1) life, (2) client autonomy, (3) communication and collaboration, and (4) the safety of society.

The worker's own value/ethical stance follows the feminist ethics of care. Noting the courage and resilience of this client in her life struggle and her specific vulnerabilities, a position of compassionate and empathic caring seems appropriate and justified. Consonant to this ethic, the worker's bias is to see her graduate from this program and successfully complete her parole, goals that might not be met if she is reported for a

(*continued*)

CASE STUDY 6.3   CONTINUED

possible violation of gun laws. A personal values hierarchy includes (1) wisdom, (2) compassion, (3) mindfulness, (4) non-injury, (5) family love, (6) integrity, (7) faithfulness, (8) generosity, (9) human relationships, and (10) right effort. These values support nonreporting and encouraging Jocelyn to complete the program safely. This value supersedes the worker's support of a total ban on guns nationwide.

A number of options or choices are available to deal with this situation, as illustrated in Figure 6.1. After confirming the presence of a concealed weapon, the worker may

- Notify parole officer, who may arrange to have subject searched and arrested outside the premises of the clinic.
- Per precedent, warn client individually, warn as part of group (discreetly, without identifying her), or both that concealed weapons are forbidden on the premises.
- Update clinic policy to include ban on weapons, then publicize policy with clients.
- Recognize imminent danger to clients and colleagues and disarm client with staff assistance.

There are also several options that do not require the worker's personal confirmation of a concealed weapon. The parole officer could be notified of a suspicion only and could proceed with the investigation. The worker could also do nothing, either with or without supervisory consultation. This worker would not be comfortable attempting to disarm the client himself, as in the previous agency experience. In addition to the option selected, it would be beneficial to the agency if discussions were held, and a formal policy written, on the subject of handguns in the agency setting or in clients' possessions.

Notifying the parole officer of the confirmed presence of a concealed weapon on the client would no doubt lead to negative consequences for the client, such as cancellation of contract to participate in therapy, revocation of parole, and/or reincarceration. However, such a notification might also promote the safety of clinic staff, clients, and society at large, as well as Jocelyn's own. This option would remove the decision making from the agency and/or the worker. Other clients could view the agency's reporting as punitive and as a breach of confidentiality, thus straining some of the therapeutic alliances, especially when the clinic program is seen as a last resort between a client and jail. However, being truthful with parole office colleagues throughout the process of a client's rehabilitation is an important reciprocal component of the working relationship between the agency and law enforcement officers. Also, doing nothing would not keep the clinic weapon-free, address the present problem, or remove the risk to the wider society, which is a clear social work responsibility.

The worker's choice of a course of action includes, first, consultation with the supervisor. Regardless of whether there is a stated agency policy, the carrying of a concealed weapon by an ex-offender on clinic premises is a grave matter, and the agency hierarchy should be made aware of the potential risks. Second, since agency policy does

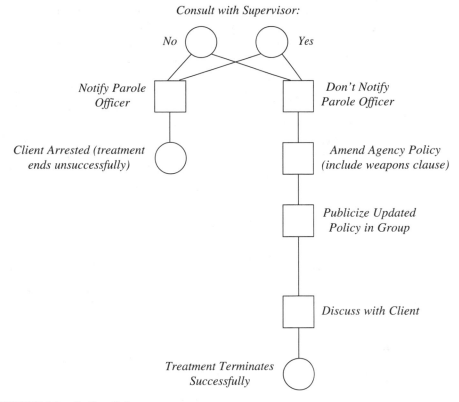

FIGURE 6.1   Option Schema.

not currently address this problem, an appropriate action would recommend updating it to specifically include a caveat against carrying concealed weapons and incorporating that into contracts with clients. Third, the policy change should be announced in each group session with clients, and a one-hour presentation on the issues raised by owning or carrying a weapon where prohibited by law should be created. This presentation should focus on safety concerns and should be reinforced by a description of the consequences on parole status. Fourth, the worker should approach the Jocelyn nonconfrontationally on an individual basis and remind her of the new policy in relation to her previously stated comments.

QUESTIONS FOR THOUGHT AND DISCUSSION

1. Do you believe that people who live in high-crime areas should be able to protect themselves from harm by carrying concealed weapons? If not, what alternatives would you suggest to ensure the safety of these residents? If yes, at what age and under what circumstances should people be able to carry firearms?

2. Social workers are also at risk when working in high-crime areas. Yet, these areas often include the poor and vulnerable populations that our profession serves. Do you think you should be asked to go into areas where you feel personally unsafe? If yes, how would you protect yourself? If no, how would services to clients in these areas be provided?

3. Does your program train and educate students about safety issues before field instruction begins? If it does not, how might you initiate a change in program to incorporate this education?

4. The safety issues facing children in high-crime areas is acute. Children are especially vulnerable members of society, and as social workers we have a special obligation to their protection. If you were a child welfare worker, what role do you think the neighborhood in which a child lives, or might potentially live, should have in your decisions about the child's ultimate welfare?

5. With a group of classmates, discuss gun control and some of the major arguments for each side. Consult *Social Work Speaks*, NASW's compendium of position papers, and search for statements that define social work's official position, if any, toward gun control.

CASE STUDY 6.4

OUTPATIENT COMMITMENT: MUST MENTAL DISABILITY PRECLUDE CIVIL LIBERTY?

Abstracted from an unpublished paper by Kimberly Platt, MSW

PRACTICE CONTEXT AND CASE PRESENTATION

Program development and social policy implementation and analysis can pose unique ethical questions, affecting the whole of the population being served. Legal advocacy for homeless persons with mental disabilities poses a particular kind of ethical challenge, one undertaken by the Advocacy Center.

A recent study estimates that, on any given day in the United States, there are 600,000 homeless people (Kassebaum, 1995). Another study shows that between one-fourth and one-third of these homeless people are severely mentally disabled (Cohen & Thompson, 1992). Kanter (1989) believes that psychiatric problems may result in homelessness, although homelessness may also induce or prompt the symptoms of mental disability. The number of chronically mentally disabled homeless has increased over the years, largely due to policies of deinstitutionalization where the patients move from institutions to inadequate community-based mental health services (Cohen & Thompson, 1992). As a result, a whole population of homeless could theoretically benefit from mental health services, whether inpatient or outpatient, voluntary or mandatory. *Outpatient commitment* is a procedure in which an individual deemed harmful to him- or herself or others is court-ordered to receive treatment in the community (Kanter, 1989).

In July 1995, Nancy Kassebaum (R-KS), Chair of the Senate Committee on Labor and Human Resources, proposed a bill that would have required outpatient commitment of mentally disabled homeless persons who are gravely disabled (Kassebaum, 1995). The bill defines the gravely mentally disabled as individuals "who are at risk of death, harm, or illness because they are too mentally ill to secure food, clothing, shelter or medical care" (Kassebaum, 1995, p. 2). Senator Kassebaum believes that this population remains homeless because they lack mental health services and adequate housing (Kassebaum, 1995). If they were required to receive treatment, Senator Kassebaum believes that their number would be drastically reduced. She feels that legislation is needed to require outpatient commitment because a current lack of treatment facilities hinders this commitment.

While a large number of the chronically mentally disabled are homeless and do require services that are often not available, some advocacy groups believe that outpatient commitment is not the answer. The Advocacy Center also feels that the commitment laws violate the constitutional right of equality by discriminating against people with disabilities (Goldman, 1995).

The ethical dilemma faced in this case may be stated as:

Society's Obligation to Ensure Optimal v. Individual Rights to Freedom Well-Being for All

(continued)

CASE STUDY 6.4   CONTINUED

RESEARCH AND RELATED LITERATURE

Scheid-Cook (1987) believes that outpatient commitment is a compromise between the individual's right to freedom and the need for society to care for its mentally disabled. Because of outpatient commitment, patients may live in the community rather than in hospitals. Scheid-Cook (1987) defends outpatient commitment because the mentally ill have "no insight into their mental illness they would not voluntarily comply with treatment" (p. 174). The author advocates laws that not only protect society from the individual and the patient from him- or herself, but also represent a lesser deprivation of liberty. Scheid-Cook (1987) studied court-ordered outpatient commitment and its effectiveness, finding that most individuals in outpatient commitment were chronically mentally disabled, usually schizophrenic males in their mid-thirties with a history of frequent hospital admissions and medication refusal. Mental health professionals successfully used involuntary commitment as leverage to enable community mental health centers (CMHC) to keep patients on medication and in programs (Scheid-Cook, 1987).

Wilk (1988) calls involuntary outpatient commitment "the legal and psychosocial process whereby an allegedly mentally disordered and dangerous person is forced to undergo mental health treatment or care in an outpatient setting" (p. 133). The dangerous person can be a danger to him- or herself, not just a danger to society. Citing the American Psychological Association, the author considers whether mental health professionals should hold liberty and privacy issues in higher regard than all other interests.

Wilk also analyzes various studies that test the effectiveness of involuntary outpatient treatment and raises many related issues. One is the worker's personal safety and the safety of the patient. In an inpatient setting, dangerous patients may be restricted and more closely supervised than in an outpatient setting, where the therapist will often see the patient alone in an office (Wilk, 1988).

Liability is another issue: Questions of responsibility if a client is harmed or harms another person, the duty of the worker to warn a potential victim, and potential worker responsibility if the patient is not taking medication or complying with a treatment plan need to be addressed before the worker treats an involuntary outpatient (Wilk, 1988).

The forced nature of the treatment also raises issues: The fear here is that social workers will be nothing more than monitors of medication (Wilk, 1988). Forced treatment is another phrase for involuntary commitment. With all that we have learned about starting where the client is, how effective would the social worker be with a client who is court-ordered to be there and is not only noncompliant but also frequently misses appointments?

Wilk (1988) states in summation that involuntary commitment requires more time from judges and other professionals, more resources, and more monitoring of commitment practices. Even after these are considered, involuntary commitment may only be beneficial to a small number of patients (Wilk, 1988).

Belcher (1988) believes that social workers face a dilemma when trying to meet the needs of clients without violating their rights. The author notes that the profession relies heavily on liberty and dignity of clients, and to stay true to those values and provide appropriate care to the individual, the worker may have to supersede other rights. Belcher (1988) cites Judge Bazelon, who believed that commitment should "be interpreted more narrowly to refer to treatment that is in the best interest of the individual" (p. 398). When considering involuntary commitment, the possibility that the person's quality of life will ultimately be improved through treatment must be considered (Belcher, 1988). Belcher (1988) argues that although the mentally disabled homeless may be exercising their rights, they "are able to determine little for themselves and are unable to self-direct their lives" (p. 398). Committing people may be a violation of their right to self-determination, but failing to commit the homeless mentally disabled may eventually lead to their death. While advocating for the right to self-determination, one must also advocate for physical well-being (Belcher, 1988).

McGough and Carmichael (1977) believe that involuntary commitment is a deprivation of liberty, justified if an individual is a harm to others, but not without due process and equal protection under the law. Beyond liberty there is the person's right to "self-determination and bodily integrity" (p. 316). However, mental illness may preclude the ability to exercise these rights in one's own best interest (McGough & Carmichael, 1977).

Kanter (1989) states that most states legally allow involuntary commitment if the person is a harm to themselves or others. The author cites the American Psychiatric Association's (APA) stance that states should reject the danger to themselves and others criterion and replace it by saying that the person is "likely to suffer substantial mental or physical deterioration" (p. 93). This new criterion shifts the focus from harm to others to harm/neglect of self. It also shifts the decision for commitment from the legal to the medical community (Kanter, 1989). The APA defends its position of commitment without consent, saying that "patients have the right to treatment that is the most appropriate and therapeutic available" (Kanter, 1989, p. 93). Overall, the author believes that involuntary commitment does not address the needs for housing, treatment, and other services for the homeless population (Kanter, 1989).

AUTHOR'S REFLECTIONS, REASONING PROCESS, AND RESOLUTION

Freedom and well-being are two concepts valued by our society. The Supreme Court has stated that liberty is not an absolute right but "freedom from restraint" should be equally enjoyed by everyone (McGough & Carmichael, 1977, p. 309). McGough and Carmichael (1977) quote John Stuart Mill's *On Liberty,* which says that "freedom is pursuing our own good in our own way, so long as we do not attempt to deprive others of theirs" (p. 309). Mill also writes that "each is the proper guardian of his own health, whether bodily, or mental, or spiritual" (p. 309).

Gewirth believes in two basic rights: freedom and well-being (Loewenberg & Dolgoff, 1992). Loewenberg and Dolgoff (1992) state, "Coercive intervention may be justified when (1) there is grave threat to basic social values or to fundamental social institutions or (2) when there is a clear and present danger that very great or irreversible harm will be done or will occur unless preventative action is taken" (p. 99).

Gewirth (Reamer, 1990) believes that freedom and well-being are the two basic fundamental rights of human beings, but at times these two rights conflict with one other. In *Reason and Morality,* Gewirth writes that people must develop a hierarchy of

(continued)

CASE STUDY 6.4   CONTINUED

values in times of conflict (Reamer, 1990). He offers guidelines for making ethical decisions: (1) Basic goods come first; (2) an individual's right to well-being takes precedence over another person's right to freedom; (3) an individual's right to freedom takes precedence over his or her right to well-being; (4) the obligation to obey laws, rules, and regulations to which we have freely and voluntarily agreed takes precedence over our freedom; (5) an individual's right to well-being may override laws, and regulations; and (6) the obligation to prevent basic harm and protect basic goods overrides the right to retain one's property (Reamer, 1990).

In summary, Gewirth believes that an individual's right to self-determination and freedom takes precedence over all, even the person's own well-being, except when their freedom hinders another individual's well-being. This position is in consonance with this author's personal values, which strongly support freedom and liberty.

The Code of Ethics addresses the present population and dilemma issues in several sections. First of all, there is a commitment on the part of the social worker to the client's interests as primary (section 1.01). However, in this case the application of this guideline is unclear: Is the primary obligation to freedom or to (society's and/or the worker's conception of) well-being?

Immediately after the primacy of client interest, the Code addresses self-determination and the obligation of the worker to support client self-determination, except in cases of "serious, foreseeable, and imminent risk to themselves or others" (1.02). It would seem that, if a worker wanted to follow this obligation, he or she would need to consider each client on a case-by-case basis: There may not *always* be such risk involved for the client. One issue with the population of mentally disabled homeless involves decisional capacity: "When social workers act on behalf of clients who lack the capacity to make informed decisions, social workers should take reasonable steps to safeguard the interests and rights of those clients" (1.14).

Should it be assumed that mental disability *de facto* makes one incompetent, and that, therefore, the worker, or "society," is justified in making decisions for such clients? Are there variations in the degree of mental disability, in the type of mental disability, in the client's particular circumstances, that can justly affect decisional capacity, or must one rule hold for all? Social workers are obligated to "promote the general welfare of society" and to "advocate for living conditions conducive to the fulfillment of basic human needs" (6.01). They should

> Engage in social and political action that seeks to ensure that all people have equal access to the resources, employment, services, and opportunities they require to meet their basic human needs and to develop fully. (6.04a)
>
> Act to expand choice and opportunity for all people, with special regard for vulnerable, disadvantaged, oppressed, and exploited people and groups. (6.04b)
>
> Act to prevent and eliminate domination, exploitation, and discrimination. (6.04d)

From these sections, it seems clear that the social worker has a responsibility to support and advocate for the mentally disabled, as a vulnerable and disadvantaged population. freedom, civil liberty, and well-being seem to be supported by the Code's positions.

Court-ordered outpatient treatment makes the recipients involuntary clients. Subsection 1.03d addresses these clients specifically, obligating social workers to: "provide information about the nature and extent of services and about the extent of clients' right to refuse service." This would seem to "expand choice and opportunity" (6.04b), but might be compromised by the client's mental disability, which can affect decisional capacity, thus returning the primary obligation for ensuring client rights and well-being to the worker.

The worker in this case believes that people have both the right to freedom and self-determination and the right to well-being. However, individuals cannot make decisions and exercise self-determination when they are trapped inside the mental illness. To be able to exercise the right of self-determination, a person must be competent to make decisions. If the mentally disabled homeless person is initially forced into treatment and becomes stable, then refuses treatment, the right to self-determination should override society's obligation to well-being. However, treatment may be required in order to ensure the validity of such decision making. Involuntary commitment might thus be a necessary step in the process of ensuring optimal self-determination.

QUESTIONS FOR THOUGHT AND DISCUSSION

1. Since the determination of "well-being" must always be a subjective one, can one ever justify abrogating an individual's freedom and self-determination in the interest of his or her well-being?
2. You have one concept of well-being for your client. Your client has another idea. You present the case at a case conference or team meeting and succeed in obtaining the agreement of other professionals to your concept of well-being. Does that make your concept "right"?
3. Competence is also a subjective judgment. What system, if any, do you believe would operate most fairly in determining "competence"? Why?
4. Deinstitutionalization of the chronically mentally disabled has now been in process for many years. What, do you think, was the original rationale for the program? Do you feel that it has succeeded in meeting the objectives?
5. If you were given the responsibility of writing a policy for this population, what kind of policy, if any, would you write? What principles, concepts, values would you appeal to in formulating such a policy? Would you separate the mentally disabled homeless from other homeless in writing your policy? Why or why not?

■ ■ ■ ■ ■

CASE STUDY 6.5

GENETIC RESEARCH: FOR THE GOOD OF THIS SUBJECT OR FOR (FUTURE) SOCIETY?

Abstracted from an unpublished paper* by Daniel W. Wilson, MSW

PRACTICE CONTEXT AND CASE PRESENTATION

SDI conducts a wide range of research projects, many of them funded by the U.S. Department of Health and Human Services (DHHS). Federal Regulations for the Protection of Human Subjects (45 CFR 46) mandate that all DHHS studies involving human subjects be reviewed and approved by an Institutional Review Board (IRB). IRBs must assess and weigh the risks and benefits to prospective study subjects against the intrinsic worth of the proposed research; they have binding authority to approve study implementation.

SDI's IRB composition is comprised of eight members: four senior staff, one attorney on retainer to SDI, two outside physicians, and one outside social worker. The IRB is chaired by an SDI executive officer.

In 1994, following review and approval by SDI's IRB, the New Genes Study (NGS) was initiated as a long-term, nontherapeutic study with an immediate objective to collect and store blood specimens from targeted populations in anticipation of sequencing newly discovered genes as they became available. The study's goal is to identify genetic biomarkers for specific cancers and disorders.

With the imminent cloning of the breast cancer gene, NGS staff began identifying and locating subjects diagnosed with breast cancer and with a high probability of having genetic mutations. Per study protocol, each potential subject was sent a letter explaining the goals and objectives of NGS, the reason she had been selected, the voluntary and confidential nature of her participation, and the foreseeable benefits and risks associated with participating. Each subject signed an informed consent document affirming her understanding that (1) blood specimens would be stored for future analyses on yet-to-be-cloned genes and (2) given the nontherapeutic and experimental nature of this research, preliminary results would not be reported.

In December 1994, a gene was cloned that many believed to be *the* breast cancer gene (Nowak, 1994). Early in 1995, sequencing of this gene was begun on stored NGS specimens, and soon thereafter the research team decided to augment the study population with cancer-free, first-degree adult relatives (controls) of current subjects with cancer (cases).

When giving its original approval, the Board had agreed that minimal risks existed for subjects diagnosed with a highly mortal disease, reasoning that subjects and their families would have been apprised of hereditary risks by medical caregivers. However, with the inclusion of cancer-free subjects, the Board is reassessing whether more

*To protect the identity and ensure the confidentiality of the organization conducting the genetic research described in this case, both the name of the specific organization and of the specific project have been changed.

than minimal risks exist for the control group. The social worker wonders whether genetic counseling might be made available to minimize psychological risks to subjects
and their families. The Chair shares this concern, recalling an instance of a patient's
committing suicide after being told she had a genetic defect. The attorney raises liability concerns created should either SDI and/or subjects possess genetic test results. The
Board almost unanimously favors providing subjects with test results, albeit clinically
meaningless; the majority also feel that genetic counseling should be made available.

However, provision of test results and genetic counseling would involve considerable expense, thus jeopardizing the study itself and the benefits that could accrue to
society in the future as a result of the research. The choice to provide services not in the
original study design would incur expenses that would have to be met by curtailing
numbers of patients or depth of research. One the one hand, there is a clear ethical
obligation to the subjects of the research; on the other, an ethical obligation to society,
which is providing the funding for the research.

The dilemma may thus be formulated as:

Good of the Individual Subject v. The Future Potential Good for Society

RESEARCH AND RELATED LITERATURE
Theoretical Perspective. Since IRB regulations generally consider populations of research subjects rather than individual subjects, IRB policy tends to be universally focused and absolute. It can be argued, therefore, that a deontological theory might be
applicable. Indeed, Gewirth's theory of basic human duties and rights (as detailed in
Reamer, 1990) provides a good model for allowing one to consider this problem from
both the individual and societal perspective. Gewirth holds that moral actions are those
that permit others to pursue their goals with freedom and well-being. He holds that there
are three core goods: The highest one, basic goods, includes the focal rights of this
dilemma: life and health. Duties are seen as actions or inactions that optimize the provision and guarding of rights. Germane to this ethical dilemma is Gewirth's belief in the
voluntary nature of communal associations, believing that "all members must voluntarily consent to membership and rules" (Reamer, 1990, p. 60). He provides a useful set
of guidelines for balancing and ordering duties and rights when they are in conflict.

On the other hand, the juxtaposition of individual and societal rights raises a teleological question, one asked by rule utilitarians, concerning which rules provide the
greatest good for the greatest number of people (Varga, 1978). This question seems not
to be entirely incompatible with Gewirth's guidelines, which occasionally require individual rights to be sacrificed for those of society.

General Background. In the past two decades, regulations guiding ethical research on
human subjects has slowly evolved, as summarized in Lederer and Grodin (1994). Following the revelation of Nazi atrocities brought to light at the Nuremberg Trials, the
Nuremberg Code of 1947 was drafted as a first attempt to protect human subjects. Building on this code, the World Medical Association in 1989 drafted the Declaration of
Helsinki IV, which more specifically detailed basic principles of biomedical research
ethics—for the first time making a distinction between therapeutic and nontherapeutic
research. Then in 1974, in response to public outcry over the Tuskegee syphilis study,

(continued)

CASE STUDY 6.5 CONTINUED

the federal government signed into law the National Research Act, creating the National Commission for the Protection of Human Subjects of Biomedical and Behavioral Research, charged with identifying ethical principles and moral actions related to such research. This commission published its deliberations in 1978 as the Belmont Report, citing three ethical principles: respect for persons, beneficence, and justice, principles compatible with Gewirth's. Also in 1974, the government created detailed guidelines (45 CFR 46) for clinical research. IRB members, including the social worker, are held accountable to all three of these codes, as well as to the laws of the United States. The social worker is also bound by the NASW Code of Ethics (1996).

Rights of Study Subjects. Subjects of the New Genes Study participate voluntarily as confirmed by their signing an informed consent document. In so doing, they waive their right to information regarding results as well as to genetic counseling. However, knowing whether one has genetic deficiencies will help subjects to make informed decisions about the frequency and nature of disease surveillance and diagnostic examinations (e.g., mammogram), the type of therapy to use for specific diseases (e.g., chemotherapy), whether to take prophylactic measures (e.g., mastectomy), and whether to have children (BRCA1, 1995; Kolata, 1995; Lerman et al., 1995; Nowak, 1994).

Several codes of ethics lend support to the subject's right to full disclosure. The 1947 Nuremberg Code protects a subject's right from suffering physical or mental health and from "even remote possibilities of injury, disability, or death" (Item 7). The Declaration of Helsinki IV (1989) requires that a study's worth be proportional to inherent risks to the subject (Item I.4) and, germane to this dilemma, places a subject's interest above society's (Item I.5). This latter point is reiterated in Section III, which specifically addresses nontherapeutic biomedical research, such as that conducted by NGS: "The interest of science and society should never take precedence over considerations related to the well-being of the subject" (Item III.4). Federal regulations (45 CFR 46) that bind SDI's IRB require that subjects be placed at no more than minimal risk when balanced against benefits of the research (46.111).

NASW's Code of Ethics (1996) also favors the subject's right to full disclosure. These are addressed in subsection 5.02. The following obligations seem relevant to the present dilemma:

> Social workers engaged in . . . research should obtain voluntary and written informed consent from participants, . . . and with due regard for participants' well-being, privacy, and dignity. Informed consent should include . . . disclosure of the risks and benefits of participation in the research. (5.02e)
>
> Social workers should take appropriate steps to ensure that participants . . . have access to appropriate supportive services. (5.02i)
>
> Social workers should protect participants from unwarranted physical or mental distress. . . . (5.02j)

Consistent with all these codifications are two tenets of religion that honor an individual's well-being: "Love your neighbour as yourself" (Matt. 22:39, *New English Bible,* 1971), and "Treat others as you would like others to treat you" (Luke 6:31).

Genetic screening is a pioneering endeavor, and little precedent exists to substantiate a subject's rights to immediate and full disclosure. One case, however, is noteworthy. In a recent genetic study of Huntington's disease, subjects received pre- and post-counseling concerning the probability of their inheriting a mutated gene associated with that disease (Wiggins et al., 1992). While these subjects were better educated than the general population, study findings indicate that, irrespective of test results, subjects benefited psychologically from counseling, experiencing less uncertainty and being better prepared to plan for the future. Beauchamp and Childress (1994) note, without citing specific studies, that concerns over the negative effects of disclosure generally are proven to be unwarranted. If replicable, these findings might assuage the NGS researcher's fear that subjects would be psychologically distressed by knowing test results.

An informal poll taken of IRB members indicated that, if given an either-or choice, they would side with the subject, arguing that control subjects in particular are immediately at risk for developing breast cancer and have been gracious in giving their blood. Additionally, two female colleagues with family histories of breast cancer (confidential communications, 7/13/95) concurred that while they would probably participate with or without counseling and receipt of test results, they would prefer to have both. This desire seems to be motivated as much by concern for their daughters and granddaughters as for themselves.

An IRB decision requiring genetic counseling and full disclosure of study results would meet Gewirth's requirement for maintaining one's basic right to health and life; would consequentially benefit the greater number (present and future generations of family); and, from a caring perspective, would strengthen relationships of mutual interdependence between researcher and subjects while tending to the emotional well-being of both.

Rights of Society. Society at large also has a right to the advantages to be gained from biomarker research. Society can only possess this right once data have been collected and analyzed. The construction of this body of knowledge depends entirely on the few research subjects volunteering to participate in research for the good of all. In this current dilemma, an IRB decision to provide subjects with counseling and test results could have cost consequences that go beyond all available funds. Thus, the world could be denied one of Gewirth's basic goods—the right to health.

Gewirth (1978) might argue that when society's basic goods are threatened, individuals have a responsibility to assist by relinquishing their own freedom. He would, however, qualify that one must give such assistance only if it is "at no comparable cost to himself" (p. 218). This reasoning lacks the ethics of care proffered by ethicists such as Gilligan and Baier, and it overlooks the consequential effects of giving individual rights priority over societal rights.

From a utilitarian point of view, Robert Cooke (1994) notes that, given the "enormous genetic heterogeneity that exist in humans [a few may be among] a handful of potential subjects for research that could lead to future prevention and alleviation of that disorder" (p. 207). Cooke goes on to wonder how the genetic puzzle will ever be solved if such subjects do not participate in research. For balance, it is helpful to look to a principle supported by Rawls and Dworkin, that of justified paternalism (Beauchamp &

(continued)

CASE STUDY 6.5   CONTINUED

Childress, 1994). Along with Abramson (Loewenberg & Dolgoff, 1992), they espouse relying on paternalism to resolve such conflicts, giving weight to the benefits derived, even if at the expense of autonomy.

Societal rights are defended, albeit with less vigor, by the same codes of ethics protecting individual rights. The 1947 Nuremberg Code stipulates that research should be done "to yield fruitful results for the good of society" (Item 2). The Declaration of Helsinki IV (1989) in Item I.3 is quasipaternalistic in assigning ultimate responsibility to the researcher, although it remains silent on societal rights when addressing non-therapeutic research per se. Federal regulations (45 CFR 46.111) allow a study to be judged of sufficient value to society as to place the subject at reasonable risk. Although applicable to research with children, 45 CFR 46.406 supports the stand taken by Cooke (1994), discussed above, that occasionally a few must submit to research for the good of all.

Section 6 of NASW's Code of Ethics specifically addresses a social worker's ethical responsibility to society. Social workers are obligated to promote the "general welfare" of society, "from local to global levels" (6.01). They should also "act to expand choice and opportunity for all people, with special regard for vulnerable, disadvantaged . . . people and groups" (6.04b).

Without the possible benefits that could result from this research, opportunity for people with the genetic conditions being studied would be curtailed, leaving them both vulnerable and disadvantaged.

An admonition from religious tradition summarizes codified arguments favoring the rights of society: "If you love only those who love you, what reward can you expect?" (Matt. 5:46). If one's obligation to care extends beyond one's self and those held dear, then self-sacrifice for society's sake is justifiable and occasionally necessary.

Historical precedent supports society's right to demand that a few serve as research subjects for the benefit of all. Many improvements in society's well-being have been accomplished because a few research subjects took risks on behalf of all. Similarly, exploratory research on HIV required the consent and participation of subjects who gave blood for blinded analyses, meaning that researchers had no idea whose blood had positive or negative antigens, and they could report no findings to subjects. Such anonymous research has made HIV screening tests available worldwide.

The belief that test results currently have no clinical usefulness is substantiated by a number of respected genetic researchers who have challenged the contrary claims of private manufacturers of genetic tests (BRCA1, 1995; Kolata, 1995; Nowak, 1994; Weiss, 1995). Similarly, studies on the effects of genetic counseling are contradictory and raise concern about its effectiveness. One study in particular challenges using counseling for NGS. Lerman et al. (1995) studied the effects of individual genetic counseling of women with a family history of breast cancer, and their results confirmed findings of several earlier studies. Over time and overall, subjects better understood that they were at risk; but the majority, *after* counseling, overestimated lifetime risks and showed increased anxiety. Coupled with the questionable efficacy of genetic counseling are certain documented manifestations of psychological stress associated with possessing information about one's genetic deficiencies. For example, physicians report that patients told of genetic defects (with no implications for clinical intervention) have expressed death anxiety and guilt about possibly giving their children a disease. Some women have had prophylactic mastectomies; and one woman, upon learning she had a mutation in BRCA1, attempted suicide. Finally, it is noteworthy that advice not to report test results at this time comes from two of the professional genetics community's most respected members: the Human Genome Council and the Breast Cancer Coalition (Kolata, 1995).

In querying genetic researchers about the issue of revealing test results to subjects, several favored not disclosing results. The ethics committee of one leading cancer research center has taken the position that, until clinically useful data are available, it is ethically wrong to give subjects information. They reason that such information could cause individuals to act or not act in such a way as to produce psychological and social harm. For example, a child with a known genetic defect that predisposes (but does not condemn) her to developing brain cancer, might be treated differently by the family, discouraged from pursuing advanced education, and/or have difficulty receiving health insurance. Others feel that, as with early research for HIV screening tests, analyses should be blinded, making reporting a moot issue.

In summary, society's future right to the basic goods of health and life appears to be achievable only at the expense of research subjects' immediate and individual rights. Since the barrier to society's rights (genetic counseling and test results) holds questionable consequences for individual subjects, caring and compassionate researchers would be hard pressed to give priority to the current rights of the subject, knowing that continued experimentation could eventually provide the same rights to the entire world.

AUTHOR'S REFLECTIONS, REASONING PROCESS, AND RESOLUTION

Influenced by U.S. culture, the subject, researchers, and IRB members tend to hold many common values that reflect our national paradox of cherishing community as well as individualism. For ease of comparison, basic values germane to genetic research are noted below in tabular form. Within each group, priorities have been set for a value's worth relative of the dilemma discussed above. Dashes indicated "no relevance."

VALUE	ALL SUBJECTS	RESEARCH TEAM	THE IRB
Justice	2	1	1
Liberty	1	2	2
Equal Opportunity	—	—	4
Individualism	4	—	3
Pioneering Adventure	6	3	7
Hard Work	7	5	—
Competition	—	4	—
Vigor/Health	3	7	6
Knowledge	5	6	5

(*continued*)

CASE STUDY 6.5   CONTINUED

As can be noted, there is agreement among all three groups concerning the primacy of two core U.S. values: justice and liberty. While subjects are more concerned about being at liberty to have immediate access to genetic test results, they nevertheless concur that justice must also prevail. Both the team and the IRB assign primacy to justice but give liberty (autonomy) the second highest mark. Similarly, knowledge is valued almost equally by all three entities. Agreement on ranking other values disintegrates at this point.

Subjects who either have or are in danger of developing cancer cherish health (their own and that of their families) over the remaining values. Vis-à-vis the dilemma, hard work is important to the extent that results are achieved quickly; equal opportunity and competition are not relevant values to subjects.

On the other hand, not surprisingly, the research team, working in a highly competitive, rapidly evolving area of research, values discovery, competition, and hard work. It is interesting that health, the team's *raison d'être,* is listed last.

The IRB's concern, predictably, is not with hard work or competition. As shown earlier, the Board's regulations tend to favor the rights of subjects over those of society. A common value of all of humanity appears to be life.

Upon reflection, it seems that the worker, like this nation, draws the majority of primary values from Anglo-Christian faith; these include: truth, charity, duty, equality of all, and justice. Other values—such as exploration/pioneering, individualism, perseverance, hard work, and liberty (but in a Banhoefferian sense)—appear to be derived from national identity.

From a Native American heritage, the worker has learned to value harmony, especially the oneness of all life. And from personal experiences, the worker cherishes values such as nonviolence, caring, compassion, communalism, fidelity, spirituality, humor, and journeying (a lifelong quest for self-knowledge). Perhaps the value that enfolds all the others and respects both society and self is charity. Charity includes love of self and of others, requires justice, demands equality, and thus can direct all ethical decisions toward right actions.

This worker admits that his first, impulsive reaction would have been to take a utilitarian approach, siding with society to provide the greater good to the greater number—expecting a trivial percent of humanity to bend to the needs of us all. In the midst of researching this dilemma, however, it became obvious that, when in doubt, based on various codes and regulations, the worker is duty-bound (in a deontological sense) to defer to an individual's rights. Consequently, the dilemma intensifies, leading to "intellectual ambidexterity" (Reamer, 1990, p. 234), considering the worth of both sides but unable to decide on a course of action.

Indeed, weighing the rights of individuals against those of humanity, this worker's scale tips toward the individual. And when regretting that individual rights might deny society an opportunity for advanced, state-of-the-art health care, he is reminded of a comment by Hans Jonas: "progress is an optional goal" (cited in Capron, 1991, p. 82S). Gallegos and Mrgudic (1993), in describing the role of IRBs over time, have noted that the ethical focus is moving away from beneficence and paternalism toward autonomy and self-determination. The worker notes the same shifts within himself.

The following approach not only guards an individual subject's right to health and life but also provides a means for society to reap the same benefits. Therefore, the following ethical option is recommended by this social worker to the IRB. Each potential study subject should

1. Be fully informed (in lay terms) of the pros and cons of this experimental, non-therapeutic research.
2. Be apprised of the reasons researchers are hesitant to provide data that are useful only in an epidemiologic (not a clinical) sense.
3. Be given the option, as new genes are cloned, to decide gene-by-gene whether they wish to have their blood specimen sequenced.
4. Be given assurances that, should findings of clinical significance be made, they will be notified, with the following two qualifiers:
   a. Since costs associated with offering genetic counseling and with re-analyzing and reporting test results would prohibit the conduct of this important study, regrettably neither will be provided.
   b. When meaningful findings are obtained, every effort will be made to locate subjects in order to refer them to clinics in their area where, at their own expense, they may seek genetic counseling and testing.

By giving informed consent and volunteering to submit to the study protocol, individual subjects are exercising their right of self-determination. In a real sense, they are entering into a social contract with the researchers and with society at large and in a certain way are allowing their personal rights to be subsumed by society. Schulte (1991) warns that, in terms of psychological harm to subjects, there is a danger in investigators' under- or overcommunicating information. But most ethicists and philosophers (ranging from the Buddha to Aristotle to Chief Black Elk) are wont to give humans credit and responsibility for making intelligent decisions. This option attempts to maximize the amount of information subjects need to do just that.

This approach achieves the social worker's goal of promoting the well-being of both individuals and society. Besides giving subjects more information than ordinarily provided for giving informed consent, it effectively checks the research community's tendency to paternalism, and it engages subject and researcher in constructive and honest dialogue. This ethical option honors a number of this worker's values, not the least of which are truth, integrity, community, and justice. Moreover, it fosters a value that appears to embrace both self and society and enfolds all other virtues—charity. Above all, this option promotes one of humanity's fundamental values—life.

QUESTIONS FOR THOUGHT AND DISCUSSION

1. It is assumed in this case that "good" will result to the society of the future from the current research. However, this "good" exists only in potential: It is not definite or

absolute. Should this factor be a consideration in weighing the two sides of this dilemma?

2. A subject might be able to provide a valid informed consent if asked to waive access to specific information that might be determined by the study. Can a subject provide informed consent to waive such access if the information to be determined is not yet known or specific?

3. As an outside social worker member of an IRB, whom should the worker consider his employer? His client? Should the answers to these two questions bear any influence on the social worker's position in this case?

4. Is there a substantive difference in ethical position between arguing for the individual versus a presently existing society and an individual versus a future society? Do we have a similar responsibility to both? How can the differences, if there are any, be defined in ethical terms?

5. Are the ethical issues the same if the research is being privately sponsored and financed? Do the individual subjects and "society" occupy the same position in relation to each other in these different kinds of settings?

■ ■ ■ ■ ■

CASE STUDY 6.6

A COMMITMENT TO SOCIAL JUSTICE: SOCIAL WORK
AND IMMIGRATION POLICY

Abstracted from an unpublished paper by M. Thérèse Jones, MSW

PRACTICE CONTEXT AND CASE PRESENTATION

Experience with immigrants has focused the worker's attention on the ethics of U.S. immigration policies. She is concerned with the extension of social justice beyond the immediate borders of the United States to a consideration of our societal responsibility toward those whose lives have been disrupted by the intervention of the United States in their countries. As a social worker concerned with both national and global issues, the author feels a commitment to explore social justice from the perspective of immigration with a view to advocacy in this area.

Specifically, the worker questions whether a just policy means the provision of equal opportunities to all immigrants, or the provision of preferential treatment to immigrants from countries in which the United States has been involved militarily. As a profession, social work has traditionally taken positions in support of human rights and social justice, nonviolence, and peace. The profession has made its voice heard on many other social issues; the worker believes that immigration is a valid issue that must be addressed. In order to address these competing concerns, they must first be stated:

Equal Opportunity to All	**v.**	**Preferential Opportunity for Immigration to**
Desiring Immigration		**Persons from Nations Where the United**
		States Has Been a Military Presence

This dilemma presents a choice between two equal and competing goods. One position is that all immigrants deserve equal treatment that requires an even-handed approach for immigration policy, regardless of an immigrant's country of origin. On the other hand, giving preferential treatment to certain groups is justified to make amends for the destruction (physical, emotional, and spiritual) the United State has caused in their homelands.

RESEARCH AND RELATED LITERATURE

History of Immigration Policy. The history of U.S. immigration policy may be described as occupying three separate phases. The first phase, from the colonial era to the 1920s, consisted of a generally open-door policy to persons of European origin, premised on the perception by business and government that such immigration was needed for continued economic growth. In the 1920s, tight restrictions on immigration were imposed, based principally on wide acceptance of theories of racial inferiority. During this second phase, strict quotas were placed on immigration from countries outside the Western Hemisphere. The third phase, beginning in the mid-1960s, saw the end

(continued)

CASE STUDY 6.6 CONTINUED

of quotas based on nationality and the advent of greater acceptance of refugees from Southeast Asia, Afghanistan, and Central America (Muller, 1993).

Current Immigration Policy. Under current law, the United States admits up to 465,000 immigrants each year (8 U.S.C.A. § 1151[c][West Supp., 1995]). It also admits up to 112,000 refugees (59 *Fed. Reg.* 52393 [1994]) and a varying number of persons who qualify for political asylum (8 U.S.C.A. § 1158 [West Supp., 1995]). Although the law distinguishes between these groups, the worker will treat potential immigrants, refugees, and asylum seekers as a single class because it includes all foreigners who wish or need to live in this country, for whatever reason.

The U.S. law provides, with certain exceptions, that "no person shall receive any preference or priority or be discriminated against in the issuance of an immigrant visa because of the person's race, sex, nationality, place of birth, or place of residence" (8 U.S.C.A. § 1152 [a][1] [West Supp., 1995]). These exceptions include preferences for family-sponsored (up to 226,000), employment-based (up to 140,000), and diversity immigrants (up to 55,000). Employment-based immigrants are classified into several categories: (a) priority workers (aliens with extraordinary ability, superior professors and researchers, and certain multinational executives, 28.6 percent); (b) professionals with advanced degrees or persons with exceptional abilities (28.6 percent); (c) skilled workers, professionals, and other (unskilled) workers (26.8 percent); and (d) special immigrants (7.1 percent). Diversity immigrants are selected from low-admission states from the following six regions: Africa; Asia; Europe; North America (other than Mexico); Oceania; and South America, Mexico, Central America, and the Caribbean (8 U.S.C. § 1153 [West Supp., 1995]).

In addition to these immigrants, the United States also admits entry to a limited number of refugees for humanitarian reasons, the number of which varies from year to year, and an unspecified number of persons who qualify for political asylum. Currently, the United States admits up to 112,000 refugees per year, on the finding that they present "special humanitarian concerns," as follows: 7,000 from Africa; 40,000 from East Asia; 48,000 from former Soviet Union/Eastern Europe; 8,000 from Latin America/Caribbean; 5,000 from Near East/South Asia; 2,000 unallocated (59 *Fed. Reg.* 52393 [1994]).

This current law provides for differential treatment of persons seeking immigration based on their family, employment, place of origin, and refugee and political status.

Equal Treatment to All Immigrants. Equal treatment of immigrants is defined literally. No preference will be given to individuals based on who they are, where they are from, or what they do. This definition is consistent with the nondiscrimination principle in the U.S. law. It does not, however, recognize the exceptions (preferences) that also exist in the law.

The equal treatment principle is similar to the principle that freedom of movement is a fundamental human right, a view that has support among some liberal egalitarian philosophers and in natural law theories (Carens, 1992; Dummett, 1992). Their basic position is that a person generally has a right to immigrate to any country, although public policy may justify certain restrictions (Carens, 1992; Dummett, 1992). If any restrictions are imposed on individual freedom of movement, such as when the consequences of open borders is a greater harm,

> the natural way of respecting the force of this right, within an egalitarian framework, would be some policy that can be justified in terms of equal treatment of all who wish to exercise their right (e.g., a lottery system that gives every prospective immigrant, rich or poor, an equal chance to enter, or some other system that embodies some other relevant notion of equality of opportunity or access). (Woodward, 1992, p. 61)

Current law reflects this equality principle to a limited degree because it provides for equal treatment of potential immigrants within delineated categories, although the categories create certain inequalities. By treating each potential immigrant within a particular category as equally entitled to enter this country, the law favors the principle of equal treatment. A major consequence of not having equal treatment of all in the right to immigrate is that the immigration issue becomes dominated by political and economic concerns. For example, the potential immigrant could be viewed as an asset or a liability to the United States in terms of political and economic policy. For these reasons it is sometimes said that "U.S. immigration policy is domestic foreign policy" (D. A. Katz, personal communication, July 6, 1995).

Among the prima facie duties that W. D. Ross (1963) postulates are the duties of nonmaleficence, beneficence, and justice. Each of these duties can be used to support a policy of equal treatment of all immigrants. The obligation of nonmaleficence is relevant because a discriminatory immigration policy inherently inflicts harm on potential immigrants who are refused entry. It may also inflict harm in particular cases if it discriminates against people who are trying to emigrate from politically repressive countries or economically depressed areas. Finally, institutionalizing a discriminatory policy within the U.S. code of laws is antithetical to democratic principles. The obligation of nonmaleficence requires that U.S. policy avoid these harms.

The obligation of beneficence supports an equal treatment policy because it promotes the welfare of potential immigrants; that is, it is an action that the United States should be doing because it benefits these individuals. The beneficence obligations also support that policy because it promotes diversity and the continued enrichment of the country's pluralistic society.

The prima facie obligation of justice supports equal treatment because fundamental elements of the Bill of Rights are equal protection and due process of law. Although substantive constitutional rights (such as equal protection) are not granted to immigrants, in recent years procedural due process (the right to legal procedures) has been used to an extent that approximates providing actual substantive rights (Motomura, 1992). Even if not formally recognized in the Constitution, justice should require equal treatment and blindfolded decision making.

Preferential Treatment to Immigrant Groups Due to U.S. Involvement. Over the past forty-five years the United States has engaged in or supported military action in

(*continued*)

CASE STUDY 6.6   CONTINUED

other countries primarily for the purpose of protecting U.S. interests (economic and/or political). These countries include, for example, Haiti in the 1950s; Vietnam, Cambodia, Laos, and Cuba in the 1960s; Guatemala, Nicaragua, El Salvador, and Angola in the 1970s and 1980s; Panama and Iraq in the 1990s; and Afghanistan and Iraq in the 2000s. In these interventions there was substantial destruction to lives and property and in some instances many people have been displaced from their homeland.

Significant populations from these countries continue to account for large numbers of the world's refugees and asylum seekers. As of December 31, 1994, these figures were as follows: Vietnam 294,900; Cambodia 30,250; Angola 344,000; Guatemala 45,050; Nicaragua 22,750; and Iraq 635,900 (wide variation reported). Refugee numbers for Haiti were less than 20,000 but still substantial (U.S. Committee for Refugees, 1995). As of the same 1994 date, the United States hosted 181,700 refugees and asylum seekers. Twenty-nine thousand, two hundred of these people were from Cuba, 4,500 were from Haiti, and the remainder were from various other countries (U.S. Committee for Refugees, 1995).

Extensive research in the late 1970s through the 1980s by Congress, the Select Commission on Immigration and Refugee Policy, and others has led to development of a bipartisan consensus supporting five principles of immigration policy (Fuchs, 1993). One of these principles is that the United States "should accept its fair share of refugees and asylees" (Fuchs, 1993, p. 172).

Currently, U.S. policy toward refugees is based primarily on providing "safe havens." The United States has provided a safe haven for Haitians and Cubans at Guantanamo military base. The problem with this policy is that

> safe havens work only as an interim form of protection until refugees can safely return home. When the causes of refugee flows have proven intractable and refugees have remained stranded in camps for years, the results have been breakdowns of the social order among the refugees, and ever escalating tendencies toward apathy, dependency, and despondency, accentuated by domestic violence, crime, and political fanaticism. (U.S. Committee for Refugees, 1995, p. 25)

Although current U.S. law provides for immigration by refugees and persons seeking political asylum and (also provides for other preferences), there is no provision for giving preferential treatment to persons who have been displaced as a result of U.S. involvement. A position should be taken that the United States should give preferential treatment to those persons who have been displaced from their homelands as a result of U.S. involvement.

Related to the idea of giving preferential treatment to immigrants who have been displaced because of U.S. involvement is the principle that the United States should gear immigration policy to assist immigrants who are fleeing poor economic or political conditions. Liberal egalitarianism provides that economic, political, and social inequalities should be reduced as much as possible (Carens, 1992), and giving immigration preference to these individuals would address these concerns.

W. D. Ross's prima facie obligations of nonmaleficence, beneficence, and reparations can be applied to support the above principle. Nonmaleficence is relevant because denying immigration to individuals living in poor economic and political conditions is a wrongful act. Denying these people immigration and forcing them to live in politically unstable and/or poverty-stricken areas may result in a lack of basic living necessities or physical harm, as evidenced in Haiti.

The beneficence obligation is applicable because allowing these people to immigrate promotes their personal and psychological welfare. Immigration allows them to take advantage of relatively stable economic and political conditions in the United States and thereby lead productive lives.

The duty of reparations directly supports providing preferential treatment to these immigrant groups because in many instances the immigrant's plight is caused by U.S. foreign policy and military intervention. In our legal system, the duty of reparations requires that a person who causes harm to another must repair that harm. One way for the United States to make reparations for the harm caused to foreign countries and their residents would be by giving them priority to immigrate.

AUTHOR'S REFLECTIONS, REASONING PROCESS, AND RESOLUTION

There are several prominent values embedded in U.S. society that apply to the immigration issue, including freedom, justice, and equal opportunity. Freedom is the cornerstone of the U.S. democracy because it relates to thought and action. The values of political freedom, religious freedom, freedom of speech, and freedom of association are recognized in the law and cultural theory.

Justice is the principle in which all members of the society are treated fairly in accordance with the recognition that people have certain rights that should be fulfilled by society. A just society is one in which all needs are met and persons are rewarded for their good efforts and punished for harming others and other wrongdoing. Justice means that when people are needy, they receive what they need; persons who are sick get medical attention; society provides for people who have no food or shelter; and when people are lonely, they are comforted.

The value of equal opportunity allows for all women, men, and children to actualize themselves in the society. This includes equal opportunity in education and equal opportunity in employment, not just at entry levels but also for higher education and career advancement. The very concept of democracy is premised on the idea that every person is equal. For some, equal opportunity means providing special treatment for persons who are economically, culturally, and physically stigmatized. Without special treatment, stigmatized groups may be prevented from having equal access to education, housing, and jobs.

These three principles—freedom, justice, and equal opportunity—are intrinsically related to immigration issues. When considering equal treatment to all immigrants, the value of equal opportunity could indicate that each potential immigrant would have the same opportunity to live in the United States legally. Conversely, equal opportunity could also indicate that we should give priority to those countries who historically have not had access to this country or to persons who have been disadvantaged (displaced) due to our involvement in their homelands.

(continued)

CASE STUDY 6.6   CONTINUED

Freedom relates to both sides of the dilemma. This country is a country of immigrants. The principle of freedom of movement is central to our very existence as a nation, whether it is viewed as a melting pot or as a pluralistic society. Persons should be free to immigrate regardless of their country of origin or their motives. This freedom supports the idea that all immigrants should be treated equally. At the same time, giving immigration priority to persons displaced because of U.S. involvement would promote political freedom, a central precept of this county.

Assuming that there is a right to immigrate, justice might support a policy that allows anyone who wishes to immigrate to this county to do so. However, if one assumes that there needs to be some restrictions on immigration, justice could still support a policy in which each potential immigrant was given the same chance to reside in the United States legally, supported by an equal opportunity principle such as a lottery. Such a system would not address the past wrong caused by our involvement in destruction of a foreign country.

Several provisions of the NASW Code of Ethics are relevant to this dilemma and consideration of immigration policy, especially Section 6, which addresses the social worker's ethical responsibility to the broader society. Subsection 6.01 obligates the social worker to "promote the general welfare of society" and to "advocate for living conditions conducive to the fulfillment of basic human needs." Social workers are also asked to

> engage in social and political action that seeks to ensure that all people have equal access to the resources . . . services, and opportunities they require to meet their basic human needs and to develop fully. Social workers should be aware of the impact of the political arena on practice. (6.04a)
> . . . act to prevent and eliminate domination of, exploitation of, and discrimination against any person, group, or class. (6.04d)

These two principles tend to support an immigration policy in which all immigrants are treated equally and not discriminated against.

However, other provisions of the Code of Ethics support the other side of the dilemma.

> Social workers should act to expand choice and opportunity for all people, *with special regard* for vulnerable, disadvantaged, oppressed, and exploited people and groups. (6.04b, author's emphasis)
> Social workers should . . . promote social, economic, political, and cultural values and institutions that are compatible with the realization of social justice. (6.01)

Two divergent positions can be drawn from the Code of Ethics that, when applied to immigration issues, inherently conflict. The first is that the social worker should prevent discrimination and promote conditions of equal opportunity. The second position would be that the social worker should promote social justice, which involves giving priority status to certain individuals and groups.

The good, for this social worker, requires consideration of the motive behind an action, the means to achieving an end, and the end itself. Although in many cases the end (result) is the clearest indicator of whether an action is good, the means and/or motive for achieving that end may be unethical.

Because of this definition of the good, justice is this worker's highest value, closely followed by nonviolence. Nonviolence is defined as not inflicting physical, emotional, or spiritual harm on any individual or group. Freedom and equality, compassion, integrity, and tolerance and acceptance of others are important values to this worker and to the profession as a whole.

Resolution of this dilemma begins with a recognition that the United States has obligations to persons wishing to immigrate to this country. These obligations, which stem from both law and historical tradition, require that the United States treat potential immigrants justly and continue to admit immigrants each year. The United States also has certain obligations relating to how it interacts with other countries. Societal, professional, and personal values indicate support for additional obligations, which arise as a consequence of military intervention.

When the United States becomes involved militarily in another country, additional ethical obligations must be considered. In other words, it must be recognized that not all potential immigrants can be viewed as similarly situated. Thus, the obligation of reparation should take precedence over the obligation to treat all potential immigrants equally. It is necessary to repair, or at least attempt to repair, the harm caused by military involvement in order to promote social justice.

The profession should therefore strongly consider its obligation to take a position advocating for preferential treatment for immigrants to whom the United States owes the duty of reparation.

QUESTIONS FOR THOUGHT AND DISCUSSION

1. NASW has issued several official position statements in recent years, on HIV/AIDS, end-of-life decisions, rights of children, and other subjects. Do you feel that such advocacy is the responsibility of the profession? Are you comfortable in letting the profession speak for you?

2. Beyond NASW position statements, do you think that individual social workers have a responsibility to advocacy? How should workers meet this obligation?

3. The United States has taken a strong global position on human rights. This has been viewed in other countries as interference in their internal affairs. Do you think that the United States has a responsibility to ensure the human rights of citizens of other countries?

4. Are we "our brother's keeper" in global issues of hunger, poverty, disease, education, shelter?

5. The United States, too, has limited resources. There are those who advocate that we must take care of those in need within our country before addressing global concerns and needs. Do you think this is a valid position? How would you balance the needs of citizens against the needs of the global community?

REFERENCES AND BIBLIOGRAPHY

Case Study 6.1

Cohen, E. D. (1990). Confidentiality, counseling, and clients who have AIDS: Ethical foundations of a model rule. *Journal of Counseling and Development, 68*(3), 282–286.

Harding, A. K., Gray, L. A., & Neal, M. (1993). Confidentiality limits with clients who have HIV: A review of ethical and legal guidelines and professional policies. *Journal of Counseling and Development, 71*(3), 297–305.

Kain, C. D. (1988). To breach or not to breach: Is that the question? A response to Gray and Harding. *Journal of Counseling and Development, 66*(5), 224–225.

Kermani, E. J., & Weiss, B. A. (1989). AIDS and confidentiality: Legal concept and its application in psychotherapy. *American Journal of Psychotherapy, XLIII*(1), 25–31.

Knapp, S., & VandeCreek, L. (1990). Application of the duty to protect HIV-positive patients. *Professional Psychology: Research and Practice, 21*(3), 161–166.

Kopels, S., & Kagle, J. D. (1993). Do social workers have a duty to warn? *Social Service Review, 67*(1), 101–125.

Lamb, D. H., Clark, C., Drumheller, P., Frizzell, K., & Surrey, L. (1989). Applying *Tarasoff* to AIDS-related psychotherapy issues. *Professional Psychology: Research and Practice, 20*(1), 37–43.

Morrison, C. F. (1989). AIDS: Ethical implications for psychological intervention. *Professional Psychology: Research and Practice, 20*(3), 166–171.

National Association of Social Workers. (1996). *NASW Code of Ethics.* Washington, DC: Author.

Ryan, C. C. (1989). The social and clinical challenges of AIDS. *Smith College Studies in Social Work, 59,* 3–20.

Tomasi, J. (1991). Individual rights and community virtues. *Ethics, 101*(3), 521–536.

Watkins, S. A. (1989). Confidentiality and privileged communications: Legal dilemma for family therapists. *Social Work, 34*(2), 133–136.

Wiener, L. S. (1986). Helping clients with AIDS: The role of the worker. *Public Welfare, 44,* 38–41.

Yu, M. M., & O'Neal, B. (1992). Issues of confidentiality when working with persons with AIDS. *Clinical Social Work Journal, 20*(4), 421–430.

Case Study 6.2

Beauchamp, T. L., & Childress, J. F. (1994). *Principles of biomedical ethics.* New York: Oxford University Press.

Calabresi, S., & Lawson, G. (1992). Foreward: The Constitution of responsibility. *Cornell Law Review, 77*(5), 955–958.

Forer, L. (1986). Autonomy and responsibility: A search for new bases of legal rights and obligations. *Utah Law Review, 1986*(4), 665–693.

Hatch, O. G. (1992). A departure on the people. *Cornell Law Review, 77*(5), 959–963.

Loewenberg, F., & Dolgoff, R. (1992). *Ethical decisions for social work practice.* Itasca, IL: F. E. Peacock.

Moore, S. E. (1994). Confidentiality of child and adolescent treatment records. *Child and Adolescent Social Work Journal, 11*(2), 165–175.

National Association of Social Workers. (1996). *NASW Code of Ethics.* Washington, DC: Author.

Reamer, F. (1990). *Ethical dilemmas in social service.* New York: Columbia University Press.

Seelig, J. M. (1990). Privileged communication. *Journal of Independent Social Work, 4*(4), 75–80.

Case Study 6.3

Blackstone, W. (1996, Fall). Commentaries. In N. Lund, The past and future of the individual's right to arms. *Georgia Law Review, 31*(1). Available: www.lawsch.uga.edu/lund.html

Caplan, T., & Thomas, H. (1995). Safety and comfort, content and process: Facilitating open group work with men who batter. *Social Work with Groups, 18*(2/3), 33–51.

Chafee, J. H. (1992, Fall). It's time to control handguns. *Public Welfare, 50*(4), 18–22.

Gilligan, C. (1982). *In a different voice.* Cambridge, MA: Harvard University Press.

Hobbes, T. (1651). *LEVIATHAN, or the matter, forme, and power of a common-wealth, ecclesiasticall and civill.* London: printed for Andrew Crooke at the Green Dragon in St. Pauls Church-yard. (Reprinted 1958). London: Oxford at the Clarendon Press.

Journals of the House of Commons, 1688–1693 (10:21-22). In J. L. Malcolm (1994), *The right to keep and bear arms.* New York: Harper and Row.

Lewis, N. (1988, October 6). Rowan won't be retried on gun charges: D.C. corporation counsel says jurors were confused in case of unregistered weapon. *The Washington Post,* p. B1.

Mace, J. P. (1989, March). The effect of attitude and belief on social worker judgments concerning potentially dangerous clients. University of California at Los Angeles, DSW dissertation.

National Association of Social Workers. (1996). *NASW Code of Ethics.* Washington DC: Author.

Star, B. (1984). Patient violence/therapist safety. *Social Work, 29*(3), 225-230.

Tully, C. T., Kropf, N. P., & Price, J. L. (1993, Spring/Summer). Is field a hard hat area? A study of violence in field placements. *Journal of Social Work Education, 29*(2), 10–99.

Case Study 6.4

Belcher, J. R. (1988). Rights versus needs of homeless mentally ill persons. *Social Work,* 398–402.

Center for Mental Health Law. (1994). *Civil rights and human dignity* [Brochure]. Name Withheld. Author.

Cohen, C. I., & Thompson, K. S. (1992). Homeless mentally ill or mentally ill homeless? *American Journal of Psychiatry, 149*(6), 816–823.

Goldman, H. H. (1995, July). Testimony on behalf of the Judge David L. Bazelon Center for Mental Health Law before the Committee on Labor and Human Resources:

United States Senate on the Reauthorization of the Substance Abuse and Mental Health Services Administration. Washington, DC.

Kanter, A. S. (1989). Homeless but not helpless: Legal issues in the care of homeless people with mental illness. *Journal of Social Issues, 45*(3), 91–104.

Kassebaum, N. L. (Senator). (1995, June). *Homeless mentally ill in the SAMHSA Reauthorization, Flexibility Enhancement, and Consolidation Act of 1995.* Testimony given to the Senate Committee on Labor and Human Resources. Washington, DC.

Loewenberg, F. M., & Dolgoff, R. (1992). *Ethical decisions for social work practice.* Itasca, IL: F. E. Peacock.

McGough, L. S., & Carmichael, W. C. (1977). The right to treatment and the right to refuse treatment. *American Journal of Orthopsychiatry, 47*(2), 307–320.

National Association of Social Workers. (1996). *NASW Code of Ethics.* Washington, DC: Author.

Reamer, F. G. (1990). *Ethical dilemmas in social service.* New York: Columbia University Press.

Scheid-Cook, T. L. (1987). Commitment of the mentally ill to outpatient treatment. *Community Mental Health Journal, 23*(3), 173–182.

Wilk, R. J. (1988). Involuntary outpatient commitment of the mentally ill. *Social Work,* 133–136.

Case Study 6.5

Beauchamp, T. L., & Childress, J. F. (1994). *Principles of biomedical ethics* (4th ed.). New York: Oxford University Press.

Beauchamp, T. L., & Pinkard, T. P. (1983). *Ethics and public policy: An introduction to ethics* (2nd ed.). Englewood Cliffs, NJ: Prentice-Hall.

Bieseker, B. B., Hadley, D. W., & Struewing, J. (1994, September). *Clinical research protocol: Initial review application: Outcomes of education and counseling for BRCA1 testing.* (Available from Medical Genetics Branch, National Center for Human Genome Research, Building 10, Room 10c101, Bethesda, MD 20892).

BRCA1 breast cancer screening test. (1995, March 29). *The Blue Sheet,* pp. 12–13.

Capron, A. M. (1991). Protection of research subjects: Do special rules apply in epidemiology? *Journal of Clinical Epidemiology, 44*(Supplement I), 81S–89S.

Cooke, R. (1994). Vulnerable children. In M. A. Grodin & L. H. Glantz (Eds.), *Children as research subjects: Science, ethics, and law* (pp. 193–214). New York: Oxford University Press.

DHHS Policy for Protection of Human Subjects. (1991). *56 Federal Register, 28003* (June 18), codified *45 CFR 46,* Subpart A. (cited as 45 CFR 46).

Donagan, A. (1983). Informed consent in therapy and experimentation. In T. L. Beauchamp & T. P. Pinkard (Eds.), *Ethics and public policy: An introduction to ethics* (pp. 343–365). Englewood Cliffs, NJ: Prentice-Hall.

Gallegos, T., & Mrgudic, K. (1993). Community bioethics: The health decisions community council. *Health and Social Work, 18*(3), 215–220.

Gewirth, A. (1978). *Reason and morality.* Chicago: University of Chicago Press.

Joseph, M. V. (1983). A model for ethical decision-making in clinical practice. In C. B. Germain (Ed.), *Advances in clinical practice* (pp. 207–217). Silver Spring, MD: National Association of Social Workers.

Kolata, G. (1995, March 27). Test to assess risks for cancer raising questions. *The New York Times,* p. A1.

Lederer, S., & Grodin, M. A. (1994). Historical overview: Pediatric experimentation. In M. A. Grodin & L. H. Glantz (Eds.), *Children as research subjects: Science, ethics, and law* (pp. 3–25). New York: Oxford University Press.

Lerman, C., Lustbader, E., Rimer, B., Daly, M., Miller, S., Sands, C., & Balshem, A. (1995). Effects of individual breast cancer risk counseling: A randomized trial. *Journal of the National Cancer Institute, 87*(4), 286–292.

Loewenberg, F. M., & Dolgoff, R. (1992). *Ethical decisions for social work practice* (4th ed.). Itasca, IL: F. E. Peacock.

National Association of Social Workers. (1996). *NASW Code of Ethics.* Washington, DC: Author.

National Commission for the Protection of Human Subjects of Biomedical and Behavioral Research. (1978). *Belmont report.* (GPO No. 867-609). Washington, DC: U.S. Government Printing Office.

New English Bible, The. (1971). Nashville, TN: Thomas Nelson.

Nuremberg Code. (1947). In M. A. Grodin & L. H. Glantz (Eds.), *Children as research subjects: Science, ethics, and law* (Appendix B, pp. 218–219). New York: Oxford University Press.

Nowak, R. (1994, December 2). Breast cancer gene: Many mutations may make test difficult. *Science, 266,* 1470.

Reamer, F. G. (1990). *Ethical dilemmas in social service: A guide for social workers* (2nd ed.). New York: Columbia University Press.

Rubin, A., & Babbie, E. (1989). *Research methods for social work.* Belmont, CA: Wadsworth.

Schulte, P. A. (1991). Ethical issues in the communication of results. *Journal of Clinical Epidemiology, 44*(Supplement I), 57S–61S.

Singer, P. (1983). Animal rights and animal research. In T. L. Beauchamp & T. P. Pinkard (Eds.), *Ethics and public policy: An introduction to ethics* (pp. 387–410). Englewood Cliffs, NJ: Prentice-Hall.

Varga, A. C. (1978). *On being human: Principles of ethics.* New York: Paulist Press.

Weiss, R. (1995, April 7). Gene discrimination barred in workplace. *The Washington Post,* p. A3.

Wiggins, S., Whyte, P., Huggins, M., Adam, S., Theilmann, J., Bloch, M., Sheps, S., Schechter, M., & Hayden, M. (1992, November 12). The psychological consequences of predictive testing for Huntington's disease. *New England Journal of Medicine, 327,* 1401–1405.

World Medical Association Declaration of Helsinki IV. (1989). In M. A. Grodin & L. H. Glantz (Eds.), *Children as research subjects: Science, ethics, and law* (Appendix C, pp. 220–223). New York: Oxford University Press.

Case Study 6.6

8 U.S.C.A. Section 1151 *et seq.* (West Supp. 1995).

Carens, J. (1992). Migration and morality: A liberal egalitarian perspective. In B. Barry & R. E. Goodin (Eds.), *Free movement: Ethical issues in the transnational migration of people and money* (pp. 25–47). University Park: Pennsylvania State University Press.

Clinton, W. J. (1994). Determination of the president. No. 95-1. 59 *Fed. Reg.* 52393.

Dummett, A. (1992). The transnational migration of people seen within a natural law tradition. In B. Barry & R. E. Goodin (Eds.), *Free movement: Ethical issues in the transnational migration of people and money* (pp. 167–180). University Park: Pennsylvania State University Press.

Fuchs, L. (1993). An agenda for tomorrow: Immigration policy and ethnic policies. *The Annals of the American Academy of Political and Social Science, 530,* 171–186.

Isserman, A. M. (1993). United States immigration policy and the industrial heartland: Laws, origins, settlement pattern and economic consequences. *Urban Studies, 30*(2), 237–265.

Motomura, H. (1992). The curious evolution of immigration law: Procedural surrogates for substantive constitutional rights. *Columbia Law Review 92*(7), 1625–1704.

Muller, T. (1993). *Immigrants and the American city.* New York: New York University Press.

National Association of Social Workers. (1996). *NASW Code of Ethics.* Washington, DC: Author.

Ross, W. D. (1963). *Foundations of ethics: The Guilford lectures delivered in the University of Aberdeen 1935–1936.* London: Oxford University Press.

U.S. Committee for Refugees. (1994). *World refugee survey—1994.* Washington, DC: Author.

U.S. Committee for Refugees. (1995). *World refugee survey—1995.* Washington, DC: Author.

Woodward, J. (1992). Commentary: Liberalism and migration. In B. Barry & R. E. Goodin (Eds.), *Free movement: Ethical issues in the transnational migration of people and money* (pp. 167–180). University Park: Pennsylvania State University Press.

CHAPTER SEVEN

APPLYING THE NASW ETHICAL STANDARDS OF PRACTICE

Your Turn!

INTRODUCTION

Provisions of Code

The previous six chapters have presented some of the essential elements of each of the six standards of the NASW Code of Ethics and provided the reader with examples of the kinds of dilemmas that might arise for social workers as they practice in varied, complex, and challenging contexts and practice settings. As we have seen, each standard focuses of a specific area of ethical responsibility.

This final chapter provides the reader with the opportunity to explore the Code and her or his own personal values, ideals, rationale, and reasoning by presenting twelve cases for practice. These are drawn from a variety of settings to encourage exploration beyond the boundaries of one's own areas of greatest comfort and competence.

In order to competently assess ethical issues in each of the cases presented, readers must be familiar with the Code of Ethics in its entirety. The Code is provided for this purpose in the Appendix and should be reviewed in preparation for the exercises in this chapter.

Application of the Decision-Making Process Structure

Cases in this textbook have been abstracted and adapted to illustrate the major issues each social worker tried to address. The full decision-making process was explicated in the Introduction. While readers are of course free to develop their own formats for analysis and discussion, using the procedure and sequence provided may provide a helpful structure. It may be helpful to reread the Introduction before proceeding with the cases for practice. The steps have been outlined as

Step 1: *Describing the Case and the Context.* This step have been provided in the cases included here.

Step 2:   *Defining the Ethical Problem.* Develop a dilemma statement using the _____ vs. _____ format.

Step 3:   *Gathering Information.* Drawing from each side of the dilemma statement, research the information needed to make a competent and informed ethical decision.

Step 4:   *Determining Applicable Ethical Theories and Principles.* Select a theory and a set of principles that are congruent with your agency, your profession, and your personal values and use these to guide your thinking.

Step 5:   *Determining Relevant Elements in the NASW Code of Ethics.* Review the Code carefully and consider sections that are applicable to your dilemma.

Step 6:   *Defining Personal Values and Biases.* Explore your personal values hierarchy and determine how this may impact on your perception of the problem, your consideration of your client and client system, and the options you might consider. It is important to recognize any personal biases that might affect decision making.

Step 7:   *Considering the Values of the Affected System.* These may include the client's, the client's support network's, the agency's (both formal and informal), the community's, the program's, and those of the broader society.

Step 8:   *Defining and Considering Options.* Using all of the information, define several options for action. Using a cost-benefit framework, consider each option, eliminating those least beneficial and analyzing the others in depth.

Step 9:   *Selecting an Option.* From the several possibilities you have considered in depth, select the one that maximizes benefits to all involved.

Step 10:   *Planning Implementation.* Develop you plan for implementation.

The Cases

The cases have been selected to present a broad variety of contexts and ethical issues that affect individuals, families, groups, communities, and program development. They include ethical dilemmas in the fields of health, mental health, child welfare, family, forensics, therapeutic groups, policy, social justice, and a collegial ethical issue. Each will offer the reader an opportunity to explore complex and interwoven ethical issues similar to those regularly encountered in practice.

It is hoped that these exercises will offer readers an opportunity to both explore and practice their personal decision-making process and validate the expertise they have gained in the process of these readings.

CASE STUDY 7.1
FLORA MENDEZ

Flora is 43 years old and has a moderate developmental disability. She lives in the home where she has resided with her parents since early childhood. Her father died eight years ago, and her mother a year ago, and for the past year she has lived by herself. Flora now has some forgetfulness, but in general seems able to shop and cook for herself, maintain herself on her medications once they are sorted and placed in her large plastic dosage system, and keep good personal hygiene with a once-a-week homemaker to help with baths, laundry, and housecleaning. She has poor vision and is quite unsteady on her feet, but refuses to use a cane, walker, or other assistive device. Flora enjoys TV and remains at home during the day. She has no known visitors.

Flora's home is in a rural setting. While there are no houses on either side of her, there is a 24-hour grocery store across the street, from which Flora purchases necessities with her SSDI check. There's not much left over, however, and over the years Flora's home has fallen into disrepair. The roof is leaking, there is mold on the wall in the kitchen, and in the bathroom tiles are cracked and the water drains excessively slowly. She is unable to maintain the lawn, and the outside of her house is overgrown with weeds which often reach six feet in height. At night, the neon lights from the grocery store shining in through the tall weeds create eerie patterns on the walls.

Her case manager visits weekly. She monitors the homemaker service, helps sort out medications and prescriptions, ensures that there is adequate food in the house, and checks the wrist monitor Flora wears to ask for help in emergencies. Lately, the case manager has become increasingly concerned with the condition of Flora's house, her deteriorating vision and increasing frailty, and her lack of a community support system. She suspects that employees from the store across the street, the only community support Flora has, do come to assist her across the street, but she worries about Flora's safety. Flora accepts the case manager's visits, but does not share much personal information. There are no known family members involved with Flora's care since the death of her parents.

Twice, the case manager has found alternative housing for Flora. The housing, in the same area, is an assisted living complex that has a mixture of older and younger disabled residents and provides many health and community support services and activities. While Flora appears to be interested and willing to move when the subject is raised with her, when the actual housing is located she adamantly refuses to move. The worker suspects she does not want to give up her home, nor the support of the grocery store across the street.

■ ■ ■ ■ ■ ▬

CASE STUDY 7.2

KENNY STROBER

Kenny is an 84-year-old widower who lives alone in a senior citizen housing complex. He suffers from Parkinson's and has poor vision. He is friendly and sociable, attends many activities, takes his meals in the complex's dining hall, and loves to sit outside on the bench in front of the building with neighbors. He has a son who pays his bills, but they are not close, and Kenny does not share any of his daily life or concerns with his son, who visits monthly.

Kenny fell seven months ago in his apartment, fracturing a hip. After several weeks in the hospital, he was discharged to a convalescent center, with the plan of returning to his apartment as soon as he was rehabilitated and able to walk again. Kenny worked hard with the physical therapist and returned home recently, using a cane for stability. He has a walker, too, "just in case." He was thrilled to be back and has returned to his friends and his daily activities. As part of his discharge planning, he was referred for case management services.

In assessing Kenny's condition, his apartment, and his needs, the case manager found several issues of concern:

1. Kenny kept the blinds drawn "to keep it cool in here," because he did not like using any air conditioning, even though it was July. She was concerned that the darkness would further limit his already poor vision.
2. Kenny had a very long telephone cord running through his apartment. He had one phone and moved it from place to place—bed to chair to couch to kitchen—leaving long loops of cord curling along the floor. His phone, he told her, was his "lifeline." It rang frequently as friends called socially and to check on him.
3. Kenny seemed unsteady on his feet. While he could sometimes be convinced to use the cane outside of the house, he didn't think he needed any support in his apartment. Passageways were often narrow and cluttered with pieces of furniture and boxes of papers and it was hard to get around.

The case manager felt that these problems constituted a real safety hazard for Kenny. She carefully discussed each item with him, suggesting more light, a cordless phone, and getting help to rearrange his furniture and belongings. Kenny refused all of her suggestions.

Three months have passed. Kenny has fallen once. Although he was taken to the emergency room, his fall resulted only in a bruise and he was not hospitalized. The worker has discussed safety concerns with him repeatedly. When she asked for permission to discuss his problems with his son, Kenny refused adamantly. The blinds remain drawn; the telephone cord wraps around chair legs, under tables, and across hallways; and Kenny's unsteadiness is increasing, albeit slowly.

CASE STUDY 7.3
JASON MARSHALL

Mr. and Mrs. Marshall have brought their 16-year-old son Jason to your agency for counseling. They were concerned about Jason following a report card that indicated a serious slippage in grades. During a subsequent parent–teacher conference, they learned that Jason appeared tired and uninterested in class, and that he had skipped school several times, forging their name on excuse forms.

Jason appears to be in good general health, though he complains often of tiredness. He has just gotten his driver's license and has obtained a job in a pizza restaurant in the local shopping mall. His job often keeps him away from home until late in the evening, since he must clean the ovens and the salad bar after the mall has closed to the public.

He has many friends and is quite popular with girls. He generally attends parties or goes out with his friends on Saturday evenings in his car. Jason has used his savings to purchase an audio system for his car, and he has a wide selection of CDs that he enjoys playing for his friends as they drive around town.

Although Jason does not feel that he needs any counseling, he attends sessions regularly and appears willing to speak freely with you. He shares his boredom with school, his impatience with his teachers and parents' expectations of him, his love of music and having a good time, and his desire to be free of parental controls and "on his own."

His parents check in with you every few weeks to be sure that he is attending counseling, but they have not demanded that the counselor share any specific information about the content of the sessions. They have had no problems with Jason at home, although Jason appears to be home less and less due to his work and social schedule. They are pleased that his grades in school have improved slightly and that he does not seem to be skipping days as he had been. They attribute these improvements to counseling and are pleased with your interventions with him.

Recently, you have become concerned about Jason's excessive lateness in returning home and his seemingly endless supply of CDs, which appear out of proportion to his earnings in the pizza restaurant. Upon engaging in a discussion of these issues, you learn that after the mall's closing hours Jason "sometimes" visits a friend who works at the mall's music store. He "takes extras" of some of the CDs he likes. In justifying himself, Jason says that "lots of times the CDs are open or they are returns that would be thrown away anyway." He says he often gives these CDs away to his friends, if they indicate that they like a particular one when he plays it for them in his car.

■ ■ ■ ■ ■ ▬▬▬▬▬▬▬▬▬▬▬▬▬▬

CASE STUDY 7.4
VIOLET SANCHEZ

Violet Sanchez, 91 years old, is a resident in a long-term care facility where you are the social worker. She is friendly and very sociable and participates in all activities programs. She has no immediate family; a distant cousin, Paolo Sanchez, and his wife Margarita are her only relatives. They visit her weekly, always bringing a candy bar because Violet loves sweets. She waits excitedly for their visit, is always delighted to see them, and introduces them to everyone as "my family." She tells the staff and other residents often that she considers herself lucky to have such loving cousins, saying "after all, they don't really have to visit me. I'm just a cousin. But if they didn't visit me there would be nobody who cares about me. That would be terrible. They are really wonderful to me!" You as well as other staff members notice the warmth and affection between Violet and her cousins.

Violet is slightly confused and has given the Sanchez cousins power of attorney over her affairs. She receives public funds for her care and is also eligible for SSI, but you have never explored her financial arrangements, as all her needs appeared to be met.

However, Violet now needs new clothes. The nurses tell you that her underwear is worn to shreds and her dresses are old and faded. She especially needs shoes. You are asked to check into her SSI in order to purchase clothing for Violet the next time that the clothing store people visit the facility.

A careful check of Violet's chart, as well as her office business files, yields no information regarding the existence of SSI funds. You call the Sanchez cousins to ask about Violet's funds. You are surprised to find them evasive and closed when you approach them with her needs. They say they know nothing about any SSI funds and suggest that you explore charitable donations of clothing on Violet's behalf. They say that they would like very much to help, but have no funds of their own for their dear cousin, because they too are living on Social Security.

Your suspicions are aroused. Calmly and gently you approach Violet for permission to contact SSI, explaining that you are trying to gets some funds to buy her new clothing and shoes. She is excited about the possibility of "going shopping" and agrees immediately to your request.

Your call to SSI reveals that the Sanchez cousins have applied for, and have been receiving, SSI in Violet's behalf for the past two years. It is obvious that they have been using the funds themselves, aside from the token candy bar they bring Violet during their weekly visits. When you approach SSI with your problem, you are informed that the recipient herself (Violet) is the only one who can lodge a complaint regarding the misuse of funds.

■ ■ ■ ■ ■

CASE STUDY 7.5
"MAC"

You are with an outreach program that attempts to address the basic needs of homeless men by offering food, blankets, shelter arrangements, and assistance with applications for programs and resources. You are assigned to a neighborhood that you visit every day.

Some of the men accept assistance willingly and utilize the resources offered by your program. They smile, exchange greetings, and occasionally ask questions. Others refuse to interact in any manner and will not even pick up a sandwich left next to them on the sidewalk where they are sitting. Still others do not speak or make eye contact, but will accept items that you leave for them. These men, however, do not acknowledge your presence, or your assistance, in any manner; it is as though you and your offerings are not connected in any way.

You know Mac's name only because other men have mentioned him to you. He does not interact or react to your presence, but does accept items left next to him, like others in the third category of the local homeless population. Recently, he accepted a sweater and a cap that you placed next to him as he sat on the sidewalk, face turned down to the street to avoid acknowledging your presence.

Two men who say they are friends of Mac have told you that he is seriously ill and in need of attention. He coughs constantly and lately has been coughing up blood. They try to tell him he must go to the emergency room, but he does not reply and simply walks away. They do not appear concerned about being exposed to whatever illness Mac is carrying; they are only concerned about him. They believe that he will die if he does not get help. They ask you to intervene and help Mac get medical treatment.

Your program has emergency care arrangements for this homeless population with a hospital located two blocks away. Often, you have taken men who have been ill or injured there. You know that Mac will be treated with understanding, kindness, and compassion, and that no pressure to change, reform, or alter his behavior or lifestyle will be exerted on Mac—only medical care will be rendered.

You have sat down next to Mac, explained what the men have told you, and asked him to walk with you to the emergency room for care. Mac continues not to acknowledge your presence in any way. He makes no move to get up or to respond.

CASE STUDY 7.6
MELINDA HASSAN

You are assigned to Family Court, and your job is to determine whether children who have been removed from their parents due to abuse or neglect and placed in foster care should be returned to live with them. The parents have all attended classes in parenting, demonstrated that they have the facilities (bed, dresser, food, and clothing) to care for their children, and made arrangements for their children to be cared for while they are at work. They are now petitioning the court for the return of their children, and the judge has ordered you to assess and make recommendations.

Melinda Hassan has three children—Sam, age 5, Charlene, age 6, and LaTonya, age 9. They were removed from her care a year ago due to neglect (leaving children at home alone while she worked or was out in the evening) and possible abuse (excessive hitting and punishment observed by neighbors). Sam and Charlene were placed in one foster home, LaTonya in another. The children have had little contact with each other because the foster homes were not near each other and visits were difficult to arrange. They all have had monthly visits with their mother. The children state that they miss each other and their mother and that they want to return home. Melinda wants very much to reunite her family under one roof once again.

She has prepared for the return of the children by finding a job as a waitress in a restaurant where the tips are good and the hours fairly regular. She has arranged to work only on weekdays, so that she can spend weekends with them. She has attended parenting classes and has received praise from her instructors. She recently moved to an apartment near her parents, and she has arranged for them to care for the children in their home while she is at work. They have agreed to supervise homework and to provide a warm evening meal while Melinda is at work. She will pick the children up by 9 o'clock each day and take them home.

Melinda is eager to cooperate with you to get her children back, and you quickly establish a good rapport and mutual trust and respect. In working with her, you spend some time talking about her own growing-up experience in order to understand the potential effects on her parenting and disciplining of Sam, Charlene, and LaTonya. Melinda tells you of a childhood filled with abuse. Her father sexually abused her from the age of 6, until she moved out of her home and in with an aunt at age 13. Her mother never noticed or acknowledged this abuse. She was also beaten regularly and denied food as a punishment. Her parents drank heavily, and there were constant fights. She often became the pawn and the victim at these times.

She became pregnant with LaTonya at 14, in her first sexual relationship with a person other than her father. Determined to protect LaTonya from what she had experienced, she never lived with a man, staying single and working hard to support LaTonya, and later Charlene and Sam. She admits to losing her temper with them and hitting them excessively, but says that this was due to her frustrations with her own life situations, which she has now resolved. She left them alone, she states, in order to earn money to support them.

Her parents, in the meantime, have stopped drinking, and they no longer fight. They are living stable lives while her father works construction. She has been able to develop a good relationship with them and is confident that they will take good care of her children. The children like them and are happy to be with them. Her parents have offered to care for the children without payment, thus enabling Melinda to provide for four people on her salary.

CASE STUDY 7.7
PATRICK DONNALLY

Patrick Donnally is a 36-year-old forensic patient who exhibits extreme paranoia. He was committed to the hospital following three assaults of varying severity, all related to his paranoid ideation. He had lived alone, was very socially isolated, and received disability due to his mental status. He sat in his house all day and stared out the window, watching for people who wanted to "know my private business." Consequently, he had assaulted a mailman who was delivering mail to his building, a telephone repairman working on a line across the street from his building, and a neighbor who had paused outside his door to catch her breath on the way up to her own apartment.

On the ward, Patrick's paranoia continues. He sits in the dayroom all day and stares in at the glassed nurse's station, watching over the chart that he had determined to be "his." Over the course of his six months' hospitalization, Patrick has slowly and reluctantly learned to trust the familiar faces he sees at the nurse's station every day: the doctors, the nurses, the social worker, the psychologist, and the pharmacist, and no longer becomes agitated if they touched his chart. However, on one occasion, an outside consultant had come to the nurse's station to review all of the charts. Although he had been informed of the visit in advance, and been reassured repeatedly regarding the consultant's purpose in reading his chart, Patrick had become extremely agitated. He had begun banging on the glass, screaming incoherently, and pushing and shoving the other residents in the dayroom, who had become angry and agitated as well. This had caused a serious incident on the ward.

The hospital's regular reaccreditation survey was underway, and the social worker knew that, at any time, the surveyors would enter this ward and pick up any charts, at random, that they wished to review. She had attempted to prepare Patrick for this visit, only to find him adamant: No one, except for the people he had learned to trust, could have access to his chart. No one could even touch it. If anyone tried to touch it, he would "go crazy." He had a right to say who could and couldn't read his chart.

There were no precedents, as far as the social worker knew, for denying access to a patient's chart. Limiting the freedom of the surveyors to review the charts they chose could create problems at various levels. It could limit the surveyors' ability to pursue their own responsibilities unimpeded. It could jeopardize the reaccreditation itself, thus putting the entire hospital at risk. It could create a problem with other patients, also agitated and with some paranoia, if special exceptions were made for Patrick. It could create problems for other workers who might feel justified for other reasons in requesting that a particular chart not be reviewed.

CASE STUDY 7.8
MATHILDA CASTILLO

Mathilda Castillo, age 40, had been admitted to an acute care hospital as a referral from an out-patient clinic for indigent and homeless adults. She suffered from severe pneumonia, malnutrition, and debilitation. Upon examination, doctors noted signs of battering and sexual abuse as well, and some evidence of schizophrenia. Mathilda had been supporting herself by prostitution, but her illness had rendered her work almost impossible.

After a three-week hospital stay, her pneumonia had cleared. IVs and an enriched diet had improved her nutritional status, and physical therapy had helped her regain strength. Psychiatric consultation showed that there was no active psychosis. Mathilda was referred to social service for discharge planning.

Discussing her living arrangements, the social worker learned that Mathilda had no permanent home. Her belongings were in a corner of a friend's living room, and she showered and rinsed out her clothes there when needed, but slept in various hotels. The clinic had referred her to a shelter, but she had refused to go because of the dangers and the unhygienic conditions. She preferred to be free. She denied any battering or sexual abuse. Mathilda also adamantly refuses referrals for counseling and assistance.

Mathilda wishes to return to her former living and working arrangements. The hospital is concerned about bed utilization and costs, and prompt discharges following doctors' orders are the rule. Traditionally, the social work department has followed the hospital's policies.

■ ■ ■ ■ ■ ▬▬▬▬▬▬▬▬▬▬▬▬▬▬▬▬▬▬▬▬▬▬▬▬▬▬▬▬▬▬▬▬▬▬

CASE STUDY 7.9
MEN'S GROUP

A therapeutic group for men who have been sexually violent or abusive meets with a social worker weekly. It is a closed group, in which members agree to participate, share, and learn to trust each other to work on their issues over a six-month period. Members are screened prior to beginning the group, affording the social worker an opportunity to get to know the clients individually, discuss and set individual goals, and prepare clients for the group experience.

Group members discuss their behavior, examine and explore reasons and alternative behaviors, and develop ways to make appropriate changes. An important goal of the group is always the establishment of trust among members, which is fostered by honesty and full disclosure of the problems that have brought them to the group. Thus, as part of the early work of the group, members take turns sharing with others the incidents and behaviors that have brought them to this particular group at this time.

It has been the experience of this agency that men who are or become known to group members as pedophiles arouse rage and anger among members of the group. This extremely negative reaction creates massive problems for the pedophile in terms of developing relationships, establishing a valid place in the group, and addressing the specific aberrant behavior. The group members' reactions encourage withdrawal, low self-esteem, and also a reactive hostility. Because pedophilia in and of itself does not occur frequently enough to support all-pedophile groups in this community setting, social workers routinely suggest during the pregroup screening interviews that the age of the victims not be discussed by either the pedophile or the worker. Thus, there exists a tacit understanding between worker and client that confidentiality will be maintained in the interests of protecting the client and enabling therapeutic change to occur. There is no agency policy regarding keeping information confidential about pedophilia or any other potential client behaviors known to the agency and group leaders.

■ ■ ■ ■ ■

CASE STUDY 7.10

REHABILITATION CENTER

A privately owned inpatient rehabilitation center that accepts insurance as well as public funding treats mental illness in an urban community. Publically funded and insurance-funded patients are mixed together and are treated equally in terms of accommodations, activities, treatment resources, and length of stay.

However, difficulties arise when patients are preparing for discharge. The public funding provides significant assistance to patients upon discharge into the community. Halfway houses, educational opportunities, special needs, supportive ongoing treatment, and community support groups funded through the local department of health provide an excellent continuity of care for these patients. Additionally, through a special grant, patients who choose to do so may remain in contact with the rehabilitation center and may periodically see the psychiatrist, psychologist, or social worker they were seeing in the hospital. Workers and clients are able to set up and maintain elaborate plans utilizing the public network to support community reentry.

Insurance patients do not have access to these kinds of services, because these are not included in most insurance plans. When the discharge process begins, frustrated social workers must scramble through the meager general community resources available. Because it is assumed that patients with insurance have housing and basic needs met, little exists in the community to support these patients through the transition process of community reentry. The period of illness, during which no income was earned, and/or the illness itself, often leave these clients in economic distress, and they cannot afford to pay privately for these "uncovered" services. Thus, most private insurance patients who are discharged from the rehabilitation center are left on their own, or with only a referral for counseling to a local nonprofit agency. Some social workers at the center continue to see these insurance patients, since they believe that some support services are essential. However, they must do so without the knowledge of administration, because this violates the center's policy, which specifies that workers can only see clients when there is funding available for these additional services.

This unequal treatment has been a part of the rehabilitation center's difficulties since it opened its doors six years ago, with the mission of serving the needs of the entire local community.

■ ■ ■ ■ ■

CASE STUDY 7.11

MEGAN'S LAW

The issue of disclosure of status of sex or violent-crime offenders when they are released from prison and settle in a community arouses strong feelings in every sector of the population in the United States. Arguments in favor of privacy maintain that people have "paid for" their crime, served time that was imposed, been rehabilitated, and should be free to pursue the rest of their lives without the burden of their past activities. These arguments maintain that it is an unfair burden to continue, in effect, to punish people for crimes that have already been punished by prison terms. The kind of ostracism, hatred, fear, and avoidance that public exposure brings can completely impede, or severely restrict, the ability of persons to lead "normal" lives anywhere. Where such individuals' status is made public, they are generally hounded out of the community by furious residents, are unable to find employment, and are unable to develop social networks. Such persons are often forced to move repeatedly from community to community, seeking the ever-elusive peace to which they believe they are entitled.

Arguments against privacy cite the public's right to know about any dangers or threats that exist within the community and the right to be free of such dangers. They note the recidivism of highly publicized ex-prisoners and fear for their children and for themselves. They do not believe that time served in prison necessarily has "cured" the offenders and that they have given up certain rights forever due to their past behavior.

Mental health professionals are often asked to take a position upon this issue, because it is presumed that such professionals have special knowledge and training in this area. In particular, social workers have a double responsibility that impacts upon this issue: They have an obligation to the individual, to assist and enable well-being, and to the public, or to the "common good," to ensure safety, stability, and well-being for the community at large.

As a social work organization, NASW is often asked to take positions on issues that involve special populations and the common good, or national interest. Panels of social workers are empowered to explore all of the issues, consult with experts, and develop a position that is then officially adopted for the organization and its members as a whole. Recently, NASW officials have begun to consider whether an "official" stance should be developed on this difficult issue.

CASE STUDY 7.12
MARCIA AND FRANCINE

Marcia is a social worker at a family agency. Over the five years of her employment, she has developed a close colleagial relationship with Francine, another worker assigned to the same unit. The women often lunch together and sometimes participate in activities outside of work. Within the agency setting, however, their relationship remains professional, because they share team meetings, consultations, committees, as well as a supervisor.

At the time that they met, both Marcia and Francine were married, about the same age, and mothers of two children in the elementary grades. Both were juggling work and home responsibilities, and both shared a dedication to the agency's clients. However, about four years ago, Francine began confiding her marital problems to Marcia. When, two years ago, Francine's husband finally left her alone with the two children and disappeared seemingly without a trace, Francine was devastated. Marcia was a good and supportive friend and confidante, and spent hours listening to Francine and offering what help and support she could.

Francine had always enjoyed a cocktail, and Marcia sometimes joined her in this after-work ritual. Lately, however, Marcia has become aware that Francine is having much more than one cocktail in the evening. Tired, lonely, overwhelmed by work, children, and housekeeping responsibilities, Francine has turned to alcohol for temporary relief and a feeling of relaxation.

Marcia has attempted to address the problem with Francine, and Francine has begun to see a therapist to address her many serious problems. The work is proceeding very slowly, although Francine does attend sessions regularly. Marcia often takes Francine's children to her home overnight, to offer Francine an evening off, and also to "keep an eye out for problems." The children have an grandmotherly babysitter who watches them in the afternoon, helps with homework, and also cares for them when Francine is out in the evening. Thus far, the children appear to be functioning with minimal difficulties related to Francine's behavior. Francine is walking a delicately balanced line, maintaining her economic stability, caring for her children, and addressing her problems with regular therapy sessions.

However, Marcia has noticed that Francine's problems with alcohol have affected her at work. She often arrives late, looking weary. She appears overwhelmed by the constant demands of her caseload, is late returning phone calls, and does not respond appropriately to emergencies. When she feels herself falling too far behind, she documents telephone calls as home visits. Marcia is concerned about the well-being of the parents and children with whom Francine is working. Francine, when confronted, says she knows she is not providing the services needed by her clients, but that things will get better soon and that she is, after all, in therapy to address her problems. "After all," she asks Marcia, "What else can I do?"

THE NATIONAL ASSOCIATION OF SOCIAL WORKERS CODE OF ETHICS
(Revised 1996)

PREAMBLE

The primary mission of the social work profession is to enhance human well-being and help meet the basic human needs of all people, with particular attention to the needs and empowerment of people who are vulnerable, oppressed, and living in poverty. A historic and defining feature of social work is the profession's focus on individual well-being in a social context and the well-being of society. Fundamental to social work is attention to the environmental forces that create, contribute to, and address problems in living.

Social workers promote social justice and social change with and on behalf of clients. "Clients" is used inclusively to refer to individuals, families, groups, organizations, and communities. Social workers are sensitive to cultural and ethnic diversity and strive to end discrimination, oppression, poverty, and other forms of social injustice. These activities may be in the form of direct practice, community organizing, supervision, consultation, administration, advocacy, social and political action, policy development and implementation, education, and research and evaluation. Social workers seek to enhance the capacity of people to address their own needs. Social workers also seek to promote the responsiveness of organizations, communities, and other social institutions to individuals' needs and social problems.

The mission of the social work profession is rooted in a set of core values. These core values, embraced by social workers throughout the profession's history, are the foundation of social work's unique purpose and perspective:

- service
- social justice
- dignity and worth of the person
- importance of human relationships
- integrity
- competence

This constellation of core values reflects what is unique to the social work profession. Core values, and the principles that flow from them, must be balanced within the context and complexity of the human experience.

PURPOSE OF THE NASW CODE OF ETHICS

Professional ethics are at the core of social work. The profession has an obligation to articulate its basic values, ethical principles, and ethical standards. The NASW Code of Ethics sets forth these values, principles, and standards to guide social workers' conduct. The Code is relevant to all social workers and social work students, regardless of their professional functions, the settings in which they work, or the populations they serve.

The NASW Code of Ethics serves six purposes:

1. The Code identifies core values on which social work's mission is based.
2. The Code summarizes broad ethical principles that reflect the profession's core values and establishes a set of specific ethical standards that should be used to guide social work practice.
3. The Code is designed to help social workers identify relevant considerations when professional obligations conflict or ethical uncertainties arise.
4. The Code provides ethical standards to which the general public can hold the social work profession accountable.
5. The Code socializes practitioners new to the field to social work's mission, values, ethical principles, and ethical standards.
6. The Code articulates standards that the social work profession itself can use to assess whether social workers have engaged in unethical conduct. NASW has formal procedures to adjudicate ethics complaints filed against its members. In subscribing to this Code, social workers are required to cooperate in its implementation, participate in NASW adjudication proceedings, and abide by any NASW disciplinary rulings or sanctions based on it.

The Code offers a set of values, principles, and standards to guide decision making and conduct when ethical issues arise. It does not provide a set of rules that prescribe how social workers should act in all situations. Specific applications of the Code must take into account the context in which it is being considered and the possibility of conflicts among the Code's values, principles, and standards. Ethical responsibilities flow from all human relationships, from the personal and familial to the social and professional.

Further, the NASW Code of Ethics does not specify which values, principles, and standards are most important and ought to outweigh others in instances when they conflict. Reasonable differences of opinion can and do exist among social workers with respect to the ways in which values, ethical principles, and ethical standards should be rank ordered when they conflict. Ethical decision making in a given situation must apply the informed judgment of the individual social worker and should also consider how the issues would be judged in a peer review process where the ethical standards of the profession would be applied.

Ethical decision making is a process. There are many instances in social work where simple answers are not available to resolve complex ethical issues. Social workers should take into consideration all the values, principles, and standards in this Code that are relevant to any situation in which ethical judgment is warranted. Social workers' decisions and actions should be consistent with the spirit as well as the letter of this Code.

In addition to this Code, there are many other sources of information about ethical thinking that may be useful. Social workers should consider ethical theory and principles generally, social work theory and research, laws, regulations, agency policies, and other relevant codes of ethics, recognizing that among codes of ethics social workers should consider the NASW Code of Ethics as their primary source. Social workers also should be aware of the impact on ethical decision making of their clients' and their own personal values and cultural and religious beliefs and practices. They should be aware of any conflicts between personal and professional values and deal with them responsibly. For additional guidance social workers should consult the relevant literature on professional ethics and ethical decision making and seek appropriate consultation when faced with ethical dilemmas. This may involve consultation with an agency-based or social work organization's ethics committee, a regulatory body, knowledgeable colleagues, supervisors, or legal counsel.

Instances may arise when social workers' ethical obligations conflict with agency policies or relevant laws or regulations. When such conflicts occur, social workers must make a responsible effort to resolve the conflict in a manner that is consistent with the values, principles, and standards expressed in this Code. If a reasonable resolution of the conflict does not appear possible, social workers should seek proper consultation before making a decision.

The NASW Code of Ethics is to be used by NASW and by individuals, agencies, organizations, and bodies (such as licensing and regulatory boards, professional liability insurance providers, courts of law, agency boards of directors, government agencies, and other professional groups) that choose to adopt it or use it as a frame of reference. Violation of standards in this Code does not automatically imply legal liability or violation of the law. Such determination can only be made in the context of legal and judicial proceedings. Alleged violations of the Code would be subject to a peer review process. Such processes are generally separate from legal or administrative procedures and insulated from legal review or proceedings to allow the profession to counsel and discipline its own members.

A code of ethics cannot guarantee ethical behavior. Moreover, a code of ethics cannot resolve all ethical issues or disputes or capture the richness and complexity involved in striving to make responsible choices within a moral community. Rather, a code of ethics sets forth values, ethical principles, and ethical standards to which professionals aspire and by which their actions can be judged. Social workers' ethical behavior should result from their personal commitment to engage in ethical practice. The NASW Code of Ethics reflects the commitment of all social workers to uphold the profession's values and to act ethically. Principles and standards must be applied by individuals of good character who discern moral questions and, in good faith, seek to make reliable ethical judgments.

ETHICAL PRINCIPLES

The following broad ethical principles are based on social work's core values of service, social justice, dignity and worth of the person, importance of human relationships, integrity, and competence. These principles set forth ideals to which all social workers should aspire.

Value: *Service*

Ethical Principle: *Social workers' primary goal is to help people in need and to address social problems.*

Social workers elevate service to others above self-interest. Social workers draw on their knowledge, values, and skills to help people in need and to address social problems. Social workers are encouraged to volunteer some portion of their professional skills with no expectation of significant financial return (pro bono service).

Value: *Social Justice*

Ethical Principle: *Social workers challenge social injustice.*

Social workers pursue social change, particularly with and on behalf of vulnerable and oppressed individuals and groups of people. Social workers' social change efforts are focused primarily on issues of poverty, unemployment, discrimination, and other forms of social injustice. These activities seek to promote sensitivity to and knowledge about oppression and cultural and ethnic diversity. Social workers strive to ensure access to needed information, services, and resources; equality of opportunity; and meaningful participation in decision making for all people.

Value: *Dignity and Worth of the Person*

Ethical Principle: *Social workers respect the inherent dignity and worth of the person.*

Social workers treat each person in a caring and respectful fashion, mindful of individual differences and cultural and ethnic diversity. Social workers promote clients' socially responsible self-determination. Social workers seek to enhance clients' capacity and opportunity to change and to address their own needs. Social workers are cognizant of their dual responsibility to clients and to the broader society. They seek to resolve conflicts between clients' interests and the broader society's interests in a socially responsible manner consistent with the values, ethical principles, and ethical standards of the profession.

Value: *Importance of Human Relationships*

Ethical Principle: *Social workers recognize the central importance of human relationships.*

Social workers understand that relationships between and among people are an important vehicle for change. Social workers engage people as partners in the helping process. Social workers seek to strengthen relationships among people in a purposeful effort to promote, restore, maintain, and enhance the well-being of individuals, families, social groups, organizations, and communities.

Value: *Integrity*

Ethical Principle: *Social workers behave in a trustworthy manner.*

Social workers are continually aware of the profession's mission, values, ethical principles, and ethical standards and practice in a manner consistent with them. Social workers act honestly and responsibly and promote ethical practices on the part of the organizations with which they are affiliated.

Value: *Competence*

Ethical Principle: *Social workers practice within their areas of competence and develop and enhance their professional expertise.*
Social workers continually strive to increase their professional knowledge and skills and to apply them in practice. Social workers should aspire to contribute to the knowledge base of the profession.

ETHICAL STANDARDS

The following ethical standards are relevant to the professional activities of all social workers. These standards concern (1) social workers' ethical responsibilities to clients, (2) social workers' ethical responsibilities to colleagues, (3) social workers' ethical responsibilities in practice settings, (4) social workers' ethical responsibilities as professionals, (5) social workers' ethical responsibilities to the social work profession, and (6) social workers' ethical responsibilities to the broader society.

Some of the standards that follow are enforceable guidelines for professional conduct, and some are aspirational. The extent to which each standard is enforceable is a matter of professional judgment to be exercised by those responsible for reviewing alleged violations of ethical standards.

1. Social Workers' Ethical Responsibilities to Clients

1.01 Commitment to Clients
Social workers' primary responsibility is to promote the well-being of clients. In general, clients' interests are primary. However, social workers' responsibility to the larger society or specific legal obligations may on limited occasions supersede the loyalty owed clients, and clients should be so advised. (Examples include when a social worker is required by law to report that a client has abused a child or has threatened to harm self or others.)

1.02 Self-Determination
Social workers respect and promote the right of clients to self-determination and assist clients in their efforts to identify and clarify their goals. Social workers may limit clients' right to self-determination when, in the social workers' professional judgment, clients' actions or potential actions pose a serious, foreseeable, and imminent risk to themselves or others.

1.03 Informed Consent
(a) Social workers should provide services to clients only in the context of a professional relationship based, when appropriate, on valid informed consent. Social

workers should use clear and understandable language to inform clients of the purpose of the services, risks related to the services, limits to services because of the requirements of a third-party payer, relevant costs, reasonable alternatives, clients' right to refuse or withdraw consent, and the time frame covered by the consent. Social workers should provide clients with an opportunity to ask questions.

(b) In instances when clients are not literate or have difficulty understanding the primary language used in the practice setting, social workers should take steps to ensure clients' comprehension. This may include providing clients with a detailed verbal explanation or arranging for a qualified interpreter or translator whenever possible.

(c) In instances when clients lack the capacity to provide informed consent, social workers should protect clients' interests by seeking permission from an appropriate third party, informing clients consistent with the clients' level of understanding. In such instances social workers should seek to ensure that the third party acts in a manner consistent with clients' wishes and interests. Social workers should take reasonable steps to enhance such clients' ability to give informed consent.

(d) In instances when clients are receiving services involuntarily, social workers should provide information about the nature and extent of services and about the extent of clients' right to refuse service.

(e) Social workers who provide services via electronic media (such as computer, telephone, radio, and television) should inform recipients of the limitations and risks associated with such services.

(f) Social workers should obtain clients' informed consent before audiotaping or videotaping clients or permitting observation of services to clients by a third party.

1.04 Competence

(a) Social workers should provide services and represent themselves as competent only within the boundaries of their education, training, license, certification, consultation received, supervised experience, or other relevant professional experience.

(b) Social workers should provide services in substantive areas or use intervention techniques or approaches that are new to them only after engaging in appropriate study, training, consultation, and supervision from people who are competent in those interventions or techniques.

(c) When generally recognized standards do not exist with respect to an emerging area of practice, social workers should exercise careful judgment and take responsible steps (including appropriate education, research, training, consultation, and supervision) to ensure the competence of their work and to protect clients from harm.

1.05 Cultural Competence and Social Diversity

(a) Social workers should understand culture and its function in human behavior and society, recognizing the strengths that exist in all cultures.

(b) Social workers should have a knowledge base of their clients' cultures and be able to demonstrate competence in the provision of services that are sensitive to clients' cultures and to differences among people and cultural groups.

(c) Social workers should obtain education about and seek to understand the nature of social diversity and oppression with respect to race, ethnicity, national origin, color, sex, sexual orientation, age, marital status, political belief, religion, and mental or physical disability.

1.06 Conflicts of Interest

(a) Social workers should be alert to and avoid conflicts of interest that interfere with the exercise of professional discretion and impartial judgment. Social workers should inform clients when a real or potential conflict of interest arises and take reasonable steps to resolve the issue in a manner that makes the clients' interests primary and protects clients' interests to the greatest extent possible. In some cases, protecting clients' interests may require termination of the professional relationship with proper referral of the client.

(b) Social workers should not take unfair advantage of any professional relationship or exploit others to further their personal, religious, political, or business interests.

(c) Social workers should not engage in dual or multiple relationships with clients or former clients in which there is a risk of exploitation or potential harm to the client. In instances when dual or multiple relationships are unavoidable, social workers should take steps to protect clients and are responsible for setting clear, appropriate, and culturally sensitive boundaries. (Dual or multiple relationships occur when social workers relate to clients in more than one relationship, when professional, social, or business. Dual or multiple relationships can occur simultaneously or consecutively.)

(d) When social workers provide services to two or more people who have a relationship with each other (for example, couples, family members), social workers should clarify with all parties which individuals will be considered clients and the nature of social workers' professional obligations to the various individuals who are receiving services. Social workers who anticipate a conflict of interest among the individuals receiving services or who anticipate having to perform in potentially conflicting roles (for example, when a social worker is asked to testify in a child custody dispute or divorce proceedings involving clients) should clarify their role with the parties involved and take appropriate action to minimize any conflict of interest.

1.07 Privacy and Confidentiality

(a) Social workers should respect clients' right to privacy. Social workers should not solicit private information from clients unless it is essential to providing services or conducting social work evaluation or research. Once private information is shared, standards of confidentiality apply.

(b) Social workers may disclose confidential information when appropriate with valid consent from a client or a person legally authorized to consent on behalf of a client.

(c) Social workers should protect the confidentiality of all information obtained in the course of professional service, except for compelling professional reasons. The general expectation that social workers will keep information confidential does not apply when disclosure is necessary to prevent serious, foreseeable, and imminent harm to a client or other identifiable person or when laws or regulations require disclosure without a client's consent. In all instances, social workers should disclose the least amount of confidential information necessary to achieve the desired purpose; only information that is directly relevant to the purpose for which the disclosure is made should be revealed.

(d) Social workers should inform clients, to the extent possible, about the disclosure of confidential information and the potential consequences, when feasible before the disclosure is made. This applies whether social workers disclose confidential information on the basis of a legal requirement or client consent.

(e) Social workers should discuss with clients and other interested parties the nature of confidentiality and limitations of clients' right to confidentiality. Social workers should review with clients circumstances where confidential information may be requested and where disclosure of confidential information may be legally required. This discussion should occur as soon as possible in the social worker-client relationship and as needed throughout the course of the relationship.

(f) When social workers provide counseling services to families, couples, or groups, social workers should seek agreement among the parties involved concerning each individual's right to confidentiality and obligation to preserve the confidentiality of information shared by others. Social workers should inform participants in family, couples, or group counseling that social workers cannot guarantee that all participants will honor such agreements.

(g) Social workers should inform clients involved in family, couples, marital, or group counseling of the social worker's, employer's, and agency's policy concerning the social worker's disclosure of confidential information among the parties involved in the counseling.

(h) Social workers should not disclose confidential information to third-party payers unless clients have authorized such disclosure.

(i) Social workers should not discuss confidential information in any setting unless privacy can be ensured. Social workers should not discuss confidential information in public or semipublic areas such as hallways, waiting rooms, elevators, and restaurants.

(j) Social workers should protect the confidentiality of clients during legal proceedings to the extent permitted by law. When a court of law or other legally authorized body orders social workers to disclose confidential or privileged information without a client's consent and such disclosure could cause harm to the client, social workers should request that the court withdraw the order or limit the order as narrowly as possible or maintain the records under seal, unavailable for public inspection.

(k) Social workers should protect the confidentiality of clients when responding to requests from members of the media.

(l) Social workers should protect the confidentiality of clients' written and electronic records and other sensitive information. Social workers should take reasonable steps to ensure that clients' records are stored in a secure location and that clients' records are not available to others who are not authorized to have access.

(m) Social workers should take precautions to ensure and maintain the confidentiality of information transmitted to other parties through the use of computers, electronic mail, facsimile machines, telephones and telephone answering machines, and other electronic or computer technology. Disclosure of identifying information should be avoided whenever possible.

(n) Social workers should transfer or dispose of clients' records in a manner that protects clients' confidentiality and is consistent with state statutes governing records and social work licensure.

(o) Social workers should take reasonable precautions to protect client confidentiality in the event of the social worker's termination of practice, incapacitation, or death.

(p) Social workers should not disclose identifying information when discussing clients for teaching or training purposes unless the client has consented to disclosure of confidential information.

(q) Social workers should not disclose identifying information when discussing clients with consultants unless the client has consented to disclosure of confidential information or there is a compelling need for such disclosure.

(r) Social workers should protect the confidentiality of deceased clients consistent with the preceding standards.

1.08   Access to Records

(a) Social workers should provide clients with reasonable access to records concerning the clients. Social workers who are concerned that clients' access to their records could cause serious misunderstanding or harm to the client should provide assistance in interpreting the records and consultation with the client regarding the records. Social workers should limit clients' access to their records, or portions of their records, only in exceptional circumstances when there is compelling evidence that such access would cause serious harm to the client. Both clients' requests and the rationale for withholding some or all of the record should be documented in clients' files.

(b) When providing clients with access to their records, social workers should take steps to protect the confidentiality of other individuals identified or discussed in such records.

1.09   Sexual Relationships

(a) Social workers should under no circumstances engage in sexual activities or sexual contact with current clients, whether such contact is consensual or forced.

(b) Social workers should not engage in sexual activities or sexual contact with clients' relatives or other individuals with whom clients maintain a close personal relationship when there is a risk of exploitation or potential harm to the client. Sexual activity or sexual contact with clients' relatives or other individuals with whom clients maintain a personal relationship has the potential to be harmful to the client and may make it difficult for the social worker and client to maintain appropriate professional boundaries. Social workers—not their clients, their clients' relatives, or other individuals with whom the client maintains a personal relationship—assume the full burden for setting clear, appropriate, and culturally sensitive boundaries.

(c) Social workers should not engage in sexual activities or sexual contact with former clients because of the potential for harm to the client. If social workers engage in conduct contrary to this prohibition or claim that an exception to this prohibition is warranted because of extraordinary circumstances, it is social workers—not their clients—who assume the full burden of demonstrating that the former client has not been exploited, coerced, or manipulated, intentionally or unintentionally.

(d) Social workers should not provide clinical services to individuals with whom they have had a prior sexual relationship. Providing clinical services to a former sexual partner has the potential to be harmful to the individual and is likely to make it difficult for the social worker and individual to maintain appropriate professional boundaries.

1.10 Physical Contact

Social workers should not engage in physical contact with clients when there is a possibility of psychological harm to the client as a result of the contact (such as cradling or caressing clients). Social workers who engage in appropriate physical contact with clients are responsible for setting clear, appropriate, and culturally sensitive boundaries that govern such physical contact.

1.11 Sexual Harassment

Social workers should not sexually harass clients. Sexual harassment includes sexual advances, sexual solicitation, requests for sexual favors, and other verbal or physical conduct of a sexual nature.

1.12 Derogatory Language

Social workers should not use derogatory language in their written or verbal communications to or about clients. Social workers should use accurate and respectful language in all communications to and about clients.

1.13 Payment for Services

(a) When setting fees, social workers should ensure that the fees are fair, reasonable, and commensurate with the services performed. Consideration should be given to clients' ability to pay.

(b) Social workers should avoid accepting goods or services from clients as payment for professional services. Bartering arrangements, particularly involving services, create the potential for conflicts of interest, exploitation, and inappropriate boundaries in social workers' relationships with clients. Social workers should explore and may participate in bartering only in very limited circumstances when it can be demonstrated that such arrangements are an accepted practice among professionals in the local community, considered to be essential for the provision of services, negotiated without coercion, and entered into at the client's initiative and with the client's informed consent. Social workers who accept goods or services from clients as payment for professional services assume the full burden of demonstrating that this arrangement will not be detrimental to the client or the professional relationship.

(c) Social workers should not solicit a private fee or other remuneration for providing services to clients who are entitled to such available services through the social workers' employer or agency.

1.14 Clients Who Lack Decision-Making Capacity

When social workers act on behalf of clients who lack the capacity to make informed decisions, social workers should take reasonable steps to safeguard the interests and rights of those clients.

1.15 Interruption of Services

Social workers should make reasonable efforts to ensure continuity of services in the event that services are interrupted by factors such as unavailability, relocation, illness, disability, or death.

1.16 Termination of Services

(a) Social workers should terminate services to clients and professional relationships with them when such services and relationships are no longer required or no longer serve the clients' needs or interests.

(b) Social workers should take reasonable steps to avoid abandoning clients who are still in need of services. Social workers should withdraw services precipitously only under unusual circumstances, giving careful consideration to all factors in the situation and taking care to minimize possible adverse effects. Social workers should assist in making appropriate arrangements for continuation of services when necessary.

(c) Social workers in fee-for-service settings may terminate services to clients who are not paying an overdue balance if the financial contractual arrangements have been made clear to the client, if the client does not pose an imminent danger to self or others, and if the clinical and other consequences of the current nonpayment have been addressed and discussed with the client.

(d) Social workers should not terminate services to pursue a social, financial, or sexual relationship with a client.

(e) Social workers who anticipate the termination or interruption of services to clients should notify clients promptly and seek the transfer, referral, or continuation of services in relation to the clients' needs and preferences.

(f) Social workers who are leaving an employment setting should inform clients of appropriate options for the continuation of services and of the benefits and risks of the options.

2. Social Workers' Ethical Responsibilities to Colleagues

2.01 Respect

(a) Social workers should treat colleagues with respect and should represent accurately and fairly the qualifications, views, and obligations of colleagues.

(b) Social workers should avoid unwarranted negative criticism of colleagues in communications with clients or with other professionals. Unwarranted negative criticism may include demeaning comments that refer to colleagues' level of competence or to individuals' attributes such as race, ethnicity, national origin, color, sex, sexual orientation, age, marital status, political belief, religion, and mental or physical disability.

(c) Social workers should cooperate with social work colleagues and with colleagues of other professions when such cooperation serves the well-being of clients.

2.02 Confidentiality

Social workers should respect confidential information shared by colleagues in the course of their professional relationships and transactions. Social workers should ensure that such colleagues understand social workers' obligation to respect confidentiality and any exceptions related to it.

2.03 Interdisciplinary Collaboration

(a) Social workers who are members of an interdisciplinary team should participate in and contribute to decisions that affect the well-being of clients by drawing on the perspectives, values, and experiences of the social work profession. Professional and ethical obligations of the interdisciplinary team as a whole and of its individual members should be clearly established.

(b) Social workers for whom a team decision raises ethical concerns should attempt to resolve the disagreement through appropriate channels. If the disagreement cannot be resolved, social workers should pursue other avenues to address their concerns consistent with client well-being.

2.04 Disputes Involving Colleagues

(a) Social workers should not take advantage of a dispute between a colleague and an employer to obtain a position or otherwise advance the social workers' own interests.

(b) Social workers should not exploit clients in disputes with colleagues or engage clients in any inappropriate discussion of conflicts between social workers and their colleagues.

2.05 Consultation

(a) Social workers should seek the advice and counsel of colleagues whenever such consultation is in the best interests of clients.

(b) Social workers should keep themselves informed about colleagues' areas of expertise and competencies. Social workers should seek consultation only from colleagues who have demonstrated knowledge, expertise, and competence related to the subject of the consultation.

(c) When consulting with colleagues about clients, social workers should disclose the least amount of information necessary to achieve the purposes of the consultation.

2.06 Referral for Services

(a) Social workers should refer clients to other professionals when the other professionals' specialized knowledge or expertise is needed to serve clients fully or when social workers believe that they are not being effective or making reasonable progress with clients and that additional service is required.

(b) Social workers who refer clients to other professionals should take appropriate steps to facilitate an orderly transfer of responsibility. Social workers who refer clients to other professionals should disclose, with clients' consent, all pertinent information to the new service providers.

(c) Social workers are prohibited from giving or receiving payment for a referral when no professional service is provided by the referring social worker.

2.07 Sexual Relationships

(a) Social workers who function as supervisors or educators should not engage in sexual activities or contact with supervisees, students, trainees, or other colleagues over whom they exercise professional authority.

(b) Social workers should avoid engaging in sexual relationships with colleagues when there is potential for a conflict of interest. Social workers who become involved in, or anticipate becoming involved in, a sexual relationship with a colleague have a duty to transfer professional responsibilities, when necessary, to avoid a conflict of interest.

2.08 Sexual Harassment

Social workers should not sexually harass supervisees, students, trainees, or colleagues. Sexual harassment includes sexual advances, sexual solicitation, requests for sexual favors, and other verbal or physical conduct of a sexual nature.

2.09 Impairment of Colleagues

(a) Social workers who have direct knowledge of a social work colleague's impairment that is due to personal problems, psychosocial distress, substance abuse, or mental health difficulties and that interferes with practice effectiveness should consult with that colleague when feasible and assist the colleague in taking remedial action.

(b) Social workers who believe that a social work colleague's impairment interferes with practice effectiveness and that the colleague has not taken adequate steps to address the impairment should take action through appropriate channels established by employers, agencies, NASW, licensing and regulatory bodies, and other professional organizations.

2.10 Incompetence of Colleagues

(a) Social workers who have direct knowledge of a social work colleague's incompetence should consult with that colleague when feasible and assist the colleague in taking remedial action.

(b) Social workers who believe that a social work colleague is incompetent and has not taken adequate steps to address the incompetence should take action through appropriate channels established by employers, agencies, NASW, licensing and regulatory bodies, and other professional organizations.

2.11 Unethical Conduct of Colleagues

(a) Social workers should take adequate measures to discourage, prevent, expose, and correct the unethical conduct of colleagues.

(b) Social workers should be knowledgeable about established policies and procedures for handling concerns about colleagues' unethical behavior. Social workers should be familiar with national, state, and local procedures for handling ethics complaints. These include policies and procedures created by NASW, licensing and regulatory bodies, employers, agencies, and other professional organizations.

(c) Social workers who believe that a colleague has acted unethically should seek resolution by discussing their concerns with the colleague when feasible and when such discussion is likely to be productive.

(d) When necessary, social workers who believe that a colleague has acted unethically should take action through appropriate formal channels (such as contacting a state licensing board or regulatory body, an NASW committee on inquiry, or other professional ethics committees).

(e) Social workers should defend and assist colleagues who are unjustly charged with unethical conduct.

3. Social Workers' Ethical Responsibilities in Practice Settings

3.01 Supervision and Consultation

(a) Social workers who provide supervision or consultation should have the necessary knowledge and skill to supervise or consult appropriately and should do so only within their areas of knowledge and competence.

(b) Social workers who provide supervision or consultation are responsible for setting clear, appropriate, and culturally sensitive boundaries.

(c) Social workers should not engage in any dual or multiple relationships with supervisees in which there is a risk of exploitation of or potential harm to the supervisee.

(d) Social workers who provide supervision should evaluate supervisees' performance in a manner that is fair and respectful.

3.02 Education and Training

(a) Social workers who function as educators, field instructors for students, or trainers should provide instruction only within their areas of knowledge and competence and should provide instruction based on the most current information and knowledge available in the profession.

(b) Social workers who function as educators or field instructors for students should evaluate students' performance in a manner that is fair and respectful.

(c) Social workers who function as educators or field instructors for students should take reasonable steps to ensure that clients are routinely informed when services are being provided by students.

(d) Social workers who function as educators or field instructors for students should not engage in an dual or multiple relationships with students in which there is a risk of exploitation or potential harm to the student. Social work educators and field instructors are responsible for setting clear, appropriate, and culturally sensitive boundaries.

3.03 Performance Evaluation

Social workers who have responsibility for evaluating the performance of others should fulfill such responsibility in a fair and considerate manner and on the basis of clearly stated criteria.

3.04 Client Records

(a) Social workers should take reasonable steps to ensure that documentation in records is accurate and reflects the services provided.

(b) Social workers should include sufficient and timely documentation in records to facilitate the delivery of services and to ensure continuity of services provided to clients in the future.

(c) Social workers' documentation should protect clients' privacy to the extent that is possible and appropriate and should include only information that is directly relevant to the delivery of services.

(d) Social workers should store records following the termination of services to ensure reasonable future access. Records should be maintained for the number of years required by state statutes or relevant contracts.

3.05 Billing

Social workers should establish and maintain billing practices that accurately reflect the nature and extent of services provided and that identify who provided the service in the practice setting.

3.06 Client Transfer

(a) When an individual who is receiving services from another agency or colleague contacts a social worker for services, the social worker should carefully consider the client's needs before agreeing to provide services. To minimize possible confusion and conflict, social workers should discuss with potential clients the nature of the clients' current relationship with other service providers and the implications, including possible benefits or risks, of entering into a relationship with a new service provider.

(b) If a new client has been served by another agency or colleague, social workers should discuss with the client whether consultation with the previous service provider is in the client's best interest.

3.07 Administration

(a) Social work administrators should advocate within and outside their agencies for adequate resources to meet clients' needs.

(b) Social workers should advocate for resource allocation procedures that are open and fair. When not all clients' needs can be met, an allocation procedure should be developed that is nondiscriminatory and based on appropriate and consistently applied principles.

(c) Social workers who are administrators should take reasonable steps to ensure that adequate agency or organizational resources are available to provide appropriate staff supervision.

(d) Social work administrators should take reasonable steps to ensure that the working environment for which they are responsible is consistent with and encourages compliance with the NASW Code of Ethics. Social work administrators should take reasonable steps to eliminate any conditions in their organizations that violate, interfere with, or discourage compliance with the Code.

3.08 Continuing Education and Staff Development

Social work administrators and supervisors should take reasonable steps to provide or arrange for continuing education and staff development for all staff for whom they are responsible. Continuing education and staff development should address current knowledge and emerging developments related to social work practice and ethics.

3.09 Commitments to Employers

(a) Social workers generally should adhere to commitments made to employers and employing organizations.

(b) Social workers should work to improve employing agencies' policies and procedures and the efficiency and effectiveness of their services.

(c) Social workers should take reasonable steps to ensure that employers are aware of social workers' ethical obligations as set forth in the NASW Code of Ethics and of the implications of those obligations for social work practice.

(d) Social workers should not allow an employing organization's policies, procedures, regulations, or administrative orders to interfere with their ethical practice of social work. Social workers should take reasonable steps to ensure that their employing organizations' practices are consistent with the NASW Code of Ethics.

(e) Social workers should act to prevent and eliminate discrimination in the employing organization's work assignments and in its employment policies and practices.

(f) Social workers should accept employment or arrange student field placements only in organizations that exercise fair personnel practices.

(g) Social workers should be diligent stewards of the resources of their employing organizations, wisely conserving funds where appropriate and never misappropriating funds or using them for unintended purposes.

3.10 Labor–Management Disputes

(a) Social workers may engage in organized action, including the formation of and participation in labor unions, to improve services to clients and working conditions.

(b) The actions of social workers who are involved in labor–management disputes, job actions, or labor strikes should be guided by the profession's values, ethical principles, and ethical standards. Reasonable differences of opinion exist among social workers concerning their primary obligation as professionals during an actual or threatened labor strike or job action. Social workers should carefully examine relevant issues and their possible impact on clients before deciding on a course of action.

4. Social Workers' Ethical Responsibilities as Professionals

4.01 Competence

(a) Social workers should accept responsibility or employment only on the basis of existing competence or the intention to acquire the necessary competence.

(b) Social workers should strive to become and remain proficient in professional practice and the performance of professional functions. Social workers should critically examine and keep current with emerging knowledge relevant to social work.

Social workers should routinely review the professional literature and participate in continuing education relevant to social work practice and social work ethics.

(c) Social workers should base practice on recognized knowledge, including empirically based knowledge, relevant to social work and social work ethics.

4.02 Discrimination

Social workers should not practice, condone, facilitate, or collaborate with any form of discrimination on the basis of race, ethnicity, national origin, color, sex, sexual orientation, age, marital status, political belief, religion, or mental or physical disability.

4.03 Private Conduct

Social workers should not permit their private conduct to interfere with their ability to fulfill their professional responsibilities.

4.04 Dishonesty, Fraud, and Deception

Social workers should not participate in, condone, or be associated with dishonesty, fraud, or deception.

4.05 Impairment

(a) Social workers should not allow their own personal problems, psychosocial distress, legal problems, substance abuse, or mental health difficulties to interfere with their professional judgment and performance or to jeopardize the best interests of people for whom they have a professional responsibility.

(b) Social workers whose personal problems, psychosocial distress, legal problems, substance abuse, or mental health difficulties interfere with their professional judgment and performance should immediately seek consultation and take appropriate remedial action by seeking professional help, making adjustments in workload, terminating practice, or taking any other steps necessary to protect clients and others.

4.06 Misrepresentation

(a) Social workers should make clear distinctions between statements made and actions engaged in as a private individual and as a representative of the social work profession, a professional social work organization, or the social worker's employing agency.

(b) Social workers who speak on behalf of professional social work organizations should accurately represent the official and authorized positions of the organizations.

(c) Social workers should ensure that their representations to clients, agencies, and the public of professional qualifications, credentials, education, competence, affiliations, services provided, or results to be achieved are accurate. Social workers should claim only those relevant professional credentials they actually possess and take steps to correct any inaccuracies or misrepresentations of their credentials by others.

4.07 Solicitations

(a) Social workers should not engage in uninvited solicitation of potential clients who, because of their circumstances, are vulnerable to undue influence, manipulation, or coercion.

(b) Social workers should not engage in solicitation of testimonial endorsements (including solicitation of consent to use a client's prior statement as a testimonial endorsement) from current clients or from other people who, because of their particular circumstances, are vulnerable to undue influence.

4.08 Acknowledging Credit

(a) Social workers should take responsibility and credit, including authorship credit, only for work they have actually performed and to which they have contributed.

(b) Social workers should honestly acknowledge the work of and the contributions made by others.

5. Social Workers' Ethical Responsibilities to the Social Work Profession

5.01 Integrity of the Profession

(a) Social workers should work toward the maintenance and promotion of high standards of practice.

(b) Social workers should uphold and advance the values, ethics, knowledge, and mission of the profession. Social workers should protect, enhance, and improve the integrity of the profession through appropriate study and research, active discussion, and responsible criticism of the profession.

(c) Social workers should contribute time and professional expertise to activities that promote respect for the value, integrity, and competence of the social work profession. These activities may include teaching, research, consultation, service, legislative testimony, presentations in the community, and participation in their professional organizations.

(d) Social workers should contribute to the knowledge base of social work and share with colleagues their knowledge related to practice, research, and ethics. Social workers should seek to contribute to the profession's literature and to share their knowledge at professional meetings and conferences.

(e) Social workers should act to prevent the unauthorized and unqualified practice of social work.

5.02 Evaluation and Research

(a) Social workers should monitor and evaluate policies, the implementation of programs, and practice interventions.

(b) Social workers should promote and facilitate evaluation and research to contribute to the development of knowledge.

(c) Social workers should critically examine and keep current with emerging knowledge relevant to social work and fully use evaluation and research evidence in their professional practice.

(d) Social workers engaged in evaluation or research should carefully consider possible consequences and should follow guidelines developed for the protection of evaluation and research participants. Appropriate institutional review boards should be consulted.

(e) Social workers engaged in evaluation or research should obtain voluntary and written informed consent from participants, when appropriate, without any implied or actual deprivation or penalty for refusal to participate; without undue inducement to participate; and with due regard for participants' well-being, privacy, and dignity. Informed consent should include information about the nature, extent, and duration of the participation requested and disclosure of the risks and benefits of participation in the research.

(f) When evaluation or research participants are incapable of giving informed consent, social workers should provide an appropriate explanation to the participants, obtain the participants' assent to the extent they are able, and obtain written consent from an appropriate proxy.

(g) Social workers should never design or conduct evaluation or research that does not use consent procedures, such as certain forms of naturalistic observation and archival research, unless rigorous and responsible review of the research has found it to be justified because of its prospective scientific, educational, or applied value and unless equally effective alternative procedures that do not involve waiver of consent are not feasible.

(h) Social workers should inform participants of their right to withdraw from evaluation and research at any time without penalty.

(i) Social workers should take appropriate steps to ensure that participants in evaluation and research have access to appropriate supportive services.

(j) Social workers engaged in evaluation or research should protect participants from unwarranted physical or mental distress, harm, danger, or deprivation.

(k) Social workers engaged in the evaluation of services should discuss collected information only for professional purposes and only with people professionally concerned with this information.

(l) Social workers engaged in evaluation or research should ensure the anonymity or confidentiality of participants and of the data obtained from them. Social workers should inform participants of any limits of confidentiality, the measures that will be taken to ensure confidentiality, and when any records containing research data will be destroyed.

(m) Social workers who report evaluation and research results should protect participants' confidentiality by omitting identifying information unless proper consent has been obtained authorizing disclosure.

(n) Social workers should report evaluation and research findings accurately. They should not fabricate or falsify results and should take steps to correct any errors later found in published data using standard publication methods.

(o) Social workers engaged in evaluation or research should be alert to and avoid conflicts of interest and dual relationships with participants, should inform participants when a real or potential conflict of interest arises, and should take steps to resolve the issue in a manner that makes participants' interests primary.

(p) Social workers should educate themselves, their students, and their colleagues about responsible research practices.

6. Social Workers' Ethical Responsibilities to the Broader Society

6.01 Social Welfare

Social workers should promote the general welfare of society, from local to global levels, and the development of people, their communities, and their environments. Social workers should advocate for living conditions conducive to the fulfillment of basic human needs and should promote social, economic, political, and cultural values and institutions that are compatible with the realization of social justice.

6.02 Public Participation

Social workers should facilitate informed participation by the public in shaping social policies and institutions.

6.03 Public Emergencies

Social workers should provide appropriate professional services in public emergencies to the greatest extent possible.

6.04 Social and Political Action

(a) Social workers should engage in social and political action that seeks to ensure that all people have equal access to the resources, employment, services, and opportunities they require to meet their basic human needs and to develop fully. Social workers should be aware of the impact of the political arena on practice and should advocate for changes in policy and legislation to improve social conditions in order to meet basic human needs and promote social justice.

(b) Social workers should act to expand choice and opportunity for all people, with special regard for vulnerable, disadvantaged, oppressed, and exploited people and groups.

(c) Social workers should promote conditions that encourage respect for cultural and social diversity within the United States and globally. Social workers should promote policies and practices that demonstrate respect for difference, support the expansion of cultural knowledge and resources, advocate for programs and institutions that demonstrate cultural competence, and promote policies that safeguard the rights of and confirm equity and social justice for all people.

(d) Social workers should act to prevent and eliminate domination of, exploitation of, and discrimination against any person, group, or class on the basis of race, ethnicity, national origin, color, sex, sexual orientation, age, marital status, political belief, religion, or mental or physical disability.

INDEX

282   INDEX

Professional integrity
    v. client self-determination, 173–176
Prolongation of biological life
    v. quality of life, 38–43
Protection of life, principle of, 10
Public emergencies, code provisions, 277
Public participation, code provisions, 277

Quality of life
    principle of, 10
    v. prolongation of biological life, 38–43

Rape reporting, 177–179
Rawls, John, 7
Recovery
    professionals in, 156–161
Referral for services, 269–270
Rejection, threat of, 62
Relationships
    dual, 156–158
        or multiple, 153
Reporting
    drug dealing, 206–209
    rape, 177–179
Respect
    for colleagues, 268–269
Roe v. Ingraham, 105
Roe v. Wade, 181
Ross, W.D., 7, 33–35, 107
Rule utilitarianism, 91

Sanctity-of-life principle, 38–39
Scarce resources, efficient use of, 190–191
Schloendorff v. Society of New York Hospital,
    100
Screening, genetic, 225
Self-actualization, 103
Self-determination
    adoption and, 173–176
    client v. professional integrity, 173–176
    code provisions, 262
    as fundamental right, 51–52
    mentally disabled client and, 51–54
    quality of life decision and, 37–43
    right to, 82
    suicide and, 147–151
    v. agency policy, 110–115
        for Cambodian client, 110–115
    v. health and safety, 162–166

    v. obligation to prevent harm, 51–54
    v. obligation to report colleague
        misconduct, 81–86
    v. obligation to vulnerable population
        (unborn child), 181–186
Self-protection, right to, 211–215
Service
    to others, 261
    value of, 13
Sexual abuse
    of foster-care child, 25–29
Sexual harassment, 22, 72–73
    code provisions, 267
    with colleagues, 270
Sexual relationships, 72
    code provisions, 266–267
    with colleagues, 270
Shaw v. Glickman, 100
Sibling relationships, 31–32
Slippery slope argument, 39
Social and political action, code provisions,
    277
Social health model, 133–134
Social justice, 198–199, 231–237, 261
    value of, 13
Social welfare, code provisions, 277
Social worker
    obligations/responsibilities
        to clients, 21–71
        code, provisions of, 72–73
        to colleagues, 72–93
        to profession, 170–197
        to self, 156–161
        to society, 198–242
    professional responsibilities
        acknowledging credit, 275
        competence, 273–274
        discrimination, 274
        dishonesty, fraud, and deception, 274
        impairment, 274
        misrepresentation, 274
        private conduct, 274
        solicitations, 274–275
    safety concerns, violence, 211–215
Social work profession
    ethical responsibilities to, social workers'
        (Standard Five), 170–197, 275–276
    code provisions, 170–171
    obligations of, 153